THE ILLUMINATED MAN

THE ILLUMINATED MAN

Life, Death and the Worlds of J. G. Ballard

Christopher Priest
and Nina Allan

BLOOMSBURY CONTINUUM
LONDON · OXFORD · NEW YORK · NEW DELHI · SYDNEY

BLOOMSBURY CONTINUUM
Bloomsbury Publishing Plc
50 Bedford Square, London, WC1B 3DP, UK
Bloomsbury Publishing Ireland Limited,
29 Earlsfort Terrace, Dublin 2, D02 AY28, Ireland

BLOOMSBURY, BLOOMSBURY CONTINUUM and the
Diana logo are trademarks of Bloomsbury Publishing Plc

First published in Great Britain 2026

Copyright © Christopher Priest and Nina Allan, 2026

Christopher Priest and Nina Allan have asserted their right under the Copyright,
Designs and Patents Act, 1988, to be identified as Authors of this work

For legal purposes the Acknowledgements on pp. 446–7 and Photo Permissions on pp. 474–5
constitute an extension of this copyright page

All rights reserved. No part of this publication may be: i) reproduced or transmitted in any
form, electronic or mechanical, including photocopying, recording or by means of any information
storage or retrieval system without prior permission in writing from the publishers; or ii) used or reproduced
in any way for the training, development or operation of artificial intelligence (AI) technologies, including
generative AI technologies. The rights holders expressly reserve this publication from the text and data
mining exception as per Article 4(3) of the Digital Single Market Directive (EU) 2019/790

Bloomsbury Publishing Plc does not have any control over, or responsibility for, any third-party websites
referred to or in this book. All internet addresses given in this book were correct at the time of going to
press. The author and publisher regret any inconvenience caused if addresses have changed or sites have
ceased to exist, but can accept no responsibility for any such changes

A catalogue record for this book is available from the British Library

Library of Congress Cataloguing-in-Publication data has been applied for

ISBN:	HB:	978-1-3994-1749-5
	EBOOK:	978-1-3994-1747-1
	EPDF:	978-1-3994-1748-8

2 4 6 8 10 9 7 5 3 1

Typeset by Lumina Datamatics Ltd
Printed and bound in Great Britain by Clays Ltd, Elcograf S.p.A

To find out more about our authors and books visit www.bloomsbury.com
and sign up for our newsletters
For product safety related questions contact productsafety@bloomsbury.com

The book you are about to read should not exist.

In January 2023, my husband, the writer Christopher Priest set aside the novel he had been writing to begin working on a biography of J. G. Ballard. Six months later, he was diagnosed with terminal cancer. We believed even then that he would have time to complete the book, or at least a passable draft of it. Sadly, we were wrong. When it became obvious that Chris would run out of time, we agreed between the two of us that I would finish what had — so tragically and unexpectedly — turned out to be his final work, and that the story of how that work came into being should itself become a part of it.

The book that has resulted is very different from the one Chris set out to write. Chris's initial inspiration for writing Ballard's biography was his desire to consolidate Ballard's position in the literary pantheon. He always believed that Ballard remained under-discussed within circles of criticism, pushed to the side or ghettoized as so-called cult writers frequently are, precisely because of their lack of conformity with the established canon. Chris wanted to write about Ballard as one of the most significant English-language novelists of the twentieth century, as well as discussing in detail the special qualities, both of his writing and of his subject matter, that made him such a grounding inspiration for Chris personally.

I first read Ballard when I was still in my teens, some twenty years before Chris and I met. Then, as now, it was his use of language, his development of a unique lexicon of words and images — a kind of unhinged poetry — that captured my imagination and critical engagement in equal measure. When Chris and I eventually did meet, Ballard was one of the writers we first bonded over. Our discussions of his work prompted us both — separately and together — to reignite our mutual enthusiasm through rereading. When Chris first spoke of tackling Ballard's biography I was thrilled. I believed he had a unique perspective from which to write, that his insights would be not just valuable, but unrepeatable, a particular combination of place, time and talent that was his alone.

Even before we knew he was unwell, I found myself increasingly trying to persuade Chris to put more of himself into the book. I insisted that his presence amongst its pages was essential, that readers would be interested in the biography at least partly because *he* had written it. Chris was more ambivalent. He loved to talk about writing but, like many of the best writers, he was at once tirelessly devoted to his vocation and completely self-effacing about what he had achieved. He kept fobbing me off; he was 'getting to it', he said, and we can at least be grateful that he got to some of it. Chris and Ballard shared many similarities in their working methods. But I have come to believe they are alike in other ways, too, most notably their intense dislike of scrutiny around their private life, an abnegation of self that is both a protection and a refusal.

Through the autumn of 2023, it became increasingly clear to both of us that much of Chris's part in this story – his creative kinship with Ballard as well as the many and occasionally unnerving correspondences between their lives and work – would be told by me. Chris was prepared for this to happen; more than that, he was relieved not to have to set down those chapters himself. As things turned out, we each ended up writing the parts of this book that we wanted to write. The result – which given Chris's abiding fascination with twins as a literary device seems uncannily fitting – is a beast with two heads, a species of twin biography that is itself an exploration of the form.

Chris was able to complete some 65,000 words of this narrative before he died. Those chapters that are his – minor copy-edits aside – remain untouched and completely intact, the way he wrote them. The rest is down to me. We came to think of this book as ours, a shared endeavour that sustained us and maintained our togetherness even as Chris's work and life came to an end.

(Nina Allan, Rothesay, December 2024)

For J. G. B and C. M. P.

CONTENTS

PROLOGUE: 'The White Hotel' — 1
Introduction: 'The Paradises of the Sun' — 9

1. 'Journey Towards the Rain Planet' — 13
2. 'The Eve of Pearl Harbor' — 25
3. 'A Landscape of Airfields' — 39
4. 'A New Arrival' — 55
5. 'The Man with the White Smile' — 65
6. 'The Abandoned Aerodrome' — 69
7. 'The Unlimited Dream Company' — 73
8. 'Exit Strategies' — 79
9. 'Out of the Night and into the Dream' — 97
10. 'Danger in the Streets of the Sky' — 109
ELEVEN. 'The Children's Sanctuary' — 117
12. 'The Naming of New Things' — 125
THIRTEEN. 'Appointment with a Revolution' — 137
FOURTEEN. 'The Sign of the Crab' — 147
15. 'The Depot of Dreams' — 159
SIXTEEN. 'Preparations for Departure' — 165
17. 'A Season for Assassins' — 171
EIGHTEEN. 'The House of Women' — 185
19. 'The Burning Car' — 203
20. 'The Causeways of the Sun' — 217
21. 'A Decline in Property Values' — 225
22. 'The Evening's Entertainment' — 247

23. 'Giving Himself to the Sun'	263
24. 'The Great American Desert'	279
TWENTY-FIVE. 'The Third Nile'	289
26. 'Through the Crash Barrier'	303
27. 'I Give Myself Away'	309
TWENTY-EIGHT. 'The Road to Shanghai'	315
29. 'The Predatory Birds'	323
THIRTY. 'Too Soon, Too Late'	333
THIRTY-ONE. 'The Upholstered Apocalypse'	351
THIRTY-TWO. 'Absolute Zero'	371
THIRTY-THREE. 'A Task Completed'	391
THIRTY-FOUR. 'The Illuminated Man'	425
Acknowledgements	446
Bibliography	448
Chapter Titles	451
Notes	453
Photo permissions	474
Index	476

PROLOGUE

'THE WHITE HOTEL'

On 10 December 2022, Chris and I set out from our home on the Isle of Bute to drive to Selkirk in the Scottish Borders. We were on our way to visit J. G. Ballard's bibliographer David Pringle, a meeting that had been planned some weeks in advance, though was now somewhat in jeopardy owing to the vagaries of the Scottish climate. So early in December, and snow already forecast. We decided we would set off anyway. We would not get another chance to make the journey until the new year, and this meeting was important to all of us. We went the slow way, along the back roads through a landscape of chilly fields, bare and hardened beneath a low sky. Wishaw, Carluke, then Peebles and the true border country. The temperature was dropping and by the time we arrived in Selkirk it was close to freezing.

The town seemed quiet, folded in on itself. The café I had earmarked for lunch turned out to be closed and so I ran the length of the High Street to look for another. Chris could not walk far because of his arthritis, and I did not want him to set off until I knew for certain where we were going. The place I found was bright and welcoming with the scents of coffee and frying bacon. We sat in the warm and ordered paninis and began to talk, as we were doing constantly by then, about the Ballard project. Chris looked happy because I was happy, pleasantly amused as he always was by the constant, steadily unfolding joy I have always experienced in ordinary things.

We arrived at David's home just after two. A modest Scottish cottage, grey stone under a slate roof, previously the home of David's parents and where he now lived with his son, who was recently divorced. The house looked down across the town's western outskirts, its door a vibrant pillar-box red, the colour chosen by David's mother and father after they moved in. The interior reminded me instantly of my grandparents' house: the particular scent and atmosphere of long habitation, the old-fashioned furnishings, knick-knacks that have stood so long in the same place the idea of moving them or getting rid of them is a kind of sacrilege.

There was something antiquated about it, a house lost in time, and my relationship with time has always been tricky. From the age of six, I have been consciously aware of time's passing and the sense of loss that comes with it. I have a deep love of time's flotsam and jetsam: mementoes, souvenirs and keepsakes that say as much about where and when they came from as of the people who owned them. I am drawn instinctively to old things, yet the older I become myself, the less comfortable I feel with accumulating objects in general. I have kept very few of the letters sent to me over the years and those that I have kept I can never reread. The sense of recall is so immediate and so agonizing it is hard to take. A letter need not contain anything difficult or sad. A simple place name, an item of clothing worn to a party, the name of a colleague, forgotten for years but now instantly present – such details throw me back into the past with such casual violence I find it overpowering. This kind of time travel is unbearable because the time you are returning to is irretrievably lost.

Yet some of my favourite works of literature are biographies, which deal with the passing of time as a central concern. As a literary genre, the biography is as various in form as the authors who work within it and has the same potential for being innovative as anything in fiction. I was sixteen when I read my first one: Anne Stevenson's *Bitter Fame*, the first sustained attempt to write the life of Sylvia Plath. As a reader, I came to treasure the feeling of closeness to a subject I cared about – like going through a tea chest filled with documents in search of long-lost relatives. I felt creatively energized and not-alone, the sense of impotence in the face of time's transit temporarily assuaged.

Reading David Pringle's exhaustive chronology of Ballard's life just weeks before our trip had been similarly affecting. I had found it devastating to observe through the chronology as if in real-time the diminishing number of days that were left for Ballard to live, the cancelled events and appointments, the brute fact of a billion possibilities becoming finite. I had cried as I read, because I cry easily when I am alone and because I still, on some instinctive level, refused what was happening. I remember the relief I felt when I realized I could go back to the beginning – to Ballard's birth in Shanghai – and run the film of his life again whenever I wanted.

Ballard had never visited David's house, yet he was here, nonetheless, in this convergence of time-streams, the ineradicable ways in which their lives had become connected. Now Chris and I were here also – two more time-travellers, complicating things further. Observing the multitude of disparate objects on display in David's hallway and living room, I could not escape the feeling that David had simply arrived back in Selkirk and set himself down, that this was the home of someone who did not give much thought to his domestic surroundings so long as he found them comfortable and fit for purpose. That his mind was elsewhere and otherwise occupied. My first sight of David's workspace confirmed this. A kind of half-room off the main sitting room, stuffed with books and files, thrumming with the energy of work in progress, with a sense of engagement and conviction that stood in contrast to the stasis that defined the rest of the house. This was the space that mattered; the rest was just stage setting. The likeness to Ballard's own working environment was interesting to notice.

David Pringle was born in Selkirk, in 1950. He was fourteen when he first read a story by Ballard, 'Track 12', in Brian Aldiss's 1961 anthology *Penguin Science Fiction*. 'It did not impress me greatly,' David writes of this first encounter. His eyes were fully opened a year or two later, during a school trip to the Holy Land in 1965:

> At my father's suggestion I took just one book with me to read on the trip – Cervantes' *Don Quixote*. After a few days at sea I was hungering for something else to read. I noticed an older boy lying on his bunk reading a brand-new SF paperback – the Penguin edition of Ballard's *The Four-Dimensional Nightmare*. Suddenly I was desperate to get hold of that book, and I badgered him into lending it to me. It was my first real experience of reading Ballard. The book just amazed, mystified and delighted me. I didn't understand it all, but I wanted to

understand it. I reread 'The Voices of Time' slowly. The atmosphere of it and the other stories seemed so intense, so original... I saw the Lebanon, Jordan and Israel through Ballardian eyes. Sand, concrete, beat-up American automobiles, barbed wire, new apartment blocks in the desert, gun emplacements ... It all seemed so apt. Having been obsessed with the concept of style in literature (under the influence of reading Hemingway and Bradbury), I was now seized with the idea of imagery. Good writing had to contain 'relevant' images, appropriate to the present day, and Ballard's work was full of them. I had to return that book to its owner at the end of the cruise, but I did so reluctantly – I even offered to buy it from him at the full price.[1]

This epiphany was to determine the future direction of David's life as a writer, editor, bibliographer and 'Ballard expert'. He corresponded with Ballard regularly throughout his life, conducted seven in-depth interviews with him, wrote the first ever monograph on Ballard,[2] and compiled the first bibliography of Ballard's work.[3] I first corresponded with David in the early 2000s, while he was still editor of the British science fiction magazine *Interzone*. Chris, of course, had known him for decades.

David was reserved, a man of thoughtful silences, much shyer in person than I had expected from his precise and detailed emails. He struck me as a typical letter-writer: more comfortable conversing in print than in person. He made us tea, passing to and from the kitchen more times than seemed necessary, as if the activity was strange to him, a ritual he had once indulged in but forgotten how to practise.

We had come to Selkirk because Chris wanted to talk to David about the book he was planning to write. His decision had come about suddenly, and was partly my doing. I had been commissioned to produce an essay exploring Ballard's approach to writing about the future, though Ballard never wrote about the future, not really; what interested him was the present, or as Ballard himself famously put it, the next five minutes. It was this – Ballard's radical approach to what is usually termed science fiction – that I wanted my essay to be about. As I began rereading Ballard's early disaster novels I became transfixed, as I always had been, by his use of language, his unique blend of harshness and lyricism, his transformative imagery.

It was not long before I began talking with Chris about my renascent enthusiasm, a running commentary on my thoughts and discoveries, points that had to be made, ideas that should be explored. This was what we did, how we operated. Our conversation was a fire we never stopped feeding, an indelible and constant excitement at what words might do. In the course of our discussions, Chris emailed me a document he had on his hard drive, a segment of a complete chronology of Ballard's life.

'David Pringle's been working on it for years,' he said. The section he showed me covered the mid-fifties to the late sixties, the years of the British New Wave in science fiction and the beginnings of Ballard's most radical period as a writer. Chris was then a young Turk, a decade and more younger than Ballard and just beginning to publish his first stories. There were multiple references to him in the chronology, and David had originally sent it to him for fact-checking.

'I'd forgotten I had this,' Chris added. 'You might find it interesting.'

That turned out to be an understatement. Over the next couple of weeks I became obsessed with it. The chronology, which David began working on soon after Ballard's death, runs to some 400,000 words in length and covers every year of Ballard's life. It forms a significant historical record, not only of the events, publications and people directly connected with Ballard, but also the political, sociological and artistic landmarks of the time he lived through and highlighting those – celebrity car crashes, key moments in the space race, technological advances and controversies – that might be said to have a 'Ballardian' inflection.

I fell into the chronology as into a novel, a historical epic, one of the most powerful evocations of my own time I had read. And I could not shut up about it. When I emailed David, asking if I might read the rest of what he'd compiled, he sent me the remaining sections just a few hours later. 'There's a book here,' Chris said, after he had read them also. He wrote to David, asking if he was intending to turn the chronology into a biography.

We had both assumed this would be his plan – if anyone was in a position to write such a book it was David. But he replied to Chris's email saying that if he once had plans to write Ballard's biography, they were now indefinitely on hold. In 2017, David had been given radiosurgery for a brain tumour, followed by repeated brain scans to verify the results.

Although the treatment was a success and he was in full remission, the experience had left him feeling that he no longer had the energy for what was bound to be a lengthy and exhausting undertaking.

'How do you feel about the idea of me writing it?' Chris said to me then. 'The biography, I mean. Of course, we'll have to ask David about using the chronology.'

I was sitting on the floor in his office. Chris was leaning back in his chair, turned away from his desk and towards me. We held hands from time to time, the way we often did when we were discussing things that mattered to us. I felt energized, validated, as if something that was supposed to happen was finally happening. Chris – like David – had been reading Ballard from the beginning. He had always cited Ballard as one of his key inspirations for becoming a writer. They had shared space in the same magazines. They had met numerous times, and occasionally corresponded.

More than any of that, there was a creative sympathy between them, a peculiar symmetry that arose from the particular way they looked at the world. In spite of their very different backgrounds, they were somehow alike.

'You have to write it,' I said. I felt certain that David Pringle would not only agree that we could make use of his material, but that he would be pleased.

These memories are still painful, because they feel so present. I suppose they always will be.

We were staying at the Philipburn, a pleasantly refurbished country house hotel situated to the west of the town centre and surrounded by dense woodland. We asked David to have dinner with us there, an invitation he readily accepted, adding that it would be the first time he had eaten out since the lockdowns ended.

His best outdoor shoes, when he put them on, were coated with dust.

The hotel was not particularly busy but the restaurant, which served local produce cooked to an excellent standard, was clearly popular with locals and soon became lively. David – who had not been out for a beer since COVID, either – was clearly enjoying himself. Chris had already explained to him how he envisaged the project, and David had agreed that he could make use of the chronology as a background guide. We finished our meal in good spirits, promising to be back in touch again after Christmas.

It snowed heavily during the night. We stepped out of the lobby to find the car park deserted except for our black Volkswagen, now blanketed in white. Chris went ahead of me down the steps, unhurried but confident, I remember that. For a few brief moments, it seemed as if the car tyres might not gain purchase on the sloping exit ramp, but then they did, and we were away, moving steadily through the snowy, gold-tinted landscape of a Farquharson Christmas card, the same vistas of sheep and rutted farm tracks I fell in love with when I was a child.

A plantation of spruces sparkling with ice, the roads bare of traffic. Sunday frozen to the bone. No one was going anywhere. Rooks bloomed like ink dropped into water across the colourless sky.

A magical quietude, we both remarked on it. We felt excited, close to jubilant. Our mission had been accomplished and the work could begin.

We entered the new year – 2023 – with the same sense of purpose. Chris had already written an outline – preliminary notes, chapter headings – while I completed the second draft of my own work-in-progress.

It was in early March that Chris began having significant issues with his mobility. His back was causing trouble – a recurrent problem – and for the first time I could remember he was in pain while driving. I felt anxious, because I did not understand what was happening to him or why. I had always worried about his fitness, to an extent. Chris was never what you would call an outdoors person. His natural habitat was his office, the space behind his desk. He loved the natural world profoundly, but he was not a walker.

This new situation seemed different, though. Chris's deterioration seemed too rapid and without explanation. He had not fallen, he had not been ill. I remember looking at him one evening while he was getting undressed. He'd had mild scoliosis for most of a decade but now he seemed bent out of shape to an unnatural degree, his spine steeply curved, his chest caved in on itself.

He was tired. More so than usual, and I remember thinking that he looked old. Old in a way he had not been even six months ago.

He is eighty this year, I reasoned, silently. Of course he looks old.

This was the moment when our lives were cast upon a different trajectory. I observed that moment – I would tell Chris's consultant about it, later – though I did not recognize it for what it was and I did not mention to Chris at the time the strange feeling I had, that he was vulnerable suddenly, at greater risk of harm than he had been previously. That he had been interfered with.

All of this is true, though I am conscious, as I write, of constructing a narrative. Of trying to make sense of things, of twisting time, to make it fit a pattern.

The days then were radically different from the way they are now. Our story still ongoing. He, still with me.

Still, we continued as normal. We had work to do.

INTRODUCTION

'THE PARADISES OF THE SUN'

Let us begin with a contention about J. G. Ballard. There are those who will agree with it, but many will be surprised, some will undoubtedly think it eccentric. It is however the belief on which this book is founded. I contend that Ballard was one of the most important writers in English of the twentieth century. Always a well-regarded writer, his books were published in multiple languages, attracting the interest of film makers as well as large numbers of readers. Most of his novels and stories remain in print. He even became a genre: the Collins English Dictionary defines 'Ballardian' as *resembling or suggestive of the conditions described in the works of J. G. Ballard*. In all of this he is not so different from many successful novelists – his reputation is secure.

However, I believe he has so far not been afforded the final step: the acknowledgement of true and permanent greatness. I suspect this is largely to do with his avowal of science fiction, which he maintained throughout his life. Science fiction is a largely unregarded, misunderstood and sometimes despised form of writing, but Ballard tackled its stimulating material with great intelligence, a lyrical imagination and original use of language. He is one of the finest writers to have emerged from the genre.

In 2016 the Nobel Prize in Literature was awarded to a writer whose work had for half a century been beguiling, enchanting and inspiring hundreds of thousands of people around the world. This writer was of course Bob Dylan. Ballard's achievement, seeing the world through a particular lens and reporting it in inimitable style, may be said to be the equal of Dylan's, and covering a similar period of time. It is of course too late for him to be recognized by the Nobel committee, but the Nobel is not the only route into the Pantheon.

J. G. Ballard was the writer of around twenty novels, and more than a hundred short stories, the recipient of multiple awards and honours. He was a famous controversialist, certain examples of whose work were found by some to be shocking or even dangerous to read. Ballard is most popularly recognized for two of his novels. One is *Empire of the Sun*, a semi-autobiographical account of his adolescence, spent through part of the second world war in a Japanese internment camp in China. The other is *Crash*, a supposedly pornographic novel about the alleged psychosexual content of automobile accidents. Both of these books brought him disproportionate fame and, in the case of *Crash*, notoriety. His other novels and short stories are not as widely known, but they are central to this contention and comprise a unique body of work.

Materially, Ballard enjoyed commercial success. In literary terms he was a member of the small elite of authors, past and present, by whose enduring work we set the value of what constitutes great literature. But with Ballard there was another ingredient, something unique, something beyond the worldly greatness that made him famous. This is a quality of deep personal commitment many readers have felt on discovering his work. Much of what he wrote could induce feelings of 'otherness', that there was an extra dimension of reality in his fiction, another view possible, a sense that an enlightening clue to understanding had just been set forth. It was the quality now generally known as 'Ballardian', a mysterious and imprecise word that no one could define but which was readily understood by those who experienced it.

This book is a celebration of the work of one of the most varied, unpredictable and entertaining authors of the decades that covered the end of the twentieth century and the beginning of the twenty-first. But it is also an attempt to understand the Ballardian effect by closely examining his work and the aspects of his life which fed subtly into the work.

In person he was something of a paradox. He was a quiet and serious family man, who lived in a small house in a modest suburban town and worked hard all his life. He travelled rarely, and personal appearances in public were unusual. He was a man of ideas, a rational thinker and a social observer with an uncanny ability to imagine and accurately predict the unexpectable. Yet some of those ideas were superficially shocking, or treated as such, because most of them challenged popular assumptions. Many of those ideas are valid today, and oddly define the complex society in which we live now, the world of unreliable mass media, authoritarian governments, environmental catastrophe and human migration.

Behind his writing was a turbulent world: a childhood passed while war flared around him. He was a close witness to at least two violent murders, and led a difficult life afterwards as a young adult trying to adjust to the prosaic, inhibiting world of postwar Britain. Ballard died prematurely of cancer: he was seventy-eight years old, but in full possession of his powers, a book project in hand and other works expected that were never to be.

Ballard's fiction both challenges and rewards the reader. His unique landscapes often summon locations familiar from television and films, sometimes also from personal experience or travel. All are heightened into unfamiliarity by the vivid visual imagery of his fiction and quietly obsessive descriptive passages: dense rainforest, vibrant light, shopping malls, river systems, sites irradiated by nuclear blasts, white-haired goddesses of the film world, errant doctors, gated communities of oligarchs and ultra-rich fund managers, psychopaths, the freeways around and across cities, rocket launching zones, flooded cities, beach resorts, drained swimming pools, desert wastes.

This book is also, from time to time, a personal memoir. I am Christopher Priest, a novelist whose work could be said to be adjacent to Ballard's, while not claiming any kind of false equivalence. Certain factual similarities between us exist. We were both conceived in the same place, albeit more than a decade apart: Stockport, a town within Greater Manchester in the north-west of England. Neither of us holds a university degree. As young men we had a passing interest in aviation, and both took flying lessons. (Neither of us qualified as a pilot.) We both discovered American science fiction in similar circumstances, which led to us becoming writers. In my case the science fiction I discovered a few years later significantly included Ballard's early work, which had a transforming and inspirational effect on me. In time I met and knew Ballard during the years I lived in London. Although we did not become close personal friends, I had reason to correspond with him from time to time and was honoured to include a new short story by him in an anthology I edited,[4] published by Faber & Faber in the UK, and Scribner in the USA.

To say one writer influences another does not mean that imitation takes place. H. G. Wells was heavily influenced by the work of Charles Dickens when he began writing, but none of that influence shows. Wells took from Dickens his interest in the small or unimportant person who makes good, but he wrote *Kipps* and did not try to rewrite *Great Expectations*. The work of an influential writer demonstrates to others what might be possible, suggests situations or characters, creates a mood or a style, some of which might stimulate the imagination of another writer, but that is about all.

Like many other writers I have always acknowledged the influence of J. G. Ballard. For those of my generation he made impossible dreams into plausible fantasies.

One of that generation is my colleague David Pringle, an editor and scholar who has studied Ballard's writing over multiple decades. Pringle knew Ballard in person much better than I did – Ballard himself often remarked that Pringle knew more about him than he did himself. He was editor of the magazine *Interzone* for twenty-two years and published many of Ballard's later short stories. Pringle's intricately researched biographical chronology has been the armature around which this book has been wound.

James Graham Ballard was known to friends and family by several variations of his first name: Jamie, Jim, Jimmie, Jimmy, James. He is most often addressed throughout this book as 'Ballard', which I consider to be a term of respect, affection and seriousness.

I

'JOURNEY TOWARDS THE RAIN PLANET'

It was the early winter of 1945, the second world war still fresh in memory, but at last even the Pacific War had concluded after the Japanese surrender in August. A youth, an adolescent only just past his fifteenth birthday, stood by the rail of a steamship as it moored in Southampton harbour. He was full of hopeful anticipation: he was British but all his childhood and teenage years had been spent in China while the war ran its course.

He had heard so much about Britain, his home country. Surrounded by other British expatriates he had listened to their stories about former lives in Britain, memories tinged not only by nostalgia and a certain national pride but also by their sense of faded entitlement. As the war progressed a picture had slowly formed in his mind of what the British at home had been going through: the bravery of ordinary people under the onslaught of nightly bombing in the Blitz, the heroic Battle of Britain, the long wars in the African deserts and the jungles of Burma, the triumph of D-Day and the fall of the Hitler regime. Now at last he was able to discover the country for himself.

But the sky was overcast and grey, a faint drizzle misted the view. The air was cold and smelled of coal smoke. The houses were small and cramped-looking. The few people he saw looked tired, thin, unhealthy and distinctly unheroic. And what were those small wheeled vehicles, painted black, parked along the side of the roads?

This was the homecoming for Jamie Ballard, the future author J. G. Ballard. It was a moment of disappointment and the first instinct of the disillusion that was going to dominate his life for a long time to come. Eventually, it would be a significant influence on his writing.

The end of 1945 was a time of release and recovery for the thousands of expatriates – British, Dutch, Belgian and American – interned by the Japanese army in Shanghai. For everyone there was a pressing need for freedom, a return to the lives that had been interrupted by the war. Young Jamie, his parents and his eight-year-old sister Margaret were little different from others.

For many of the adults coming out of internment, who before the war had been leaders of the expatriate community – business people, lawyers, teachers, administrators – an early priority was to find out what could be restored of their former lives. They were all residents of the International Settlement, a Western commercial enclave within the city of Shanghai. The Settlement had been created by Britain and the USA during the nineteenth century, and survived anomalously well into the twentieth century. What might be recovered of that?

In practice, not much. In February 1943 the Settlement had been formally dissolved and the mandated territory inside the city returned to the Chinese, but because of the Japanese occupation the handover was unenforceable.

With the end of the war the formalities were at last being slowly sorted out by a Liquidation Commission. In spite of this a semblance of the past seemed a possibility to some. For most of the business people the Settlement had been a thriving and prosperous trading zone until the Japanese arrived. It was also a home. By the end of the war many of the large houses formerly occupied by expatriates had been damaged in some way by the occupying forces: some had been physically ruined, others desecrated, many of them robbed of their contents. Unusually, the house where Jamie Ballard and his parents had lived, at the Home Counties-like address of 31 Amherst Avenue, was still intact.[5] After the family were released from internment they resumed living there. Fresh food was obtainable. Servants were employed, a chauffeur re-hired, a car was bought.

Like many ex-internees, Jamie Ballard's mother Edna was anxious to return to Britain, and she booked passages home for herself and her two children. Just before his fifteenth birthday Jamie Ballard therefore boarded the steamship *Arawa* in the zone of the International Settlement next to the Bund called Hongkew (now Hongkou).

James Ballard senior remained behind in Shanghai. He was a businessman, widely recognized as a tai-pan, and before the war had much influence within the British Settlement. His selfless work and attempts to improve the conditions in the camp meant his prominence had continued while interned. He was one of many who felt the need to get their firms working again, or at least wound up coherently and safely. It seemed to him that with the inherent instability of the Chinese government, and the increasing influence of the communists, it was important to restore the economic independence of the Settlement, perhaps even to resume trading in the newly liberated city. His business was a calico printing process called the China Printing and Finishing Company. It was a subsidiary of a company in Britain, and James Ballard's management enterprise had made the firm prosper before the war.

The departure of the *Arawa* was a huge event: almost everyone who for the time being was remaining in Shanghai turned out at the Hongkew dock to wave farewell. Jamie's father was among them. Edna and Margaret took up a position at the midship rail. As the ship moved slowly back from the quay Jamie stepped away from the other two and went to stand by the stern rail. He could see James senior on the dockside, waving up in the direction of his wife and daughter, but then turning towards the stern of the ship, shading his eyes, clearly seeking a sight of him. His father waved. For some reason Jamie did not wave back. He never really knew why, and later said that he regretted that inexplicable inaction for the rest of his life.

The situation in Shanghai soon turned out to be far worse for the former residents of the Settlement than at first it had seemed. Jamie's father found it extremely difficult to leave China, and he and his son were destined not to meet again for three more years. By that time Jim Ballard was on the brink of adulthood, already determining his own life ahead. His father became a much reduced influence on him.

The *Arawa* steamed slowly down the Whangpoo River (now called the Huangpu), heading for the estuary of the Yangtze and the open sea. Many American boats and small ships accompanied them, with deafening blasts of their sirens.

A voyage of more than six weeks lay ahead.

It is difficult to try to imagine Jim Ballard's thoughts as the sea journey home began. In his autobiography[6] Ballard says only that life on the ship resembled a sort of seaboard version of the Lunghua camp, where he had been interned. As he describes the camp as a positive experience, it is reasonably safe to assume he felt the same way about being aboard the *Arawa*. In the camp he had been used to roaming around, sometimes alone, sometimes looking for adult company for chess games and other distractions. On the ship with him were around a thousand British internees heading home, many of whom he would already have known from the camp. Although the ship was full it was not unpleasantly crowded. Most of the adults were women. There were many young people of his own age, but he remained by nature a loner.

As the ship sailed south – the first port of call was at Hong Kong – the weather warmed and many passengers changed into beachwear. The ship's officers were in tropical white. The ship had been converted into a troop carrier during the war, but before then it had been a refrigerator ship carrying food and other provisions. Refrigeration piping still lined the decks and holds.

To speculate about Ballard's state of mind during the voyage is legitimate, partly because of his recent past experiences but also because of what he was to become.

First of all, China was the place in the world he knew best. He had been born there in 1930, although conceived while his parents were still living in England, shortly before they departed. He had lived almost all his young life in Shanghai, with only two breaks, neither of which he seemed able to recall in any detail in later years.

The first of these was when he was three years old: a four-month visit to his maternal grandparents in West Bromwich. (Jamie was also to meet his paternal grandparents, Ernest and Emma Ballard, who lived in Blackburn, Lancashire, during this visit. Sadly it would be their only encounter, as both Ernest and Emma died before the war. Ballard had no memories of ever having met them.) But he was taken back to England again when he was eight years old, a visit to which he never referred. According to shipping records Edna Ballard's second trip with her children took place in 1939: after they spent Easter with the maternal grandparents, young Jamie was placed for the summer months in

Sompting Abbotts Preparatory School, on the English south coast. One assumes nothing of much note took place, other than the stresses of being in a new school for a while. Ballard's only adult reference to this is the fact that he did remember meeting up again with his father on the way back to China, via Vancouver, just as the second world war started in Europe.[7]

At the time he boarded the *Arawa* in November 1945 we can therefore presume that his significant memories were of his life in China. His formative experiences all took place within the false sanctity of a post-colonial enclave in a foreign city at a time of turbulence and aggressive warfare. As an expatriate he was already more 'British' in outlook than most of the people living in Britain, but even though he was only in his mid-teens he must also have been hardened and alienated by the dangerously fluid political chaos of Chinese society.

His family led a privileged life in the International Settlement: they lived in a large house, had many servants, a chauffeur, a leading position within the business and social worlds, and were existing in an economic and social structure that enabled them to set the wider reality of the place where they lived at a slight distance. It unerringly suggests a complex psychological profile in a highly intelligent and sensitive adolescent boy.

The 1930s and 1940s were a time of immense social upheaval throughout China. The civil war between the nationalist government of the Kuomintang and the Chinese Communist Party had dragged on since 1927. It would not end until 1949, at least on the mainland. Introducing chaos to confusion the Japanese invaded Manchuria in 1931, and the violent and unrelenting war spread across the country, notably with the massacre of more than two hundred thousand civilians in Nanjing, and the Battle of Shanghai, both of which occurred in 1937.

When fighting broke out around Shanghai the Ballards felt themselves to be in danger. The house in Amherst Avenue was not actually within the known boundaries of the International Settlement, but just outside. In later years, looking back at this period, Ballard described how shells from the artillery batteries of both the Japanese and Chinese forces flew low over the house. The family moved to the comparative safety of a rented house in the French Concession (another enclave, directly adjacent to the International Settlement). This house had been neglected by its owner. Ballard later remarked, no doubt with the benefit of hindsight, that he was interested to discover the swimming pool in the garden was leaking and slowly draining away.[8]

They remained in the French Concession until the fighting died down. Jamie's sister Margaret was born while they were living in this house.

After winning the battle for the city, the Japanese took control of Shanghai. The International Settlement remained in theory inviolate, and the Ballards returned to Amherst Avenue, but much of the rest of the city was in turmoil. More than ten thousand buildings had been destroyed by shelling or bombing. People who remained in the city suffered hunger, oppression or death, but thousands of refugees poured into Shanghai every day, mainly from the smaller towns and villages overrun by the Japanese. The immigrants also included a huge number of Jewish people fleeing the Nazis.

Jim Ballard was attending the Cathedral School, sometimes being driven by the chauffeur in the family, Packard, his hapless White Russian governess beside him as an ineffectual protection from possible kidnap. When he was a little older he was even able to ride his bicycle to school. Every day he would pass armed soldiers and barricades, but also see street beggars, starving children and the unburied dead. He was not directly affected by the crisis in Shanghai, but he certainly witnessed it.

Other matters would have been on his mind during the voyage, while the *Arawa* slowly crossed the Indian Ocean, but these are more ordinary, ones that can be imagined. He would, for instance, have been looking forward to seeing Britain for what probably felt like the first time.

The state of Britain, the condition of being British, was a constant in the outlook of the expatriate adults in Shanghai. Everyone still had relatives at home, everyone had memories, and there was a general feeling of stubborn pride in what Britain meant in the world, the benign influence, the benefits of British outlook, the feeling that the moral culture and language and general sense of fairness was respected around the world. The shock of the Japanese invasion had if anything briefly challenged these assumptions, but from an expatriate point of view it was the Chinese who had capitulated and suffered most. Britain, on the other side of the world, had grimly fought a war and won. Ballard would have grown up surrounded by these attitudes, not brainwashed by them but experiencing them on a daily basis from everyone he knew.

When the victorious Americans arrived in Shanghai at the end of summer, with their sharp uniforms and impressive aircraft, but also, and more interestingly to a young boy, with their comics and magazines and candy and jeeps, Ballard had greatly admired them. For a time he had even developed a grudging admiration for the Japanese soldiers and airmen he had seen around the internment camp. He expected that England would no doubt be riding high on the outcome of the long hard battle in Europe.

He was surely anticipating a greater independence from his parents. The accommodation in the Lunghua camp had been cramped and restrictive: for two and a half years the whole family had lived, eaten and slept in one small room, often curfewed away from other internees. The frustrations of a teenage boy confined for so long, in such a way, are all too imaginable.

Finally, most simple and comprehensible of all, six weeks aboard a passenger ship, crossing oceans, can be an unexciting experience. He was almost certainly keen to escape shipboard tedium and start his new life in England as soon as possible.

Briefly varying the tedium the *Arawa* did call at several ports en route. One of these was a stop at the port in Colombo, Ceylon. In his autobiography Ballard names the place as Rangoon, but Irene Duguid Kilpatrick, eighteen years old and a passenger on the same ship, said more convincingly that it was Colombo. A glance at a map of the Indian Ocean and the known destination seems to confirm the likelihood of this.[9]

Before the ship docked, the officers issued a lock-up-your-daughters warning to the passengers. Some thirty battle-hardened British soldiers, veterans of the Burma campaign, were joining the ship for the last part of the voyage to Britain.

Ballard was eager to find new heroes from the war and hung around the men after they had boarded, hoping to hear how they had slain the Japanese soldiery. However, the British squaddies, tough-faced but exhausted by the gruelling campaign through the Burmese jungles, and perhaps also after the long journey down to Ceylon to pick up the ship, were in no mood for bravado. Each morning they made for the saloon bar on the upper deck, bought dozens of bottles of beer, then spent the rest of the day in the leather armchairs, quietly drinking. When they spoke of the fighting they mentioned only the comrades killed beside them at the end of the campaign during the suicidal attacks of the starving Japanese soldiers. Were the Japanese soldiers heroes? Ballard wanted to know. The answer was curt: no, they were staring mad, off their rockers. But, he pressed, were they brave? Alas the idea of bravery meant nothing to these exhausted young soldiers. They had fought the enemy to a standstill, the job they had had to do.[10]

At the end of November, after a month at sea, the *Arawa* called in at Aqaba. Situated at the head of the gulf of the same name, Aqaba was the only seaport in the Protectorate of Transjordan. Administered by the British, Aqaba was used by them as a base in the Middle East. The protectorate remained under the Mandating Powers until the following year, when it gained independence and became the Hashemite Kingdom of Jordan.

Although the *Arawa* was arriving in winter, the warm sun and the temperature in the mid-sixties Fahrenheit were for the British people on board reminiscent of a pleasant summer's day in England. Many of the passengers went up to the outside decks to look at the view. Jim Ballard was one of them. It was his first experience of a desert landscape, and the sight of the dunes stretching away to the horizon was to remain with him as a signifying image that informed his fiction throughout his career.[11]

After Aqaba the ship returned to the main part of the Red Sea, sailed through the Suez Canal and entered Mediterranean waters.

She arrived in the Solent on 14 December and docked in Southampton. Meteorological records tell us that the Southampton area was experiencing the sort of dull winter weather familiar to most British people: temperature in the mid-forties Fahrenheit, a low and cloudy sky, light rain, a chilling breeze. Once again, Jim Ballard was at the rail of the ship, eager now for his first sight of Britain.

His reaction was one of profound disappointment, almost disbelief. It was not the England he had read and heard so much about. The few people he could see on the dockside looked small and shabbily dressed, their faces grey with exhaustion, or from breathing the chill air. The narrow streets of mean housing visible from the deck were lined with tiny, black-painted vehicles with doors – they looked to him like perambulators, or some sort of wheeled equipment used for bunkering the ships. He soon realized that these were British cars, which in 1945 would have dated from the pre-war era. To a teenage boy who had grown up in a city where most of the cars were American-made, with their extravagant size and styling, chrome-plated details, and bright and colourful paint jobs, this was one more revelation of a sad reality that would haunt him for many years of his life.[12]

Nor did things improve as they travelled north, first to London. He was shocked by the degree of devastation the city had suffered, not just damage to buildings but the hundreds of acres where everything had been levelled to the ground. Wild flowers grew rampant in the rubble. London had a shattered look. The people were tired and badly nourished, dressed in clothes that were shapeless and patched. They looked like they were survivors of ruthless enemy occupation.

After London they moved on to the Birmingham area, to stay with Edna's parents in West Bromwich. Ballard was struck by the smell and appearance of the murky, foggy air, caused by the thousands of chimney pots belching out coal smoke. He could not see the sun, could barely see even to the end of the road. Rationing was still in force and the people they met were obsessed with the small quantities of food they were allowed to buy: a tiny ration of butter or sugar or cheese, a minute portion of tough stewing steak ruthlessly weighed to the exact limit, the careful paring out of fresh vegetables or fruit.

His long months imprisoned in the Japanese internment camp had made Ballard used to being physically deprived, but he was far more disturbed by the degree of psychological deprivation from which the English were suffering on a daily basis. The people he met all talked as if they had won the war but acted as if they had lost it.[13]

No relief from this gloomy assessment was to be found in his new, if temporary, home. His maternal grandparents, Archibald and Sarah Annie Johnstone, both now in their seventies, were teachers of music. Their home was filled with dark and heavy Victorian furniture. From Ballard's point of view they were rabidly conservative, socially and politically. His grandfather in particular seemed to Ballard to be a straitlaced puritanical Edwardian gentleman. He later realized that at this time Archibald and Sarah were facing what must have felt to them like the apocalypse of the newly elected Labour government's socializing policies. Everything in their world had been shattered.[14]

Similar feelings were obsessing their unwelcome teenage visitor. Ballard's adolescent dream of a glorious and victory-celebrating Britain meant nothing to people like his grandparents. To them, Britain had become a place whose position in the world was greatly reduced by six years of war, where all the nation's money had been spent and international loans were due to be repaid, where many of the cities and other centres of business or culture had been laid waste by bombing, where most of the young men were still under arms or serving abroad, where there was a socialist government bent on reform, where there was little food to spare – the list went on and on.

For this imaginative teenager an internal revolution was taking place. The old assumptions, which he had only ever picked up from the people around him in Shanghai, were being upset by a new awareness.

Ballard was not alone in this. In the ten or fifteen years following the end of the second world war a number of novelists and playwrights were to emerge in Britain, expressing the frustrations and anger they felt. These social-realist writers were all young, predominantly male and were drawn from both the middle class and the working class. They confronted the conservative, hypocritical, small-minded and unambitious society in which they found themselves.

The names include John Braine (who emerged as a writer in 1957), Kingsley Amis (1954), Stan Barstow (1960), Arnold Wesker (1957), David Storey (1960), John Osborne (1958), Alan Sillitoe (1958), Shelagh Delaney (1958), John Wain (1953), Keith Waterhouse (1957) and Colin Wilson (1956). Many of these writers peaked early, some settled down into a more general literary career, others faded from view. Most of them, because they were individualists, disowned any connection or identifying link with any of the others, as of course they would. However, with the benefit of the passage of time their work, considered collectively, can now be identified as giving a literary voice to that uncomfortable period of austerity and postwar recovery through the 1950s.

J. G. Ballard (first published story 1956, first novel 1961) is an immediate contemporary of these writers, and clearly shared their social concerns if not always their politics. He has never been identified with them, either singly or as part of a group. Kingsley Amis spotted Ballard's talent soon after he emerged and for a while was a stout supporter of his work, but later changed his mind. None of the other writers of that 'angry young man' period ever recognized Ballard's talent, emerging adjacently to theirs, and for many years barely any critics of the time understood his work. He was perhaps noted as a genre oddity, lost somewhere in what was perceived to be the commercial phenomenon of science fiction. Only the more percipient or adventurous critics in the genre of science fiction itself, and precious few of those, had a clear understanding of this young writer's groundbreaking work. Yet Ballard's motives for becoming a writer were no different from those of his contemporaries. It was a clear demonstration of the assumptions that surround not only the world of genre fiction, but also the fenced-in nature of realist or contemporary literary fiction. The numinous and the quotidian rarely meet on equal terms.

The rejection was two-way, interestingly. In later years, in a remark that was typical of his unconventional thinking, Ballard said that the laying down of the M1 motorway – the first long freeway through Britain – was much more important than John Osborne's fulminations about what Jimmy Porter's father-in-law thought about this or that. The motorway system had a much bigger influence on freedom and possibilities for ordinary people.[15]

While these literary contemporaries were launching frontal attacks on the mundane world, ranting against people and institutions regarded as unworthy, Ballard was different. Osborne used sarcasm and declaration, Barstow gentle satire of the working class, Wilson verbose literary analysis. All railed against the establishment, bad housing, employers, class barriers, landlords, National Service, universities and so on. Ballard did not.

Ballard grew to believe that the English were self-deluding, and had paid a terrible price for it. He saw them as victims of the condition in which he found them after the war, rather than progenitors. They accepted rather than acted. The mood was evidenced by the grime, rubble and despair he encountered everywhere: putting up with it all, making grim jokes about it. His grandparents' three-storey house was icy cold: there were only a couple of single-bar electric fires, parsimoniously used, and a coal fire which sent dust into the room and most of the heat up the chimney. Outside, people had to queue in the streets for everything, but everything was almost nothing.

All such matters depressed him but did not antagonize him. His experiences of the violence of war and internment in China soon receded, began to seem distant, not on the same overwhelming scale as this all-consuming state of mute acceptance.

Once he was back in England new questions circled endlessly in his mind: 'Who are we?', 'what's the nature of reality?', and 'who am I?' He realized that during his years of internment he had been wrapped up in the war in ways that most other people had not been.[16] Now it was over, so where was the England that had charged his dreams – *Boy's Own Paper*, A. A. Milne, *Just William*, *Chums* annuals? Where were the British who had fought back at the Nazis? Some element of national grit and willpower had contributed to the greatness and stability of the mandated territory in the chaos of Shanghai – where was the evidence here of that?

People were exhausted by the war and expected no improvement in the future, but it was the future that tempted Ballard with its possibilities. Instead of raging against the present, Ballard felt himself becoming an outsider and a maverick, interested in society, interested in science, interested in the dynamics of change. It was an attitude that was to persist throughout his life. He said that it was this period of readjustment that steered him towards predicting and, if possible, provoking change. Change was what England needed.[17]

What had happened to him in China was to provide him with the creative energy of his adult writing career, but those drab postwar years of austerity were not the right time to dwell on it. The images and memories of his childhood and adolescence had to be packed away.

2

'THE EVE OF PEARL HARBOR'

At the beginning of April 1930 James and Edna Ballard sailed from Liverpool to Canada, en route to Shanghai. They crossed Canada on the Canadian Pacific Railway, then boarded a ship in Vancouver for the rest of the journey to China. Their ship docked in Shanghai at the beginning of May, and they moved into a rented apartment in Great Western Road. Edna was at this time approximately two and a half months pregnant.

James and Edna had met while staying at a hydro hotel in the Lake District – this was a kind of holiday popular with young people during the 1920s.[18]

James, born in 1901, came from Blackburn in Lancashire, a town where his family had lived for many years, and had a degree in chemistry from London University. He was employed as a Works Chemist in a Manchester firm of textile manufacturers, the Calico Printers' Association, and he and Edna had travelled to Shanghai for him to take up a management post in the subsidiary owned by that firm: the China Printing and Finishing Company.

Edna Johnstone, born in 1905, was from West Bromwich, part of a large family. For a brief period before marriage she worked as a teacher in a junior school in West Bromwich, and was appalled by the dreadful poverty of many of the children.

James and Edna were married at Stockport Register Office on 9 August 1929. The groom's parents were Ernest and Emma Ballard – Ernest was a master tailor. The newly married couple took their honeymoon in Paris (Edna's only trip abroad before she went to China), and just before Christmas they renewed their vows in a Church of England ceremony in West Bromwich.

James Graham Ballard was born on 15 November 1930 in the Country Hospital Shanghai, after a difficult but safe delivery. In the first few weeks of the following year, his birth was registered with the British Consulate, and he was baptized at the Holy Trinity Church, Shanghai. He now had formal identity as British, but also was one of around thirty-nine thousand foreign residents known informally as 'Shanghailanders'. They inhabited an area of Shanghai called the International Settlement, about nine square miles in area, just to the west of the city centre.

The International Settlement was a treaty zone, a consequence of Britain's victory in the first Anglo-Sino War (otherwise known as the First Opium War). The war had been fought over Britain's presumed unilateral right to trade opium to the Chinese. In 1842, under the Treaty of Nanking, as well as losing the argument over opium, the Chinese government was forced to make many wide-ranging concessions, including the ceding of Hong Kong to Britain, and the opening of five coastal cities as treaty ports to enhance British trading with the Chinese. Shanghai, a former fishing and market town, was soon the most successful of these free ports, and numerous British, French and American business enterprises opened there.

The Second Opium War, fought between 1856 and 1860 with the same end in mind, that is, the right to supply opium to the Chinese, produced an Anglo-French victory over China, after which many more concessions were demanded and met. The most substantial of these was that the warships of foreign navies were allowed to patrol the great Chinese rivers. This meant a huge area of the interior of China now became subject to Western interests and military dominance.

In the period after the Second Opium War the Americans and British combined to form the International Settlement, while an adjacent area of Shanghai became the French Concession.

An era of internal conflict and confusion began in 1911 when the last Emperor of the Qing Dynasty died. A temporary republic was set up and run from Peking (Beijing), but in 1919, the celebrated diplomat and political philosopher Sun Yat-sen re-established the Kuomintang in the French Concession. The communist revolution had already begun, threatening the Kuomintang government, and in 1931 the Japanese invaded Manchuria. Events of extreme violence, cruelty and destruction followed.

This is a brief and incomplete account of the monumental chaos in the vast Chinese country, but it indicates the constant background to J. G. Ballard's childhood.

Under the various treaties, the two foreign concessions in Shanghai were not treated as colonies, but were accepted as self-governing territories with their own laws, police forces, languages and administrations. At the time Ballard was born the International Settlement was managed by the Shanghai Municipal Council (SMC), a representative body of leading businessmen and landowners, elected by a kind of democratic process. These tai-pans of the Settlement employed a form of gerrymandering: the voters were all Shanghailander property owners, and under their variant of democracy they had a vote not only for themselves but also for each property they owned, or for each tenant occupying the property. As only three per cent of the residents of the Settlement were wealthy foreigners (the remaining ninety-seven per cent being Chinese or Japanese), the SMC was inevitably dominated by the minority interests of the Westerners.[19]

In spite of the political inequality inside the two concessions, and because the trade was important to the Chinese economy, the territories remained intact and more or less inviolate through the various warring upheavals that China was enduring. Many attacks, attempted invasions and insurrections occurred during Ballard's childhood, including the full-scale Battle of Shanghai, fought literally over the heads of the people in the International Settlement. Nor was Britain ever taken to task for the imperial assumptions that had led to the creation of the Settlement. That accounting was to come later, but only when the Japanese interceded during the second world war. It has continued since, with, for example, the British handover of Hong Kong to China in 1997.

Inside the Settlement the Shanghailanders enjoyed what they thought of as an ideal and privileged way of life. They had little or no sense that they were doing anything wrong. The British lived in the gin-and-golf-club world of an idealized memory of Virginia Water or Guildford, for the French the Concession was a reminder of the Parisian boulevards and café life, and the Americans enjoyed the familiar material comforts of home.

Even many of the street names were uncannily Western. As well as Amherst Avenue there were streets named Ward Road, Winchester Road, Miller Road, Lloyd Road and Park Lane. The French Concession included avenue Pétain, avenue Joffre, rue Corneille, route Lafayette, rue Auguste Boppe, and so on.

Few Shanghailanders spoke Chinese or even heard it spoken, although they employed numerous local people as domestic servants. They were driven in their chauffeured Chryslers and Packards through the streets of Shanghai crowded with rickshaws, bicycles and thousands of pedestrians, but did not engage with that rambunctious world at any point. They did not eat Chinese food, observe local customs or holidays, made little attempt to understand Chinese culture.

This tiny and anachronistic residue of empire was the extraordinary society that Ballard knew and in which he went through his childhood.

In his autobiography written towards the end of his life, and in several interviews and essays over the years, Ballard described his life in China in the pre-war era.

In October 1939, after they arrived back from their six-month visit to England, the Ballard family moved into a new and more spacious house: 31 Amherst Avenue. This had been built in the early 1930s in the classic stockbroker-Tudor style of the English Home Counties. The interior was more like that of an American household, with five bathrooms, air conditioning and a kitchen that seemed to be the same size as a squash court.[20]

Writing in his autobiography with the benefit of hindsight, the cruel ironies of privilege were clearly not lost on Ballard. He described how an emaciated old man crouched outside the gate to the Ballard house, rattling his Craven A begging tin. He died there when the weather turned wintry. When Ballard asked his mother why they had not been able to feed the man to keep him alive, she pointed out that had they done so more and more beggars would cluster by the gate. However wealthy the Shanghailanders might have seemed in comparison to the poor Chinese, they could not solve the problems of the city with a few bowls of soup, or a couple of coins dropped into a tin. Thus, another aspect of Kipling's white man's burden.

The shopping streets were lined with beggars displaying their sores and wounds. Those who died were often left where they had lain. Meanwhile, the SMC trucks toured the streets every day, picking up the coffins that had been put out overnight. Many of them were children's coffins. Corpses floated down the Whangpoo River.

Like all Shanghailanders the young Ballard could not help witnessing what was going on around him, but it was from a distance, from within his luxury household, from behind the windows of a car. He was not entirely protected, though: his parents knew the prevalence of violence was real but they could not fully shield him. When he was by himself in the family car, as he was when being driven to and from school, they always made sure his White Russian nanny was with him. After the Japanese invasion he sometimes saw the soldiers brutally controlling crowds, swinging their rifles and thrusting their bayonets. How much help the frightened young nanny would have been if the soldiers turned against him was never clear.

Ballard remarked in his autobiography that by the time he was fourteen he had become as fatalistic about death and hunger as the Chinese.

There was another side to life in Shanghai. Violence and poverty in the streets were not the whole story. Although the Japanese were surrounding the city, even before the attack on Pearl Harbor, it was apparent that they had decided Shanghai was of value to them as a thriving commercial and industrial centre. They held back from risking a showdown with the West. The International Settlement was where most of the city's department stores were situated, all the best restaurants, the cinemas, radio stations, theatres, brothels and nightclubs. The racecourse was in the Settlement, and horse and greyhound racing were obsessions not only of the Shanghailanders but the Chinese too.

From the perspective of a British boy growing up in Shanghai, life in the city seemed to be an endless round of adult cocktail parties, lavish weddings, bizarre advertising campaigns, swimming club galas, film shows at the British Embassy, movie premieres – all under the bayonets of the Japanese who guarded the perimeter checkpoints around the Settlement. Ballard enjoyed childhood treats: parties, a gymkhana, a display by American Hell Drivers lurching and crashing around the racecourse, magic shows, and discovery of the jai alai stadium with its hordes of Chinese gamblers and ball games of tremendous speed and athletic agility. During some of the feverishly hot Shanghai summers he and his mother and his baby sister would sail northwards to Tsingtao, a beach resort with a pleasantly temperate climate.[21]

For all this activity going on, Ballard was still a sub-teen child, often alone, especially inside the house where none of the Chinese servants ever spoke to him. He made good use of the relative freedom his life gave him. He became close friends with an English family called the Kendal-Wards, who lived at the far end of Amherst Avenue. During school holidays he would cycle over and spend most of a day with them. There was his friend Malcolm, whom he knew from school, as well as his three brothers, Clifford, Vernon and Hugh. But it was their parents, Arthur, who was CFO of the Shanghai Power Company, and his wife Grace who had the most powerful and lasting effect on him. The Kendal-Ward house was the complete opposite of the stiff emptiness of 31 Amherst Avenue. The Kendal-Wards' cheerful muddle, casual habits and general feeling of informality was a lasting influence.[22] Years later, most visitors to Ballard's untidy home and office in Shepperton remarked curiously but pleasantly on the timeless and dusty chaos in which he lived and worked.

At other times, declaring he was going to visit the Kendal-Wards, Ballard rode away and bicycled through the Settlement, following an ever-widening arc of exploration, dodging the confusion of traffic, zigzagging around the French streetcars. Sometimes he rode as far as the Bund, looking across at the Japanese cruiser *Izumo* and the British and American gunboats, HMS *Peterel* and USS *Wake*. The British tommies manning their sand-bagged emplacements sometimes invited him to join them, giving him their regimental cap badges to try on and showing him how to clean a rifle with pull-throughs. In his many excursions he was somehow never challenged or threatened by the crowding forces of repression or poverty. He believed that he soon came to know his neighbourhood in more detail than either of his parents, who invariably travelled around in the rear compartment of their fast-moving chauffeured car.

More dangerous was the time he went with his parents and their friends for a Sunday afternoon trip to look at the recent battlegrounds on the outskirts of Shanghai. A convoy of chauffeur-driven Packards, Chryslers and Cadillacs moved through the shattered landscape. In the rear compartments the men wore straw hats and their wives were veiled against the sun, in their silken best. The older British among them must have been chillingly reminded of the battlefields on the Western Front: the endless network of trenches, the shell holes, the crumbling earth blockhouses, the stripped and blasted trees, the abandoned houses. When they climbed down from the cars they found that the ground was littered with the bright gold of spent cartridges, machine-gun ammunition belts, webbing and backpacks. Dead horses still lay by the roadside. In the abandoned paddy fields were the corpses of Chinese soldiers, more of them lying in the waterways, their legs stirring eerily as the current flowed through the reeds.[23] Ballard was tempted by the feast of military souvenirs, but he was not allowed to pick up even a bayonet. Other Western sightseers had been there before them, some of them killed or injured by stepping on unexploded shells. One of the boys Ballard knew at school had lost a hand when a grenade exploded.[24] Finally the convoy turned around, heading back to the familiar safety of the Country Club and an afternoon of pink gins.

On another occasion he was taken by his parents to visit friends in the countryside to the west of Shanghai. There was a large lunch party, after which the children were left to themselves. Ballard slipped away, ducked through a gap in the fence and ran across two dried-out rice paddies to an abandoned Chinese military airfield. On the edge of the field, forgotten in the long grass, was the shell of a fighter plane. He managed to scramble up into the cockpit. He sat on the low metal pilot's seat, surrounded by the grimy controls. It was for him a magical experience. He was alone with this stricken but mysterious craft, an authentic dream of flight. He returned to the old aircraft three or four more times whenever he was brought to another lunch party at the house. On his last visit several Japanese soldiers were there, inspecting the hangar. He was spotted, and ordered away. Years later, this small airfield became the site of Shanghai Hongqiao International Airport.[25]

Because of the American presence in the Settlement, always culturally modern if not socially dominant, some of the reading material he came across would not at that time have been read by children in Britain. Ballard eagerly devoured comic books about Superman, Flash Gordon, Buck Rogers and the early appearances of the Batman, but most of his reading was more conventional. He read children's versions of *Alice's Adventures in Wonderland*, *Gulliver's Travels* and *Robinson Crusoe*, then when he was a little older *Treasure Island*, *Arabian Nights* and the short tales and fables of the Brothers Grimm and Hans Christian Andersen. He also read *The Water Babies* by Charles Kingsley, which years later he described as 'one of the most unpleasant works of fiction I have ever read'. He considered Stevenson and Kingsley were as important an influence on his writing as Joseph Conrad and Graham Greene, filling him with feelings of fright and morbidity.[26]

Once back in Shanghai after the visit to England in 1939, Ballard and his father often listened together to news from London on a short-wave radio. Now that war had broken out in Europe nothing about it could be ignored, even though it was a long way away. During that first winter they were gripped by the story of an almost invincible pocket battleship being hunted by the Royal Navy. In his autobiography Ballard describes this as the loss of HMS *Hood* during the chase and final sinking of the *Bismarck*, but that important event did not occur until 1941. It seems more likely that the naval battle he listened to was the heroic pursuit of the *Graf Spee*, and the eventual scuttling of the German battleship in the estuary of Rio de la Plata.[27]

And then there was school. From the age of five he attended the Cathedral Boys' School, where the teachers were British and the headmaster was a Church of England clergyman, the Reverend P. C. Matthews. Jamie's mother, a former teacher, had taught her son to read before he started school, which put him at a slight advantage in the early years.[28] The school was run along English lines, offering an education equivalent to similar schools in Britain, with an emphasis on Latin and the scriptures. The boys were worked hard, with much homework having to be completed in the evenings.

Ballard disliked the Reverend Matthews, whom he thought sadistic. This perhaps overstates the case, but Matthews was at least a fierce disciplinarian. He was free with the cane and frequently slapped boys, even small ones, across the face. Because of his father's prominence in the expat community Ballard noticed that Matthews only assaulted those boys who had fathers from more modest backgrounds. He himself managed to escape the headmaster's physical wrath. But he was routinely punished along with everyone else, often for the most trivial infraction, with the imposition of five hundred lines. The boys were expected to copy out long chunks of books by authors like G. A. Henty, the Victorian adventure writer and moralist.

One day Ballard was painfully copying the tenth page of one of these interminable books when he suddenly realized it would be easier and faster to make up his own lines. Later, Matthews said to him, 'Next time you copy out your lines, don't pick some trashy adventure story.' Ballard gleefully described this as his first review, spurring him on. He knew he was doing the right thing.[29]

He also noted that a few years later, when the British civilians were interned together, Reverend Matthews was quick to remove his dog collar, spent hours sunbathing outside the camp buildings and revealed himself to be something of a ladies' man.[30]

Ballard was eleven years old when the Japanese attacked Pearl Harbor, the provocation of war with the United States, Britain and other Allied countries. Inside China, already occupied, the Pearl Harbor attack was also the event that initiated a determined Japanese action against what remained of Chinese resistance. Soon, they were in occupation of the whole country. Shanghai fell to the Japanese at the same time as the attack on Pearl Harbor, but because of the International Date Line the date was one day later.

In the early hours of 8 December 1941 the Japanese attacked the two river gunboats, one British and one American. These had been stationed in Shanghai waters as symbolic protectors of the International Settlement, but which were mostly used by the Shanghailanders as a means of maintaining radio contact with home. First, the Japanese boarded the USS *Wake*. The crew surrendered and were taken captive. (The *Wake* was the only US Navy vessel captured during the second world war. Under another name she was to serve in the Japanese Imperial Navy for the rest of the war.[31]) The Japanese then boarded the Royal Navy gunboat HMS *Peterel*. The crew here fought back, and after a brief exchange of fire the *Peterel* capsized and sank. There were six fatal casualties but the rest of the crew, including the captain, Temporary Lieutenant Stephen Polkinghorn, were taken into captivity and interned for the rest of the war.

Soon after this, Japanese tanks entered the International Settlement, clanking down the streets. This was both alarming and thrilling to young Ballard, and also a relief: he was spared the scripture exam he was supposed to have been taking that day.[32]

The presence of Japanese troops in Shanghai was already familiar long before Pearl Harbor. Back in 1937, even before the Battle of Shanghai, the Japanese had consolidated their hold on the city by setting up a puppet regime in the Greater Shanghai Municipality. This extended to all areas outside the International Settlement and the French Concession, meaning they continued to respect the neutrality of the foreign zones, at least for the time being. (In July 1940, after the German conquest of France, things had changed for the inhabitants of the French Concession. When the French State was set up under Marshal Pétain – Vichy France – the Concession was deemed to be allied to Germany, an ally of Japan, and therefore able to enjoy a certain amount of independence.)

Once war was fully declared the Kempeitai, the Japanese military police or gendarmerie, roughly equivalent to the Nazi Gestapo, became active. Life in the International Settlement was disrupted as much as everyone expected, with several hundred British and American men being rounded up and interned. Ballard's father was not among them, though, and his company was allowed to continue trading. In some respects the inviolability of the Settlement continued to seem secure, if only observed by lip service. The Ballard family continued to live in their house in Amherst Avenue. They kept on all their servants, apart from the chauffeur, who had to be let go because all civilian cars were confiscated. (He was re-employed by the Ballards after the war.) James senior had to buy a bicycle to take him to and from his office. The world of tennis parties, bridge clubs, swimming regattas and film premieres was ended. They could no longer go to the department stores. The Country Club was converted to a Japanese officers' club. Adult civilians were required to wear identifying armbands, red with a number.[33]

Oddly, the incursion of the Japanese at first benefited Ballard. Once the Battle of Shanghai was over, his school had merged with the Cathedral Girls' School, on the western edge of the Settlement. This placed his schooling within easy bicycling distance of home, meaning that he no longer needed to be chauffeured in the family car. Better still, he was free of the indignity of being watched over by the nanny, compared with which the constant presence of armed Japanese troops and time-consuming roadblocks seemed a minor inconvenience.[34]

Two days after the attacks on the small gunboats in Shanghai, news came in of a greater disaster: two of Britain's finest capital ships, the battlecruiser *Repulse* and the battleship *Prince of Wales* were sunk in the South China Sea, off the coast of Malaya. Eight hundred and forty seamen were lost. Two months later Singapore fell to the Japanese, an even greater humiliation to the British, who now lacked influence, political or military, anywhere in the entire Pacific region. The British residents of the International Settlement were isolated, defenceless, totally under the domain of the Japanese invaders.

As some of the people managed to slip away from Shanghai, heading for the presumed greater safety of Canada or Australia via Hong Kong or Singapore, several of the big houses in the neighbourhood were left abandoned. Ballard, still making his bicycle expeditions, realized how many of these had swimming pools in the grounds, drained by the residents before they left. The first pool he had noticed was during his temporary stay in the French Concession, but now the sight was being repeated around places and areas with which he was familiar. He held a tremendous schoolboy admiration for the Japanese soldiers he saw about the streets, but he was intensely patriotic and he and his family felt the pain of the loss of British prestige. He was beginning to see these intriguing white-tiled and pale-blue-painted excavations as symbolic of the power that was draining away.[35]

In later years images of drained swimming pools became a recurrent motif in Ballard's fiction.

Those freedoms that remained were gradually eroded. The Japanese segmented Shanghai into various districts, bounded by barbed wire, so that movement from one zone to another was impossible except at certain times. Sometimes Jamie was joined by his father on his way to school. One morning they found that all the checkpoints were closed. Undeterred, James senior wheeled his bicycle through the crowd and set off towards a house belonging to English friends. Their long garden ended at the barbed-wire fence first erected around the Settlement in 1937. They lifted their bicycles over the loosened wire and stepped into the grounds of a derelict casino and nightclub. This was named the Del Monte. Concerned that there might be Japanese in the building, his father told Jamie to wait and walked through an open rear door. After a few minutes Ballard could no longer hold back and followed, walking quietly through the silent gaming rooms. The floor was covered with broken glass and betting chips. A roulette table lay on its side, exposing the machinery inside. Gilded statuettes propped up the canopy of the bars that ran the length of the casino, and on the floor ornate chandeliers cut down from the ceiling tilted among the debris of bottles and old newspapers. Everywhere gold glimmered in the half-light, transforming this derelict casino into a magical cavern from the tales of the Arabian Nights.

But for Ballard it held a deeper meaning, a sense that reality was itself a stage set that could be dismantled at any moment. No matter how magnificent anything appeared, it could in a few moments be swept aside into the debris of the past. He began to believe that the ruined casino, like the city and the world beyond it, was now more real and meaningful than it had been when it was thronged with gamblers and dancers.

Then his father reappeared and led the way to the rear door. They parted at the ramshackle gates of the casino. James senior cycled off to his office while Ballard rode the few hundred yards to the Cathedral School and another day of Latin unseens.[36]

Abandoned houses and office buildings held a special magic for him. On his way home from school he would often pause to stare up at the blank windows of an empty apartment block. This haphazard rearrangement of the city gave him his first taste of the surrealism of everyday existence.

In general, life in the Settlement was becoming more difficult. Inflation was eating into the value of everyone's money, and banks were allowing only small withdrawals of cash.[37] Money was therefore increasingly scarce and accommodation was becoming crowded. The sense of luxury began to be seen as a thing of the past. The one hope that all Westerners shared was that their distant governments would send ships or aircraft to repatriate them. They dreamed of liners docking in the harbour to collect them, large seaplanes skimming down to the Whangpoo River. Hugh Collar, chairman of the British Residents' Association, knew that there was constant contact with the Swiss Consulate. Negotiations for repatriation were in hand and snags were slowly being ironed out. Numbers were fixed and a tentative date mentioned. There would be so many places for British, so many for Dutch, so many for other nationals. It was all being arranged.[38] But only slowly – those distant governments had other priorities.

One of the people feeling the gradual restrictions on freedom was a woman called Peggy Pemberton-Carter. Following the deaths of her adoptive parents she was financially independent, living alone in a luxurious penthouse apartment in Shanghai. She was a talented pianist and spoke several languages. When the war broke out she began a diary and managed to maintain it during the time she was interned. Although her diary does not mention Jimmy Ballard at any point her experiences in the internment camp run parallel to his. Knowing what was inevitably to come she began selling off her more valuable furniture and property, and made sure her Chinese servants, who had been with her for many years, would be provided for.

Her diary was later published under her married name: Peggy Abkhazi.[39]

In August the neon lights of Shanghai were turned off for the duration. At the same time the people the Japanese referred to as enemy subjects – meaning mostly the British and Americans – were barred from cinemas, nightclubs, the racecourse, the jai alai court and the huge sporting track and stadium known as the Canidrome. The expatriates were feeling the steady deterioration of the world they knew, and the tightening grip of repression.[40]

Since the end of the Battle of Shanghai in 1937 the British had been allowed to continue to govern the Settlement themselves. Their methods might seem quaint, but had a ring of familiarity to anyone who has lived in the middle-class shires of England. The Shanghai Municipal Council acted rather like a parish or borough council, dominated by well-meaning but self-interested business leaders and professionals. At a slightly lower level, representing the ordinary expat, was the British Residents'

Association, or BRA. This apparently reasonable form of administrative democracy, comprehensible to all property-owning Brits, clearly could not sustain itself against the power of the Japanese Army.

It was therefore not long before change came and after that it was obvious who was now in charge. The first step was a take-over of the SMC, by the same quasi-democratic means that had been used by the British incumbents to gain power: the Japanese out-manoeuvred the committee on voting rights, and brutally backed up their new ascendancy: when the Chairman, Mr W. J. Keswick, stood up to speak, one of the Japanese delegates pulled out a gun and shot him. Transition of power was immediately understood to be complete. (Mr Keswick was taken to hospital, where he recovered.[41])

At the beginning of 1943 Britain and the United States signed treaties relinquishing their 'extra-territorial' rights in parts of Shanghai and other ports. Under the treaties these were formally handed back to the Chinese Nationalist government, now based in Chungking, although in reality the Japanese controlled Shanghai and most of the other ports. Shanghai's International Settlement therefore ceased formally to exist. A few months later the Vichy government of France would also renounce the Concession that it had held in Shanghai since 1849.

The expatriate life in Shanghai was definitively at an end, and all those who dwelt in its anachronistic pleasures were totally at the mercy of the Japanese. J. G. Ballard was still only twelve years old.

3

'A LANDSCAPE OF AIRFIELDS'

From the end of January 1943, the removal from Shanghai of 'enemy subjects' was carried out in an orderly manner by the Japanese occupiers. There was a discipline to it, almost a formality, but it was also compulsory. The first camps to be set up were called Ash Camp and Pootung: the Lunghua camp, where the Ballards were designated to be sent, was opened later, but at first only men were taken there.[42] It was based at the former Kiansu Middle School, a teacher training college in Minghong Road.

The buildings at the centre of the Lunghua compound had become dilapidated after neglect and military action. The male internees did what they could to carry out necessary repairs. In the middle of April the Ballard family, along with the remaining foreign inhabitants of the Settlement, were removed from the city. They were therefore among the last to be interned.

They had to make their own way to the American Club near the Great Western Road, where they assembled by the swimming pool. Ballard remembered that several of the women had wrapped themselves in fur coats in spite of the warm weather, sitting around the pool surrounded by their suitcases.[43] Some people came with nothing more than the clothes they were wearing, but others brought many possessions. Ballard's parents, with foresight, had carefully packed textbooks for their children: Latin, science, history, Shakespeare, an anthology of English poetry compiled by Robert Lynd.[44]

A long wait followed until a convoy of French-owned coaches arrived to pick them up. Guarded by Japanese troops they were driven south to an area several miles from the centre of Shanghai, a zone of abandoned paddy fields and drained canals. The camp was close to a malarial swamp and next to a military airfield.

A local landmark, the Lunghua Pagoda, stood nearby.

First impressions of the camp were that what had once been a college campus had been seriously damaged by the fighting. It was a rough, treeless area, much of it still covered by broken rubble. Some of the main buildings survived, although they carried the evidence of past fighting in the pockmarks, bullet scars and broken windows. Long wooden huts had been recently erected, and there were quarters where the Japanese guards were housed. There was a pervasive smell of sewage.

With the final tranche of internees there were now about two thousand people in the camp. Most were British, but there were also a few Dutch, Russians, South Africans, Belgians and French. A few months later a small group of American sailors joined them: their freighter had been seized by the Japanese, and they were transferred to Lunghua from Pootung camp.[45]

The men who had been moved to the camp earlier had worked to prepare for this huge new influx, clearing away rubble, repairing the doors and floors, servicing the water system. Floors were cleaned. Beds were set out. Hot water and electric lights were working. Someone with a thin sense of humour had put up a banner with the words *WELCOME HOME*. The men came out to the buses to help with moving people and their heavy luggage into the buildings. They had already made a start on preparing a list of basic facts about what people would need to know, minimizing the chaos created by so many people arriving at once.[46]

The Japanese directed the single women to the wooden huts, already partly in use as dormitories and soon filled to capacity. Single men and couples with no children were housed in what were now designated E Block and F Block. Families with children were allocated to rooms within the main building. The Ballards were assigned to a single small room in G Block – they were to spend the next two and a half years crammed into this tiny space, formerly a lodging for one student. Ballard remarked later that it was the same size single room that had been given to servants in Amherst Avenue. Inside this cramped space two adults, a teenage boy and a five-year-old girl had to eat, sleep, relax, undress and dress, and spend long hours trapped inside by the overnight curfew and blackout.

Immediately after arriving Ballard went exploring – he knew his parents would be glad to see the back of him for a while. He wanted to make contact with people he knew from school, who would have arrived on some of the other buses. He discovered almost at once that outside the overcrowded buildings the camp was the sort of place for a slightly rough-and-ready holiday. Most of the men, whom he had normally only ever seen in business suits or leisurewear for the social club, were now walking around in cotton shorts, open-necked shirts and sunhats. Some of the women too, even the ones he recognized as the rather formal young mothers he had seen collecting their children from school, were in beachwear and sunglasses. Sports teams were being picked. The cinder paths across the rubble had been awarded names like 'Piccadilly', 'Oxford Street' and 'the Strand'. Various amenities in the temporary buildings were given sarcastic labels: 'Bubbling Well' (the washroom), 'Loose Women' (the huts for single women), and so on. A dry and gently self-mocking British sense of humour prevailed.

In his autobiography Ballard described his experiences in the camp as 'my last real childhood home', where he spent two and a half 'largely happy years'. He sometimes said it was the best time of his life. He depicted himself as a friendly, optimistic boy, eager to make friends, pleased to run errands in return for the loan of an old copy of *Life* magazine, or going around with a chess set, challenging anyone who was willing to play a few games with him. He soon had regular opponents, glad of the temporary relief from the endless boredom of captivity. Some of these friends of his parents affectionately called him *Shanghai Jim*.[47]

Over the weeks he also befriended some of the Shanghailanders he had previously found it impossible to meet, screened off as he had been by his privileged childhood. He immediately liked these 'devious and unscrupulous characters' who had habituated the bars, the hotels, the kitchens, the laundries, the car repair shops, the racecourse. He found they had what he described as a colossal vitality. They spoke entertainingly of scams and rackets, rigged bets, casual jobs for quick money, shady property deals they had known about or been involved with. They were not at all as repressed as the British middle class. They amused him, gave him new insights, and were more generous with the share of the sweet potatoes they offered him than the missionaries, the teachers, the business people.[48]

The food the internees were provided with in the camp was unappetizing, but it kept them alive. Staples produced by the Japanese included congee (a kind of rice porridge, stewed into a pulpy liquid), a weak vegetable soup in which tiny pieces of gristly horse meat might sometimes be found, hard black bread that tasted as if it contained floor sweepings, and sweet potatoes and cracked wheat, normally given to cattle as fodder. Ballard loved the sweet potatoes. In the early days in the camp, people drew on the supplies of fresh and tinned food they had brought with them, and these helped eke out the prison rations for a few weeks. Once the camp was established a slow but reasonably steady supply of Red Cross parcels also brought some variety to the dull diet. Because the parcels included sugar, chocolate and cigarettes, they offered a reminder of simple luxuries. These were sometimes enjoyed for what they were, but also provided valuable items of barter.[49]

In the last months of the war, food supplies were to worsen even more. The rice was full of what the family called 'weevils', which they pushed to the side of the plate. Ballard described a rim of the small white slugs, some sort of insect larvae, lining their plates. Then his father pointed out they were a protein source, all they were likely to see that day.[50]

There was a large, apparently unused area next to the main camp, cordoned off. The hastily convened camp council (on which Ballard's father was soon a leading figure) persuaded the Japanese to allow them to use one of the buildings as a schoolhouse. This was seen as urgent: there were four or five hundred children in the camp with hardly anything to do all day. Sense prevailed and it was quickly arranged: every day the barricade was drawn back so the teachers and children could cross over into this extra space.

The school, soon named as the Lunghua Academy, Shanghai, was one of the more successful features of life in the camp. The driving force and headmaster was a missionary named George Osborn, who according to Ballard did a good job. An experienced teacher himself, the Reverend Osborn found abundant extra teaching skills from amongst the many professionals interned. Although there were never enough textbooks available, the quality of education was comparable with that of an English school. They were even able to set exams recognized by the University of London. When Ballard eventually returned to Britain and mainstream schooling, his academic attainments turned out not to have suffered.[51]

The adults were for the most part pleased with the activities of the school. Even the Japanese guards realized its social importance, and its function as a means of managing behaviour in the camp. Closing the school and returning the children to the main camp all day was sometimes used as a sanction against the adults if they were perceived to have broken the rules, such as by attempting escape. Towards the end of the war there were in fact sporadic attempts at this, but sometimes the mere threat of a school closure was enough of a deterrent.

Peggy Abkhazi (née Pemberton-Carter) managed to keep a diary throughout her internment, at some personal risk. It was published as a book in Canada in 1981 under the title *A Curious Cage*, and reprinted in the UK in 1995 as *'Enemy Subject'*. Ballard was invited to write a Foreword for this edition. In it he said how much he wished he could remember the author. She had taught him French, he said, but she had left no personal imprint on his memory.

Abkhazi's diary does not mention Ballard – he was just one young teenage boy amongst many, after all.[52] It is only reasonable that half a century after certain events nearly everyone who was interned should have only a hazy memory of details. Of course no one then, including Ballard himself, could have realized that this obviously intelligent and imaginative teenager was going to grow up to become a world-renowned novelist. The invisibility of childhood temporarily cloaked him.

At least one of the former internees chose to forget him. Ballard was friendly for a while with a boy about four years older than him, separated from his parents because they had been taken to another camp. His name was Cyril Goldbert, and he had acting aspirations. Ten years after they left the camp Ballard and he had a brief reunion in a London pub, and Cyril told him that he had changed his name to Peter Wyngarde. Ten years after that, by which time Wyngarde had become a celebrated television actor, they happened to bump into each other again in a London park. Cyril cut him dead.

Others did remember him, although mostly because of his father's influence in the camp. Isaac Abraham remembered James Ballard senior as a larger-than-life character who acted as a leader in the camp, which was modelled along the lines of an English village. Spokespersons were appointed to negotiate on various matters with the Japanese, and Ballard's father was one of those. A troupe of players was formed called the Lunghua Sophomores: they mounted Gilbert & Sullivan productions like *The Pirates of Penzance* and *Trial by Jury*. In one they modified the lyrics to harmlessly lampoon the more prominent Lunghua characters. One of the songs went: *'They are serving beer at Waterloo, that's the rumour today. Ballard and Braidwood are first in the queue, that's the rumour today.'*

It wasn't summer camp by any means, Mr Abraham said. It could have been a lot worse, but there was no liberty. They lived under a regime of curfews and roll calls, and there was a constant threat of punishment from the notoriously mercurial guards. The worst thing was not knowing when it would end.[53]

Ballard himself looked back on these theatricals with pleasure. He said they were performed on a stage at the end of the dining hall, with full costumes and scenery, ingenious by-products of the endless hours of time the internees had to pass. He said he was mesmerized by the shows, and vividly remembered them years later.[54]

Around the time the Japanese were opening their civilian internment camps, the war had started to turn against them. At the beginning of 1943 the Americans had re-taken Guadalcanal, a strategically important island in the Solomons. This was the beginning of a long and painful military and naval campaign by the USA, moving slowly from one fiercely defended group of Pacific islands to another, heading ultimately towards the Japanese home islands. Guadalcanal was followed by the taking of New Guinea, the Gilbert and Marshall Islands, the Mariana and Palau Islands, the Philippines, and the Volcano and Ryukyu Islands.[55]

Little of this became known to the internees of Lunghua camp. To them the war seemed likely to last for many years, with no certain outcome. Holding on to a semblance of daily normality was their main preoccupation.

Ballard was becoming familiar with his life in Lunghua. He described the camp as a slum, a place where teenage boys ran wild. If this led to his own wildness he remained discreet afterwards, but he pointed out that with so many other children of his age hanging around it was almost impossible not to have a good time. He came to puberty during his time in the camp – the uninhibited attitudes gave him his first experiences of physical contact with girls. He saw it as one of the best possible results of internment.[56]

The conditions were far from ideal, but Ballard's own viewpoint was a particular one and he made the best of things. He began to befriend some of the Japanese guards. Off duty, when no NCOs were around, they were amiable enough. They let him try on their kendo armour, and fenced with him with wooden weapons – every stunning blow to the helmet and face mask raised friendly cheers from them. (On duty, when officers or NCOs were present, the same young men were brutal and unpredictable.) Ballard was in a prison, but paradoxically it was a prison where he felt free. It suited him, it was compatible with his outlook. He was never a misfit in the camp; he only became a misfit later, when he moved back to Britain.

The sewage stench never really vanished but became a norm, and there was nothing anyone could do about the lack of trees or other shade plants. Attempts at growing fruit or vegetables were only fitfully successful. During the long hot season the air at night was full of mosquitoes, necessitating the use of nets over the beds. Towards the end of the war there was an informal estimate that something like three-quarters of all internees were infected with malaria, but Ballard and his family managed somehow to avoid this.[57]

Things were arguably less acceptable for the adults. The missionaries, and many of the professional businessmen, away from their roles, were given physical tasks as their contribution to the overall effort. Ballard's father was included in this. It meant becoming a latrine emptier, road builder, garbage collector, stoker, cook, butcher and kitchen slave. There was no alcohol available anywhere in the camp – the forced abstinence was noticeably problematic for the habitual heavy drinkers after their days and nights in the clubs and bars of the International Settlement.

The presence of so many academics, engineers and teachers meant the camp had an almost unlimited resource of potential lecturers. Ballard attended many of these lectures, relishing the unexpected information about such diverse subjects as Roman roads or how to build an airship.

His agnostic father gave a talk on 'Science and the Idea of God', which Ballard found impressively tactful, and which led to several conversations later with parsons, who had felt challenged but also involved by the talk.

Perhaps worst of all, because more subtle, these adults were disempowered by being held in captivity. Children instinctively look up to their parents for guidance, for protection, for advice. The experience of seeing parents under stress, not free to make decisions, no longer having authority of any kind, was an education in itself, bought at a heavy price. By the time Ballard was on board the *Arawa*, sailing home to Britain with his mother and sister, he felt distant from his father, even while having admired his fortitude during the last two and a half years.

Years later, when he was raising his own children, Ballard often thought back to this period, hoping he was not inadvertently repeating the process. But he said the crowded, friendly conditions in the tiny room in Lunghua had given him a taste for domestic slackness; he insisted that tidiness of the home was a matter of not letting it become a fetish.

His bed placed him close to his mother at night. He loved lying silently next to her a short distance away, as she huddled under her mosquito net. When the electric supply was still working she often read while the others slept. One night a Japanese officer, passing the building, noticed a chink of light coming through their home-made blackout curtain. He burst into their room and drew his sword. He was only inches away from Ballard. The officer shouted threats at her and ruthlessly slashed away the mosquito netting and smashed her lightbulb. He stamped off down the narrow corridor. The people around them must have been woken by the commotion, but there was a deep, fearful silence along the corridor.[58]

A firm agnostic and rationalist, James Ballard senior was a powerful influence on his son, at least in the early days of childhood. He used the frustrating months in captivity to try to make things better for other people. He worked uncomplainingly and tirelessly at the menial tasks he had to share with the other men. He thought of small solutions to real problems: for instance the school building had many broken windows, making the rooms freezing cold in winter. He improvised insulation by begging scraps of fabric from other internees and soaking the pieces in melted candle wax. The lightweight boards that he made stopped many draughts.

He was also a man of principle. James senior's negotiations with the camp commandant, a man called Hyashi, had given him respect for the elderly Japanese. Hyashi was a civilized man, willing to try to meet the internees' demands, although sometimes without much success. Towards the end of the war, and following the escape of several internees from Lunghua, Hyashi was abruptly sacked, to be replaced by a man called Yamashita. The new commandant's stiff manner gave the impression that he was a strict disciplinarian, but he turned out to be more yielding to requests.

When Mr Hyashi was later put on trial for war crimes, Ballard's father flew down to Hong Kong to testify as a witness for his defence. Hyashi was acquitted and released.[59] After the war it became known that Mr Yamashita's entire family had been killed when Hiroshima was atom-bombed.[60]

The end of the war was fast approaching. This was known to a handful of the internees from a hidden radio, but for security's sake they could not reveal the information to most of the others. There was little anyone could do about the conditions, which continued to worsen. It was not just the matter of the food supplies running out, but of the rumours that were going around the camp. These stemmed from the Swiss authorities, who had reason to believe that all Western inmates were soon to be transported to somewhere in the heart of China, and there disposed of.

American air raids on Shanghai became frequent and the Japanese airfield close to Lunghua was bombed several times. Low-flying aircraft from island bases and American carriers often flew directly overhead. Ballard described in his autobiography how he and others stood on the balcony of G Block to watch the explosions, and heard and saw the bombers and the anti-aircraft fire stream above them. The upper decks of the Lunghua Pagoda had been taken over as a flak tower – the flash of constant gunfire lit up the building like a Christmas tree.[61]

The young Ballard felt admiration for his father during the long months of detention, but also became increasingly distant from him. Ballard felt unable to look to his father for guidance or advice, and this lack of closeness was to contribute to Ballard's sense of disappointment and isolation living in his grandparents' house during the drab winter weeks following his return to Britain. Later, when his father strongly warned him against becoming a writer, Ballard ignored him.

The experience of internment in Lunghua Camp was to become the principal source of Ballard's best-known novel, *Empire of the Sun*, published in 1984. Two years after the book appeared, it was adapted for the cinema, largely by Tom Stoppard, and filmed by Steven Spielberg. Many details of life in the camp differed in both these versions, not only from the reality of the experience, as summed up in this chapter, but also from each other. Some of the differences are trivial, some not.

Both the novel and the film will be discussed later. For now we concentrate on what really happened.

The only witness to Ballard's time in the camp is Ballard himself. Neither of his parents left a written record. Although a few accounts of life in Lunghua have been written or posted online by other people, they contain nothing that either confirms or denies what Ballard says about himself, or the physical conditions he experienced.

One of the most vocal critics of Ballard's story of his days in Lunghua was a fellow internee called Irene Kilpatrick (née Duguid). She wrote that Ballard's description of the behaviour of the internees in *Empire of the Sun* was 'outrageously inaccurate', but her remarks were made in 2007, the year before Ballard published a factual account of his internment in *Miracles of Life*. Kilpatrick added that she knew and remembered the young Jimmy Ballard, and that he seemed 'to live in a dream world making up tales about talking to the Jap pilots of the planes in the nearby aerodrome, which was impossible',[62] though in an earlier letter, published in *The Times*, Mrs Kilpatrick had said nothing about remembering Ballard.[63] Interestingly, she went on to describe the running of the camp in more or less the same general terms as Ballard in *Miracles of Life*.

We can therefore accept Ballard's account as published in *Miracles of Life* to be true and factual, given two or three minor errors of fact about dates and names, easily discoverable and corrected here. Naturally, this present chapter has drawn extensively on Ballard's descriptions.

Ballard's story might be true, but is it complete?

In a 1992 review of a book of interviews by the psychiatrist Dr Anthony Clare, Ballard let slip this intriguing remark: '... after some four hundred interviews on *Empire of the Sun* I have never yet explained why it took me forty years to write the novel.'[64]

He does not go on to say why, so one's curiosity is piqued but left unsatisfied.

Much of the work of a novelist is in coming to terms with personal experience: for instance, how much should one use memories when writing a book, and in what way? There is a need to understand not only the reality of events but because they have assumed memorative strength (so have become established in the semi-conscious) the symbolic nature of them. Are these experiences remembered accurately, or are they liable to have been finessed in memory by time? How might the events themselves have affected our memory of the context? (You might remember a painful accident, but do you also recall what you were doing a few minutes before it happened?)

Most of this can be said of anyone drawing on memories, but a novelist is working at a slightly more sophisticated level. There is a point to this: the act of writing it down, making it public.

Common examples of reportable events include falling in love, going through a divorce, bringing up children, an involvement in war, a scientific discovery, a meeting with a remarkable person, and so on. Merely to state the facts as they occurred is not enough – a novelist seeks to understand the context, what happened before, what followed, what changed as a result, how the author and other people were affected, how it could be best expressed and, ultimately, how it relates to the literary instinct.

This is a slow process: it can take years for a novelist to come to some kind of personal or psychological position about their experience. But forty years?

In the case of the events in the Lunghua camp, Ballard is not selecting single memories or a string of them, but a whole period of his life, summed up in some detail in a couple of chapters of his autobiography.

How then can such an account be challenged as to its completeness?

As Ballard's autobiography is the sole literal account of this experience, it would be presumptuous to argue that certain facts or incidents have been left out or amended in some way. How would we know?

But if the account does include reports of certain events while glossing over them, or does not draw significance from them, or omits telling details, we are surely entitled not only to point this out but to speculate about the reason. And we cannot turn to the novel in search of more information: fiction is fiction, even in a semi-autobiographical novel like *Empire of the Sun*.

Ballard's statement that his time in the camp was a happy one, his last real childhood home, seems to sit at odds with his remark that four decades of reflection were needed before he could write about the experience.

It's important to note that *Miracles of Life* was written fifty-five years after he left the camp, and twenty-one years after Spielberg's film was made. It was twenty-four years after *Empire of the Sun* was published (and when Ballard received public criticism from people who had been interned with him). *Miracles* is the factual account (2008), and the film is probably what most people remember (1987), but they appeared in reverse order and the novel came first (1984).

There are two descriptions of events in his autobiography that seem to reveal a deeper, more troubling experience. Ballard does not gloss over them, but neither does he give much emphasis and he certainly does not discuss them in depth. They both involve his witnessing of murder.

At the beginning of 1945 Ballard was just fourteen years old. The war was still on and there was as yet no clear indication that the Japanese would be defeated. Ballard describes an incident in which two of the Japanese guards arrived at the camp, driven in a rickshaw. They turned on the Chinese rickshaw driver and gave him a beating. They set about kicking his rickshaw to pieces, and as the man fell to his knees and sobbed they renewed their attack on him. They kicked and beat the man to death.

This took place about ten yards from where Ballard was standing. He was in a small group of male internees, and they witnessed the whole incident from beginning to end in silence. Ballard said he knew, as the rest of the men knew, that if they had tried to intervene there would be other reprisals on the civilians in the camp. He said he experienced a feeling of deep deadness. One of his father's friends belatedly noticed he was there, and led him away from the scene.[65]

Ballard places this event in the context of the general breakdown of order in China, caused partly by the weakening hold of the Japanese but also by the thousands of refugees moving about in the countryside. Institutionalized by two years in captivity, Ballard had started to see the camp as a place of safety, the barbed-wire fence more a means of keeping other people out than of keeping the internees in. He said he felt glad when he saw some of the Japanese mending and strengthening the fence.

The death of the rickshaw driver was the first violent murder he closely observed. Then there was a second.

A few months later (Ballard was still only fourteen years old) a state of interregnum had descended on the camp. For reasons that are historically controversial the USAAF dropped atomic bombs on the Japanese cities of Hiroshima and Nagasaki. News of this reached the people in the camp through the secret radio, and they were in no doubt about its importance to them. In common with many people who were involved in the Asian war, civilians as well as servicemen, Ballard was convinced these actions saved his life and those of all the internees in the Shanghai area. He said that if the Americans had been forced to land at the mouth of the Yangtze there would have been the most terrible slaughter. Everyone dreaded the violent consequences of the no-surrender creed of the Japanese Army. It was all too easy to anticipate a horrific suicidal land war that would have been fought for months across the vast Chinese interior.[66]

Five days after the destruction of Nagasaki, Emperor Hirohito broadcast his acceptance of the Potsdam Declaration, surrendering unconditionally. The war was emphatically over, but for a few days the Japanese guards stayed on at the camp. Then they began to drift away

The internees also remained in the camp, free now to leave but aware that many Japanese forces were in Shanghai and were still moving about in the surrounding countryside. When some of the male internees decided to trek into Shanghai on foot they were intercepted by Japanese military police, beaten badly and returned to the camp. Meanwhile the Red Cross continued to supply rations to the camp, and the USAAF parachuted in canisters of food and medical relief. Ballard remarks in his autobiography on the feeling of deep uncertainty that prevailed because of the dangerous state of affairs. This feeling of uncertainty continued to dog him for several years afterwards.

One day he decided to walk alone to Shanghai. He wanted to see what the city looked like after the Japanese had left, and in particular to find out if the house in Amherst Avenue was still standing. He left the camp without informing his parents of what he was doing. After walking for about an hour he came across the Hangchow–Shanghai railway line that ran to the west of the city; following this he reached a small wayside station. A group of fully armed Japanese soldiers was standing on the platform. One of them had captured a young Chinese man, and was using a length of telephone wire to truss him to a telegraph pole. When he was tied securely, the soldier began slowly strangling the man using another length of wire. Ballard was transfixed by the sight of what was happening. He was close to the actions. The soldier saw Ballard standing there and demanded he should give him the plastic belt he was wearing, so he handed it over. A petty demand in a moment of terrible mercilessness.

Ballard believed then, and still did at the time of writing his record of this, that these troops, and presumably thousands more like them, had lost the rigid discipline imposed on them by the conditions of war. They were aware that their lives were already over, that nothing now mattered. After several more minutes of increasingly weak struggle the Chinese man finally fell silent and died. Ballard judged it safe to walk away.

Ballard describes himself as badly shaken by the incident, and became aware that a vast cruelty must be spreading around the world.

He continued his walk, found their former home in Amherst Avenue and in due course returned to the camp.[67]

It seems an inescapable fact that Ballard's close witness of these atrocities would have had a traumatic effect on him, deeper and more lasting than the feeling of being badly shaken, and would have persisted for much of the four decades he mentioned.

Consider the wider context. He was a young teenager, he had been deprived of his freedom for more than two years, as a child he had been privileged and protected, he had been cut off from most of the normal social connections and experiences young people encounter as they pass through adolescence, he had no conception of what his future life was going to be like, he was sensitive, highly imaginative and intelligent, open to suggestion, underfed, surrounded by armed military action that was entirely unpredictable, in a country where he did not speak the language. The two murders he witnessed close at hand were brutal, random, unspeakably cruel and pointless.

Although normal parental controls and comfort had largely been lost to the exigencies of captivity, he had at least been with his parents through much of that time. Perhaps a clue to his resilience, and a glimpse of his own doubt about it, can be found in a review he wrote in 1991 of Robert Capa's war photographs: 'Children, as long as they are with their parents or adults they trust,' he wrote, 'can feel untouched by war even during the most violent and terrifying times.'[68]

By the middle of September, he and his parents and young sister were back in their old house in Amherst Avenue, which was still miraculously intact. Two months later, in mid-November, he set sail for Britain aboard the *Arawa*. This was the teenage boy who landed in Southampton.

4

'A NEW ARRIVAL'

Just before Christmas Mrs Edna Ballard, who had recently arrived back in England with her two children, wrote to Dr W. G. Humphrey, headmaster of The Leys School, Cambridge. She was requesting a place for her son, James, to start in January 1946, and enclosed a letter of introduction written for her in September by the Reverend George Osborn:

> My son is just fifteen. I am very anxious to get him back into normal school life after he has missed so much & has had the misfortune to be interned. I wonder if by any chance you have a vacancy & could take him after the Xmas holidays or even later? I realise that he is at least a year older than you would like him to be & that he would be breaking into the school year, also that I am giving you very short notice. If you could overlook this & give his case special consideration I should be most grateful. As regards his standard of work, I do not think you would find him too backward as we were fortunate in having a highly qualified staff in the camp which carried on nobly under Mr Osborn's direction in very difficult and trying circumstances. I am so sorry to bother you in the middle of your holidays – I realise we have arrived in England at rather an awkward time. Would you be kind enough to let me have an early reply, which I do hope will be favourable.

She evidently received a positive reply from Dr Humphrey, because at the beginning of the following month she filled in an application form for the registration of her son James as a pupil at The Leys School, Cambridge.[69]

In mid-January, Ballard became a boarder at the school, which he entered halfway through the fourth form year. While the war had gone on the school had been evacuated to the Atholl Palace Hotel in Pitlochry in Scotland, but at the time Ballard enrolled it was just re-establishing itself in its own campus in Trumpington Street, Cambridge. In this period The Leys was a progressive private school of the highest quality, with an indoor heated swimming pool and well-equipped science block. In Ballard's time the school was restricted to boys only, though it is now co-educational. Ballard was none too secretly glad to be moving away from his grandparents' house, and after the initial period of settling in Ballard made himself at home in The Leys, remarking that in many ways it reminded him of life in the camp, although the food was not as good![70]

As in many English schools, the boys were divided into 'houses', and Ballard was assigned to North B House. He made an early friendship with one of the boys who had been in Pitlochry, Barrie Page. It was not destined to be a lasting friendship, as Page described himself as a conforming pupil, keen on sport and on team work generally. This was not a profile that would ever fit Ballard, who never joined anything organized. Page described him as keeping clear of the Scouts and the Corps, and most of the other non-academic school activities. But even he had to do something on Wednesday afternoons, so he became a leading member of the Non-Cadets, teaming up with another North B rebel, Brian Victor Ellington Helliwell. Barrie Page remembered these two, among the fifteen or so other conscientious objectors, wandering around the Quad with shovels over their shoulders, carrying out badly organized maintenance tasks with barely concealed languor.[71]

Helliwell was from Leeds, but liked to affect an American accent, a reflection of his liking for American films and jazz. With his large stature and untidy black hair, he could be intimidating to some of the quieter boys. A contemporary of Ballard's, Tony Thornton, remembers Brian Helliwell as 'a delinquent ... and a nasty bully ... who caused Mr Morris, our housemaster, a lot of heartache.'[72] As well as the naturally rebellious Brian Helliwell, Ballard formed friendships with an Anglo-Indian boy, the son of a doctor, named Dhun Robin Chand, and Reinhard Frank, who was Jewish and had survived Auschwitz.

Although he was not unhappy at The Leys, Ballard soon discovered that he had little in common with most of the other boys. He was broadly the same physical age as those in his year, but the range and complexity of his recent experiences clearly gave him an outsider viewpoint, which in general he was trying to keep to himself.[73] Tony Thornton as well as others of Ballard's contemporaries at The Leys (Keith Wollaston, Anthony Proudman) remember Ballard as someone who identified with those who had a strong anti-authoritarian streak, but unlike Helliwell he was never a bully, and was helpful to the more conventional boys whose path he crossed.

In February 1947 Edna Ballard left Britain to return to Shanghai to be with her husband. She took Margaret with her, leaving young Jamie with only one place to stay during school vacations: with his grandparents in West Bromwich. For the next year or so the holidays he spent with them represented the lowest period in his life, 'several miles at least below the sea level of mental health'.[74] The emotional distance between the teenaged boy and his elderly relatives was such that Ballard found himself banished from their home for a time, finding refuge with the family of a friend, Bill Weight, who had been with him in Lunghua.[75] What Jamie did to upset his grandparents is unknown, though no doubt this episode did nothing to improve his negative feelings about life in England.

Presumably after parental discussions in Shanghai, James Ballard senior wrote a letter to Dr Humphrey, setting out some of their hopes for their son. Because of his disrupted childhood, he did not want Jamie to have to do National Service on finishing the sixth form (he assumed an exemption could be made) and hoped the school could use its influence to find him a place at university. He added that Jamie seemed to be developing an interest in biology, a subject which could provide a satisfactory career.

Ballard's interest in biology was genuine, although not perhaps with the same focus as his father. He was developing an interest in psychiatry, particularly psychoanalysis, a fascination that appears to have grown apace with his first discoveries of surrealist art. He knew that to become a psychoanalyst he would need a medical degree. As he was interested in biology it seemed natural to study medicine.[76]

His literary education was also beginning. He learned that the author James Hilton was a former student at his school: Hilton's bestselling novel *Goodbye, Mr Chips*, was written about one of The Leys' housemasters.

This was William H. Balgarnie, still alive and often seen about the place while Ballard was there, although by this time he was in his late seventies and semi-retired. An antecedent of still greater interest to Ballard was the author of *Under the Volcano*, Malcolm Lowry, whose father, Ballard later noted, shared the same Manchester cotton industry background as his own.[77] Other notable alumnae included the actor Michael Rennie and the flour-mill tycoon J. Arthur Rank.

But Ballard's life was no longer centred on the school. The campus was in the heart of Cambridge, with easy access to bookstores, cinemas and some of the inner colleges. He described how he would sneak off to the Arts Cinema to see all the French films of the 1940s. 'I would go to the Cambridge Film Society and soak myself in *The Cabinet of Dr Caligari* and those experimental films of the '20s. And there were always art exhibitions of various kinds on in Cambridge. Also I had two or three friends among the boys in the class above mine who went up to Cambridge University to read medicine, and through them I had an early entry into Cambridge undergraduate life. If I'd gone to a school out in a remote corner of Dorset or somewhere it would have been a bit of a strain, but being in Cambridge it was like being a member of a junior college there – which was a big help to me.'[78]

In June 1949, Ballard sat an exam for entry into King's College, University of Cambridge. He passed.[79]

It would be incorrect to describe Ballard's years at The Leys as lost or wasted time. He did well enough academically, clearly learned more about what real life in postwar Britain was actually like (even if through the prism of a select school), and no doubt found out what many of his contemporaries had themselves experienced while he was immured in China.

More interestingly, from what we know of his future development, it was the period when his unique personality, outlook and preoccupations began to take shape. In this he was little different from other intelligent and articulate people of that age group, but even before he moved on from The Leys a certain fixity of direction was starting to show, not rigidity but purpose, not contrived but generated from passions or fascinations within.

At this time his interest in psychoanalysis was almost obsessive. At the beginning of the Michaelmas Term 1949, Ballard went 'up' to Cambridge, although in practice King's College was only a short extra walking distance along a familiar road. His intended course of study was to be medicine. This would enable him to go on to study psychiatry.[80]

Ballard was a curious mix of passion for his chosen subject, and impatience with what he saw as England's mental aspect, the slow, provincial and unimaginative way that people's minds worked, the obsession with petty class distinctions, the lack of interest in twentieth-century ideas. He recognized his ambitions as a sort of adolescent dream, but insisted he was perfectly serious about them. Soon after arrival he mentioned to one of the senior dons that he was interested in psychoanalysis. The remark was greeted with gales of laughter. Sigmund Freud was still regarded as hilarious.[81]

Perhaps unsurprisingly, then, his first day in the anatomy department was something of a mixed success. There is a detailed account of the first lecture included in Ballard's semi-autobiographical novel *The Kindness of Women* (1991). Using the approach and techniques of fiction, Ballard depicts his first-person narrative character as a slightly gauche, stand-offish figure, lurking in the upper realms of the lecture hall, until spotted and embarrassingly brought forward by the professor. Years later, in his actual autobiography, Ballard confirmed the reality of the encounter, but added that he had a genuine high regard for the distinguished Professor Henry Harris.[82]

The lectures in the hall did not feature prominently as the degree course developed. Most of the teaching was conducted in the DR (dissecting room), where students working under careful supervision concentrated on the whole body dissection of the particular corpse to which they had been assigned. The donors of these cadavers seemed mostly to have been doctors. In *The Kindness of Women*, Ballard describes in great and sometimes tender detail his extended dissection of a woman doctor, whose name he learned, and with whom he appeared to form a respectful posthumous relationship. Naturally, he was again writing within the conventions of fiction, so we should be on guard against making assumptions about actuality. Outside the novel he never specified the gender of the cadaver he was engaged with – the evidence of a story like 'The Drowned Giant' (1964) suggests Ballard was more familiar with male anatomy.

Several years later, in *The Atrocity Exhibition* (1970; reprinted and annotated 1990), a book regarded with suspicion by some, Ballard presents as one of many leitmotifs the sensuous and tactile opportunities of the body of a woman. In his 1976 short story 'The Smile' Ballard's first-person narrator buys a manikin: a physically exact and detailed artificial woman, whom he takes to his apartment and there falls in irrational love. As several critics have declared,[83] because of some of his later writing, it is facile to dismiss Ballard as a sexual obsessive, but his admiration for women, both intellectual and amatory, is detectable throughout his work. In this he compares favourably with the more familiar pornographic obsessive, such as the author Henry Miller, whose contempt for women approached the visceral.

The intimate experience of the dissecting room was something even Ballard acknowledged at the time:

> I had seen a lot of corpses, unlike most of my fellow students. I remember the professor of anatomy giving the welcoming lecture and warning that a few of us would be so unsettled by the experience of dissection that we might not be able to face it. If that were so, we should go and see him quietly, and that would be that. I can understand that some people were shocked, and I was quite. You walked into this huge room, which was a cross between a butcher's shop and a nightclub, with rather eerie overhead lighting, and there were twenty tables, each with a cadaver lying on it.[84]

Outside the DR, life at King's College was a constant reminder of the perversity of aspects of British life in the late 1940s. Ballard and his new friend Bill Spencer, who had met each other at a film society or some other literary function, noticed how the Cambridge science faculties were orienting themselves towards a new technological future. The general current of liberal thought was different.

Ballard said that King's was dominated by its chapel and the musical events that surrounded it. The provost was a classicist, a pantomime parody of the eccentric don. In the dining hall they listened to a long Latin grace and sat on benches to eat execrable meals, wearing gowns after dusk and being overseen in the streets of Cambridge by a proctor and his bulldogs. They had to be back in college by ten, or perhaps earlier.[85]

Spencer added, 'There was a great deal of orthodox thinking going on at Cambridge in those years immediately following the second world war. A lot of people saw the university as a place where you went to learn some specific body of knowledge, almost by rote, and you got a qualification and you ended up with a job. But Ballard and I tended more towards the unorthodox in our thinking. I don't want to suggest that we went round waving banners or tying tin cans to things, or whatever else one does to protest: there was no outward expression of this disquiet other than what we said to each other, but I think we felt that much of the mainstream of Cambridge life was happening in some other universe. We were therefore out of alignment with the general current of thought.'[86]

Spencer shared with Ballard a dislike of F. R. Leavis's limited and dogmatic approach to literature, which made Ballard claim it was more important to go to a screening of the 1947 Hollywood noir thriller *T-Men* than to attend Leavis's lectures. Spencer: 'The senior tutor of my college Tom Henn was a devotee of Yeats. He held candlelit "Monday nights" in his rooms (modelled on the soirées of Yeats) at which members of the college were invited to read pieces they had written to the assembled gathering. Discussion then followed. This meant that we were always scratching away at some kind of writing. Attendance was restricted to members of St Catharine's, so when I later met Jim he never took part. But I remember holding at least one joint "writing session" with him in his room in King's. Curiously enough some of the stuff I was writing then was science fiction, whereas Jim was working on straight fiction.'[87]

Spencer's description of Ballard's work at the time adds an extra layer of separation between him and the few other King's students reading medicine. He said he was forced to find friends who were reading other subjects: 'One Kingsman I knew was Simon Raven, whom I would meet in the Copper Kettle after dinner. He told me many years later that he thoroughly enjoyed his time at King's. But he was actively homosexual and King's was an openly homosexual college, famously home to Maynard Keynes and E. M. Forster, with close connections to the painter Duncan Grant and the Bloomsbury Group. The ethos of the college was homosexual, and a heterosexual like myself who brought in his girlfriends (mostly Addenbrooke's Hospital nurses and free-livers all) was viewed as letting the side down, as well as having made a curious choice in the first place. This was an era when most public schoolboys met no women for the first twenty years of their lives other than the school matron and their mothers, with the result that women in general remained forever in a dead perceptual zone.'[88]

Interviewed half a century later by Alison Carter for *King's Parade*, a newsletter for King's alumni, Ballard was happy to talk, critically and at length, about Cambridge and King's in the early 1950s. He maintained it was then an institution hopelessly out of touch with the new ideas coming from America and continental Europe; he still could not forgive or forget the dons in King's who laughed at the idea of psychoanalysis. Had he made good friends? Yes, yes. With an audible nod to his own lack of political correctness and in almost confessional tone he said: 'Of course, the place was packed with pederasts.' When he smuggled his girlfriends in, fellow students backed away alarmed. 'I hated the Chapel,' he added, and detected almost fresh loathing for what he bundled together as 'all that jugged hare – and grace.' There were other contributors to the antiquated atmosphere; 'that old writer,' he said only half-jokingly (meaning E. M. Forster), and the Provost, whom he thought a ridiculous tottering figure.[89]

Inevitably, perhaps, Ballard did not complete his medical training, and left King's halfway through 1951 without sitting any examinations. A month earlier he had become the joint winner (with a student named D.S. Birley) of the *Varsity* Crime Story Competition. Winning a student writing competition might be seen as a thin basis for starting a new career direction, but it did encourage him to believe his ambition to be a writer might be achievable.

The story, called 'The Violent Noon', deals with the ambushing of a vehicle in postwar Malaya by Chinese insurgents. The vehicle's two male passengers, Hargreaves and Allison, argue about the 'throwing away' of British concessions in the Far East, while Allison's wife plays with their young daughter Susan. The horror of the attack, and the more subtle injustice that follows, are deftly conveyed and reveal Ballard's continuing interest in the post-colonial politics of those regions of the world he has so recently left behind. Although the story contains not even a hint of the fantastic it is fascinating to observe some of the core Ballardian imagery – the heat and lushness of jungle landscapes, the sudden and indiscriminate outburst of violence, Hargreaves's body, 'muscular, supple and hardened in all the swimming pools of the East' – already beginning to show itself.

Ballard's first story was published in *Varsity* magazine on Saturday 26 May 1951. A photograph of the young Ballard – styled 'J. Graham Ballard' – appears alongside. In addition to short stories, the caption reads, the prize-winning author also planned 'mammoth novels' which 'never get beyond the first page'.

His restlessness was not only created by his literary ambitions. 'I thought I'd studied enough medicine for my purposes. I had been in and out of clinical hospitals as part of the two years I did at Cambridge, and I knew that clinical medicine was demanding in time and energy. Young doctors work long hours, and though they may over the years accumulate an enormous amount of fascinating material they have no time for anything else. I felt I'd completed the interesting phase of studying medicine. I had already stocked my medical vocabulary enough for me to move on. I wanted to write – I felt the power of imagination pushing at the door of my mind and I wanted to open it.'[90]

Even so, it was not yet the end of formal education for Ballard. In October 1951 he enrolled as an undergraduate at the University of London's Queen Mary College, studying English literature. His father had said, with a chemist's logic, 'If you want to be a writer you should study English.'[91]

Sustained only by a minimal allowance from his father, and committed to the course only by a sort of silent agreement that he would take part, Ballard entered the downtrodden, footloose world of a single young man navigating bomb-damaged London in the early 1950s.

He soon felt at home – he liked London, in particular the Chelsea area with its informal cafés, lesbian pubs and rich friends of friends who took him to expensive nightclubs like the Milroy and Embassy in Mayfair.

Everything was still shabby as a result of wartime bombing, and much of South Kensington, where he found a bedsitter in Onslow Gardens, was semi-derelict. People lived in dilapidated flats but dressed as if they bought their clothes in Bond Street.[92] Ballard himself was kept on a tight rein by his father's deliberately ungenerous allowance. He realized his sort of life might one day be romanticized as bohemian, but for him the day-to-day reality was shortage of cash. Also, much more interestingly, it was a time to write a lot of short fiction, of many different kinds.[93]

In the end, the inevitable happened. His performance at an Intermediate exam in June 1952 was so dismal his QMC student card was marked 'not permitted to return'. He had been, in his own phrase, turfed out.

5

'THE MAN WITH THE WHITE SMILE'

His formal education summarily curtailed, Ballard continued to live in the bedsit in Onslow Gardens, but in November 1952 he moved to an inexpensive residential hotel in Lansdowne Walk, close to Holland Park. He was still in the general area of Notting Hill. Again he maintained that he was not living a bohemian life, although the combination of dead-end jobs and late nights working on one short story after another, does create a familiar sketch of the literary low life.

He found work as a porter in the flower market in Covent Garden, employed in the chrysanthemum department of a large wholesaler. His closest friend at the time remained William Spencer, by this time working for the Benson advertising agency in London. Spencer recalls Ballard calling round to his office in the mid-mornings, having started work every day in the early hours. He was by this time desperate for a break and a cup of coffee. Although Spencer realized Ballard was strong enough for the physical labour, he was clearly unsuited to it, and when he heard of a vacancy coming up in an associated agency he recommended his friend for it.[94]

But Ballard's second career was even less successful than the first, and much shorter: he handed in his resignation before the end of the first week. For a while he had no more contact with Spencer.

Ballard's background of failure with education, abortive attempts to find work, and unsuitable accommodation is of course fairly commonplace at the sort of age he then was (he was twenty-one when portering in Covent Garden). Many writers who go on to become known or even famous speak of their 'lost years' of late youth, working in dead-end jobs while they sought some way of determining the ambition that burned within. In Ballard's case it turned out to be a relatively short period, compared with some.

Speaking of this time three decades later, Ballard said:

> My father certainly disapproved totally of my wanting to become a writer. He regarded it as not really a profession at all, didn't think one could make a sustained career out of it. It would take years to discover whether one had the sort of talent the world would pay attention to. In many senses, of course, he was absolutely right. But even with the benefit of hindsight I wouldn't change things. It would have been much easier for me if I had, say, graduated as a doctor. I then would have been financially secure, and given the sort of imaginative pressures I was feeling I think I probably would have written. My mother agreed with my father but I don't think either of them had much influence on me. I don't think parents do have as much influence on their children as people imagine.[95]

A year later he made a second stab at the ad trade. He found a job with a solid agency called Digby Wills Ltd, where he wrote copy for among other things a cordial drink and cooking ingredient called Pure Lemon Juice. This job was slightly more of a success, in that he held it down for three or four months, but he found most of the work dull, a long slog through the chore of writing booklets and copy for manuals.[96]

Towards the end of 1953 Ballard embarked on yet another potential career, this time as an encyclopaedia salesman. For those who identify Ballard's published work as a kind of unyielding modernism, obsessed with surrealist images and a sometimes shockingly explicit sexual vocabulary, the revelation that he was for a time working on the road as a salesman comes as a disjunctive surprise. Even more interesting is that by all accounts he really liked the work, and held a genuine enthusiasm for the books he was selling. Mix into this a few minor unanswered questions, and you discover one of the more intriguing episodes in his life.

He was sent to work the suburbs of Midland towns, spending a lot of time in places like Coventry and Leicester. He grew to know those narrow streets of back-to-back terraced houses, which outwardly presented an intimidating aspect. It was the salesman's job to call at every house, a loud but politely intended hammering on the door. If no answer then a second try, but after that a move along to the next house. It was necessary to overcome the feeling that the ubiquitous lace curtains were another line of defence against importunate salesmen. Eventually, somewhere along the road a door would be opened. This was when the job changed.

Ballard described his salesman days as fascinating, one of the most interesting periods in his life. It lasted about six months. He felt that by simply going into so many people's homes he was conducting his own social survey of English life. The variety of human lives was extraordinary.

Once the front door was opened you were presented with the full richness of human life, with people's odd habits and obsessions laid out before you. One house he went to was full of budgerigars – in cages literally from the ground floor up the stairs, the upstairs rooms all packed with these birds. In a back room, the kitchen, a family was having tea surrounded by cages from floor to ceiling, the pot of tea being poured, a black-and-white TV the size of a lamp bulb in the corner – everyone totally unmindful of the birds chattering around them.

At the next house, some other bizarre set-up. It taught Ballard that people's imaginations are extraordinary, that one should never underestimate the imaginative ability of the ordinary person.

Ballard said that whenever he has written imaginative fiction he has taken that for granted. 'You light so many tapers in ordinary people's minds that are waiting there to be lit,' he said.[97]

The encyclopaedias Ballard was selling were a multi-volume set bound as *The Waverley Encyclopedia of General Information*. This was written and edited by Gordon Stowell. Ballard was probably hired to sell what was then a new edition of the books, appearing in November 1953. He said that he believed in *The Waverley* because he had read it as a boy. Whenever he was bored his mother had told him, 'Go and read the Eight Volumes.' This suggests, incidentally, that the Ballards' collection was probably an earlier version of the set he was selling in 1953, an eight-volume collection which appeared in the early 1930s, called *The Book of Knowledge, An Encyclopaedia for Readers of All Ages* (published by The Waverley Book Company).[98]

The minor unanswered questions? How did Ballard travel to and from these Midlands towns, presumably burdened by weighty sample copies? *The Waverley* was a substantial production, printed on good quality paper and bound in heavy cloth. Ballard is not known to have owned a car or to be able to drive at this early age, so he must have travelled by train. He would have subsisted with many other commercial travellers of that ilk in inexpensive hotels, before setting off down the narrow streets of back-to-back terraced houses. On these practical matters his memory was silent.

6

'THE ABANDONED AERODROME'

Because of his status as a former internee of an enemy power, Ballard was granted permanent exemption from National Service. But he had always been interested in aviation, and as a boy had been drawn on some deep level to the many abandoned or damaged aircraft that littered the landscape around Lunghua Camp. The flying skills of the American pilots who had helped liberate Shanghai made a deep impression on him.

He was suddenly keen to fly. He found the postwar advances in flying to be exhilarating. Aircraft were changing over to jet propulsion, breaking the sound barrier was only a matter of when and how, and in the field of weapons technology there was a whole new world: huge bombers carrying atomic weapons everywhere. He felt he wanted to be a part of it, wanted that experience. Also, from his particular point of view, it was a chance to get out of England, which he was desperate to do. It had been announced that after the recent formation of the North Atlantic Treaty Organization, the flight training for the Royal Air Force would be run from Canada. Ballard had known Canada briefly from travels with his parents.[99]

In July 1954, on what he described as a strange impulse, he went into the RAF Recruitment Office in the centre of London and applied to be a trainee pilot officer. He passed the assessment tests at RAF Hornchurch, and in the first week of August he began basic training at Kirton in Lindsey, in Lincolnshire.

Here, apart from going through the standard rigours of learning to march, square bashing and so on, he encountered some of the harsher representatives of the armed forces.

He said, 'When I joined the Royal Air Force, most of our instructors were veterans from the second world war. They would tell us, "Killing is such tremendous fun." They'd tell stories about how they'd machine-gun villages for the hell of it.' He added reflectively, 'To use a term like "sadism" and to construct an elaborate psychological machinery to explain this behaviour, however, is to miss the point. The fact is, we are violent and dangerous creatures. We needed to be to survive all those hundreds of thousands of years when we were living in small tribal groups, faced with an incredibly hostile world. And we still carry those genes.'[100]

Ballard's period of service with the RAF began officially the day he set sail for Canada. He was now Cadet Pilot James Graham BALLARD (4154813). Departing from Liverpool, the *Empress of Scotland*, a pre-war liner of the Canadian Pacific fleet, crossed the Atlantic unmemorably, other than through a storm which Ballard remembered with only a hint of exaggeration as 'a subarctic realm of vertical seas, deranged ice and voracious seabirds'. They docked in Montreal.[101]

He and the other cadet pilots spent a month at an RCAF base near London, Ontario, not far from Detroit and Niagara Falls, enjoying the novel experience of full-blooded North Americanness. 'This was great,' Ballard said thirty years afterwards, 'we had a lot of fun. We spent a lot of time in bars ... Part of our acclimatization was seeing Canadian Air Force and Canadian military service instructional films. We were straight off the boat from England and they made us sit in a viewing theatre and watch movies. Among them were what they described as hygiene films. At that time none of us had seen a pornographic film, because they didn't exist in England except behind closed doors ... So there we sat in a darkened auditorium, hour after hour, watching this endless stream of films on sexual hygiene which were quite explicit.'[102]

In mid-December Ballard and the others travelled north on the four-day train journey to Moose Jaw, Saskatchewan, the base for the RCAF flight training programme. It was snowing when they arrived, and all flying had been suspended. Over the weeks ahead there were to be fewer clear flying days than snowed-in ones. Inevitably daily life on the

Moose Jaw base soon became one of idleness and tedium. Like the other cadets Ballard started hanging around the bookstall at the airbase's bus station, looking for something to read. Once the thin supply of news had been exhausted he turned to the spinners where American science fiction magazines were displayed. They were easy to pass over: crammed into the wire racks they looked careworn, tousled, but they were a flash of colour and bravado in a grey world. Curiously, he picked out a couple of them.

It was a moment of singular significance in his life. Soon he was avariciously reading these cheaply printed and luridly illustrated magazines, soaking up the bizarre ideas and what he quickly recognized were images often inspired by surrealism.

Some flight training did become possible. Ballard enjoyed flying the heavy American trainer, the Harvard T-6, with its huge radial engine, retractable undercarriage and variable-pitch propeller, but the training was continually hampered by the weather.[103]

Ballard said, 'Flying is a strange experience, it's close to dreaming. The normal yardsticks, the parameters of our movements through space, are suspended. You're travelling at 150 mph, but if you're 1,000 feet up you seem not to be moving at all. Likewise, you can be travelling quite slowly coming in to land, yet you seem to be hurtling along like a Grand Prix car. The problem with light flying is that it's unstable and dangerous and also noisy, there's hardly any time to think.'[104]

During his time at Moose Jaw, Ballard recorded a total of twenty-two hours in the air. However, the actual flying he did was all 'pre-solo', with an instructor in the cockpit behind him and sharing the controls. He never went solo, never gained his wings and after all the weeks of delay would soon decide that he had had enough.

The last straw for him was an announcement that all flight training was to be transferred back to the UK. He knew the ways of the RAF well enough to suspect that this would almost certainly mean another huge upheaval followed by a posting to an isolated base in Scotland or the north of England. He had already written several science fiction stories, with a queue of others waiting in his mind. The passion to become a published writer had only intensified. He liked flying but the RAF decision would postpone everything he really wanted to do.

Accordingly, he resigned his commission, and was soon installed in a tiny couchette on the Canadian Pacific Railway train to Toronto, a long journey of endless lakes and pine forests. He spent most of the journey with pad and pencil, in a real sense writing his way across Canada, and then across the Atlantic.[105]

As he said to a friendly correspondent: 'I couldn't wait to get back to England & writing.'[106]

7

'THE UNLIMITED DREAM COMPANY'

What was it that J. G. Ballard found in those erratically printed pages, those science fiction magazines, that suddenly supercharged his ambitions? He transformed himself almost overnight, away from the aimless drifting from one job to another, the semi-bohemian lifestyle of cafés and junk food, the impulsive decisions, the lack of formed or permanent relationships. Above all, he gained a sense of literary direction, a focus on a type of writing that appealed to him.

Science fiction ('SF') would seem to many people, especially most other writers, to be an unlikely stimulus.

At the time Ballard discovered it, science fiction was widely thought of as escapism, an undemanding genre hurriedly written for an uncritical readership. Many of the regular SF writers brought a certain journalistic skill to their work, but it was not regarded as a well-written genre, nor one where literary values were considered important. It was supported by sensational artwork: battles between the inhabitants of different planets, invasions of Earth mounted by large and horrific insects, scientific experiments going tumultuously wrong. (In reality, few of the actual stories contained this kind of material.)

In the 1950s almost all science fiction was brought out by small magazine publishers. They were committed fans of the genre, but they economized by under-paying their authors, by a widespread use of journeyman material printed under a range of pseudonyms, and by using the cheapest possible printing and publishing techniques. Some mass-market paperbacks did appear from trade publishers, but the conventionally bound hardcover novel was almost unheard of in science fiction, outside a specialist or collectors' market for a few titles.

The increasingly prosperous 1950s were a time of transition in magazine publishing. The first all-SF magazines had appeared in 1926. During the years that followed, the standard format was the 'pulp' magazine, 10ins x 7ins, 128 pages printed on poor paper with untrimmed edges, aimed at lowbrow readers and heavily genre-oriented: adventure, romance, detective, cowboys, spies ... and SF. The emergence of television as a mass medium after the second world war had steadily eroded the market for the pulps. The genre magazines that survived were now mostly published in 'digest' format – based on the size of *Reader's Digest*. There was a slight concomitant uplift in the quality of the writing.

Most of the magazines Ballard bought in Moose Jaw would have been in digest format. It's difficult now to work out for certain what he read, but it's possible to make an informed guess.

For instance, the issue of *Galaxy Science Fiction* dated November 1954 would have been delivered to the Moose Jaw base just before Ballard arrived, and arguably remained sitting in the wire rack until Ballard picked it up.

There was a cover illustration by Ed Emshwiller (certainly not surrealist, but definitely abstract), and it contained a number of short stories by established SF writers of the day: Clifford D. Simak, Robert Sheckley, Edgar Pangborn and F. L. Wallace.

This was very much a line-up of writers typical of the time, whose work was hardly on its own likely to create the revolutionary change in approach that was soon to be stirred in Ballard's heart, but it is more than possible that he did read this issue. Several of the stories, such as Edgar Pangborn's, set in a drowned New York City of the near future, seem to contain pre-echoes of Ballardian themes to come.

Ballard had this to say about the discovery:

> There was nothing to do, nothing to read on the news-stands. There were no national papers, just local papers. These were packed with stuff about curling contests and ice-hockey. They relegated international news to about two columns on the back page. The papers were

packed with ads for local garages and so forth ... *Time* magazine was regarded as wildly highbrow. The only intelligent reading matter was science fiction! I suddenly devoured it. This was the heyday of these magazines, there were dozens of them, or seemed to be, some of which were really rather good. Magazines like *Fantastic Universe* – it was probably never distributed over here – published some great stuff. Plus *Galaxy*, which I thought was the best, the most tuned-in to me.[107]

And:

I was struck by how interesting science fiction was; it was highly intelligent and concerned with what was happening. The world was really changing about this time ... The first hydrogen bomb had been exploded and the possibility of thermonuclear war was very real ... I had thought SF was all Buck Rogers and Flash Gordon. But when I found these SF magazines I was stunned. They had a freshness and were about the future and the greatest concerns facing the world.[108]

The point is that Ballard liked what he found – he was not doing a bit of literary slumming or striking an attitude. His enthusiasm was genuine. He was also isolated: he makes no mention of what his fellow cadet pilots found to fill the empty Moose Jaw hours. One imagines him holed up somewhere alone with these magazines, eagerly devouring the stories for their ideas and images, while his colleagues stared out at the snowy Canadian waste, or played endless rounds of cards.

Ideas and images are what an intelligent or open-minded reader would find. Science fiction has at its heart an unstated question: 'What if ...?' That simple postulate is inspirational to some people: they do not take the future as a given, a predetermined regurgitation of the past or present. They relish the unexpected, the possibilities of change. They are prepared to speculate, to wonder, to dream.

Ballard was clearly one such. He was thrilled and inspired by the imaginatively possible.

He continued to read science fiction magazines and paperbacks throughout the winter of 1954–5 while his flight training went on intermittently. Gradually he acquired a broader view of the genre, and began recognizing the qualities of individual writers. This of course leads to a better understanding of any genre. He said:

> A lot of the American writers were very good. Ray Bradbury above all – I thought he was head and shoulders above everybody else. He had that wider dimension to his writing which the others, however good, didn't really achieve. I liked Robert Sheckley – very droll and witty. Frederik Pohl and Richard Matheson I also liked – Matheson very much, actually, because he showed you why SF wasn't about outer space, wasn't about the future. So many of his stories were psychological twist stories – the sort of standard story where the character begins to forget everything, and the story ends with 'AARGH!' and he can't remember who he is. Those were the sort of stories I liked. He did them so well.[109]

The more he read of science fiction the more Ballard understood the form, and what it was that enthralled him as a writer. At the time SF was going through something of a minor publishing boom, and almost all the various current magazines were on sale in Moose Jaw. Ballard soon realized that there were, in effect, two kinds of science fiction. He loved them both, but one of the two variants connected directly with his own outlook as a writer.

Traditional science fiction was represented by magazines like *Astounding Science Fiction*, which Ballard realized led the field in terms of prestige and sales. It revered the work of Isaac Asimov, Robert A. Heinlein, Arthur C. Clarke and many other American or American-influenced writers, who took an optimistic view of the possibilities of space exploration and a hard-edged technological future. Their stories were concerned with military activities, outer space, scientists, spaceships, time machines, galactic empires, big business. Many of the writers had a background in engineering, and several worked for the nascent NASA or Jet Propulsion Laboratory. They saw the future as a sort of American imperium which would go out and bring not only peace to the entire universe, but a cheerful suburbanism that felt to Ballard distinctly like the USA in the 1950s. Ballard noted wryly that most of the characters in this kind of SF seemed to wear uniforms of one sort or another, a tradition that continues in much present media SF, such as *Star Trek* and *Star Wars*.¹¹⁰

The other kind of science fiction was much more to Ballard's taste. He found it in magazines like *Galaxy* and *The Magazine of Fantasy & Science Fiction*. Here many of the stories were set in the present day or the very near future. They were in tune with the real world as he understood it, dealing with social and political trends, moral dilemmas, solipsism, advertising and media issues, music, paradox, art, sex, cinema, and so on. Ballard thought of this as the future in the next five minutes. He called it 'inner space'.

It deeply encouraged his ambitions about his own writing. He could hardly wait to get down to it.

Ballard frequently referred to himself as a science fiction writer, or SF writer. He saw this as an exact description of himself, and as his reputation grew in the years ahead it became a proud claim, a rallying call to others. When trying to assess his work, this statement about himself must always be factored in to whatever other evaluation is being made.

At the risk of getting ahead of ourselves, it is obvious that some of his best-known works, such as *Empire of the Sun* and *Crash,* are simply not SF by any kind of metric. Ballard never claimed them for science fiction – instead he would argue that the conventional understanding of what defined SF was itself faulty. In 1989 he said this:

> Science fiction has been hijacked by people who aren't really interested in the subject. Most SF writers are writing fantasy – all these future-earth sagas and planet eons, these tales of galactic empires, this sort of medieval futurism. It's the world of Robin Hood dressed up in space suits. It has nothing to do with science as we see it emerging around us today, infiltrating our lives, changing the psychology of the world in which we live. I can see that by the standards of Isaac Asimov and company, novels like *Crash* and *High Rise* and so on are not science fiction, but I like to think that they are ... You see, I don't consider what Isaac Asimov writes to be science fiction. I consider that to be, well he's writing a sort of technological folktale ... It's not really about the present world, it's not really inspired by science!¹¹¹

8

'EXIT STRATEGIES'

In the vindictive way that military organizations frequently adopt, the Royal Air Force treated contemptuously those who failed to 'measure up'. After his long voyage home Ballard was posted to RAF Booker, once an active station but by 1955 reduced to an unheated barracks next to a disused airstrip. (It now operates as a civilian airfield, Wycombe Air Park.) Here with several other miscreants Ballard was forced to wait. He said:

> We sat in this airfield near High Wycombe, a sort of transit camp, straight out of Kafka in a way. There were great gloomy huts by the pines on the edge of these empty runways where we reject air crew sat around, trying to keep warm by the one stove. They didn't bother to keep us warm, and there was nothing to do. There were two squadron leaders who were in charge of processing us, and they had to wait for various documents to arrive. As mine had to come from Canada I spent a long time there. Weeks went by and I sat around waiting for my name to be called. One didn't know when this was going to happen, so with all this spare time on my hands I thought, I'll write a science fiction story! Which I did.

The story was 'Passport to Eternity'.[112]

Of this story Ballard later said:

> 'Passport to Eternity' was the first SF story I ever wrote – it was written as a kind of pastiche. I think I slightly embroidered it when I came to sell it to one of the American magazines some years later, but

I was still in the RAF when I wrote that story. It was influenced by a magazine story by Jack Vance, which I remember vividly, called 'Meet Miss Universe'. That was a biological fantasy about a beauty contest; it impressed me enormously with its wit and cleverness and inventiveness – the best of that sort of American science fiction. 'Passport to Eternity' was a summary of all the American SF I'd been reading while in Canada. It's a kind of spoof, indistinguishable really from the American SF. It didn't occur to me to submit it – I don't know why, I think I had other problems on my mind. I already knew that I wanted to write a different kind of SF – that story may have been my first, but it isn't in any way typical. A few years later I typed it out again from the original typescript, the basic story unchanged, and sent it to Cele Goldsmith, the editor of the US magazines *Amazing* and *Fantastic*.[113]

Once free of the RAF, Ballard made a dash to London. One can easily imagine him throwing off the despised Cadet Pilot uniform as the train rattled along towards Paddington Station, symbolically restoring himself to civilian life. Or more exactly taking up the mantle of professional writer. He now saw his way ahead clearly.

Before even that, though, there was another urgency to deal with.

The previous summer, just before he joined up, he had been introduced by friends to a young woman named Mary Matthews. They were both lodging in a residential hotel in Stanley Crescent, and a party had been held in an untended wilderness behind the hotel. Ballard remembered the overgrown garden as a cross between Arcadia and a jungle-warfare training range.

They had exchanged a few letters while he was in Canada, but so much time had passed that he had no idea if she would still be in Stanley Crescent. He went straight to the lodgings – his old room, luckily, was vacant. He dropped his suitcase and knocked on the door of Mary's room. It was opened by a middle-aged woman in a nursing sister's uniform.

Ballard later remembered that for a few seconds his heart died – he suddenly understood the real reason he had abandoned the Air Force and travelled all the way from Moose Jaw. Then the woman told him that Mary had moved to a larger room on the first floor. A glad but initially wary reunion soon followed.

Born 25 August 1930, Mary was the daughter of Dorothy Vernon and her husband Arthur Matthews, who were well-to-do landowners in Stone, Staffordshire. Mary's father served in the Honourable Artillery Company during the Great War and was invalided out. At the time Ballard met them in 1955 they were living in a modest cottage in Dyserth, a village near Prestatyn in north Wales. They grew their own vegetables and had a simple and pleasantly provincial life together. Like Mary and her two sisters, Peggy and Betty, they were extremely generous people with strong moral principles.

> When I first met Mary she was working as a secretary for Charles Wintour; he later became editor of the *Evening Standard*, but was then a senior editor at the *Daily Express*. She was tall, with a striking figure and great presence, a woman whom men immediately noticed. In many ways she remained a girl from the Potteries, and at times appeared to be a dizzy brunette, something of an act, as she was quick-witted. All my men friends liked her enormously, and she was generally popular at the *Express*. What she saw in me I still find difficult to work out. I was probably rather 'lost' in her eyes, but she knew that I was ambitious. I lived on the floor below her in a wing of the hotel, and I worked hard at making myself useful. We began to spend increasing amounts of time in the pubs along the Portobello Road, getting pleasantly tight together. Mary was not impressed to hear that I was joining the RAF, but her eyes widened a little when I said that I was writing a novel ...[114]

Which novel he's talking about is far from clear, because all his early output was in short stories. In 1951, four years earlier, following his win of the *Varsity* Crime Story Competition, Ballard had written a novel he described as completely unreadable: a pastiche of *Finnegans Wake* and *The Exploits of Engelbrecht*. 'I was gilding the lily a little to refer to it as my first novel. When you're 21 or 22 thirty consecutive pages feel like a novel!'[115]

So probably not this one. It's a truism that most beginning writers harbour the attractive illusion of becoming a novelist, think about it more than actually start it, and let slip the necessary hints to loved and admired ones.

By midsummer Mary was pregnant, but they stayed put in their familiar lodgings. For these two it was a brief period of making sense of their rather disordered recent past and the undoubted excitement of reunion. They were happy together and Ballard was thrilled by the idea of a child coming into his life, but bearing down on them both was the need to address the matter of getting some of his work to publishers.

Mary owned a typewriter which she lent him, and as soon as possible he started typing out clean copies of all the stories he had written to this point. She read them carefully, was clearly impressed by them and seemed not in the least put off by the fact that they were science fiction. Like many people, she had never taken notice of SF before. She strongly encouraged him to carry on, although he knew that most of her friends regarded science fiction as beyond the pale. But he also knew that she was sensing that there was something original and fresh in this apparently modest genre.[116]

On 26 September 1955 James Graham Ballard, aged 24, married Helen Mary Nance Matthews, aged 25, in Notting Hill, Royal Borough of Kensington, London. The wedding was solemnized at the Parish Church of St John the Evangelist. At the time bride and groom were living a few minutes' walk away, at 13 Stanley Crescent, W11. The witnesses to the marriage were John Henderson and Dorothy Matthews.

Ballard later said:

> Mary's family, my parents and sister, and a few friends attended the church service, which moved me deeply. Three of us, in a sense, were being married – Mary, I, and our unborn child. I took the ceremony very seriously, though not for religious reasons. Mary was three months pregnant when we married, and I would lie beside her, touching the swelling of her womb, willing on this little visitor from beyond time and space. I remember the wedding ceremony as a slightly disjointed affair.

Although parents from both sides were in attendance, and politeness prevailed, what Ballard later called the old tribal defensiveness showed up. The difference in relative wealth was particularly obvious, something of which Ballard himself was acutely aware. The allowance from his father had been discontinued from long before he went into the RAF.[117]

Towards the end of the year he and Mary, now visibly expecting a baby, moved away from the Notting Hill area and found accommodation in a small flat in Chiswick: they were at 30 Fairlawn Avenue, close to Chiswick Park tube station.[118] Meanwhile, Ballard found work in a public library: 'Richmond or Sheen,' he recollected vaguely.[119]

Maybe it was both. Interviewed by *The New Review*, Ballard aired the familiar complaint of many who work in local lending libraries:

> If you've worked in a library you know that a large amount of borrowing is indiscriminate. Someone returning what they've just read, hardly even knowing its title, saying 'I want another like this one.' Very few readers have a specific title in mind when they come into a library. I remember doing my little bit, which sounds pompous but it isn't. They'd come in with a thriller, wanting another one, and I'd give them a Raymond Chandler.[120]

By March the following year Jim and Mary Ballard were still living in Chiswick, albeit in a slightly larger apartment at 69A Barrowgate Road. Their first child, a son also named James, was born while they were there. The already uxorious and family-focused Ballard observed, 'My son was born in hospital in the days, sadly, when fathers were not allowed to be there.'[121]

'Time went by very rapidly with the baby around. I spent a lot of time writing, and of course I had a young wife and child. The period of greatest financial stringency was after we were married, that was the difficult period.'[122]

Ballard was now writing SF short stories regularly, and mailing them off to the same American magazines he had been reading in Canada. He was persevering with the writing of science fiction, and it was probably around this time that he discovered the existence of the British SF magazines.

It didn't occur to him straight away to write for British ones. The American magazines of the day were more widely distributed and because he had read them closely he was familiar with the work of many of their writers. The magazine that he continued to admire most was *Galaxy*. Its greatest strength was wit – in particular in the work of Robert Sheckley, Richard Matheson and Frederik Pohl. He submitted several stories there, but they all came back.[123]

There were in fact two (later three) science fiction and fantasy magazines being published in Britain at the time, and eventually Ballard noticed them. They were published by the same firm (Nova Publications Ltd) and were called *New Worlds SF* and *Science Fantasy*; another called *Science Fiction Adventures* was to follow. Because of a combination of even slimmer production budgets, the antiquated methods by which all magazines were distributed in the UK (the trade was dominated by one large firm who had intractable notions about what the British public would buy), but also because of an innate conservatism about style and commercialization, it was not obvious from a superficial glance at the clustered titles on a typical railway bookstall what these magazines might contain.

The American magazines were, if not brash, certainly straightforward in their cover depictions of weird alien beings, scantily clad young women and paintings of immense starscapes and futuristic spaceships. The British approach was more subtle, indirect, humorous – even slightly surrealistic. Naturally, Ballard was interested.

The quality of work was also different. Although a few Americans made occasional appearances in these magazines, there was a sort of general British reserve about the material, a sense that the writer's breath was being held, that one could not go too far without straining the reader's willingness to suspend disbelief. A lot of the stories were about scientific or engineering puzzles on newly discovered planets; others mildly worked at the way human perception was not the only game in town. Some work was good; these magazines carried several early stories by future SF stars like John Brunner and Brian W. Aldiss. Ballard's interest was fully engaged.

The editor at Nova Publications, Edward John Carnell, known to all as Ted, described what followed:

Jim Ballard sent me a story, 'Escapement', in the summer of 1956 when I was editing *New Worlds SF* and *Science Fantasy*. I liked the story and offered to buy it. He then followed it up with a personal visit to my office, bringing with him a fantasy story titled 'Prima Belladonna', which I liked even better. The chemicals had begun to catalyze. In a very short time stories were flowing steadily from the versatile mind of Jim Ballard.[124]

Ballard confirms:

> I remember submitting stories to Carnell's magazines only out of desperation. And he bought the very first one. I think 'Prima Belladonna' was the first I wrote, although it may not have been the first I submitted. Whatever the case, it and 'Escapement' went to him within weeks if not days. In fact, I'm certain it was 'Prima Belladonna' because I remember getting a very encouraging letter from him, which he wouldn't have sent if it had been 'Escapement' (that was rather a humdrum story). He wrote to me saying, 'Extraordinary story, with fascinating ideas – I'm going to publish it and will pay you £2 a thousand.' I was amazed. I was twenty-five, married by then of course, and it was an extraordinary event. To have your first published work in a commercial magazine. I was overjoyed. I sent him the next story, which I'm almost certain was 'Escapement' and he took that and I was well away.[125] I can still remember the thrill of receiving the cheque for £8. At last I was a professional writer, and my wife and I celebrated by using the money to buy our baby son a new pram. Pushing it past the department stores in Chiswick High Street, a hundred ideas in my head, I felt that I had found the philosopher's stone. Looking back, it seems curious that my first short story was set in an imaginary beach resort as far removed from the grey, shabby Britain of the 1950s as one could go without actually leaving the planet. By 1956 I had spent ten years in England, but clearly had yet to put down any real roots.[126]

Which of the two stories led the way is of course entirely irrelevant. Ballard is correct in his assessment of 'Escapement', which is a well-written time mystery in a domestic setting. It was of a type already made familiar by writers like John Wyndham and John Christopher.

It's a good story with effective touches and several traces of humour, and as a 'first' story achieving publication it is remarkably able and accomplished.

'Prima Belladonna', however, is in a class of its own. Although Ballard had already adumbrated the unique location and setting of Vermilion Sands in an unsuccessful tyro effort, 'Prima Belladonna' is the first and in some ways the most successful of the nine completed stories in the cycle.

One can only imagine the reaction of Ted Carnell as he read this rich and totally original fantasy. Of course he would buy 'Prima Belladonna', of course anything more by this unknown Ballard would rise instantly to the top of his to-read list. And so it was: over the next couple of years, New Worlds and Science Fantasy published most of Ballard's early output, and quickly attracted an initially small but rapidly growing appreciative readership.

'Escapement' appeared in New Worlds 54, published in December 1956. Carnell's introductory puff said: 'Mr Ballard is a new author to our pages from whom we hope to see a lot more stories in the near future. His first story herewith (although he also has one in the current Science Fantasy) is a delightful type of time travel theme in a setting all too familiar to everyone – commercial TV.'

More interesting information about the author appeared in an unsigned profile. It would be the first ever glimpse readers would have into the background of this unusual writer. Beneath an author photograph it said, 'Ballard was born in Shanghai twenty-five years ago and has spent most of his life travelling, with the exception of two and a half years in a Japanese internment camp. He first came to England after the war. Outwardly, at any rate, he lives quietly in Chiswick with his wife and baby son Jimmie. He admits that though she doesn't actually write his stories his wife has as much to do with their final production as he has himself.'

The profile continued, in words almost certainly written by Ballard himself: 'It wasn't until he turned to science fiction that he found a medium where he could exploit his imagination, being less concerned with the popular scientific approach than using it as a springboard into the surreal and the fantastic. Most of his ideas come, if anywhere, from visual sources: Giorgio de Chirico, the expressionist Robin Chand,[127] and the Surrealists, whose dreamscapes, manic fantasies and feedback from the id are as near to the future, and the present, as any intrepid spaceman rocketing round the galactic centrifuge.' Of the genre in general he says, 'Writers who interest me are Edgar Allan Poe, Wyndham Lewis and Bernard Wolfe, whose *Limbo '90* I think the most interesting science fiction novel so far published.'[128]

More Ballard stories soon followed: 'The Concentration City' and 'Venus Smiles'; both of these originally appeared with Carnell under different titles, but are named here with the titles they were given when some time later they were collected or anthologized. 'Prima Belladonna' was picked up for one of the annual 'year's best' anthologies, a book called *SF: '57, The Year's Greatest Science Fiction and Fantasy*, edited by Judith Merril and published by the American imprint Gnome Press. Ballard was delighted. 'Thirty-five years later I can still remember the thrill of excitement, the sense of amazement that every novice writer has felt at the first sign of critical approval.'[129]

Change came again for Ballard in 1957. Carnell, knowing that Ballard was a family man in need of a day job (if only because he ruefully knew the starvation rates he was forced to pay writers), offered to find him a position within the Maclaren Group. This was the publishing firm who owned Nova Publications. Soon after, Ballard therefore became assistant editor on a trade magazine called *The British Baker*.

It was a step away from the frustrations of his job at the library, but it was not yet a new career path. There were few responsibilities, and the pay was only barely better than before. 'There were always vacancies because the firm paid so little to its employees, from the editors down. Colleagues would go out for a packet of cigarettes and never return. After six months I too moved on.'[130]

Ballard's next job was also in journalism – in the autumn he went to work as an editorial assistant on *Chemistry & Industry*, published in Belgrave Square at the offices of the Society of Chemical Industry. The editor at this time was William E. Dick, who had been in post only since the issue of 29 June.

Ballard said:

> I heard that there was a vacancy at a much better salary, and I went there. That was a good choice – apart from anything else because of all the scientific magazines which came into the office and which I devoured. The hours were pretty lax. I was there for three or four years as assistant editor. I did practically everything. This was a weekly journal of about fifty pages, including a mass of formulae and tabular material. I did all the basic subbing, marking copy up for the typesetter, dealing with the printers, doing make-up and paste-up, negotiating with the artists who drew the scientific formulae. I used to go on works visits, visits to laboratories and research institutes. I wrote a few science articles as reporter and I reviewed scientific books. But most of it was straight production. I enjoyed being at the centre of a huge information flow.[131]

Further change was to come a few years later, in 1960, when Ballard's immediate boss, Bill Dick, committed suicide, the result of a spiral of depression and alcohol abuse. 'After this I was left alone to produce the magazine and adjusted my time so that I could write in the office.'

On 24 August 1957 the Ballards had their second child, a daughter they named Fay.

Ballard, by now a fully committed family man, said:

> I was present at the birth of my two daughters, who were both born at home. Not only was I present when the girls were born but I practically elbowed the midwife aside and delivered them myself. I remember Fay's head emerging into daylight; it was an extraordinary moment. Most people imagine that a newborn child is very young, as young as a human being can be, but in fact for the first few seconds I had the sense she was immensely old. She had the whole of the human race behind her, she looked like something from Egyptian sculpture, streamlined by time. Within a few seconds she was suddenly very young.[132]

Within a couple of weeks of Fay's safe and inspirational birth, Ballard made what with hindsight seemed to him like a terrible mistake: he went to a world convention of SF fans being held in London

(6–9 September 1957). The fact that Ted Carnell was the chairman of the event almost certainly had an influence on Ballard's decision to attend. The presence of John Wyndham, president of the convention, who by this time was being recognized as a major writer, might also have given Ballard a motive for being there.

There were certain matters Ballard was probably unaware of, and others which came as a disappointment to him, perhaps through misreading the signals. Although he had published only four or five stories by this time, his unusual work had already aroused a degree of curiosity and excitement amongst the well-read minority who took SF seriously. These were the sort of people, in fact, who would willingly spend a weekend in a third-rate London hotel to discuss the subject.

Bookish people are in general not social animals, and through a habit of introversion tend to make unexpected responses to social niceties. They can seem odd. And as is commonly known, almost any large interest-centred group of people will at first seem to be intimidating to a newcomer.

Brian Aldiss, himself still a relative newcomer, sets the scene:

> Was that nondescript year really 1957, and not 1947? The convention was held in a terrible hotel in the Queensway district. A distinctly postwar feeling lingered. Bomb damage was still apparent. I went to the bar and bought a drink. Standing next to me was a slim young man who told me that there were some extraordinary types at the convention, and that he was thinking of leaving pretty smartly. He introduced himself as J. G. Ballard.[133]

Ballard continues:

> I went to the Worldcon, which took place a few months after I had my first short stories published. I was stunned by how small-minded and parochial the people attending were – I'm thinking mostly of the English fans. Most of them were semi-literate. I'm not exaggerating, one felt that they had closed minds and their whole mental attitude was rather like that of people who belong to some little fanatical UFO

> cult. Their main inspiration seemed to be Buck Rogers and Flash Gordon. I only spent one evening there – it was a pleasure to meet Brian Aldiss for the first time.[134]

And:

> Ted Carnell was always enthusiastic, urging me to break new ground, telling me to take no notice of the more vocal of the other writers (the most dingy and pathetic bunch of third-rate ex-journalists and business machine salesmen I had ever met – enough to put anyone off the written word forever) who were irritated in their usually mindless way by what now seem to be the most conventional of my short stories. Among those who were sympathetic in those early days were John Brunner and John Wyndham.[135]

The outcome of this disenchanting experience, in spite of his having had affable encounters with Wyndham, Aldiss and Brunner, was this: 'It shattered me, and then I dried up for about a year. For over a year I didn't write any SF at all.' (Two stories which appeared during these months would have been written and sold already.) 'I was disillusioned and demoralized. Carnell was the only person in the SF world I ever met, because I never went to any meetings or anything like that. The fact that I was writing and being published in *New Worlds* and *Science Fantasy* from '57 to '63 didn't alter my life in any way. It was just something I did: I wrote a story, put it in the post, got a small cheque, and the story in due course was published.'[136]

Here again is a degree of overstatement. But a certain insight emerges, if one remembers the personal traits that started to show while Ballard was at The Leys; a fixity of purpose, generated from passions within.

There was in fact a short hiatus in Ballardian publication throughout 1958 and the first half of 1959, but no writer ever has a steady rate of creation, whatever might be thought to be the case, and gaps occur. These can often be caused not by brief exposure to third-rate ex-journalists and business machine salesmen but by the arrival of babies, the growth of a family and looking after their needs, the search to find somewhere to live, and so on. All that was going on at home.

And this allegedly dried-up period, and the months that followed, were to produce three of the finest stories Ballard ever wrote, at least one of which is now recognized as an enduring classic of fantastic literature: 'The Waiting Grounds' (November 1959), 'The Sound-Sweep' (February 1960) and 'The Voices of Time' (June 1960). His first great novel, *The Drowned World*, was published in 1962.

Nearly two years after Fay's birth came the Ballards' third child: Beatrice, born during or at the end of Ballard's self-described 'dried up' writing period after the London convention. She was born on 29 May 1959, an enchanting event, recorded in fictive style in his novel *The Kindness of Women* (1991):

> The whole face had emerged, a high forehead, miniature nose and mouth, and closed eyes streamlined as if by time, by the aeons that had preceded this child down the biological kingdom. Waking into the deep dream of life, it seemed not young but infinitely old, millions of years entrained in the pharaoh-like smoothness of its cheeks and its ancient eyelids and nostrils. I looked down at the baby. She had changed yet again, more puckered and more alive, her lips moving while she slept, as if she were trying to remember a message entrusted to her by the unseen powers of creation. Within a few hours she had recapitulated her roles, from archaic messenger to slippery water sprite baptised in her mother's caul, and then a dreamy swaddling.

This clearly refers back also to his description of Fay's earlier birth, but these words are not the work of a diarist but a beautiful literary stylist conveying what few fathers ever notice or, if they do notice, they fail to comprehend. This deep and moving description of the continuity of human experience, passed on through the miracle of childbirth, is a quiet thematic constant in much of Ballard's later work.

In October of that year, after an unusually long and hot summer in Britain, Ballard's new story 'The Waiting Grounds' appeared in *New Worlds 88*. This opened a fresh and fascinating imaginative source for Ballard, with its contemplation of the essence of the universe, the elapse of cosmic time. The magazine published a new profile of the author, in which Ballard was quoted as saying that SF gave him the opportunity for 'experimenting with scientific or psycho-literary ideas. Just as psychologists are now building models of anxiety neuroses and withdrawal states in the form of verbal diagrams – translating scientific hypothesis into literary construction – so I see a good SF story as a model of some psychic image, the truth of which gives the story its merit. Examples are *The Incredible Shrinking Man*, *Limbo '90* and Henry Kuttner's "Dream's End". In general, stories with interplanetary backgrounds show too little originality, too much self-imitation.' Of this new story, his first with an interplanetary setting, he added: 'Seen as a psycho-literary model, perhaps it represents the old conundrum of the ant searching hopelessly for the end of an infinite pathway around the surface of a sphere. "The Waiting Grounds" offers it a solution, implies that instead of crawling on and on it will find the pathway's end if it just sits still.'[137]

Published nine years before the release of Stanley Kubrick's classic film, *2001: A Space Odyssey*, Ballard's 'The Waiting Grounds' substantially anticipates most of the major themes of the film (and of course the Arthur C. Clarke story and novel from which the film was developed). The climax of the Ballard story even sets out a psychedelic lightshow of cosmic images, an almost exact literary analogue of the special effects bonanza towards the end of Kubrick's movie, as well as following with a coda of a quiet existential mystery for the audience to take away and think about.

As in the Kubrick film, the human component of the plot is rudimentary, and depicted as a dispute between three men, one of whom departs. The two who remain finally confront each other physically, reason struggling against brutality, before triggering the true conclusion to the story:

> Mayer was losing control, carried away by his rage. With his big burly shoulders hunched in anger, staring up blindly at the five great megaliths, face contorted by the heat, he looked like an insane sub-man pinned in the time trophy of a galactic super-hunter.

Superficially this is the style of familiar 'men's adventure' writing of a bygone age, but the sheer simplicity of it works as a counterpoint to the almost incomprehensible super-galactic upheaval that immediately follows. The mise-en-scène is clearly analogous to the early scene in *2001*, itself the pitting of reason against brutality, as in one of modern cinema's most celebrated jump-cuts the enlightened 'sub-man' fast-tracks a broken femur into the space age.

A contrast in styles of this sort was to become for a while a trademark of Ballard's SF, especially in his early novels, but it was in 'The Waiting Grounds' that he did it first, and perhaps best.

Within the next twelve months Ballard was to publish two more long stories of almost epic imaginative energy: 'The Sound-Sweep' and 'The Voices of Time'. It should be mentioned that within the same short time-frame three other of his stories were also published by Carnell. These, under different circumstances and in perhaps another context, would have been recognized as excellent in their own right. All three were later collected or anthologized elsewhere: 'Now: Zero', 'Zone of Terror' and 'Chronopolis'. However, the sheer energy of the other two leads us away towards the culmination of Ballard's SF short story writing, thence to the appearance of his first three novels.

The first and perhaps the lesser of the two new long stories, 'The Sound-Sweep', appeared in *Science Fantasy* at the beginning of 1960. The story is remarkable for two extended scenes.

We are initially introduced to Madame Gioconda, an ageing prima donna, desperately trying to relive her days of operatic glory by surrounding herself with mementos of fame. In this she reminds the reader of Norma Desmond, as played by Gloria Swanson in Billy Wilder's 1950 drama *Sunset Boulevard*. Unlike Norma Desmond's, most of Gioconda's memories are delusional: in the noisy chaos of the overcrowded city in which she manages to survive, she believes she can still hear the wild applause, the admirers calling for encores, and so on. To sustain this illusion she employs a mute 'sound-sweep' named Mangon, who uses a device called a sonovac to clean away the superfluous racket of traffic, loud radios, overhead aircraft, shouted arguments in the street, leaving just her memories. Mangon understands there are no real sonic traces of her days of glory. The story becomes a touching but unreliable account of a growing relationship between two extremely vulnerable people.

Mangon wishes to explain to her the reality of the chaos of sounds he sweeps away from her world. He drives her out to the 'stockades', a vast area of dunes where a complicated arrangement of sound baffles and acoustic panels creates a sort of land-fill of unwanted sound pollution:

> [It was] a place of strange echoes and festering silences, overhung by a gloomy miasma of a million compacted sounds, it remained remote and haunted, the graveyard of countless private babels.

What follows is a long and most effective descriptive passage, a tour de force of imaginative writing. The world Madame Gioconda now inhabits is depicted finally as one where she no longer belongs.

If 'The Sound-Sweep' were to be concluded at this point, the story would be perfect – but a third act follows. It describes a complicated hoax played on the hapless woman by two of her rivals from the past. The outcome is a delusional last performance, in which she is tricked into revealing the true state of her once golden voice: she sounds in effect like Florence Foster Jenkins, the American socialite and untrained soprano who set up elaborate performances for her admirers but who invariably sang off-key. The story ends in disaster.

It was one of the longest stories Ballard had written to this point – perhaps he felt there might be a novel in the idea? The idea of sound having a persistent existence remains one of the most interesting ideas he came up with, with some genuinely moving characterization. The two scenes highlighted here are both magnificent and memorable. 'The Sound-Sweep', for all its flaws, should be regarded as one of Ballard's best stories.

With the long story called 'The Voices of Time', published in *New Worlds* for October 1960, we reach what might be described as the peak of Ballard's early career as a writer of SF short stories. Everything he had published up to this date fed into it. Afterwards his talent spread in many different directions, some of it a kind of denial or avoidance of the complex themes of 'Voices', while other works were apparently a tentative return to them. It is in many respects the 'key' Ballard story. It is also a story that defies interpretation, while leaving the reader grappling mentally for more.

It concerns three scientists, all of who seem to be doctors: Powers, Whitby and Anderson. They are working at the Neurology wing of a scientific research station in a desert area, which is accommodating around five hundred 'sleepers', people for whom the entropic end of the universe has been triggered because they carry the 'silent pair' – genes missing from their genomic make-up. At the start of the story Powers is reflecting on the suicide of Whitby, who created a mandala – a Jungian symbol representing the wholeness of self – by carving deep grooves in the floor of a drained swimming pool. Powers later constructs a gigantic version of this mandala using building materials on a former artillery range in the desert. Two young people, Kaldren and Coma, former patients of Powers, have been genetically altered to make sleep impossible. They now challenge Powers because he appears to be succumbing to the silent pair syndrome.

Many animals, some held for research purposes, are spontaneously evolving so that their bodies will resist the approaching cataclysm: Powers comes across a large frog whose outer integument is turning to a protective layer of lead. From the cosmos comes a series of long numbers, slowly counting down from some ninety-six trillion to zero: the exact moment when the heat-death is expected. A key event in the past is said to be the disappearance of the Mercury Seven (the first team of NASA astronauts): according to myth they travelled together to the moon where they were contacted by mysterious beings from Orion, and were never heard of again. When Powers has completed the new mandala he moves to the very centre of it, offers himself and succumbs to the countdown of entropic universal death.

'The Voices of Time', we soon discover, is a story that does not give up its secrets. If there is a plot, an underlying purpose, it constantly evades the reader. Instead, every page, every paragraph, seems charged with meaning, never clarified, never given the benefit of cause and effect. The reader is cast alone. If obscurity is art, here we find it – but 'The Voices of Time' is not obscure.

The language of the story is clear, comprehensible, constantly suggesting that elucidation will dawn. It's a maddeningly attractive story, capable of being read and reread for new discoveries each time, strange in every sense, but the engagement of the main characters is almost vernacular in style. Their obsessions with space and time are natural to them, so we accept them, but afterwards we wonder what they were on about.

Through 'The Voices of Time' we discover the authentic Ballardian.

9
'OUT OF THE NIGHT AND INTO THE DREAM'

Ballard's principal market for his fiction remained the British magazines, with their lowly payment. Selling to American outlets would be more lucrative on a payment-by-word basis, but his success here was intermittent: an occasional story to the Ziff Davis magazines edited by Cele Goldsmith, or to *The Magazine of Fantasy and Science Fiction*. Their usual payment was made not on acceptance but on publication (sometimes months in the future). Trying to manage a reliable income was therefore problematic. The need to hold down a day job was also taking its toll on his energy. It was becoming apparent that he needed a working relationship with a trade publisher: better distribution, including into bookstores, availability in print for much longer, a chance of being reviewed, and so on.

He decided the time had come to write a novel.

Easter 1961 approached, and he had two weeks' vacation due to him. He said:

> We moved to Shepperton in 1960, and one drawback was the enormous journey, to and fro, from central London. It was difficult to help in bringing up a family of young children and to travel this distance to work and to secure enough time and energy for oneself to go on writing. When I got home I had a tired young wife who wanted to go out for a drink, or round up a baby sitter and see friends, or do whatever one did then. I couldn't conceive of myself writing a serious novel while I was not getting home till eight o'clock in the evening.

His wife Mary said, 'We don't have enough money to go away anywhere. Why don't you write a novel in a fortnight?'

Through Carnell, who was now acting as his semi-agent, Ballard already had tentative supporters in the USA. One of these (probably unknown to him) was the American SF writer and anthology editor Damon Knight, whose annual collections sometimes included British writers. Knight would certainly have been aware of the series of outstanding stories Ballard was writing. His openness to non-American writers was similar in approach to Judith Merril's, who cast her net wide when rounding up the 'best' for her annual anthologies. At the time, Knight was working as part-time SF editor for Tom Dardis, who was employed by Berkley Books in New York.

Ballard said:

I had a feeling that if I wrote a novel I could sell it, even if I wasn't going to get very much money. In those days £300 could keep you going for a long time. So I decided to write a novel in ten days, six thousand words a day, during the holiday. I needed a subject, but I had this idea about a whirlwind. I thought I'd use all the clichés there are, the standard narrative conventions, and I sat down at the typewriter and I wrote the book. I kept up the pressure, and soon had a 60,000-word novel.[138]

Carnell promptly airmailed the manuscript to Tom Dardis, and in due course Berkley Books offered a contract. It's not known how much they paid as an advance, but at the time Berkley printed slim and inexpensive paperbacks for the mass market, and for them Ballard was a completely unknown and untried author. It was probably not a huge advance. His remembered estimate of about £300 was almost certainly not far off the reality.

In October, Carnell published the novel as a two-part serial in *New Worlds*, under the title *Storm-Wind*. An unsigned author profile appeared on the inside front cover, reminding readers that the serial, concluded in this issue, was 'a shortened version of Jim Ballard's first book-length novel'.

Ballard was quoted:

The cataclysmic story is particularly interesting because it shows how even a minor variation in one of the physical constants of the environment can make life totally untenable – a corollary of the biological rule that the more specialized the organism the narrower the margin of safety. Perhaps because of their climate English writers seem to have a virtual monopoly of the genre. Analysing the author's hidden motives is one of the quieter pleasures of reading – and writing – science fiction, and from the deluge in the Babylonian zodiac myth of Gilgamesh, from which come Noah and the sign of Aquarius, all the way down to *The War of the Worlds*, the real significance of the cataclysmic story is obviously to be found elsewhere. *Storm-Wind* is no exception, and anyone wondering why I've chosen to destroy London quite so thoroughly should try living there for ten years. I'm only sorry that I couldn't call it *Gone with the Wind*.[139]

The plot, such as it is, centres on the construction of a vast concrete pyramid called the Tower of Hardoon. This is intended to be one of the few buildings able to withstand the violent pressures of the storm wind. Towards the end of the story we encounter Hardoon himself, whom Ballard depicts as 'a squat, broad-shouldered man in a dark suit. His head was huge and bull-like; below a high-domed forehead were two small eyes, a short stump of nose, a mouth like a scar, and a jutting chin. The expression was sombre and menacing.'

We are again in the language of boys' adventure fiction. It turns out that the Tower is just as vulnerable as everywhere else, and predictably collapses. Soon afterwards the storm wind starts to decline.

Ballard's choice of the name Hardoon was evidently not random. Silas Aaron Hardoon was a Shanghai millionaire and property developer whose fortune was based on opium running. He had been born in Baghdad, was educated in Bombay, and from about 1911 became a major speculator in Shanghai property dealing. He died worth $150,000,000.[140]

Ballard himself remembered:

My father showed me the vast Hardoon estate in the centre of the International Settlement, created by an Iraqi property tycoon who was told by a fortune teller that if he ever stopped building he would die, and who then went on constructing elaborate pavilions all over Shanghai, many of them structures with no doors or interiors.[141]

The truth is that *The Wind from Nowhere* is not at all a good novel. It is, as Ballard described, riddled with narrative clichés, and the haste with which it was written is evident on almost every page. There are scenes of violence: people punching and bashing each other. Conversations are frequently angry, with much gesturing. The plot with its descriptions of the massive storm wind makes no logical sense – nor is the catastrophe given any kind of symbolic meaning. It is just 160 pages of people clambering around as buildings are blown down around them. On a line-by-line basis it is good enough, but even a sympathetic rereading, knowing what else Ballard was capable of, creates a sense of disappointment.

However, it certainly had the desired effect. Whatever the publisher paid as an advance gave the young family a financial breathing space, but better still Berkley Books followed up by publishing three collections of Ballard's short stories: *The Voices of Time* (1962), *Billenium* (1962) and *Passport to Eternity* (1963). They also published his next three novels.

Ballard said later, 'Of course *The Wind from Nowhere* opened a few little doors. It led to my tie-in with Berkley Books and to short story collections. It was a convenient arrangement because they published almost everything I'd written, volumes of stories which were then republished all over the world and gave me the income to make the final break.'[142]

Those slim paperbacks, published more than six decades ago, which I bought with increasing excitement from an import bookstore, are now frail and losing their covers, but as the first collections anywhere of those stories they are priceless.

The Wind from Nowhere was Ballard's first novel, though he himself never regarded it as such, referring instead to the three books that followed as his debut novels.

In 1962 Ballard delivered the manuscript of his next novel, *The Drowned World*. Berkley Books in New York promptly put it into production as a paperback, labelling it 'A Berkley Original'. In Britain the response was rather more measured.

The novel had also been submitted by Carnell to the long-established firm of Victor Gollancz Ltd, then gaining recognition as the premier publisher of SF in the UK, albeit one which drew almost exclusively on American writers: Algis Budrys, Frederik Pohl and Hal Clement, among many others.

The author Kingsley Amis was already in contact with Hilary Rubinstein, the editor at Gollancz, because the firm had published Amis's book-length survey of SF, *New Maps of Hell*, the year before. Amis said, 'I have been a fan of J. G. Ballard's ever since I noticed his stories in *New Worlds*, and I am most impressed by *The Drowned World*. So much so that I would willingly be party to any sort of scheme that might bring the book to notice: talking to Ballard on TV, etc., if it could be arranged.'[143]

After he had read the full-length novel, Amis wrote again, this time more fully:

> Ballard, we all agree, is a very promising lad who may really be something, and he is worth judging by the most serious literary standards. At the same time *The Drowned World* is an SF novel and Ballard's career until now has been that of a straightforward SF writer, publishing in SF magazines. In fact he is the first instance in England of what people like me have been waiting for, the serious writer who works within SF. It seems a pity that when SF throws up a good writer he is, so to speak, whipped away into a different sphere. This encourages the false view that when a book is good it cannot really be SF, which is what highbrows say about *Nineteen Eighty-Four*. The point is that, taking the long view, we surely all want to establish SF as a serious art form which educated people can read without lowering themselves, which can be recommended by the Book Society, etc. Ballard's book is first-rate propaganda for this idea.[144]

Gollancz took Amis's advice seriously and published the novel in hardback, described as science fiction, eventually selling nearly 15,000 copies. I myself bought one of them.

Both Gollancz and Amis, while being genuinely and extravagantly complimentary about the book, added the semi-jocular remark, intended as a further compliment, 'Of course, you've stolen the whole thing from Alejo Carpentier and Joseph Conrad.' Ballard was unimpressed: he claimed to have read neither of them and that he did not think much of them when he did.[145]

A brief and incomplete synopsis of the plot:

Following a massive increase in global temperatures in the future, with a concomitant sea-level rise, the only remaining habitable parts of the world are the North and South Poles. Dr Robert Kerans is on a field trip with a scientific expedition under the command of a Colonel Riggs, studying the state of the tropical flora and fauna now flourishing in the overheated and flooded remains of London. The city is covered by a deep, tropical lagoon. Ancient carboniferous plants crowd and cluster. Weird animal and marine forms lurk in the deeper areas. After one of the party abandons the work and heads south, the team breaks up. Kerans and two other scientists, Dr Beatrice Dahl and Dr Alan Bodkin, decide to remain. Kerans takes up occupation of a penthouse apartment in the Ritz Hotel where the air conditioning still works and food can be kept. He has an uneasy relationship with the other two, but both men are inevitably drawn to Beatrice Dahl.

There is an invasion of pirates led by a man named Strangman, whose intention is to drain the massive lagoons covering the city and loot the buildings of valuables. There are violent interludes: Dr Bodkin is killed, Beatrice Dahl is taken away and Kerans is captured and tortured. The lagoons are drained, leading to Kerans trying (and failing) to break the new flood defences to restore what he now understands as an evolutionary process. After an intervention by Riggs, Kerans believes they are about to be rescued, but rather than punish Strangman Colonel Riggs cooperates with him. Kerans, angered and frustrated, succeeds at last in re-flooding the lagoon. He abandons the city, heading south towards the torrid zone of the Equator.

This summary reveals that at no time can *The Drowned World* be read as a straightforward narrative. The plot exists as a platform for what amounts to a series of landscapes, bizarre confrontations, and strange and nihilistic meetings between unlikely characters. Little can prepare the reader for the scenes and events that come to the author's hand almost at random. What is 'deep time' and how does it impact on Kerans, for example? This slightly jarring effect adds to the general ambience of otherness. The structure of the plot is at best mechanical, and for many of the early pages the characters react to each other like automata. Dr Bodkin for some reason spends several long paragraphs explaining scientific theories to Kerans: 'I am convinced that as we move back through geophysical time so we re-enter the amniotic corridor and move back through spinal and archaeopsychic time,' and so on. Overall there is again the detectable sense of a melodramatic scenario, a formula for violent action, which seems to be a hallmark of Ballard's storytelling during this period.

Graham Matthews wrote:

> Ostensibly set in London, the novel presents a panorama of department stores and apartments emerging out of swamplands evoking the landscape of Shanghai in the 1930s and 1940s. This is reflected by descriptions of the Ritz that are reminiscent of the Peace Hotel on the Bund and by repeated references to bamboo groves, lush vegetation, huge rivers, canals, and flooded paddy fields. Just as various characters in the novel steadily devolve into primordial forms, *The Drowned World* reaches back in time to Ballard's own 'archaeopsychic' past and to the formation of his creative imagination.[146]

Ballard tosses narrative clichés around. They are not for him to make sense of, but for us to contemplate. The physical, allegedly practical, setting was never intended to be real. This is not fiction of global warming, nor even the kind of 'catastrophe' SF novel still in vogue in the early 1960s. The characters in *The Drowned World* go through the motions of normal life, but in fact they have no apparent interest in struggling against the catastrophe. Instead, they enter a state of reverie, a lowered threshold of involvement. Many of the events have a dreamlike quality, while not being dreams. A case in point is the explosive arrival of a ghostly white Strangman roaring across the surface of the lagoon, his hydroplane bouncing over the waves and throwing up a spume of spray, while hundreds of albino alligators swarm around him – it is intended literally, as Strangman soon becomes an active character in the story, but at the same time he and his arrival represent an extreme idea, a disruption.

The business of preparing for the next evolutionary step, a return to the climate and ecology of the Triassic Age, continues to dominate the unconscious motives of the others.

Ballard said that the landscape south of Shanghai, which lay between Lunghua camp and what he could see of the city in the near distance, frequently looked like a drowned zone. 'It was a very interesting zone psychologically, and it obviously had a big influence – as did the semi-tropical nature of the place: lush vegetation, a totally waterlogged world, huge rivers, canals, paddies, great sheets of water everywhere.' He recalled being able to see the taller buildings of the French Concession reflected in the dark waters.[147]

Written in heightened language, rich in compelling similes and metaphors, the central image of the dreaming swamp that London has become is paradoxical, impossible, utterly memorable. Ballard was soon recognized as one of the most unusual of novelists, certainly in the SF field but also in the wider literary world.

The narrative format of Ballard's next novel, *The Drought* (1964), was at first more naturalistic. The title of the US edition was *The Burning World*.

We are introduced to a number of characters in a reasonably recognizable circumstance: a long drought has caused severe water shortages and people are wondering how they can continue with their lives. However, it is not long before this conventional scenario breaks down. As in *The Drowned World*, Ballard is not particularly interested in the actual crisis, nor even how it might develop and eventually be resolved. His cast of characters, depicted in extremity, have chaotic, mysterious, self-harming motives of their own. There is no unity of purpose between any of them – they form a sort of mutually antagonistic chorus of perplexing wishes and actions, reflecting the breakdown of the psyche as an ingredient of the larger disaster. Danger threatens all of them, but somehow most of them survive, perversely transformed into something either lower or higher than they were before.

The plot: Following the accidental or even deliberate creation of molecular film pollutant, the oceans cannot evaporate and the world is rapidly desertifying. Lakes and rivers dry up. The sea remains.

Dr Ransom, initially reluctant to join the exodus from the cities, is finally forced to move towards the coast when the city in which he lives is razed either by arson or wildfire. Subject to constant threats and physical attacks he travels in a mixed, squabbling party of neighbours and hangers-on. They face many dangers en route and discover on arrival at the coast that survival by forced desalination of sea water is the only social order. Ransom's party seek refuge in the 'dune limbo' of the seashore and take their places in a world dominated by the need to extract fresh water from the reluctant sea.

The military authorities control activities on the beach with the use of live ammunition; many are killed. Violence is commonplace as water is manually paddled to the treatment works. Here, Ransom finds, people are simply marking time and fighting a hopeless rearguard action. Ten years pass. An unforeseen consequence of desalination is the constant build-up of waste salt deposits. Beneath the salty crust lie the remains of civilization: buried homes, shops and cars. Mining this resource keeps a form of survival possible. In the final section of the story, Ransom goes inland again to see what has become of the city and its last few inhabitants. These people, mad and monstrous, have found a new way of life, hideous but somehow appropriate to the universal drought, which is an aridity of the soul as well as of the land. As hope finally fails, Ransom feels the first drops of a return of rainfall.

While it is in some ways the most symbolically satisfying of these three loosely connected novels (there are references to the surrealist art Ballard himself most likes) the waywardness of the action and the constant nihilism of the characters often make *The Drought* hard to identify with. Then you notice the extended descriptive passages, and although they often seem inconsistent or even illogical, they cannot be ignored.

Sometimes Ballard's prose rises to the heights – what he sees and describes is always unexpected: it is his observant eye that leads us, and gradually the reader becomes embroiled in a perverse, extremely original and persuasive reading experience. Whether or not the story ends with the return of rainfall is added almost as an afterthought. The 'story' of the true drought, obliquely meant by the title, is described by Ballard as being internal, psychological and unconscious. The process we observe as the erratic plot takes us along is about the narrowing of identity, memory and deep wishes, not at all about external events.

The first appearance of the material at the heart of Ballard's next novel, *The Crystal World* (1966), was in a novella called 'The Illuminated Man', published in *The Magazine of Fantasy and Science Fiction* in 1964. That story is set in the Florida Everglades, and is told by a scientific investigator, one of a team, who lingers too long in a part of the forest turning to crystal: apparently a reaction to some sort of effect arriving on Earth from a distant star system. It is called the 'Hubble Effect'. The narrator enters the forest but he is impacted by the Hubble Effect and his body starts turning to crystal. After a quasi-religious experience he manages to escape the forest and throw off the effect, but afterwards is drawn irresistibly to return. 'The Illuminated Man' was later included in the short fiction collection *The Terminal Beach* (1964).

An expanded version of 'The Illuminated Man' appeared as a two-part serial in consecutive editions of *New Worlds* in May and July 1964. It was now called 'Equinox', and was different in almost every way from the earlier story. It being too short to be published in book form, Ballard later set about a further expansion, and *The Crystal World* was the result.

In a way familiar from *The Drought*, Ballard sets up a plot outline that from the start seems as if it could develop into a conventional story: a doctor, Sanders, is sailing up-river through the Cameroon Republic, intending to join the staff of a leprosy clinic. A diamond mine, guarded by soldiers, is close by. Two of his colleagues are already working at the clinic. On board the riverboat with him are Father Balthus, an apostate priest, and the man with whom he has shared a cabin: Ventress, a secretive businessman whose gun Sanders accidentally finds. Our attention shifts from the journey to the travellers and the various tensions between them, especially as there is a delay on arrival.

A letter from Suzanne, a former lover and now one of his colleagues, has tempted Sanders to the leprosy clinic with a dreamy description of the transcendent calm that has descended as the rainforest turns slowly to crystal. She hints at the peacefulness of death. But Sanders is unable to reach the clinic immediately. He discovers Ventress is in a bitter feud with a man named Thorensen who has seduced his wife. Sanders has a brief affair with Louise, a young French journalist. Suzanne when he finds her is showing the first signs of having contracted leprosy: is the crystallization of the forest a metaphor for the disease? Father Balthus suddenly decides to succumb to the thanatos of the crystals; as Sanders becomes deeply involved with the cross-currents between these people he discovers he too has started to develop crystals on parts of his body.

He saves Ventress from an attempt on his life, he makes love to Louise, he discovers a dead man's body whose arm has been changed to a crystal mass. Although he arrives at the clinic he discovers it is in the hands of the military. They are intent on violently protecting the valuable diamond mine. Sanders learns that the water of the river has a cleansing, neutralizing effect on the crystallization. He abandons the clinic and the various struggles between the people there, tries to escape by running through the forest but with only partial success – the river water removes the crystals but scours the body of flesh. Suzanne has gathered around her a group of leprosy sufferers, who now seek the immolation of crystallization, deep in the forest. Sanders finally makes good his escape to safety, but soon he is feeling the irresistible pull of the crystal world. Inevitably, he finds another riverboat and sets off upstream.

Once again Ballard has produced a novel unique to himself. With its unmistakable assumption of Conradian quest to the heart of darkness, and Graham Greene's hesitant leprosy doctor and dissolute priest in *A Burnt-Out Case*, it seems at first that it will conform to the expectations of the literary novel of despair and redemption. But it soon turns into a weird, almost unfathomable blend of violent events and actions. The world of the crystallizing forest is a unique landscape, but also it is an extension of inner landscapes: it fulfils wishes, seems to offer peace or psychic fulfilment. It is at least shockingly beautiful and dangerous.

The changes forced on the characters, while damaging and superficially hurtful, lead them to their psychological goals. There are images rarely glimpsed before: a world of prisms, reflections and the crystal perfection of a diamond, the cessation of time, a deadly relief. It is unquestionably a novel not of outward action (although there is plenty, including sexual encounters) but of inner peace, the inner space that Ballard so often called upon in writing his fiction.

10

'DANGER IN THE STREETS OF THE SKY'

Around the time Ballard delivered the manuscript of *The Drowned World*, life for the young Ballard family had reached a state of comparative stability, their main worry being the constant one suffered by all relatively new writers: chronic shortage of money. However, they were settled into their new home at 36 Charlton Road, Shepperton, and Ballard himself was working steadily through the three novels that were to set down early markers of his fame. He bought his first car: a ten-year-old Armstrong-Siddeley Typhoon (traded in a year later for the slightly larger Armstrong-Siddeley Sapphire). The children were thriving. Even the worries about money began to recede, because of the success of *The Drowned World* and the fact that many of his short stories were being reprinted and translated abroad.

Denied a proper childhood in Shanghai, where everything took place in a luxurious but unwelcoming house under the silence of Chinese servants, after he was married Ballard threw himself into the joyful muddle of family life: 'Our home in Shepperton was a chaotic, friendly brawl, as a naked parent dripping from the bath broke up a squabble between the girls over a favourite crayon, while their brother triumphantly strutted in his mother's damp footprints. Mayhem ruled.'[148]

His increasing success as a writer widened Ballard's social circle. In 1962 he formed what was to be an important friendship with the writer Michael Moorcock, who also had three children with his then wife, the writer Hilary Bailey, and the two families would often spend Sundays together at the Moorcocks' large maisonette in Ladbroke Grove. At other times, Ballard, Mary and the children would drive out to visit Brian and

Margaret Aldiss in Oxford, or Kingsley Amis and Elizabeth Jane Howard at their flat in Maida Vale. Ballard later reflected that this fairly low-level literary society was probably not what Mary had expected from married life. He always imagined that what she had left behind from her days as a single woman was the affluent country life of hunt balls, prosperous farmers, lavish private parties, fast cars. If she felt she was missing any of that, or even if it had actually existed, she never showed it.

She was committed to what Ballard was writing, actively supported him in it, and when she wrote to her friends she described how proud she was of his achievements.[149]

In the summer of 1963, following a series of pain attacks, Mary was admitted to hospital in Ashford and underwent an operation to remove her gall bladder. The procedure did not go smoothly and she recovered only slowly from the operation. There were worries an infection might have set in. Ballard, looking after the children alone, was anxious for her to return home. At this time he was working hard on a series of new short stories, key among them being one called 'The Terminal Beach'.

This explored radical new material, yet another departure from the sort of stories he had written before. Several other stories from the same period, all with a similar relationship to SF (that is, a remote one), would ultimately form the collection *The Terminal Beach*. Finally, Mary was discharged from hospital, and life at Charlton Road was restored to normal.

The following year, with *The Terminal Beach* coming out and Ballard thinking of further expanding 'Equinox' into what would become *The Crystal World*, he and Mary agreed they should take a long family holiday during the summer. Mary did say quietly a couple of times that she hoped she was going to be well enough to go, as she was looking forward to the trip. By the time of their departure, she seemed fully recovered. They loaded up the large old Armstrong-Siddeley, and at the beginning of August drove the long way down to El Campello, San Juan, close to Alicante on the Costa Blanca. They planned to stay abroad for at least a month.

Many of the stories included in *The Terminal Beach* (1964) either had their first appearance in the collection itself, or were published in magazines very close to the time the book came out. This gave the collection a welcome sense of newness, a feeling that it accurately represented Ballard's most recent work and was not simply a random selection of existing stories, true of many other author collections, including his own. It was published in the USA by Berkley and by Victor Gollancz in the UK.

Only two of the stories bore any resemblance to traditional SF: these were 'Billennium' and 'Deep End'. The latter of these depicted a world where the great oceans had been drained in the cause of urgent interplanetary needs for water: it offered the unusual setting of the dried-up seabed close to Bermuda. From here the former archipelago loomed on the skyline:

> Twenty miles away he could see the symmetrical peak of Hamilton, nearest of the Bermuda Islands, rising off the dry ocean floor like a flat-topped mountain, the narrow ring of white beach still visible in the sunset, a scum-line left by the sinking ocean.[150]

'Billennium', a much simpler story, is a satirical horror story about an overcrowded future world.

Of the rest, 'The Venus Hunters' is not an SF story but in some respects it is *about* science fiction, or at least it deals with one of the subjects some people think science fiction is about. It's the story of Andrew Ward, a leading astronomical scientist, who becomes attracted to the story told by a local man called Charles Kandinski. Kandinski claims to have seen a spacecraft on a patch of open ground, and made contact with the Venusian who arrived in it. Ward, a professional sceptic about such claims, at first ridicules Kandinski, but because of the man's plausible insistence that his story is true, later falls prey inevitably to intense curiosity.

This story broadly follows the consequences of a similar claim by a man called George Adamski. He claimed that in the late 1940s he had observed many 'flying saucers' (now called UAPs – Unidentified Anomalous Phenomena) in the Californian skies, and even visited a spacecraft on the ground and made contact with the being inside. He stuck to his story all his life, and wrote a book about the incident, backing it up with photographs he alleged had been taken at the time. Nothing was ever shown to be true.

Ballard's rendition of this unlikely story is told sympathetically and naturistically, a study of character rather than phenomenon.

At the centre of this new book, though, was the title story, 'The Terminal Beach'.

Again, it broke new ground for Ballard's fiction. It was not SF in any sense, nor did it have cosmic consequences. It was set on the Eniwetak Atoll (at the time Ballard wrote the story the main island was called Eniwetok). Between 1948 and 1958, the USA tested, that is detonated, a total of forty-three nuclear weapons on Eniwetok. 'The Terminal Beach' is the story of a man named Traven, who has come to the ruined island on some inner quest, said to be the search for his wife and son, almost certainly killed in an automobile accident. It is therefore a tale of tragic delusion, but the delusion takes a complicated and perhaps guilt-ridden quality.

Once on the island Traven dreams of burning American bombers falling through the air, of concrete bunkers half destroyed by nuclear blasts, of American USAF crew members trying to atone for their involvement, of the bodies of Japanese soldiers who had once occupied Eniwetok. The island had been ruined and desolated by the nuclear hell, and was now almost bare of trees, a man-made desert as barren as an endless network of abandoned freeways and blind concrete intersections, where everything had been devastated forever. It was a place where the Cold War (what Ballard called 'the pre-Third') had actually been fought.

Written in an impressionistic way, with realistic details unreliably reported, Traven's survival always in question, and his encounters with would-be rescuers who might be imaginary, 'The Terminal Beach' is a sustained prose poem, unlike any anti-nuclear fiction written before or since. It is one of Ballard's finest achievements.

The long family visit to Spain went on. It was the first real holiday Ballard had ever taken, and it was focused on the simple pleasures of a warm climate, childhood and beach life. Ballard himself described it as 'the kind of holiday where the high point is the day Daddy fell off the pedalo.'[151]

An inveterate letter writer, Mary wrote to Margaret, Ballard's sister. She said they expected to be home by 15 September and described how the family had discovered a 'rio seco' in a dried-up creek that ran close to their rented apartment in El Campello. The children had already found, to their delight, colonies of beetles, tormenting the adults when they took them indoors. Ballard himself became fascinated by the dried-up riverbed as it wound between low, rocky banks. Mary said it made him talk about writing a 'BIG' book – he wandered along it, perhaps remembering the drying out of the rivers and lakes in *The Drought*.

But in spite of the positive tone of her letters Mary was not feeling well. Some kind of infection, perhaps ultimately related to her post-operative condition from the year before, took hold. Her immune system may have been compromised by the operation.

The symptoms worsened and she took to her bed in the apartment, while the illness swiftly turned into severe pneumonia. She was put on an oxygen supply. The family gathered around her. In spite of the attention of a local doctor, a male nurse who was constantly with her and a consultant from Alicante, she continued to weaken. Fay Ballard said, 'I remember my father said, *Go out, go out*. And I remember thinking: my mother is dying.'[152] Ballard himself said, 'Towards the end, when she could barely breathe, Mary held my hand and asked: "Am I dying?" I'm not sure if she could hear me, but I shouted that I loved her until the end. In the final seconds, when her eyes were fixed, the doctor massaged her chest, forcing the blood into her brain. Her eyes swivelled and stared at me, as if seeing me for the first time.'[153] Fay added, 'My father came out of the room, called the three of us, hugged us tightly, and said, "She's dead." I remember him crying in despair, "What do I do now?"'[154]

It is all but impossible to imagine, and especially to describe, the shock of tragedy that must have run through Ballard and his young children. It was a disaster off the scale of anything that might have been expected, or could be fully understood.

There were practical problems to solve: there had to be a funeral. But funds were low and they were a long way from home in a foreign country. They located a small graveyard in Alicante, where a few British holiday-makers were buried, victims of accidents while yachting, swimming and so on. A handful of English residents from the apartment block where they had been staying watched alongside Ballard and his children. A Protestant priest presided over a simple ceremony. Mary's body was moved to the graveside on an iron-wheeled cart pulled by a horse. Both Fay and Bea Ballard have said they would remember the sound of the hooves and the creak of the wheels for the rest of their lives. After a brief service the priest rolled up his sleeves, took a spade, and filled in the grave alone.

Summer was over – the wind coming down from the mountains was chill. The beaches were empty, holiday apartment buildings were closing. Ballard was determined to get the children home as soon as possible, and so three days after the burial service they loaded everything into the car and set out on the long drive back to Shepperton. Fay, sitting beside her father in the passenger seat, remembers that Ballard said not a word about Mary the whole way home, but that he kept having to pull the car over to the side of the road, consumed by weeping.

'It happened very quickly and I think I was never able to come to terms with it properly. Even when the grieving process was over, a year or two later, I was faced with this huge conundrum, *why*?'[155]

Speaking to Tom Shone in 1997, Ballard said:

> She was so young, thirty-four, that I felt a crime had been committed by nature, against her. And it reminded me of all those terrible crimes that I'd seen during the war in the Far East, and it reminded me in a peculiar way of the Kennedy assassination, which had taken place the previous year and had been televised endlessly. And there was the whole culture of sensational violence that had grown up in the 1960s. What I was trying to do was make sense – I think, I think – to some extent, of this meaningless death. If I could give it some meaning, make sense of Kennedy's death – all these other deaths – I could possibly find a rationale for my wife's death.[156]

Here Ballard was articulating the change of mood and subject that was to characterize much of his fiction in the months and years ahead.

The feelings of his own responsibility and vague guilt led to one of the most important decisions of his life: although Mary's mother and sisters quickly raised the possibility that the two girls at least could come and live with them, Ballard was determined that the loss of his wife would not lead to a break-up of his family. After the long journey, as they returned to the house in Shepperton, he was firm in his resolve. He would continue to raise all three of the children, be both mother and father to them as far as humanly possible. He acknowledged that he probably needed them more than they needed him.

Of course, close friends clustered around, offering help. Dorothy Matthews and the two aunts gave real support, as did Ballard's sister and brother-in-law, all offering their presence and family experience, opportunities for periods of relief, sometimes taking the children for short breaks. But in the months and years ahead, the cheerful homely chaos in Shepperton was what all three children knew best. Maybe the unusual arrangement could have led to endless problems, even to trauma, but all four of the people involved declared it a miracle: a word used in the title of Ballard's autobiography, referring to his children.

He wrote in that book:

> A year or so after Mary's death I saw her in a dream. She was walking past our house, skirt floating on the air, smiling cheerfully to herself. She saw me watching her from the doorstep of our house and walked on, smiling at me over her shoulder. When I woke I tried to keep these moments alive in my mind, but I knew that in her way she was saying goodbye, and that at last I was beginning to recover.[157]

ELEVEN

'THE CHILDREN'S SANCTUARY'

'I knew that the children were braver than I was,' Ballard writes in *The Kindness of Women*. 'During the long drive home they had never once mentioned their mother, the first of the unspoken pacts which we made in the coming months ... My own recovery took longer, delayed by the well-meaning refusal of almost everyone to refer to Miriam's death. A gentle conspiracy existed among my friends and publishing acquaintances, as they feigned not to notice that Miriam had vanished through a window of time and space. This silence reminded me of the cruel childhood game in which we pretended, without telling him, that one of our friends no longer existed ... I envied the public mourning rituals of the Chinese, the public wailing of the widow on which Europeans so looked down.'[158]

In an interview for the *Guardian* in 2014, Fay Ballard, who grew up to be an artist, vividly remembers the silent aftermath of her mother's death. 'My father was the most wonderful, loving, brilliant father,' she says, 'but we never talked about our mother. Not once. We couldn't discuss her with the wider family either. I never discussed her with Bea or Jim. I felt very awkward if her name ever came up. I buried the trauma deep inside of me.'[159] Beatrice Ballard insists that the subject of Mary was not out of bounds, that if her father did not talk about their mother it was because he was concerned that he might upset them.

Mary's sudden and traumatic death was a tragedy no one could have predicted, or prepared for. Within a matter of hours, Ballard's life and the lives of his children had been altered irrevocably. Fay remembers taking her mother's watch from their hotel bedroom shortly after she died. Her father must have known that she had done this, she realizes, though he never commented upon it or asked her to return it.

It was 1964. Any subject considered difficult or upsetting – sex, pregnancy, childbirth, adoption, illness, death – would not normally have been discussed in the presence of minors. The three Ballard children were young and bewildered – the future television producer Beatrice was just five at the time – and no doubt Ballard, ravaged by his own grief, believed the best thing for them would be to reinstate a version of normality as quickly as possible.

'It was such a traumatic event that we were all in complete shock,' Bea says. 'It was as if we'd been hit with a hammer – everything had been blown apart. I don't really remember coming home, walking into the house for the first time. Just that it felt desolate, empty. My mother was irreplaceable. Over a period of time, we stopped talking about her.'

Fay suggests that for their father, the experience was not unlike what he went through in China two decades before. The imperative then was simply to survive, and it was the same now. 'I think Daddy thought it would be better for us just to keep going.' She remembers being plagued by nightmares for many years afterwards, the sense of a bad thing coming closer that could not be stopped.

Ballard spoke often in interviews of the decade he spent bringing up his children, a time that was as important for him as it was for them. He always regretted the emotionally distant relationship he had had with his own parents. He liked spending time with his children, and wanted to give them the affection and sense of security he felt he had missed out on.

'It was an unconventional upbringing,' Bea says, 'but he got the important things right. He was very loving. He made sure we were properly looked after. He gave us plenty of affection and lots of support. He was an amazing father.'

When she came to clear the house in Shepperton after Ballard's death, Fay Ballard came upon a multitude of small mementoes: there were photographs, images of Mary she had not known existed. Things that had belonged to her mother that her father had kept, or not thrown away, that had remained in the house and even on his desk throughout the time that Mary had been gone. These were the objects she documented in

'House Clearance' a series of acutely detailed pencil drawings that both record the physical presence of the objects, and in their delicacy and beauty somehow manage to convey something of the emotional significance attached to them.

One of the myths about the aftermath of Mary's death is that Ballard was left alone to bring up his children. The detail of his 'aloneness' has been repeated so often, not least by Ballard himself, that it passes unquestioned. Michael Moorcock, the person who was probably closest to Ballard in the years immediately following Mary's death, puts a different perspective, affirming that Ballard 'frequently liked to give the impression that he was raising the children alone but we often saw him without them and with a girlfriend. He almost never mentioned his adult family, but I know they played a much larger part in taking care of the children than he admitted.'

Fay remembers that Mary's sisters, Peggy and Betty, were there from the beginning, waiting at the house in Shepperton when they arrived home from Spain. Both Fay and Bea have fond memories of their grandmother Dorothy, Mary's mother, who was known as Granny Matthews.

'During the school holidays we used to go and stay with her in Wales,' Bea said. 'She had a beautiful house, which looked down over a stream. We always had a lovely time up there. My grandmother's family were farmers, landowners. She had grown up in the country. She was a real character, a very strong lady, quite mischievous. I always remember her coming down in the morning. She would light a fag – a mint Consulate – and then she would sit there in her dressing gown, smoking her cigarette. The next moment she would be outside shooing animals away from the lawn, or shelling peas at the kitchen table.'

Peggy Matthews was now Peggy Davidson, married and living with her own family in Sutton Coldfield. Ballard would often drive the three children up to stay with them, usually stopping off in Oxford on the way to visit Brian Aldiss and his family. Betty had remained at the farm and, says Beatrice, 'was always there when we went to stay. She was a lovely woman.'

Mary had been close to both of her sisters, and the summers on the farm in Wales would have been as important to the Matthews women as it was to the Ballard children. Nor was it only from the Matthews side that help was forthcoming. Ballard's sister Margaret, a museum curator, and her architect husband Tony Richardson were both a regular and important fixture in the children's lives. While Fay, Bea and Jim junior relished the freedom of running wild on a Welsh hillside, they equally enjoyed the company of their paternal aunt and uncle, both London professionals and with the lifestyle to match.

'They were enormous fun,' Bea remembers. 'It seemed very exciting and glamorous, coming up to London from Shepperton.' Fay describes her Aunt Margaret especially as being stylish and trendy in her miniskirts and hexagonal tinted glasses. 'They would take us on outings to the Natural History Museum and to Battersea fairground. When we stayed over we would listen to the Beatles and dance on the beds.'

Edna Ballard, living first in the New Forest and then later in Claygate, Surrey, also had regular contact with her grandchildren. The Ballards and the Richardsons would drive down to stay with 'Granny Ballard' every Christmas, and if Ballard's relationship with her was rather formal, it was cordial and friendly. Ballard would always bring his mother chocolates and flowers.

'I liked her,' Bea says. 'I didn't mind listening to her stories about old Shanghai. She talked a lot about those times, and I found it interesting. She was quite a feisty character.' She added that Edna was always closer to Margaret, with whom she often went on holiday.

Unsurprisingly, it was Margaret who took over the Christmas day lunch duties after Edna's death.

Margaret Ballard was born in 1937. Now eighty-seven, she has the beginnings of dementia, but she knows this book is being written, and when I speak with her husband Tony Richardson in November 2024 Margaret is there in the room with him, seated in an armchair. She is dressed smartly but comfortably in a duck-egg blue cardigan with a bold, polka-dot shirt under, her straight grey hair cut into a neat bob. The skin of her cheeks, still smooth, is a delicate pink. There is a family resemblance to Ballard, especially around the mouth. She is wearing spectacles, her eyes fixed on the screen, and she is following our conversation.

Tony at eighty-eight is lively and vigorous. He turns and speaks to Margaret from time to time, asking her if she wants to add anything or to confirm a detail. Margaret's voice is still strong, though she seems shy of speaking. I am a stranger to her, after all, and I am sure she is aware that her memory is becoming unreliable.

Anthony Richardson was born in 1936. He met Margaret in the late 1950s.

> I was a student at the Architectural Association in Bedford Square. Margaret was a student at UCL, studying Classics. We met because Margaret shared a flat with an architecture student, Sally, who was in my year. After Margaret finished her degree, she went to the Courtauld Institute to study Art History. She was taught by Anthony Blunt, the then director – Margaret admired him enormously. I used to get invited to the Courtauld dances in Portman Square, which I hated because I can't dance and never wanted to! We were together for some years before we tied the knot.

They married in October 1963, and would go on to have two daughters: Victoria (born October 1968) and Candida (born August 1970). After leaving the Courtauld, Margaret landed a job at the British Museum under the tutelage of Edward Croft-Murray, cataloguing the drawings of Hogarth, on whom she became an expert. She went on to work for RIBA, cataloguing the drawings of deceased architects for the Institute's collection. It was here that by a strange coincidence she became friendly with Michael Manser, the architect who designed the Heathrow Hilton, an icon of modernist architecture and Ballard's favourite building.[160] Tony worked first for a firm of architects in St John's Wood before going on to establish his own architectural practice, Anthony Richardson & Partners, in 1969. 'I had always wanted to be an architect,' he told me. 'From the age of about fifteen I knew that was what I wanted to do.'

To the Richardsons, Ballard was always Jamie. Tony was aware of Ballard's writing from the time he and Margaret first met, though he was not particularly impressed by his stories in *New Worlds*, and it was only after reading *The Crystal World* that he began to pay serious attention to what Ballard was doing. 'At that time, Jamie was regarded as a failure by his parents. Margaret's mother was alarmed and horrified that her son was writing for disreputable magazines, publishing science fiction, though her attitude did begin to change after Kingsley Amis praised *The Drowned World* – that really meant something.'

Before Mary's death, the two families saw very little of one another. 'We only met Mary once or twice. We did see them at Christmas, but at that time the life Jamie was living was very much not accepted by the family. Mary was never accepted either by the Ballard parents because of her farming background, and I think that hurt both of them. It became part of the distance between them.'

After Mary died, things changed, though Ballard never spoke about Mary to the Richardsons, and neither did the children. Tony remembers Fay, Bea and Jim junior once coming with them to Scotland, where they spent their summer holidays at The Manse, a house in Aberdeenshire owned by Tony's brother. The Manse lay some forty miles to the north of Aberdeen. 'It used to take us twelve hours to drive up there. We would set out at around nine o'clock in the evening and drive through the night. The children would all be asleep in the back of the car.' The house was very old and rather spooky, with vast rooms that were difficult to heat. Jim junior in particular found the place frightening at night and had bad dreams on several occasions. 'I couldn't help wondering if he missed his mother,' Tony remembers, 'though he seemed cheerful enough during the day.'

Though Ballard was glad of their help with the children, he himself remained at a distance. Tony and Margaret had different interests, and moved in different circles. Both were enthusiastic supporters of the Victorian Society, with a love of traditional British architecture and nineteenth-century English literature. Tony suspects that Ballard saw him very much as a commercial architect, out of step with the modernist aesthetic that fired his own imagination, though he still has the feeling that the architect in Ballard's novel *High Rise*, Anthony Royal, might have been based on him, at least partly. 'I was working on a high-rise project in Southampton at the time he was writing it, so you have to wonder.' It is interesting that there are almost as many architects in Ballard's novels as there are doctors.

Margaret began working at Sir John Soane's Museum in the mid-eighties, the first woman ever to hold the post of director. Although when she and Tony first met she was much more interested in making a life in London than reminiscing about her childhood in Shanghai, after they were married she talked about it a great deal. The Richardsons visited Shanghai, and the Lunghua camp, in the 1990s, as did their own children. Much of the furniture in their Camden home is originally from Amherst Avenue, part of the consignment shipped back to Britain from China in 1948. 'We are surrounded by Chinese furniture,' Tony says.

Margaret's experience of Lunghua was very different from Ballard's. Being so much younger, and a girl, she was closely protected by her parents, and rarely alone. She and Edna would undertake domestic tasks together, such as gathering coal for the stove they cooked their meals on, and Margaret attended the small nursery school that had been set up by the residents. 'Margaret was devoted to her mother,' Tony says. He describes how after James Ballard finally left China in 1947, he, Edna and Margaret sailed to San Francisco, where they bought a car and drove across America together.

What comes across most clearly is how differently Margaret and Ballard thought and felt about their parents. Tony, with his reliable income, steady working habits and more conventional outlook was quickly accepted and appreciated by Edna and James senior as exactly the kind of husband they would have wanted for Margaret. Tony in his turn still carries a great deal of fondness and admiration for James Ballard senior.

'Margaret's father was a remarkable man, a very generous man, and believed the best of everyone. Although he went to China as a servant of Calico Printers Ltd, he was a great admirer of Bernard Shaw and a bit of a socialist. He liked looking after the factory, he liked China, got on well with the Chinese and admired them. I think he would have stayed on in Shanghai if that had been possible.'

James senior was greatly supportive of Tony in his early career, putting commissions his way whenever he could and treating him very much as a second son. 'He did all kinds of things for me. I got on incredibly well with him.' There is a wistfulness in the way Tony speaks of his father-in-law, a nostalgia for a vanished time. His relationship with Ballard himself was distant by comparison.

'Because of his reticence, and because the children were always there when we were together, I never really talked to him or got to know him, and I don't think he wanted to know us.'

Later on in our conversation I discover that Margaret and Tony have visited Bute, that they were guests of the late Marquis at the neo-Gothic stately home near Rothesay built by his great-grandfather.

'We are great admirers of Mount Stuart House. We spent quite a lot of time there, and lunched in the Marquis's new dining room – he was very interested in architecture.'

They were here on the island about ten years ago, Tony estimates, when Margaret was in better health and they used to travel all round Scotland looking at Victorian buildings.

Just one of the strange coincidences that have accompanied the writing of these chapters.

Ballard used to meet his sister regularly for lunch, Fay told me. They would exchange news about their families, holidays, people they both knew. But still, it was as if they were living out their lives in different worlds.

12

'THE NAMING OF NEW THINGS'

Just before the Ballard family tragedy unfolded in Spain, a minor literary revolution was starting to take place in London. It was indirectly but innately concerned with the sort of work Ballard had been creating, his name and reputation being summoned many times. He had become a divisive figure. While some considered him to be the most innovative, unusual and stimulating writer working with fantastic fiction, others felt quite the opposite: that he was, in effect, betraying the long-established traditions of the science fiction genre. Loose battle lines were being drawn up.

This was the movement known then, and still identified as such, as the 'New Wave in Science Fiction'. It was sometimes also called the 'British New Wave', there being a roughly similar activity a year or so later in the USA, although that was different in type, intent and effect.

As things turned out it seems possible that it was I who first applied the label, although I originally intended it as a glib parallel: I was obsessed with cinema, and felt stimulated and inspired by the many postwar films then coming out of France, Italy, Germany and Japan. The French young radicals in particular declared they were bored with *tradition de qualité* (the well-made film, usually based on a classic literary or theatrical text). Instead, they reinvented themselves as a new generation, working with small camera crews and largely unknown actors – they edited their scenes in jumps and disruptive shifts and called the iconoclastic result *la nouvelle vague*.

That struck me as similar to the kind of writing that was being talked about by several upcoming writers, of whom I was one. There was general dissatisfaction with the standard canon of science fiction: too many engineers, galactic empires, puzzles, spacemen – several of us argued that there was a wealth of different and more relevant speculative material that had never been explored properly. I wrote a short essay on the idea, using the English version of the tag. Somehow it stuck. Others began using 'new wave' as a descriptor – it was perhaps an obvious connection.

Although most of J. G. Ballard's work was written in conventional prose, the underlying impression gained from reading Ballard was disturbing, fascinating and sometimes subversive: the quality of being 'Ballardian' already mentioned. Ballard's early exposure to American SF was accepted and understood, but even by the late 1950s he had moved on and was writing about Hollywood queens, surrealist art, cosmic countdowns, nuclear holocaust, drained seabeds, lost artworks, wildlife, the nature of subjective reality, the next five minutes of the future and much else. Few of these subjects had ever detained the most popular and easily 'understood' writers of the SF genre.

And remember the times, the way Western society as a whole was changing. The early and mid-1960s were thrilling years to live through: all the old social conventions were being re-examined or rejected, led by the young people who had been born in or shortly after the end of the second world war. This restlessness felt by new SF writers was not isolated. Overall, there was a stimulating climate of change and expansion. Sexual mores were being relaxed, there was widespread use of recreational drugs, women had access to an effective contraceptive, possible jobs were no longer a deadly choice between office or factory, there was a boom in rock music, the visual and dramatic arts underwent radical change.

The frequency of political independence movements increased, but also assassinations and the rise of international terrorism. The dependence of the West on imported oil, the war in Vietnam, the spread of television, the overthrow of dictatorships and the creation of new ones ... all these events, and the social reactions to or against them, were part of a much larger upheaval.

Historically, the New Wave movement can be said to have begun with a few informal lunch meetings between Ballard and the writer and editor whose name is almost synonymous with the British New Wave,

Michael Moorcock. Moorcock, born in 1939, began writing while he was still at school and landed his first editing job, on a weekly magazine for young people called *Tarzan Adventures*, at the age of seventeen. Early stories and novels in the sword and sorcery subgenre and featuring his 'eternal champion' Elric of Melniboné were popular and won him fans even among readers who preferred more traditional fantasy. It is likely that he first met Ballard in 1960, though their friendship was not properly cemented until 1962, after Moorcock returned from several months abroad in France and Sweden. He was sharing digs in London with an old friend, the writer Barrington Bayley. Barry had already read the short magazine version of 'The Drowned World' in *Science Fiction Adventures* and pointed it out to Moorcock, who found it a revelation. He realized that this Ballard, previously unknown to him in spite of having several stories published, was the real thing.

Feeling a determination that there should be more to science fiction than spaceships and alien planets, Moorcock and John Brunner decided to call a one-day conference of SF writers at the Bonnington Hotel in London, with a view to starting some kind of professional association. Barry Bayley and E. C. Tubb were present, and so was Ballard. Brian Aldiss did not appear, but several of the regular contributors of spaceship-and-alien-planets stories were there.

The meeting turned out to be disappointing. Moorcock and Brunner had hoped to hear some real ideas about how to create a new literature for the space age. Instead, most of those attending were only interested in 'how to break into new markets', or 'how to sell to TV', and so on. Everything was rather dominated by Tubb, who at the time saw himself as a leading writer. United in disappointment, Ballard, Moorcock and Barry Bayley started meeting regularly once or twice a week, most often at a pub called The White Swan in Knightsbridge, near to where Ballard was working on *Chemistry & Industry*.[161] They were sometimes joined by a colleague of Ballard's, whose identity cannot now be traced, but both Moorcock and Bayley observed how the two men had developed an almost shorthand way of communicating abstract ideas.

Looking back years later, Ballard complained that at their first meetings Moorcock was still obsessed with the high fantasy that characterized his Elric books, and did not seem able to see beyond that. Moorcock for his part felt Ballard was not well or deeply read, that he referred often to films he had seen, and artwork he liked, both of which interested him more than literature. Moorcock was a musician, a guitarist, and soon realized that Ballard was tone deaf and uninterested in any kind of music. Even so, there was a rapport, a sense of energy and ambition that was shared by both of them, and the two became friends, a bond that deepened through the intense discussions that were always a part of the regular Sunday lunches at Ladbroke Grove.

Gradually, the concept of a more ambitious and modern form of speculative writing was beginning to take shape.

In March 1964 it was announced that the Maclaren Group could no longer afford to keep publishing *New Worlds* and *Science Fantasy*, which were both losing money, so they put them up for sale. A firm called Roberts & Vinter stepped in and took over both titles: there had already been some contact between them and Michael Moorcock, who had previously sold them a couple of commercial novels.

Ted Carnell, with his advance knowledge of what was going to happen, had already made alternative arrangements – he was announced as editor of a new series of original paperback anthologies, called *New Writings in SF*, which would be published by Corgi Books. New editors were therefore needed for the magazines. *Science Fantasy* would be taken over by an Oxford antiquarian bookseller and gallery owner called Kyril Bonfiglioli, while *New Worlds* would be edited by Michael Moorcock.

It's fair to say that for a while these were seen by many writers and readers as controversial choices. Moorcock was firmly associated with commercial writing and stories of epic fantasy – neither of which seemed in prospect to be the right approach for guiding an SF magazine. Meanwhile, no one knew anything at all about Kyril Bonfiglioli, apart from the fact that he was said to be friendly with Brian Aldiss. Like all minor controversies, this quickly blew over.[162]

The first issue of *New Worlds* under the Roberts & Vinter imprint appeared in paperback at the end of April 1964. It was dated May/June 1964. Moorcock's editorial was called 'A New Literature for the Space Age', focusing on the work of William S. Burroughs, which if not a trumpet call to arms gave some idea of the thinking behind the revamp. New stories by Brian Aldiss, John Brunner and Barrington Bayley appeared, and the first episode of Ballard's two-part serial version of 'Equinox', adapted and heavily rewritten from 'The Illuminated Man'. Confirming the influence Ballard was having on Moorcock's editorial policy, this inaugural issue published an essay by Ballard, also on Burroughs, called 'Myth Maker of the 20th Century'.

The mediocre writers from the Carnell days were largely absent at first, although two of the regulars (Joseph Green and Lee Harding) were in the next issue, and more familiar writers from those days, Sydney J. Bounds, E. C. Tubb and Clifford C. Reed, appeared in the one after. It is of course likely that these stories were in the inventory of manuscripts when Moorcock took over the editorship.

Over the next three years (while *New Worlds* remained in its Roberts & Vinter stripe) the magazine gradually built a reputation for being at the cutting edge of a new approach to writing fantastic fiction. These days it is widely but erroneously assumed that *New Worlds* was publishing work of literary quality, that the stories were radical, progressive, modern. This was only partly true, and was best seen in the work of Ballard and Aldiss, although the stories that appeared from them in the Moorcock issues were not at first noticeably different from what they had been writing before and were somewhat thin on the ground. (Only three short Ballard pieces of fiction were published in the first twenty issues of the new format.)

Moorcock himself printed a great deal of his own material in *NW* (he was open about the fact that it was the only way he could keep some of the editorial fee for himself), but until the advent of the Jerry Cornelius period some years later, Moorcock's work was firmly in the tradition of adventure fiction. For instance, in the third paperback *NW* there began the serialization of his conventional science fantasy novel *The Shores of Death*.

During the next three years (until July 1967) *NW* published many examples of traditional or canonical SF, with authors who were familiar from the earlier era: E. C. Tubb, Harry Harrison, Arthur Sellings, David Rome, John Baxter, Donald Malcolm, R. W. Mackelworth, Dan Morgan and more. True, newer and younger writers did start appearing (George Collyn, Langdon Jones, Hilary Bailey, Keith Roberts, Charles Platt and notably David I. Masson) but at this time they were in the minority.

Where *NW* stood for something new or radical lay in its editorial presence. In a series of editorials, and in book reviews by 'James Colvin' (a Moorcock pseudonym), a theme was established. For example, in issue number 148 Moorcock wrote in his editorial:

> We need more writers who reflect the pragmatic mood of today, who use images apt for today, who employ symbols gathered from the world of today, who use sophisticated writing techniques that can match the other techniques of today, who employ characters fitted for the society of today. Like all good writing, good SF must relate primarily to the time in which it is written; a writer must write primarily for his own generation. He must not seek to emulate his predecessors in their own territory, neither must he write for a posterity which will anyway not remember him unless he is true to himself and his own age. He can learn from his predecessors, but he should not imitate them.[163]

Then again, the issues of *NW* that followed this particular manifesto were dominated by a conventional SF adventure novel, presumably from inventory, serialized in three parts and written by the unambitious E. C. Tubb. Much of Moorcock's own fiction, both as himself and 'Colvin', showed evidence of hasty composition. Although I myself had two short stories published in Bonfiglioli's magazines, and three in *New Worlds*, my own contributions were minor and without importance – at the time I was a nervous young writer learning the craft. My work was still developing. I have always said that during this period I was 'of' the New Wave, but never really significantly *in* it.

Throughout this transitional period, *New Worlds* looked and acted like a compromise between ideals and convention. Although there were several *New Worlds* contributions from Ballard during 1966 and early 1967, including material that would eventually be collected as *The Atrocity Exhibition*, the paperback format was starting to look restrictive and the magazine was redesigned to full-size format. The editorial team was changing and the UK Arts Council provided a small subsidy. It was better printed and laid out, it was trenchant and sometimes dizzying ... but it was oddly lacking much of the work of J. G. Ballard.

He was now selling more stories in the USA, and had started working with the doctor-writer Martin Bax on the experimental magazine *Ambit*, of which he was soon announced as the fiction editor. Much of this work was modernist and experimental in form, but it was outside the remit of *New Worlds*, and Ballard became increasingly detached from association with the New Wave as it was then understood.

A version of the New Wave soon emerged in the USA, where it predictably caused controversy, complaint and consternation among many of the older writers.

The conventions of the SF genre ran deep in American pop culture, with many famous reputations based on canonical work of space opera, time travel, alien invasions and so on. There was widespread acceptance of 'unwritten rules' about what was and what was not SF, there were traditions of narrative approach, and overall there was orthodoxy based on works perceived as favourites or classics. American writers often spoke warmly of a 'golden age' when many of these assumptions had grown up around the early works of Robert A. Heinlein, Isaac Asimov, A. E. van Vogt, Ray Bradbury and a few others.

Even so, in the USA during this period there was a similar groundswell of new and younger writers, not only aware of what had been happening in Britain, but feeling a similar restlessness themselves.

There was a fundamental difference, though. The British writers were discontented with a form of literature they felt had been commercialized, trivialized and in general written badly. They were responding to substantial social changes in the larger world, feeling the impact of that and seeking a modern literature that would address what was actually going on. Ballard's work was held up as an example.

The American response was different: much of what was written and discussed in the USA was concerned with throwing off perceived taboos, the prohibitions against certain sexual attitudes or language, the silent censorship imposed on writers by pressures of American religions, overseas military activities and the draft, fear of libel laws, political ambitions, prudish publishers and a conservative and materialistic society. American writers wished to be liberated to say what they wanted, which is not the same thing. There was no periodical in the US that was the equivalent of *New Worlds* around which a literary movement might take shape – the American New Wave is mostly identified with anthologies of new stories published in book form, and to a more austere and critical British eye much of what appeared in the USA looked opportunistic.

Ballard's stories and novels were to say the least misunderstood in America: he was often described or labelled as an avant-garde writer. Even well-respected American reviewers, apparently familiar with the potential for a broad church in SF, struggled to understand Ballard's unique approach to his subjects. The writer and editor Algis Budrys quickly passed sentence on Ballard's early novels:

> A story by J. G. Ballard, as you know, calls for people who don't think. One begins with characters who regard the physical universe as a mysterious and arbitrary place, and who would not dream of trying to understand its actual laws. Furthermore, in order to be the protagonist of a J. G. Ballard novel, or anything more than a very minor character therein, you must have cut yourself off from the entire body of scientific education. In this way, when the world disaster – be it wind or water – comes upon you, you are under absolutely no obligation to do anything about it but sit and worship it.[164]

Whatever the reasons, towards the end of the 1960s the British New Wave had more or less run its course. The spirit remained alive in some: the writer M. John Harrison emerged from within the New Wave and half a century later is still producing challenging and prize-winning fiction. Many new and formerly unknown names appeared briefly under the New Wave brand, some shone brightly; nearly all faded away with time. Sidetracking became persistent: the cult of Moorcock's continuing character Jerry Cornelius – a gender-swapping, time-travelling adventurer who exhibits both science fictional and fantasy characteristics – looked superficially if it might be radically worthwhile, but too many second hands played the game and wrote their own inferior Cornelius stories. Moorcock persisted with it.

The wave became a ripple, science fiction soon succumbed to the mighty visual and popular influence of TV companies and film studios, and this led inevitably to more generic material than ever before. They called it 'sci-fi' and it became and has remained a dominant form. Many novels written in the genre since the advent of *Star Trek* and *Star Wars* have become systematized to popular taste and expectation: once again bookstore shelves are full of space opera and epic fantasy.

Towards the end of March 1969, Ballard flew to Rio de Janeiro to take part in a science fiction event, planned as part of the then-current Third Annual International Film Festival – that was discontinued soon after, and has no connection with the present Festival do Rio, which was formed years later.

According to Brian Aldiss, the SF symposium was the brainchild of Doctors José Sanz and Fred Madersbacher, who had discovered that several members of the festival's treasury were SF fans: 'They secretly sent out invitations to their favourite writers, siphoning off the odd million cruzeiros to pay for it.'[165]

Ballard, who disliked air journeys, said, 'It was the last really long flight I took. We were flown first class and were given little slippers to put on. When the plane landed I felt fantastic: "Let's get out of this steel hearse!" But I found I couldn't put on my shoes – it was a ludicrous state of affairs; I was sitting there with these shoes in my hands. I finally managed to force them on. I felt shaky for days.'[166]

He stepped off the Aerolíneas Argentinas plane with Brian Aldiss. Both men had spent part of their young years in the hot countries of the East. Aldiss said:

> We were hit by the heat as by a sweaty sock in the face. 'Ah!' said we, and breathed deep. The tropics once more, in all their diversity. We were established in a hotel overlooking Copacabana Beach. While aged SF films were shown in the centre of Rio, and distinguished writers such as A. E. van Vogt and Robert Bloch trotted diligently to see James Whale's *Frankenstein* for the umpteenth time, Jimmy Ballard and I and another crowd of us stayed with the beach and its passing show. We used the Bar Bolero as a base, overlooking those long

beaches. Also present were Robert A. Heinlein, Damon Knight, Kate Wilhelm, Alfred Bester, Judith Merril, John Brunner, Poul Anderson, Harry Harrison, Philip José Farmer, Robert Sheckley and Arthur C. Clarke, who flew in to collect the Black Monolith awarded to the Clarke/Kubrick film *2001: A Space Odyssey*.[167]

John Brunner gave a talk on the cultural shock from which civilization was suffering, a present theme of his; Frederik Pohl spoke of the dangers to our environment. Panel discussions put the world to rights. Aldiss added, 'The supporting programme of SF films ran happily light on monsters. A particularly stylish film was the Italian-made *The 10th Victim*, starring Marcello Mastroianni and adapted from a story by Robert Sheckley. Sheckley was one of the stars of the festival, constantly interviewed and filmed by the media magnates of São Paulo.'[168]

For Ballard this week-long event was his most concentrated exposure to the intelligent middle ground of science fiction writers. Nothing could be more different from that grim fan meeting in west London twelve years earlier: he was in the company of the top American and British genre writers. It had the ostensible form of a structured conference, while in reality it was a chance to meet and mix socially with fellow professionals.

But did he feel in any way that his views on SF might have been changed by this high intensity gathering of like minds? He said:

> Most of the writers I'd never met before and have never seen since. It was a pleasure to meet so many of these people whom I'd been reading for years. Damon Knight and Sheckley and Harry Harrison. Philip José Farmer I met: I was very impressed by him – as I was by all of them. Heinlein I met. Asimov wasn't there, Bradbury wasn't there, but so many of the writers whom I'd read keenly in the fifties at about the time I was thinking of being an SF writer myself were there and it was a great pleasure to meet them. They were very good company, highly intelligent, and it was a successful gathering.[169]
>
> Listening to the leading writers speak at the Film Festival in Rio – van Vogt, Bloch, Clarke, Ellison, Poul Anderson – I was certain that I was in the antechamber of a lunatic asylum. What has to be remembered about

most of these writers (and there are many exceptions, sophisticated and lucid people like Sheckley, Harrison, Judy Merril and Brian Aldiss himself) is that the science fiction they produce represents the most ordinary face of their imaginations. Their lives are their real fictions.[170]

Buck Rogers had won. However, the career of J. G. Ballard continued on, heading intriguingly into deeper and darker creative areas. The festival in Rio was to show up again – significantly shorn of any association with science fiction – in *The Kindness of Women*. Ballard's final word on this subject came many years later. Screened behind his civil and courteous manner, Ballard's answers to a faxed questionnaire from Alexandre Matias made no mention of a lunatic asylum: 'I visited Rio in 1969 and I was surprised with its vitality, charm, and the most beautiful women in the world. Brazil has always occupied a special place in Western imagination, thanks largely to Rio, and to our image of the Amazon and its immense forests, which represent a profound dream of the primitive heart of humanity. I wish them all the best.'[171]

THIRTEEN

'APPOINTMENT WITH A REVOLUTION'

'The overall effect of "This is Tomorrow" was a revelation to me,' Ballard said of the landmark exhibition at the Whitechapel Gallery in August 1956, 'and a vote of confidence, in effect, in my choice of science fiction ... For the first time, the visitor to the Whitechapel saw the response of imagination tuned to the visual culture of the street, to advertising, road signs, films and popular magazines, to the design of packaging and consumer goods, an entire universe that we moved through in our everyday lives but which rarely appeared in the approved fine art of the day.'[172]

The exhibition consisted of twelve independently designed exhibits by some of the painters, sculptors, architects and graphic designers who came to be known as the Independent Group and who were the forerunners of British pop art. The typical response to art that is considered avant-garde does not seem to change much, and it is fascinating, now, to look at the Pathé newsreels that advertised the exhibition. The voiceover – male, and speaking with the archetypical BBC accent of the 1950s – describes the artworks on display as 'strange, yes, but exciting and provocative' while at the same time predicting that they will be 'exasperating and too much for some people to swallow'. A second newsreel takes a more humorous approach: gallery patrons dressed in the conservative suits and nipped-in waists of 1950s formal attire wander among the exhibits, perusing catalogues and appearing suitably perplexed.

The two exhibits that caught Ballard's imagination most forcefully were Richard Hamilton's collage 'Just what is it that makes today's home so different, so appealing?' – the poster used to advertise the exhibition as well as one of the defining images of British Pop Art – and an installation by the sculptor Eduardo Paolozzi in collaboration with the architects Peter and Alison Smithson, a Paolozzi collage depicting 'Nuclear Man' inside a 'terminal hut', to be used as basic habitation by survivors in the aftermath of a nuclear war.

The bold outlines and bright colours of the Hamilton collage – a brash commentary on American-style consumerism – set against the stark minimalism of the Paolozzi installation seemed to encapsulate everything about the world that had been evolving in the wake of the second world war. For Ballard, 'This is Tomorrow' was a creative turning point, cementing the ideas that had begun to form when he first started reading science fiction magazines on the air base in Canada.

The work of the painter Francis Bacon proved similarly game-changing. Ballard first encountered Bacon's art at a retrospective at the ICA in 1955, and then again at a larger exhibition at the Tate in 1962. He found the work to be 'a revelation', and came increasingly to think of Bacon as the greatest painter of the postwar world. 'His popes screamed because they knew there was no god,' Ballard writes of Bacon in *Miracles of Life*. 'Bacon's paintings were screams from the abattoir, cries from the execution pits of WWII.'[173]

Bacon, like Ballard, often referred to medical textbooks in the course of his work. His *Three Studies for Figures at the Base of a Crucifixion* (1944) in particular had a profound effect upon Ballard. These nightmare creatures, close-up portraits of the Greek Furies, or Eumenides, became key images for him, part of a storehouse of imagery that grappled with the accelerated reality of the twentieth century in a way that seemed fully authentic, probably because it aligned so closely with his own. There is something terrifying and almost obscene about those nameless, hideously pliant figures against their strident orange background, a charge of danger that makes them impossible to forget. The genius of Bacon, as Ballard recognized, is that his work speaks to everyone. The viewer may love his work or loathe it but they cannot remain indifferent.

'I knew there was a link of some kind with the surrealists,' Ballard explains, 'with the dead doctors lying in their wooden chests in the dissecting room. ... A jigsaw inside my head was trying to assemble itself, but the picture when it finally emerged would appear in an unexpected place.'[174]

That place turned out to be *The Atrocity Exhibition*. Even the title – Bacon's Furies appear to be 'exhibited' inside glass vitrines – seems to summon Bacon's spirit, the same horrified fascination with human violence that formed the core of Ballard's creative thinking throughout that most troubled period of his life, the run of work that begins with 'The Terminal Beach' and ends in *Crash*.

Chris had just turned thirteen at the time of the Whitechapel exhibition; as a schoolboy in Manchester, he would not even have been aware that it was taking place. Chris was born in 1943, exactly three months after young Jamie found himself interned in Lunghua camp. Chris had no memories of the war, though his parents, teachers and older relatives had all been impacted by it in some way or other and the details he absorbed from his immediate environment exercised a lasting influence on his imagination. Chris's passion for reading came to him early, and many of the books he first enjoyed were war stories. He had an endless fascination with the densely illustrated part-work magazines his father collected, detailing the war's most significant campaigns, weapons and personalities. His interest in aircraft, pilots and flying became – as it did for Ballard – a significant and recurring leitmotif throughout much of his writing.

Chris hated school. Like Ballard, he found the atmosphere of conformity that tends to dominate in formal education unstimulating and dispiriting. Never a natural rebel, he was one of those kids who preferred to sit at the back of the classroom gazing out of the window. Exceptionally bright, he won a scholarship to the prestigious Cheadle Hulme grammar school, but once there he found himself adrift, a puzzle and a frustration to his teachers. He did badly in his 'O' Levels, which he refused to re-sit. His father found him a place as a trainee accountant at a firm near Cannon Street, a situation he loathed, if possible, even more than school, though it was here that his luck would finally change. He became friendly with one of the other clerks through their mutual interest in reading and dislike of accountancy, and it was this similarly disaffected young man who introduced Chris to science fiction.

The effect was transformative and almost instantaneous. After years of stifling boredom and lack of direction, Chris had stumbled upon the thing he wanted to do. He set out consciously to become a writer, and within five years of stabbing out his first short story on a borrowed typewriter he had landed himself a contract with Faber & Faber.

He never did learn to touch-type; I still recall the incredulity I felt when I first saw him working on a draft, typing at incredible speed using only two fingers.

When he first started reading Ballard in the early 1960s, Chris was profoundly affected by the dreamlike, surrealistic stories first published in *New Worlds* and later collected in *The Four-Dimensional Nightmare*. At the time, he found himself out of sympathy with Ballard's move towards the avant-garde, and saw his work of that period – the condensed novels, the 'Advertiser's Announcements', the experiments with cut-up – as a blind alley, an extreme manifestation of the self-consciously '*New-Worlds*-type-story' he had himself deliberately rejected even as his own essays in that style were first finding publication. He only fell back in love with Ballard's work on publication of *Crash* in 1973.

Both Chris and Ballard had conflicted relationships with science fiction. From early in his career, Chris was seen as an agitator within SF. His dismissive attitude to what he perceived as conservative values and derivative writing did not always make him popular within the science fiction community. The demands he made of himself meant that he was often perceived as having a prickly personality – he soon fell out with Michael Moorcock, a chasm that was only bridged in the final months of Chris's life and with the writing of this book. But even as he was prepared to criticize much of what was published as SF for being insufficiently ambitious, he remained deeply appreciative of science fiction's knowledgeable, switched-on audience, the opportunities presented by SF conventions to meet and talk with readers, the democratic inclusiveness of the SF magazines, in which the stories of new writers were routinely published alongside so-called masters of the genre. All the things he found to be lacking within the literary mainstream.

Ballard, while he liked and admired a number of writers who worked within the genre, found the fannish parochialism that is an inherent part of the science fiction community – the in-jokes and feuds, the occasionally bizarre rituals and above all the acceptance of devalued literary standards as the price of an exciting plot – impossible to tolerate. After his disastrous experience at the London Worldcon in 1957, while he continued to sell stories to *New Worlds* and *Science Fantasy*, Ballard separated himself from the social infrastructure of SF more or less entirely. What drew him to SF was not the people, but the language, the arresting and sometimes queasy juxtaposition of far-out fantastical conceits with the kind of specialist, technical jargon found in science magazines such as *Chemistry & Industry*.

It was this particular deployment of language, of a particular lexicon – the aftermath of nuclear war, urban decay and suburban sprawl, environmental catastrophe, post-human modification, medical-scientific technology, space-age sexuality – that offered Ballard what he was looking for: a way of parsing his early experiences that reached beyond realism to capture something of the radical disconnect between his years in a Shanghai internment camp and the barely comprehensible landscape of the postwar era.

Nor was Ballard the only writer to recognize the potential of science fiction to ignite new possibilities in terms of language and imagery. A group of young novelists drawn together around the experimental writer and publisher John Calder – a close friend of Samuel Beckett and the first publisher to put the work of William Burroughs before a British audience – had begun to notice what was going on at *New Worlds* and to be inspired by it.

Christine Brooke-Rose (1923–2012), Alan Burns (1929–2013), Eva Figes (1932–2012), B. S. Johnson (1933–73) and Ann Quin (1936–73) all emerged from different backgrounds and with wildly differing personalities. What they had in common was a dissatisfaction with the literary establishment as they perceived it: dominated by men with Oxbridge pedigrees and in thrall to nineteenth-century literary conventions that bore little relevance in a world that had experienced the detonation of nuclear weapons. B. S. Johnson, who became the unofficial spokesperson for the group, provided them also with a suitable mantra: 'to write as if it matters'.

Eva Figes (née Unger) was born in Berlin but grew up in London, a refugee from the Nazis. Her grandparents died in the Holocaust; she herself was bullied at school for having a German accent. Figes never fully recovered from the destruction of her childhood and writing for her was both a passion and a necessity. Following the breakdown of her marriage, she was left with little money and two children to care for. From her depression and uncertainty she fashioned a new way of writing, a bald transcription of her daily reality that resulted in *Equinox*, a suitably Ballardian title for a work that stripped the novel bare, laying the ground for later works such as *Konek Landing* and *Nelly's Version* that tip over from hyperreality into the fantastic.

Christine Brooke-Rose was born in Switzerland and was fluent in several languages. During the second world war she was hired to work at Bletchley Park, decoding and translating German news broadcasts. Her early novels were semi-autobiographical, drawing on her family background and her marriage to the Polish poet Jerzy Peterkiewicz. Even then, her fascination with language and the defamiliarization of language through coding drove her away from realism and towards formal experimentation. Her search for a new mode of expression was given fresh impetus when in 1960 she attended a reading given in London by three of the foremost writers of the French nouveau roman, Alain Robbe-Grillet, Marguerite Duras and Nathalie Sarraute.

The three had been invited to Britain by John Calder, a passionate advocate of the new French writing and who was already in the process of publishing their works in English translation. For Brooke-Rose, the intense focus and scientific precision of the nouveau roman were a revelation. Like Ballard, she was convinced that for the novel to remain relevant, it needed to express the reality of the postwar environment in a language that was reflective of that environment. The novels she produced in the wake of this personal epiphany – *Out*, set in the aftermath of a nuclear war, and *Such*, which dealt with the psychological impact on astrophysicists of quantum mechanics – delivered the conceptual breakthrough Brooke-Rose had been chasing, though she was reluctant to have her work defined as science fiction.

Alan Burns's mother and brother both died during the second world war, and every novel Burns wrote features the death of either a parent or a sibling. His debut novel *Buster* (1961) deals with this trauma in a realist, semi-autobiographical mode. His second, *Europe After the Rain* (1965) sees a radical shift both formally and thematically. The novel – named for the Max Ernst painting that was a key image for Ballard also – makes use of collage techniques, and takes place against a bleak, dystopian landscape ravaged by violence. Ann Quin's *Passages*, in which a female narrator and her male lover journey through southern Europe searching for the woman's missing brother, makes a similar marriage of fractured narrative and political dystopia.

Anna Kavan (1901–68) was a generation older than the writers of the Calder circle and so not truly aligned with them, but her interest in the new experimentalism, together with her affinity for the works of Franz Kafka, produced one of the most important speculative novels of that period. *Ice* (1967) is an eerie, fragmented narrative in which an unnamed narrator describes his relentless pursuit of a young woman, 'the glass girl', through an apocalyptic landscape of steadily advancing ice-fields. His rival for the woman's affections, a Nazi-like local dictator known as the Warden, is portrayed alternately as an enemy and an ally.

Part nightmare, part fairy tale, *Ice* envelops the reader in an atmosphere of chilly unknowability, making powerful use of non-linear narrative, filmic jump-cuts and point-of-view shifts to enhance and deepen the overall sense of alienation.

Like Ballard's triumvirate of early disaster novels, *Ice* sets itself up as a work of post-apocalyptic science fiction, only to subvert the form and with it the reader's expectations. Both Brian Aldiss and Ballard admired the novel, and were interested in Kavan's work as a whole. Chris would often cite *Ice* as a key inspiration. He would later write the introduction to the novel's 2006 reissue by Peter Owen, and take part in an event at the London Review Bookshop in 2007 to celebrate the posthumous publication of Kavan's 'lost' novel *Guilty*. Alongside him on the discussion panel were Brian Aldiss and Doris Lessing. In the audience was the writer Deborah Levy, who Chris had met briefly years before when they were both commissioned to work on a TV project that never came to pass. They reconnected briefly after the talk, as they do here. Levy has long been an admirer of Ballard, and cites him as an influence.

Anna Kavan originally offered *Ice* to John Calder for publication, but he turned it down.

Ballard first read the work of William Burroughs sometime towards the end of 1963. In his essay 'Myth-Maker of the Twentieth Century', published in the first Moorcock-edited issue of *New Worlds* in April 1964, Ballard praises Burroughs's use of collage and cut-up techniques – the requisitioning of previously existing texts in the creation of something new – comparing him with Joyce and Kafka and asserting that 'his three novels are the first definite portrait of the inner landscape of our mid-century, using its own language and manipulative techniques, its own fantasies and nightmares ... For science fiction the lesson of Burroughs's work is plain,' Ballard adds. 'Once it gets "off the ground" into space, all science fiction is fantasy, and the more serious it tries to be, the more naturalistic, the greater its failure.'[175]

In his own inaugural editorial for *New Worlds*, 'A New Literature for the Space Age', Moorcock – who had first discovered Burroughs during his extended European travels in 1962 – effectively claims him for science fiction, maintaining that 'his own writing techniques are as exciting – and as relevant to our present situation – as the latest discovery in nuclear physics'.[176]

By centring the word as significant entity, the novel as construct, Burroughs does not so much enhance SF for Ballard as redefine it, and the effect was as electrifying for him as his visit to the Whitechapel Gallery eight years earlier. Ballard's vision for science fiction – that it should be and was the natural heir to modernism – was already established when he begun to experiment with collage techniques in the late 1950s. Even as he rejected the conservative values and 'realist' embodiments of traditional SF, Ballard was looking to other writers and new forms of writing that he believed could and would be science fiction's natural allies.

Where Joyce and Woolf had revolutionized the novel by seeking to replicate the ceaseless internal monologue that is human consciousness, the new experimentalists revealed the postwar human condition to be essentially one of brokenness: fractured, non-linear narratives, snippets of pre-used text jammed and jimmied together to reveal secret meanings; obsessively repeating images, jump cuts, blank spaces in lieu of words; sex acts performed in the open, the language of gunmen and medics, bomber pilots and nuclear physicists, a new kind of slang.

In the 'condensed novels' and packets of text that would ultimately become *The Atrocity Exhibition*, Ballard would lay out in fractured chunks the story of a character named alternately Travis, Tallis, Traven, Talbot, Talbert or Trabert who is trying to process and make sense of the death of his wife in an automobile accident. He is stalked and studied by Dr Nathan, a rogue psychologist with unorthodox methods and a particular interest in the psychic effects of violence.

At the periphery of the enigmatic relationship between Traven and Nathan hovers the psychotic figure of Dr Vaughan, the 'hoodlum scientist' destined to reappear as the central character in Ballard's most controversial novel *Crash*, just a couple of years later. *The Atrocity Exhibition* is in fact a dress rehearsal for *Crash*: the giant billboards, the crash test dummies, the burned-out Pontiac, the dead film stars, the wounds confused with genitalia, the motorway flyovers compared with the symbolic curvature of female bodies – the same imagery occurs and recurs, repeated and redoubled and obsessively refined.

Travis/Traven/Talbot is desperate to decipher the horrors of the twentieth century: the assassination of President Kennedy, the war in Vietnam, the death-by-fire of the crew of the Apollo 1 on the launch pad at Cape Kennedy, the nuclear bombing of Hiroshima and Nagasaki. But the true subject of his investigations lies still deeper. In summoning the dangerous instability of Shanghai in the weeks immediately following his time in Lunghua, the dried-up riverbed close to Alicante, where his children played in the dusty wilderness nearby the apartment where Mary Ballard died, Ballard seems to be offering us an encoded autobiography.

Chris met William Burroughs only once. It was in August 1969, and Chris was twenty-six. He had just finished writing his first novel, *Indoctrinaire*: surrealistic and fragmented, his arresting debut might well be described as the quintessential novel of the British New Wave. It had been acquired by Charles Monteith at Faber & Faber, and would be published the following year.

As one of the fresh young voices of the new radical science fiction, Chris had been asked to appear at the Harrogate Festival of Arts and Sciences. The invitation had arrived at short notice – he was to replace J. G. Ballard, who had decided to go on holiday to Italy with his partner

Claire instead. The American New Wave writer Norman Spinrad had been selected to replace Michael Moorcock, another no-show.

The literary conference had been organized by John Calder, with the specific aim of placing writers of his own circle in open discussion with the writers of *New Worlds* magazine. For Chris, a young writer at the beginning of his career and unused to speaking in public, the conference proved to be an unpleasant experience even before he arrived there, cementing a dislike of Burroughs and his aesthetic that never altered:

> I took the train to Harrogate in the company of the science fiction writer Norman Spinrad, a striptease dancer called Terry Champagne who was Spinrad's girlfriend and the author William Burroughs. Mr Burroughs spent most of the journey in the bar, knocking back one glass of whisky after another and telling me and the others that he was on something called the 'drinking man's diet' – as he was of cadaverous and skeletal appearance I think it's safe to say that it was a diet that worked. We were greeted on arrival in Harrogate by the publisher John Calder, who fussed and fawned over Mr Burroughs, dancing attentively on his needs, carrying his suitcase, etc. Spinrad, Terry and I followed on humbly behind. We were ushered into Mr Calder's shining and splendid Jaguar, waiting at the station entrance: Mr Burroughs was helped into the front passenger seat and the rest of us crammed in behind. We drove away from the station portal, heading across the broad concourse. Mr Calder was in a sort of rapture: talking nineteen to the dozen to the great man in the front seat, sloshing the praise out unstoppably, regarding the famous author with loving eyes. However, in the back seat the three of us could hardly fail to notice that the Jaguar was heading towards a long flight of pedestrian steps. Our cries of warning went unheeded as Mr Calder blithely accelerated on. Within moments we were rattling and clattering down the steps, with loud and expensive-sounding scrapes and bangs coming from beneath the car. Halfway down the flight, the steps levelled out briefly before resuming. Here the beautiful Jaguar at last came to a halt, rocking to and fro on its chassis, balanced on the lip of the topmost step, just like the bus at the end of *The Italian Job*. We continued our journey to the hotel on foot.[177]

FOURTEEN

'THE SIGN OF THE CRAB'

Towards the end of May 2023 I travelled down to London to attend the launch of M. John Harrison's new book *Wish I Was Here*. Chris was unhappy about me going; Mike's launch was on the Thursday evening, and on the Friday Chris was meant to be heading to Glasgow, where he had been invited to be guest of honour at a convention. I too was a guest of the convention and Chris had assumed we would be travelling there together. His anxiety over this – a ninety-minute journey he had made many times before – was proof to me that something was very wrong.

By this point I knew that anyway. Chris's mobility had continued to deteriorate, and the pain he was experiencing while walking was by now impacting many aspects of our everyday lives. The previous autumn, we had booked a holiday in Stratford-upon-Avon for the week of Chris's eightieth birthday in July. We had invited Chris's children, Elizabeth and Simon, to join us for the second half of the week. We bought tickets for a performance of *As You Like It* for Chris's birthday on 14 July.

The week before I went to London, Chris told me he was worried about the drive and that he thought we should cancel. I was devastated, but at the same time relieved. Aside from being at his desk, Chris was never more comfortable than at the wheel of a car. We had travelled thousands of miles together and I had never known him anything but confident and at ease. This not wanting to drive was entirely new. And yet for some weeks I had been feeling increasingly worried about the trip. Chris seemed so tired, and he had not driven on English motorways since before COVID.

I suggested we ask the kids if they would like to take the cottage instead of us, an offer they happily accepted, together with the theatre tickets. Chris made light of the situation, not wanting to worry them. Other than the problem with walking, he was fine. We knew he was fine, because he was working on this book and making good progress. We kept assuming that whatever was wrong with his mobility would eventually improve.

I arrived back in Glasgow on the Friday lunchtime, as planned. Chris and I were happy to see each other and aside from being tired from his walk from the station, Chris was in good spirits. That evening we ate dinner with the writer Lisa Tuttle, Chris's second wife and our good friend, who had also just returned from a trip to London. She mentioned that she was still suffering from the after-effects of a heavy cold, and might leave the convention early.

Towards the end of the following week, Chris came down with what we assumed was the same virus as Lisa's. He tested negative for COVID, but felt increasingly unwell. He was due to appear at a literary event in Edinburgh at the weekend, and expressed doubts about going. It is painful for me to recall how I urged him not to cancel. I was eager for him to meet the writer Martin MacInnes, who would also be at the festival and who I felt sure Chris would like. In this I was not wrong – he and Martin bonded instantly and their friendship, though cut horribly short, was important to both of them – but unsurprisingly the trip itself was an awful mistake.

Chris spoke well at his event – I watched the livestream – and I am sure no one in the audience would have realized there was anything wrong. But he suffered two panic attacks, one in a taxi on the way to a restaurant and another the following morning at Waverley Station. He arrived home exhausted. He had never experienced a panic attack before. He had completely lost his appetite, together with a worrying amount of weight. We put this down to the virus he had caught in Glasgow, feeling certain that with rest he would soon start to feel like himself again. He needed time to work on the book without outside distractions and both of us were adamant that he should get it. We were determined to stick close to home for the rest of the summer.

Months and months later as I am writing this, I read a report in the *Guardian* about a predicted surge in cases of prostate cancer. The number of deaths is anticipated to rise by 85 per cent by 2040. The underlying cause of this dramatic statistic is the worldwide increase in longevity for men. 'Signs that prostate cancer may have spread include back or bone pain, a loss of appetite, and unintentional weight loss,' reads the article.

Chris had all these symptoms but the idea that he might have cancer never once crossed our minds.

The crisis came a month later, during the week we were supposed to have been in Stratford. Chris's left leg was by now causing him unbearable pain whenever he put weight on it. On Tuesday 11 July, the physiotherapist we had been consulting issued him with a three-wheeled walking frame. He also told us he was going to get Chris looked over by the GP, as he wanted to make sure there was nothing more serious in play than advanced arthritis.

That evening, we were supposed to be having a meal out with friends, followed by the new Wes Anderson movie *Asteroid City*. Shortly before we were due to leave, Chris told me he would go for the meal but come home afterwards. He did not feel like sitting through the film. He assured me he would be fine and that I should stay and see the movie. Less than an hour into the film, my mobile started ringing. I dashed outside to take the call.

'I think I've broken my leg,' Chris said. 'I've had to phone for an ambulance.'

I ran to the taxi rank. By the time I arrived home, paramedics were already preparing to lift Chris on to a stretcher so they could take him to hospital. Chris told me later that when he got out of the car he had found himself unable to cross the road, that he had come to a standstill halfway to the house. Two neighbours had helped him inside, but while reaching for his walking frame, he had fallen. He could barely remember how it happened, he said, just that his leg seemed to give way suddenly. One of the paramedics told me the leg had been twisted under him, that it was almost certainly broken.

I went with Chris in the ambulance to our local cottage hospital, the Victoria. I waited while he was admitted, and left to go home shortly before midnight. Chris would be X-rayed early the following day, we were told, and then, if the leg was broken, transferred to a hospital on the mainland to have it repaired.

I did not sleep much that night. Chris was less than two miles away, but he felt unreachable.

On his second day in hospital, I brought Chris a notebook. The notebooks I like best are the size of a school exercise book, wide feint, paper-backed and preferably spiral-bound. Chris likes hardbacked notebooks the size of a pocket address book, with plain paper and an inlaid ribbon bookmark. One of the plastic storage boxes that make up his archive contains dozens of them.

The notebook I took into the Victoria was given to me by a friend a couple of years ago. It is exactly the size Chris liked, with a cover that pretends to be the new Virago edition of *The Talented Mr Ripley* by Patricia Highsmith. The design is called 'Mobiles' and is by Marian Mahler, a suspension of geometrical shapes against a charcoal-grey background. The inlaid ribbon bookmark is brimstone yellow, matching the endpapers. It is a beautiful little book, one that I had never used. A notebook that size is too small for me – my atrociously sprawling handwriting would overflow the pages. Also, I have a strange animus against those notebooks that are mocked up to look like novels, though both Chris and I are fans of Patricia Highsmith and Ripley is – of course – one of our favourites.

Chris loved the book, which was the perfect size for his writing and for his thought process. On the first blank page he has written 'THE NOTBOOK', in block capitals, and underlined it. 'Notbook' is a private joke, a word he stole from Mike Harrison's *Wish I Was Here*. 'A series of disjointed nots,' he has written beneath it. 'Christopher Priest, aged 80 today, 14 July 2023 – ?'

He will write in it every day he is in hospital, and he will keep it close to hand until the end. Some weeks after he dies, I will take it from where he left it, on his desk to the right of his keyboard and beside a pot of pens, and place it in the right-hand drawer of my own desk in my office upstairs. I do this because I am anxious about it going missing. I am not a person who invests heavily in physical objects – less and less, in fact, these days – but this notebook is precious. A line keeps coming back to me, from Stephen King's novel *Rose Madder*, which tells of a woman walking out of an abusive marriage with nothing but her handbag. 'It was the purse she brought with her out of Egypt,' King writes of Rose, and that is the feeling I have about this notebook, that it carries a great weight, and was bought at great price.

It is the last of him, our final handhold. I cannot read it – I am only three pages in before I have to stop. It brings back those weeks too clearly – a time that now seems miraculous because we still had several months ahead in which to be together. There is nothing particularly profound about what is written in it. Chris always used notebooks sparingly. Dates, place names, things that happened jotted down with economy, precision and the sparsest of details. No first-person meanderings, no snatches of conversation, no extended description. His novels-in-progress he always carried in his head; he spared no time for writing memoir, or only rarely. It is not the content, but the existence of this notebook that for me is profound – that, and the fact that I have always been able to hear people's voices when I read their handwriting – a kind of graphic synesthesia – and so Chris's voice is audible on every page.

Chris kept everything from his life in writing, from the very beginning: correspondence, interviews, draft manuscripts, carbon copies of unpublished stories, early fanzines. The archivists who acquired Chris's papers for the British Library told me his was the most complete novelist's archive they had come across in years. I have kept nothing of my own apart from my notebooks, stuffed into drawers haphazardly and never looked at.

Anna Kavan destroyed most of her personal papers before she died. I felt a wave of fellow feeling when I first discovered this. Kavan did not intend to erase herself; what she wanted was to live through the writing she had chosen to publish. The diaries I wrote in every day from the age of fourteen I dumped wholesale into the dustbin when I was twenty-one. The feeling of needing to separate from myself was urgent and insurmountable.

Retelling the story of my final months with Chris is proving more painful than I imagined it would be. Even the prosaic detail is painful: the *this happened, that happened*. This is a story we learned by heart, the two of us. We told it many times between July and December, passing the threads of the narrative back and forth as seemed fitting or necessary. Repeating it now by myself I feel sick at heart, the weight of sadness heavy as granite, the same stolid grey.

To those who will one day read and study Chris's hospital notebook, I know you will not hear his voice in the writing as I do, but you will find the words perfectly legible, and perfectly true. Chris always had fine handwriting, though it deteriorated towards the end, as the notebook makes plain.

His final written words – in a card to his son – are unrecognizable as his, and therefore heartbreaking. Remembering this still causes me sorrow. I suppose I hope that in writing it down – in preserving the memory – I can let it go.

I arrived back at the Victoria shortly after 9 o'clock the following day. Chris had already been taken for X-ray and we were told he would be transferred to the Royal Alexandra Hospital in Paisley as soon as an ambulance became available. I rushed back to the house to pack him a bag. We were given to understand that he could be in surgery that same afternoon, or failing that the following morning.

The ambulance left the island on the one o'clock ferry. When we spoke on the phone later in the afternoon, it seemed clear that the operation to repair Chris's leg would be taking place the next day. But what happened on the Thursday was nothing. Chris had been put on nil by mouth from midnight on the Wednesday evening but around nine the following morning he was told the surgery would not go ahead.

'They want to give me an MRI first,' he said when he called me. 'There's something unusual about the fracture, apparently. They won't tell me what.' He sounded exhausted, dispirited and deeply unhappy. I just managed to catch the eleven o'clock ferry, then the train to Paisley, a trip I was to repeat on alternate days until Chris returned home in the back of another ambulance six weeks later.

The ward Chris was on was an orthopaedic receiving ward, a constantly moving conveyor belt of traumatic incident. Patients appeared suddenly or disappeared, often at night. Chris told me how the guy in the bed opposite had been brought in well after midnight, clearly in agony, friends and colleagues circling nervously, tapping their phones.

'He's in TV, I think,' Chris said, 'a news journalist.'

The following morning the man seemed better, making calls. In the bed closest to the door lay a much older man with a spinal injury. He was confused and mostly silent, his neck in a brace. His wife, distraught, kept demanding to see a doctor. I remember especially a wiry Glaswegian in his fifties whose right leg had been amputated below the knee, the result of complications from diabetes. He handled his wheelchair with a graceful fluidity, as if it were a racing car. His gallus humour bounced off the windows, divots of sunlight piercing the grey like rivets through steel.

There are a lot of men like that here, guys out of Trocchi or Welsh or Kelman, street-poets.

'I can't understand a word he says,' Chris said. My mind had begun working overtime, trying to bring a sense of order to what was happening: if Chris was going to be using a wheelchair, our current home, with its stairs and tight corners, would not allow him adequate freedom of movement. If hospital visits were to become a frequent necessity, then living on an island would no longer be practical. In my head I was already making plans to get us moved to a bungalow on the mainland. I was becoming exhausted, too tired to concede that reason cannot always function as an effective weapon.

'You can't keep coming over here every day,' Chris said. 'It's taking too much out of you.' He suggested I phone Christopher Johnstone, a retired Paisley GP who had written to Chris some months earlier, expressing his admiration for one of his novels. Dr Johnstone had been in the audience for Chris's interview at the Glasgow convention in May, and had come forward to introduce himself afterwards. Chris described him to me as friendly and highly intelligent, a great reader.

'I like him, and he lives in Paisley,' Chris said. 'Ask if he might find the time to pay me a visit. It would give you a break.'

There are good angels and bad angels in every story. Dr Johnstone is one of the good ones. He answered my first email in under half an hour and visited Chris at least three times each week throughout his hospital stay.

Dr Johnstone is sturdy, energetic and loquacious, what in doctors is invariably called affable. He must have been a wonderful family physician. He is, as Chris had inferred, highly intelligent and a voracious reader. As a former member of the GMC, he is also used to cutting through NHS bureaucracy. The difference he made to our situation was incalculable.

He came into our lives seemingly by chance, as angels do. Dr Johnstone and I were in contact most days throughout Chris's time in hospital, and when I search my emails to check the date of his first visit, I discover that our correspondence forms a complete and detailed record of the four uncertain weeks between Chris's first MRI scan and his eventual diagnosis.

The first week passed in agonizing slowness: multiple postponements, misdirection, a seemingly hopeless quest for more information. I was especially concerned that Chris, his fractured leg still seemingly no closer to being repaired, could not sit up to use his computer, attach his phone to its charger or even read in comfort. It seemed to me that the longer he was kept immobile, the more his recovery would be jeopardized, a point of view I conveyed to every member of the medical staff who found time to listen. I remember one capable junior doctor in particular, James Paxton, who seemed to be on our side, acting as an intermediary between us and the orthopaedic consultants, who we rarely saw. He spoke to me as an equal. I felt less anxious when I knew he would be on duty.

Gradually we were made aware of the reasons behind the delay. The initial set of X-rays had shown that the fracture to Chris's femur was not a straightforward break, but the result of a general weakening, a friability the doctors were anxious to investigate. The first MRI revealed what they immediately suspected were cancerous deposits; a further MRI – this time a full body scan – confirmed the deposits as cancer secondaries, metastases that were present not only in the leg bone but in the lungs, kidneys and spinal column.

The orthopaedic team at the Royal Alex were by now in direct consultation with oncologists at the Beatson Cancer Centre in Glasgow. Eventually a plan emerged: the leg would be repaired, whereupon Chris would be transferred as soon as possible to the Beatson, where he would receive a dose of radiotherapy accompanied by steroid treatment to stabilize the spine.

My emails to Dr Johnstone are a catalogue of false dawns and vain hopes. The leg operation was successful – a steel pin was inserted, a tumorous mass removed and replaced with metal. Within days Chris was able to stand, then take his first steps using a walking frame. Already he was much more comfortable, able to sit up and use his computer, to send and receive emails, even to get back to work. At the end of his second week in hospital, Chris was issued with a wheelchair. We were able to get off the ward and have coffee together in the café on the floor above, with its view of the hospital car park and trees beyond. This small autonomous act felt like a major victory. There was talk of bringing Chris back to the Victoria for rehab and physio.

We latched on to every positive and were, in our own way, jubilant. The doctors suspected prostate cancer, which would be treatable even at this stage. I kept reminding Chris about my uncle, Brian Grimwood, who had been diagnosed with what we believed to be a similar disease profile and who had lived a normal life for a substantial time afterwards. I kept thinking that if Chris could only come home we would begin to make sense of things.

It is important to me to record the facts, to put them in the order in which they happened. I want the facts to be known, or rather, I do not want them to become lost, unmoored in time, though they might convey little of the experience of living through them. Chris is less hung up on exactitude – what he used to call clock-time – and his recording of things that happened tends to be more wayward. I was forever pulling him up on points of order and it drove him crazy. I frequently found his versions of events to be skewed, opaque and potentially misleading. Like Peter Sinclair's narrative of his life in Chris's novel *The Affirmation*, they were not untrue so much as partial, so subjective they could be construed as falsehoods, though they never were.

We are both, each in our way, so like our books. On Monday, 17 July, the day the word 'cancer' was definitively uttered by a medical professional, Chris called his ex-wife, Leigh, and asked her to tell their children, Elizabeth and Simon. An hour later they were all in the car and heading north. Lizzy emailed to let me know they would be in Scotland the following day. Though Chris's need to see his family was understandable, for me it was another imponderable, something else to take account of, more people. I would have preferred them to wait until he'd had the operation at least, but the Priest twins are like their father: they do what feels right at the time and not what, on further reflection, might be more practical.

They are both exceptional people: compassionate and honest in a way that makes me fear for them. They do not calculate, they feel. They will always have each other. They are so different from me.

'I want everyone together,' Chris said. 'I want to tell them about the wedding.'

At some point in the past twelve hours, we had decided to get married.

Leigh Kennedy is beautiful and piercingly intelligent. I had not seen her in person since 2011, just after she and Chris split up. In the years since the divorce, they had kept a cordial though distanced relationship, mainly centred upon their children. When I encounter her for the first time in the hospital — on the Thursday morning, the twentieth, the day after Chris's leg surgery — we embrace, we smile. I am crying, I think, a little. Leigh handles this new situation — the instant, unasked-for intimacy that has been foisted upon her — with tact and with grace, her guardedness deftly concealed beneath a wraparound warmth. She seems in every way better put-together than I am, and I find myself admiring her enormously, as I have always admired her writing, elegant and singular.

Chris is in a heightened state. He has all his people around him, and the presence of the twins is like a drug for him. They are talkative, unchained. Lizzy, who has recently begun her own writing career, publishing a series of young-adult fantasies, keeps close to her father, closer than usual, and Simon, who has organized the trip, who has transported Chris's missing personal effects from the Alex to the Beatson, who has bought his father a long-cord phone charger and brought me coffee, appears much older, suddenly. As if he has stepped into bigger shoes. As if he is finally leaving his teenaged self behind.

The pathos makes my throat tight. I feel exhausted, wrung out, ashamed of my earlier doubts about them coming.

The biggest immediate threat to Chris's recovery were the tumours that had metastasized to the spinal column. If pressure on the spinal cord increased, there was a danger that Chris might lose the movement in his legs and lower body. Steroids would counteract this, slowing the growth of the secondaries, at least for a time, though they also gave Chris nightmares and hallucinations. For most of a week, until the dose was lowered, he was obsessed with his dreams, recounting them to me at length, describing with a kind of fascinated delight the strange effects the drugs were having on his mind and vision.

Chris had never been much interested in dreams before – dream-sequences in novels especially were a thing he abhorred – but these dreams were different, a psychic irruption, a coup perpetrated against the rational mind by guerilla forces of the subconscious.

'None of this is real,' I told him repeatedly. I kept thinking of Ballard and his bad LSD trip, though I did not mention this to Chris until the side-effects of the treatment were out of his system. I was more concerned with chasing up doctors, trying to find out what had happened to the biopsy results. Chris fixated on detail while I hacked brutally through it, searching for the wider landscape. Babes in the wood, the two of us: lawyer-brain and back-row daydreamer, mismatched yet inseparable, even now.

Later, when he was out of hospital, there was an anecdote Chris loved to tell about the worst night of his steroid-induced derangement in which he temporarily lost the sense of who and where he was. The fact that his brief period of paranoia took such classic form was a source of genuine and uproarious amusement to everyone who heard it. I have no doubt that for Chris, unwell and alone in the darkness and silence of an alien place, the experience at the time was mortally terrifying. Laughter helped to assuage the fear, to rewrite the reality.

I encouraged him to write down everything he remembered. Already we were beginning to talk about the possibility of including Chris's own experiences as part of the book and this one, I insisted, was especially valuable, especially relevant. Ballard too had been treated with steroids; there was every possibility he had undergone a similar breakdown of narrative logic.

As first-person evidence of Chris's hospital stay we have his notebook, which I cannot read, and this, the story he brought with him out of Egypt. I wish that there were more, but in this as in everything else, time was not on our side.

15

'THE DEPOT OF DREAMS'

ROYAL NEPHEW NUMBER ONE
On the second night in the Beatson I had a dream: it was inexplicable, surprising and memorable. It was also short and to the point. I dreamt I was in a castle somewhere in Scotland, and came across a young man who lived there hidden away in a suite of rooms in an obscure wing. He told me earnestly that he was a semi-disowned member of the Royal Family, who was never allowed to be seen in public. The other royals referred to him as 'Royal Nephew Number One'.

I woke up. I had been allocated a room on my own, off the main ward. It was the middle of the night. All was dark and quiet.

I tried to go back to sleep but I was uncomfortable because of my sore leg. I drifted. I woke up again, fully and suddenly. I was unable to breathe. Someone had turned me over so that I was face-down in the bed. I was terrified. I struggled to move but my paralysed leg made all movement difficult. Panicking I tried to escape from the bed, but metal railings on each side prevented that. I fought against the entrapping bed, pulling off the sheets, gasping for air. Beneath the sheets the bed surface was bristly, like a brush. It scraped against my face. All I wanted to do was escape from the bed. I began shouting.

The door opened and a woman came in quickly. She was carrying a bright torch, but she did not turn on the room lights. I tried to tell her what had happened, but could not speak clearly. Very swiftly and efficiently she remade the bed, putting the sheets back on, covering me with a blanket. She was strong, capable. Somehow, without lifting me, she laid me on my back. But I was turned over! I could no longer feel the bristles beneath the undersheet. I was still gasping, but gradually calming down. It was impossible to think about anything else except the fear of suffocation.

Then she said, 'Do you know where you are?'

I looked around at the room, aware of it for the first time: everything was in shadows because of her torch. I couldn't see much, just the walls, indistinct shapes. The torchlight made the shadows waver. Was the room moving? I thought maybe it was a cabin.

I said, 'Am I on a ship?'

'No – do you know who you are?'

Blank. I could not answer.

'Can you tell me your name?'

I could not. For the first time I felt a deep fear. My memory was empty of myself.

'Do you know who I am?' I said. 'Couldn't you tell me?'

'No – you have to remember.'

I mentally floundered, now really disturbed. Who was I? What had happened to me? Who was this woman? What was she doing? Everything was still blank.

Then a thought, a ghost of a memory. I clutched at it.

'Is there any chance,' I said, 'that I'm a minor member of the Royal Family?'

She stepped back from me.

'I'll ask the duty doctor to come and see you.'

As she walked swiftly from the room I realized she was wearing a nurse's uniform. By the time the doctor arrived about ten minutes later I had recovered from what I now understood must have been a lucid nightmare. I could identify myself, my situation, which hospital I was in, and why.

He had apparently looked at my medical record before he arrived. 'You've been put on a course of steroids,' he said. 'They sometimes cause nightmares. Don't worry – we'll reduce the dose a little.' Then he was gone.

The day before I had been transferred to this specialist cancer hospital, and on arrival I was given a bed in a general ward. There were five beds. Most of the others were occupied, but the one directly opposite mine was empty. Because of my broken leg I was capable of little more than minor movement, so for some time I stared across at the bed opposite.

I closed my eyes, hoping for a nap. It was summer and the ward was full of daylight. My closed eyelids glowed red, lending that impression of seeing something while there was nothing to see.

Suddenly I realized there was something to see: against the reddish background I could make out the head and shoulders of a child: a small boy, smiling away to one side. The image was monochrome, black against the red background, the lines drawn rather like a microscopic image of body fluids. Definitely not random, though. This was exact. I 'stared' in fascination. As I did so the image slowly changed, and the head and shoulders of a girl formed as I watched. She was approximately the same age as the boy. She displaced him.

I opened my eyes, astonished. Had I fallen asleep without realizing it? Had that been a dream? I am familiar with pre-sleep hypnagogic imagery, but I had never seen anything like it before, nothing so clear and detailed. I looked around the ward: nurses were moving about, attending to some of the other patients. One of the ancillary workers was handing out cups of tea or coffee – a cup of coffee was placed on my own bed table. I sipped the warm brown liquid: it was awful!

I closed my eyes again and within a few seconds the image of the boy returned. The little girl replaced him. I continued to watch – around me I could hear the familiar noises of a hospital ward. The taste of the horrible coffee was still detectable. I was not asleep.

The image started changing again. The picture of the girl coalesced into what looked like a sheet of paper or fabric, with three dark holes in a horizontal line.

The holes then merged with each other to make only one.

This grew larger – it was as if a camera was moving towards it. When it was close up I realized the hole looked just like a navel, a tummy button.

No – it was an eye, staring back at me.

It changed yet again: this time into a plughole. While I watched, water swirled into it, circling in a familiar way.

The 'camera' moved back and now I realized the image looked like a birthmark, a mole. It was on someone's neck and I could see an ear lobe just above it, and a tuft of dark hair.

I opened my eyes. The activities in the ward were continuing. The plastic cup of hospital coffee was on my table, still warm.

I was deeply interested in what I had just witnessed, unable to explain it. Clearly it was some kind of imagining, but where did it come from? I had no idea who the children might have been. And the holes, or marks — what did they signify? Was I going mad?

I hoped not, and didn't think so. I felt rational, involved. The summer sun was still filling the ward. I closed my eyes, stared at the reddish vagueness. Within about a minute, the image of the boy formed again. The face was exactly as before. As was the little girl, then the holes ... the entire sequence was repeated as far as the mole on the neck. I 'ran' the sequence several more times, then wrote a description of it in my notebook. It never changed in any detail, and I was not at all curious about what would replace the image of the birthmark on the neck. All I knew was that the whole thing was in ordinary terms inexplicable, but I was certain it was real, not a dream, obviously some kind of delusion, but one that was rational, repeatable.

Later, while I was still wondering about this experience, I downloaded a copy of the short story 'Casey Agonistes' by Richard M. McKenna.

The story is about a small group of American ex-Navy sailors, who are confined in a TB ward in the terminal stages of the disease. This grim group are unexpectedly enlivened when one of the men (who is known for laughing to himself occasionally) reveals that he has imagined into existence a giant ape he calls Casey. With a little encouragement he helps the others to 'see' Casey: 'He looked like a bowlegged man in an ape suit covered with red-brown hair. He grinned and made faces with a mouth full of big yellow teeth.'

Soon all the men are familiar with Casey, and as a groupthink the imaginary ape gains a kind of independence. No one else but they can see him. Gradually, Casey starts to act on their behalf, sheltering them from the worst tyrannies (as they perceive them) of the head nurse and a couple of doctors. It's an astonishingly moving story.

The similarity between this eidetic imagining and what had just happened to me was intriguing, especially as I too was in a terminal condition in a hospital environment. I couldn't help wondering if at some time McKenna himself might have undergone a similar experience.

Later that same evening, after an early dinner, the ward was quiet. Because of my difficulty moving, once again I had little to do and stared across the room at the empty bed opposite mine. The long summer evening kept the ward lit.

The ward was set up so that each bed had its own television receiver. This was on a jointed, cantilever arrangement, so that the small flat screen could be pulled down and across for private viewing. When it was switched on the sound could only be heard through personal earphones. Whoever had been in the bed across the ward, or maybe one of the nurses, had folded the TV screen up and away, facing the bed below. All I could see of it was the plastic frame edge-on, down the side of the screen, halfway up the wall, a black short line, slanting slightly.

While I was looking at it I suddenly realized that from this angle it looked a little like a stick cartoon character. Now the top section had resolved into an angular hat! To my amazement a stylized cartoon arm appeared and doffed the hat in my direction.

I blinked, mentally backed away, looked around at the rest of the ward. Everything seemed normal, comprehensible. The TV screen parked opposite me was again visible only as a dark line. I felt calm and unexcited, but worried – I was seeing things! Had I imagined that? My eyes were not closed – this was happening right in front of me. I stared across at the dark line, almost willing it to do something. After about a minute it did: the cartoon character briefly reappeared, doffed the hat, then reverted. This too now blurred and as I watched a new image appear, a woman. I could not see her clearly, but she was tall and youngish, standing at the same angle as the line. She looked faintly old-fashioned. She was wearing a shapeless soft hat, and a long dress or coat that reached down to her feet. She was standing in a narrow road. In the distance behind her were some hills. At her left side, and slightly in front of her was a wooden bench seat, on the edge of the road. The sky was bright but clouded over. Wind appeared to be blowing, because it was lifting parts of her long hair not covered by the hat. The image was in colour, but muted. She seemed about to step forward, in my direction. Now she was upright, no longer at a slant. Unexpectedly, a group of small children emerged from behind her, jostled past her on the narrow road, some of them running their hands along the bench seat that stood there.

I blinked the image away, wondering what I had been seeing and why. I glanced up quickly at the TV equipment and noticed that one of the cantilever arms was positioned exactly where the back of the wooden bench seat had been, but nothing else that I had seen in the vision appeared to be related to the reality of the ward.

Of course I went back for more: I was fascinated, keen to know what was going to develop. Over the next half-hour or so I let the image play in a number of iterations. Between each one I scribbled a description in my notebook.

The woman was walking towards me. There were cars on the narrow road, following her with headlights showing. One swung off the road and disappeared to my left. I sensed there was a body of water beside the road. I could see the dark bulk of a ship, moored close by. I wanted to see the woman's face, so I held still as she came towards me. But she never came close enough for me to gain anything more than an impression of her appearance.

The day after my suffocation nightmare, I went online and looked up what I could find about the side-effects of steroids.

There were many, but only a few affected me. I did notice that corticosteroids taken by mouth could cause nightmares ... and hallucinations.

On the third and fourth night I suffered repeat nightmares, but nothing as unpleasant as the first. After that, the dose was lowered to the point where the side-effects had no serious impact on me.

I never did discover the truth about the nephew prince, trapped in his tower.

SIXTEEN

'PREPARATIONS FOR DEPARTURE'

The author of 'Casey Agonistes', Richard McKenna, was an American writer best known for his epic war novel *The Sand Pebbles*, which draws on his experiences as a naval engineer on the Yangtze Patrol. His time in the navy cast a major influence upon his writing, and his science fiction stories combine his interest in technology with themes of escape, especially of how the mind can transcend the body. In 'Casey Agonistes', Casey the invisible gorilla is unnervingly potent as a metaphor for death, and there is something pre-Ballardian in the story's furniture: the men on the isolation ward talking over 'old times in China', the proto-modern building with its 'green-gray linoleum' and 'high, narrow windows', most of all the masked doctor, 'a tall skinhead with wooden eyes and pinchnose glasses', who might easily pass for a character in *The Atrocity Exhibition*.

Chris was so preoccupied by 'Casey Agonistes' he reread it several times, both while he was in the hospital and afterwards. The Beatson is one of the top cancer care facilities in the UK, with a calm, even welcoming atmosphere, nothing like the sweltering and overcrowded TB ward described by McKenna — and yet the situation the patients find themselves in is eerily similar. The endless waiting for what will all too often be bad news, the coded language of the medical staff, the way in which time and even reality become eroded.

From the moment Chris was able to sit up in bed to use his computer, he was anxious to return to work on this book. At the time he broke his leg, he had been about to start researching his chapter on *The Atrocity Exhibition*. He had not been looking forward to it. He had never liked the work, and the prospect of writing about it brought back memories of the time when he had begun to feel increasingly out of step with the British New Wave and without a natural cohort with whom to identify.

Within days of entering the hospital, he was forming new insights. 'I know how to write about it now,' he kept saying to me. 'It's the key to everything Ballard wrote.'

He asked me to bring the novel with me when I next visited, so that he could reread it. He was soon making notes, and writing, writing. The renewed acquaintance with 'Casey Agonistes' acted as a springboard for his ideas, revealing the ways in which a significant or traumatic experience might affect an artist's work, not simply in terms of the subject matter – what it is 'about' – but in how the work is structured, even how the words might be arranged upon the page.

'I just wish that this was an experience I could live through, and learn from.' Words Chris spoke to me on several occasions during his final months, and that fill me even now not only with pain at both our losses, but with regret for the work that would undoubtedly have emerged: the altered forms, the radical imagery, the renewal of self.

Chris finally got his diagnosis on Friday 11 August, exactly one month after first being admitted to hospital with a broken femur. In one of those chaotic reversals that are common in any prolonged course of hospital treatment, he was back in the Royal Alexandra. He had been taken there initially on what was promised to be a two-hour excursion – the orthopaedic surgeon who had carried out his leg surgery wanted to check on the wound – but that inexplicably turned into a week-long detention.

Earlier that week, he had been subjected to a third CT scan, this time for the purposes of taking a full biopsy. Forced to lie on his stomach and in a position that was painful and that restricted his breathing, he found the twenty-minute procedure close to unbearable. The sense of helplessness this gave him, together with the needless disruption of being moved back to the Alex, impacted Chris severely. We were both more than ever anxious for him to be discharged; at the same time, we knew he was not really well enough.

While I was visiting Chris in the Alex on 10 July, one of the junior doctors – a warm, humorous and sympathetic man named Nick Whiteley – came on to the ward and asked if I would be able to return the following day. He told us that Chris's biopsy results had arrived, and that his consultant at the Beatson would be coming to the Royal Alexandra to discuss them with us.

Our response was one of relief – finally, some answers. We should perhaps have known that consultants do not make such journeys routinely, that Chris's doctor doing so now could not necessarily be counted on as good news. What I remember of the next day, mostly, is the waiting: waiting to get to the hospital, waiting for the consultant to arrive. Ben Fulton was young, keenly observant, emotionally intelligent and compassionate in a way that seems at least in our experience to be a defining characteristic of those who work in oncology.

He drew the curtains around the bed. 'These were not the results we were hoping or expecting to find,' he said. He told us that Chris had small cell carcinoma, a rare and particularly aggressive form of cancer, that they remained pretty sure that the primary was the prostate, but at this stage that was of lesser importance than the damage that was being done by the cancer throughout the rest of Chris's body. He said the radiotherapy Chris had been given had, for the moment at least, halted the progression of the tumours in the spine, but that the respite was only temporary.

'We can try chemotherapy,' he said, 'but that carries its own risks.'

The risks, he scarcely needed to tell us, had to do with how well an eighty-year-old would be able to withstand a full-on chemical war in which his body would form the battleground. A friend of mine who worked in medical physics later told me that patients of Chris's age and disease profile would not usually be offered chemotherapy because they were too frail to tolerate it. But Chris was worth the fight.

'What sort of timescales are we talking about?' I asked Ben Fulton. 'With and without chemo?'

Ben hesitated. 'Are you all right,' he said to Chris, 'talking about this stuff?'

Chris nodded at once. 'We might as well know what's what,' he said, or something like that. I cannot remember his exact words, which for me is unusual. As a rule, I have the vexing habit of remembering everything.

To this day, I have never looked up 'small cell carcinoma' on the internet. I know that Chris did, but I did not because I could not bear to. I listened intently to every word Ben Fulton told us, weighing them against his honesty, which I judged to be total. He said that without chemo, Chris might have seven months to live. With chemo, if it went well, he might have as much as eleven, maybe a year.

'With chemo there are no guarantees,' he added. What he meant was, the treatment might not work, and Chris's general state of health might be impacted to the extent that he would have been better off not having chemo in the first place. He offered Chris the option of trying a first dose to see how well he took it. He could then continue with the treatment, or not; it would be up to him.

'What choice would you make?' I asked him. 'If it were you, I mean?' I felt as if we were being asked to spin a roulette wheel.

'Either choice is perfectly valid,' he said. 'It wouldn't be right for me to influence you, either way.'

He left shortly afterwards, telling us it would be a good idea to take the weekend to think about things, to discuss the options between ourselves. He left us his phone number and email address so we could contact him directly with any questions.

I was cautious. I had read and heard enough about chemo to know what it could do to a person. If the time remaining was so short in any case, chemo might ruin that, might even accelerate Chris's decline. I was tending towards the view that maybe – *maybe* – it would be better to forgo the treatment and make the best of things.

Chris though had already decided. He would take the treatment. At the time I wondered if he understood the full implications. It is difficult, now, to articulate how much I love and admire him for not caring about percentages, for going for it anyway. For taking the chance. For wanting to survive even though Ben Fulton had told us that survival was impossible.

'If there's a treatment, I want to try it,' Chris said. 'It's worth a shot.'

Out of unreality, we forge something real.

In the space of six weeks – a month – you have become a dying man.

Saturday 12 August, and the Bute Highland Games. On the *Today* programme, three guest editors are talking about grief. Grief makes you into a different person, says one of them, and although I have heard these words before, or something like them, I realize I have never believed them, that I have never understood how real grief, which is a remaking, is a proof of love.

At Wemyss Bay Station there are crowds of Games-goers: children in Highland costume, guys with muscled calves and dressed in kilts queueing for bacon rolls at the café counter. In the first hours of daylight the rain was torrential, typical Games weather, yet the feeling of warmth and festivity on and around the station forecourt is tangible, a kind of blessing. The Games are old, a bigger deal than any day on which they happen to take place, more than capable of surviving bad weather and this wet day in particular, and I have no doubt that counts for something, that it is a marker of independence and resilience.

There is a fiddle band. They are playing simple dance tunes – the kind you'd hear at a ceilidh, the kind anyone could learn to play on a flute or a recorder in less than an hour. And I find that I am crying. Walking on to the platform with my cardboard cup of tea and crying. For days and days, the idea of listening to music – those self-conscious constructions, such artifice – has been impossible, not so much too moving as irrelevant. What has been central to my life and thinking now seems beside the point, a *decoration*. A thing that can only exist in the kind of world where rules apply and can be followed, where there is time to build a concert hall, where audiences can flick through their programmes, which are mostly advertising, and buy expensive drinks in the interval or say casually to a friend at the faculty the following day, 'Did you happen to catch the Bruckner on Radio 3 last night?'

I have so much wrapped up in these rituals, so much personal investment. So much history. I find I no longer care. And yet this fiddle music seems to enfold me, to cover me in warmth and in something else – a sense of being in time and more particularly of being here, in Scotland. I am walking and crying but that is OK, that is to be expected. Even in rain. Especially in rain. This.

I am supposed to be running in the 10K road race today, but I am visiting the hospital instead. I am going to be with Chris, to hear his decision. On the Sunday he will email Ben Fulton and on the Monday he will be transferred back to the Beatson to begin his treatment. After that, we are told, Chris should finally be able to come home.

Several months earlier and long before we knew that Chris was ill, we had arranged a date to have lunch with M. John Harrison and his partner Cath Phillips. Mike was to be interviewed on stage at the Edinburgh Book Festival and although we would not be able to stay for the gig – his event was in the evening, and overnight accommodation in Edinburgh at festival-time is ridiculously expensive even if you can find any – we were looking forward to meeting up, especially as Chris had not seen Mike in person since we moved to Scotland in 2017.

As with our trip to Stratford, the lunch never happened. But when we realized that Mike and Cath's weekend in Edinburgh would more or less coincide with Chris's discharge from hospital, we hurriedly arranged for them to visit us on their way back to Shropshire. They arrived on Bute in the late afternoon of Sunday 20 August. Chris would be coming home the following day.

I ached to see them. To talk. To eat in a restaurant. To be normal.

'How is he?' Cath said. 'How are *you*?'

'He's dying,' I said, the first time I had admitted it out loud. I began to weep. Mike stepped forward to hug me, a moment of mute acknowledgement I will never forget. Later, in the restaurant, I began telling them about this book.

'It sounds like you should be writing it,' Cath said. She was responding, I suppose, to my enthusiasm for the project, for the excitement I still felt for it, in spite of everything. I laughed and shook my head. I told her Chris was determined to finish the book himself, that he had everything in hand.

17
'A SEASON FOR ASSASSINS'

This book is a work of biography, focused on the life and work of one writer. It is not a psychological analysis, nor an investigation into the consequences of real or alleged traumatic events. My concern throughout this book is to examine and evaluate the literary work J. G. Ballard produced in his lifetime, taking into account only known events or experiences that might have had an impact on the work, or the lives of other people close to him who can be shown to have had a significant influence on his writing.

While still at The Leys, when he was a teenager, Ballard had read Sigmund Freud's major works. He developed early ambitions to become a psychiatrist.[178] He went on to read medicine at Cambridge University with that ultimate intent. He continued with the course for two years before abandoning it: he later said, self-critically, 'I could have done some *real* damage if I had become a psychiatrist!' His youthful faith in psychoanalysis appeared to be fading.

Ballard's early life contained many extreme or at least unusual experiences, most of which have been described here.

In summary: His childhood was privileged, and the middle-class expatriate social circumstances of his birth were restrictive. He was raised in a luxurious but emotionally chilly household where much of the parenting was handed over to Chinese servants. He was educated at an English-speaking religious school inside a Western enclave in a foreign country, of which he knew nothing, did not speak the language nor even eat the local food. War and invasion occurred around him before he was ten years old – he witnessed the uprooting of thousands of people and would have known of the many more who were massacred by the

Japanese as they swept across Manchuria and China. He said he saw thousands of dead Chinese in the streets of Shanghai. He was interned in a Japanese prison camp when he was in his early teens, suffering loss of freedom, poor diet and limited horizons of ambition. He witnessed at close hand at least two violent murders: there were possibly more that he did not record. On his return to the UK he felt abandoned and adrift, failed at two university courses, could not find proper work for years, and finally joined the RAF for a few months before backing out.

Only once he was free of the RAF and started writing did a recognizable structure enter his life. He became a writer. This was without premonition a step forward into a more conventional way of life, an author's career. That was immediately enhanced by falling in love and producing three healthy children with his wife Mary. In 1964 her sudden death created the major crisis of his life, one he often said took years to come to terms with.

All of this experience must at least be considered as we move on to the next stage in his unique writing career. This was when he wrote and published *The Atrocity Exhibition*.

Ballard was a self-aware man. In 1997, he was contacted by David R. Kopacz, an American doctor and psychiatrist who writes about wellness, trauma, post-traumatic growth, healing and spirituality, transformation, holistic health, and the healing power of story and creativity. Dr Kopacz asked Ballard several questions about the possible effects of traumas he was believed to have suffered, which were answered in some detail:

> I ought to say first that there seems to be an underlying assumption by both you and the received wisdom of the day that all disturbing or violent experience is inherently damaging – that experiences such as the death of a spouse or child, death of a parent, the stress of being uprooted from one's home, the hunger and privations of war, will all leave indelible fracture lines that run through the wounded psyche like a crack through a glass pane, and that even the lightest tap is capable of inflicting irreparable damage. I very much doubt this, although I seem to be opposed to the entire apparatus of twentieth-century psychotherapy. The fact is that throughout most of their evolution, human beings have been exposed to constant threats and ordeals,

both physical and mental, of every kind, and the majority of people recuperate and in due course make a full recovery. I'm not sure that I have ever suffered irreparable trauma. Of course the death of my wife was a devastating blow, and to some extent I still mourn her over thirty years later. I think its 'inexplicable' cruelty (in fact, sadly, mortality – often unexpected – is the ocean we swim in) led me to embark on *The Atrocity Exhibition*, with its attempt to make sense of another inexplicable death, that of JFK.[179]

To Kopacz, Ballard was therefore maintaining a rational view of the possible effects of trauma. He meant that *The Atrocity Exhibition* and other books of his which were soon to appear, most of them considered by some to be sexually deviant and psychologically disturbing, should be seen as the product of conscious creative choices, the untraumatized work of a professional writer.

On the other hand, he frequently did allude to the possibility of trauma.

In 2008, not long before the end of his life, he described to James Naughtie the many dead Chinese he had seen: 'When I came to England in 1945 I think I was carrying a huge cargo of death. I couldn't understand why this had happened. I think my wife's death was a reminder that you couldn't pretend that death had left the stage.'[180]

So maybe he was hinting at the possibility of 'received wisdom' of the effects of trauma? On the other hand I believe there is evidence that what he said to Kopacz was in fact closer to the truth.

Even as early as 1958 Ballard had been experimenting with what he called 'condensed novels'. He made up several posters using cut-out display typography from the trade magazine he worked for, and mounted them around his office with an overall title 'Project for a New Novel'. These were the precursors of the material that went into *The Atrocity Exhibition*. His wife Mary took a photo of Ballard in front of his 'Project' in around 1960, with several others, taken by a newspaper photographer, appearing in 1965. One was later published by Ted Carnell on a cover of *New Worlds*, which has since appeared in other places.

The original individual constituent, or 'condensed novel', from the book was called 'You and Me and the Continuum', which appeared in the first-named issue of *Impulse* published by Kyril Bonfiglioli. (Michael

Moorcock, who believed he and Ballard had been discussing the story with a view to it going into *New Worlds*, felt let down when Bonfiglioli was offered the story.[181]) Similarities between the story as published and some of the text dimly discernible in the photograph of the 'Project' do exist, but they are unreliable. Ballard anyway has said that he wrote 'You and Me and the Continuum' as a piece of fresh work. It was eventually presented as the ninth item in the contents table of *The Atrocity Exhibition*.[182]

Over the next three years or so more constituent pieces appeared, by no means confined to publication in *New Worlds*. Four of them were carried by *Ambit*, but the rest were scattered around: one in *Encounter*, another in *Transatlantic Review*, yet another in *International Times*. One appeared in a student magazine, another was handed out as an 'event-sheet', a programme leaflet from the Institute of Contemporary Arts in London.

Interspersed with these were more conventional Ballardian stories, later collected in book form: these included two excellent new *Vermilion Sands* stories, 'Cry Hope, Cry Fury!' and 'The Cloud-Sculptors of Coral D'.

The overall picture is not of a tormented, traumatized author, working out his hang-ups in public. Ballard continued to be a conscious literary artist. Even so, many readers found the condensed novels of *The Atrocity Exhibition* difficult – although superficially easy to read they were frequently baffling. Some of the sexual imagery was close focus and seemingly perverse or abnormal; many of the anatomical details, particularly in reference to the bodies of women, were obscure or excruciating. To those ready to be shocked or scandalized, the book provided an easy resort.

It was the precision of that level of detail that is the clue to unravelling the apparent obscurities. Ballard's vocabulary was always exact, anatomically correct: presumably he had learned much from his dissection work as a medical student, and no doubt still owned reference textbooks on the subject.

Two later additions, first published in *New Worlds* and *Ambit* in 1969 and 1970 but included as part of the 1990 annotated edition of *The Atrocity Exhibition*, were based directly on texts written by plastic surgeons about a facelift and a breast reduction operation, in which Ballard reproduced the grisly details of the procedure but instead of using the word 'patient' he replaced it with the name of a famous woman, creating a parallel with the way Andy Warhol used the images of celebrities or canned food to depict his pop-art portraiture.

The common pornographer blurs the reality of sexual description by using clichés or slang or generalizations: if you come across an unusual word or description in *The Atrocity Exhibition* and look it up, you will find precisely what Ballard meant.

What were his motives for such work? He said repeatedly that he was trying to come to terms with the unexpected death of his wife, feelings which were complicated, distorted, by the similarly inexplicable assassination of President Kennedy a few months before. Both of these events he would have seemed to dismiss as lasting personal traumas, and in any case the sheer practical awareness of writing tends to steer an author into the realities of literary composition, rather than an uncontrolled release of pent-up emotion.

Because of the overall circumstances in which *The Atrocity Exhibition* came into being, it seems likely that the apparent motives were more the result of creative freeing.

He had been considering such work over a period of months and years, long before the need to make sense of the death of either his wife or President Kennedy. The circumstances now lent themselves to it.

So what are the components about, and how may we try to understand them?

The first UK edition of *The Atrocity Exhibition* was published by Jonathan Cape in 1970. Each of the component pieces appeared 'bare', without much of a guide for the reader. The seeming lack of narrative cohesion (i.e. very little cause and effect), plus the fact that several characters had interchangeable names, and that most of the individual components were broken up into short passages with no clear link between them, did create real problems of comprehension in readers.

At different times Ballard tried to offer help. For instance, when 'You and Me and the Continuum' was published in *Impulse*, Ballard added a prefatory note:

> The theme of sacrifice led me to think of the Messiah or, more exactly, the idea of the second coming and how this might take place

in the twentieth century. In my version, which I would describe as a botched second coming, the Messiah never quite managing to come to terms with the twentieth century, I have used a fragmentary and non-sequential technique ... and have tried to invoke some of the images that a twentieth-century Messiah might see. You'll notice that the entries are alphabetized.[183]

As Ballard had never before shown much interest in Christian mythology, and the alphabetization of the entries was obvious but unexplained, this did not exactly help.

In an 'Author's Note' to the 1993 UK paperback edition of the original 1990 annotated edition he suggested opening the book at random, allowing one's eye to fall on a particular passage, then reading around from that point. Again, few readers or critics found this made things any clearer, although Ballard insisted that it was a way of reading the book in much the same way as it had been written. A warning of a kind was implied.

It was reviewed in the *Financial Times* by Isobel Murray, who said, 'J. G. Ballard is increasingly admired for his powerful writing in a field which for want of a clearer term is vaguely described as science fiction. The possible terrors of post-nuclear life have been made startlingly probable by his ingenious, precise, almost clinical prose. A terrible kind of poetry of violence.'

An American edition of *The Atrocity Exhibition* had been arranged with the publishers Doubleday & Company in 1969. However, fearing legal action from some of the notables named in the book, the CEO of the company, John Turner Sargent, personally cancelled publication and had all printed copies destroyed.[184] It was published two years later by Grove Press, under the title *Love and Napalm: Export USA*.

Twenty years after it first appeared, the annotated edition of *The Atrocity Exhibition* came into being, largely through the intelligent attention of persistently supportive Ballard admirers, in which the author was encouraged to elucidate some of the thinking that had gone into it. The annotated edition has itself gone through various iterations since, but it is now the standard text and although obscurities remain, one sees the process of much of Ballard's thinking.

Take his interest in violence, for instance. He was apparently obsessed with car crashes, particularly with deaths in car crashes, and pointedly in car crashes where someone famous or celebrated was killed. Was this a kind of voyeurism? But he indicated the general way in which violence, sometimes extreme violence, was routinely celebrated not only in films and on television, but throughout the wider media. Car crashes were frequently enacted on the screen, often with horrific detail, but in the real world these crashes were something to which nearly all of us were vulnerable, a fact most people secretly understood and dreaded. It was a genuine kind of serious violence that threatened us all.

He also referred to the death of a Vietcong suspect, shot in the head by a police chief in front of a live camera – a truly sickening and shocking image from that terrible war. Ballard pointed out: 'It was soon used by the London *Sunday Times* as a repeated logo keying its readers to Vietnam features in the paper. If I remember, the tilt of the dying man's head was slightly exaggerated, like a stylized Coke bottle or tail-fin.' Within twenty-four hours the image had been made into popular media.[185]

One of the constituent pieces, 'The Generations of America', was originally presented without explanation as a list of one named person after another shooting someone else, who themselves had shot someone else, and so on. It ran on in like fashion for something like six pages. In the annotated edition Ballard explained that every name he used was a real one, taken from the editorial mastheads of three leading US magazines: *Look*, *Life* and *Time*. These were 'the mass-magazines that helped to create the media landscape at the heart of *The Atrocity Exhibition*.'[186]

One way of comprehending the material in *The Atrocity Exhibition* is to treat the text of each constituent as a sort of lexicon of Ballardian themes and phrases.

For example, here is a short list of references extracted more or less at random from two or three of the condensed novels. They are listed here in each case because they appear more than once:

white safari suit
white gown

shabby flying jacket
wound area
white Pontiac
auto disasters
camera or hands exploring the body of a naked woman
pine needles
the excitement of pain and mutilation
a speculative geometry
multi-storey car park
white medical coat
motorcade
gold-tipped cigarette
white shirt
drained swimming pool
delta
pudenda
mouth-parts
(Many more could be added to this list, but it is merely for illustration.)

Note the number of times 'white' is used: white safari suit, gown, car, medical coat and shirt. Ballard's fiction frequently dresses the characters in white, gives them extremely white skin or hair, or white eyes. (White is the colour of everything light and pure. In some regions it has stood for purity, innocence and cleanliness, and in others death, mourning and the passage to new life; in many, it represents the divine or ethereal.)

Body parts: wound area, body of a naked woman, pudenda, mouth-parts.

Abstract formations or designs, or simply patterns: pain and mutilation, a speculative geometry, multi-storey car park, motorcade, pine needles, gold-tipped cigarette, drained swimming pool, delta.

An overwhelming majority of Ballard's leading characters are doctors, and named as such.

All writers refer to recurring images, summon them in different guises or with a slight change of vocabulary, depend on them for metaphorical life or allegory. Ballard is no different, but there is a distinct oddness to his choice of images and he uses them in a unique way.

By no means is he the only novelist who will from time to time refer to the presence of a swimming pool drained of its water, to take a classic image. But when a reader comes across one in Ballard's fiction it is immediately imbued with a range of possible meanings: the passage of time, the loss of value, the decay of society, the scene of vandalism, a change in technology, neglect, barbaric damage, the moving on of an old order – even, in one astonishing Ballard story, a means of communication with entropy and the heat death of the universe.

The Atrocity Exhibition lies at the heart of Ballard's fiction: enigmatic, sometimes annoying, oblique, mystifying, explanatory, sexually explicit, challenging – but in the end superbly original. It is an inscrutable, unique key to everything he wrote, not only before but after. Everything refers back to it, or from it.

Many years after *The Atrocity Exhibition* was written and published, a film was made of it: a valorous attempt to recreate in visual imagery the tangle of Ballardian obsessions, phrases and iconic moments. The director was Jonathan Weiss, and it was written by Michael Kirby in collaboration with Weiss. J. G. Ballard was sent a videotape while the project was still a work in progress – apparently, Mr Weiss was hoping for words of encouragement that might not only enable him to complete the film but gain attention for it.

Ballard was supportive. He said:

Dear Jonathan: I've just watched your film of *The Atrocity Exhibition* again, and I'm even more impressed than I was when I first saw it. It's a remarkable piece of work, clearly a great labour of love, and a unique kind of cinema in its allusiveness, poetic imagination and a vast repertory of powerful effects that are freely available to film today but rejected in favour of the star-driven vehicles that monopolize the highways of the film-going mind. I'm delighted that it follows so strongly in the sequence of films adapted from books of mine – Steven Spielberg's *Empire of the Sun* and David Cronenberg's *Crash*. Watching it closely, I was so impressed by the way in which every scene made some kind of original and imaginative point, often lasting only a few seconds and probably lost to the spectator at first screening, but adding to the huge tapestry you've woven. How imaginatively, with what I assume were limited resources, did you flesh out the images cited in the book – Duchamp, the periodic table, X-rays, geometric models and so on. It's an extraordinary achievement, and the film deserves to be shown as widely as possible. Congratulations! Sincerely, J. G. Ballard.[187]

* * *

Such was Ballard's ambition for science fiction. But the fertile, febrile marriage of the speculative-moderns was not to last. In August 1973, Ann Quin ended her own life, walking into the sea off Brighton beach not far from the seaside boarding house run by her mother. In the years following the success of her astonishing debut novel *Berg*, Quin had suffered a series of disappointments: financial problems, romantic betrayals and steadily decreasing sales. Her unwilling return to a place she had fought hard to escape came as one reversal too many. She was thirty-seven years old.

Just three months later B. S. Johnson followed, slitting his wrists at his home in Islington. His failure to achieve the kind of success he had been hoping for – to break through to a wider public awareness – had left him depressed and embittered. Quin's death seemed to confirm Johnson's own sense of futility.

The suicides of Quin and Johnson undoubtedly signalled the end of something. Alan Burns left for Australia to take up a teaching post. Christine Brooke-Rose, who was already teaching at the University of Paris, made France her permanent home. The Calder circle, once the dynamic focus of experimental writing in Britain, was effectively broken.

And over at *New Worlds*, a similar endgame had been playing out. The serial publication of Norman Spinrad's controversial and sexually explicit novel *Bug Jack Barron* led to the magazine being criticized for obscenity in the House of Commons and as a result losing the support of W. H. Smith and John Menzies, its two most important distributors. Although Smith's eventually rowed back on their decision, so much financial damage had already been done that *New Worlds* never fully recovered its equilibrium.

Michael Moorcock, exhausted by the endless pressures of keeping the magazine afloat, was forced to scale back production to a quarterly schedule before eventually handing over the editorship to lesser hands. Sporadic attempts were made to revive the magazine but the old fire was gone.

By the time *New Worlds* finally folded in 1976, Ballard had long since moved on. His vision for SF – that it would lead to a radical rethinking of what literature might achieve within a post-nuclear reality – had not come to pass, and his friendship with Michael Moorcock was starting to drift. He was also beginning to find himself constrained by the experimentalist mode. There was certainly no love lost between Ballard and B. S. Johnson, who in later recollection Ballard describes as 'a thoroughly unpleasant figure who treated his sweet wife abominably' and 'who was forever telephoning and buttonholing me at literary parties, trying to enlist me in his campaign to persuade publishers to pay a higher royalty to their authors'.[188]

In a long interview with Alan Burns in the early seventies, Ballard expresses some of the frustration he felt at the largely negative reception of *The Atrocity Exhibition* amongst readers and reviewers alike. Though he puts this down to the fact that 'people are so lazy or so rooted in established conventions in their reading that they won't make the effort',[189] there are indications also that he was feeling increasingly out of sympathy with the counterculture with which so much experimental writing and Burroughs especially was associated.

Intimations of the distance between Burroughs and Ballard had been in evidence as early as 1966, when in his essay 'Terminal Documents'[190] Ballard expresses what would seem to be an increasing impatience with Burroughs's worldview. 'In spite of its brilliant images, which revolve like chimeras in a neural jungle, Burroughs' landscape becomes an increasingly regressive one, set at an infantile level where the differentiation of physiological and cerebral functions has yet to occur. To the drug addict all events in the universe may seem coeval and conterminous, but this sense of unity, the equivalence of all objects and activities, is a result not of an enlarged but of a blunted consciousness.'

What Burroughs lacks is objectivity, the power of discernment, and for Ballard, trained in medicine and schooled in time of war, Burroughs's self-indulgent paranoia becomes increasingly tiresome. His drug use, his immersion in gay culture to the exclusion of other realities and in particular his Americanness were all aspects of Burroughs that Ballard found alienating, a clash of styles and sensibilities that could only ever grow more dissonant. Ballard's own awareness of those differing aspects of their character and working assumptions grew to such a point that although he never denied the importance of Burroughs as an inspiration, full-throttle endorsement was no longer possible.

In the spring of 1968, Ballard was asked by *Esquire* magazine to write a profile of Burroughs, a commission he found in the end he could not fulfil.

> I met him at his service flat in Duke Street, St James. Burroughs, though courteous, was very suspicious. The baleful power of media empires already obsessed him. While his young boyfriend, 'love' and 'hate' tattooed on his knuckles, carved a roast chicken, Burroughs described the most effective way to stab a man to death. All the while he kept an eye on the doors and windows. 'The CIA are watching me,' he confided. 'They park their laundry vans in the street outside.' I don't think he was having me on. His imagination was filled with bizarre lore culled from 'Believe It or Not' features, police pulps and – in the case, I assume, of the laundry vans – Hollywood spy movies of the Cold War years. When Burroughs talked about *Time* magazine's conspiracy to take over the world he meant it literally. I turned down the *Esquire* assignment, realizing that nothing I wrote could remotely do justice to Burroughs's magnificently paranoid imagination.[191]

For Ballard, the extreme imagery of *The Atrocity Exhibition* had always been just that – a series of images put on display, an artistic expression of the various assaults upon the consciousness provided by his experience of living in the twentieth century. As in the surrealist art that reached its fullest flowering in the years immediately following the first world war, the outlandish hellscapes of Ballard's condensed novels are filtered through the intellect – through knowing reference to other artworks – as much as the naked subconscious. Whereas for Burroughs, there was no gap between what he thought and believed and what he put on the page. The conspiracy theories, the 'deep state' paranoia, the drug-induced confusion between the actual and the imagined – these elements of Burroughs were, for him, part of the point and meaning of the authorial exercise.

The outdoor rock festival Phun City that took place at Patching, near Worthing in the July of 1970 seems to sum up those aspects of the burned-out New Wave Ballard was determined to get away from. Worthing now is younger and more fashionable than it was then. In 1970, the threat of invasion from thousands of hippies was almost enough to have the 'phun' and games shut down before they got underway. Originally intended as a multimedia event, featuring poets, writers and performance artists alongside the rock musicians, Phun City rapidly disintegrated into a disorganized melange of naked sunbathing and loud music.

Chris accepted his invitation to the festival solely in the hope of hearing Ballard read. There is a photograph of him there, standing alone in a field looking terminally bored. He described the event to me as 'utterly excruciating'. The Hells Angels who had been tasked with security kept calling Ballard 'Dad' – not entirely unreasonable, given that he travelled to Worthing with his children. Chris's account of the event was published in an SF fanzine three months later:

> We got past a cordon of club-brandishing Hells Angels and penetrated to the forbidden zone behind the platform. Here there was a bar, several groupies, and a cluster of windswept poets ... After an hour we were getting restless. The only three faces we recognized were our own: Mike Harrison, Graham Charnock and myself. Mike coalesced our fears into one sentence. 'What happens,' he said, 'if the heavies don't arrive?' The heavies in this instance being William Burroughs, J. G. Ballard and Alexander Trocchi who, it had been reliably rumoured, were going to do 'something with lights and film.' It was agreed, therefore, that Mike would impersonate William Burroughs, Graham would pretend to be Alex Trocchi ... and I would be Ballard. Five minutes later Ballard himself walked into the bar, looking as unfreaky and unspaced as us. 'That's me out of a job,' I muttered. Time passed. A few more familiar faces turned up: John Brunner,

Max Jakubowski, Bill Butler, Mike Dempsey, Anthony Haden-Guest. The atmosphere was still tense, a little nervy. No one knew what was going to happen, what we were supposed to do. I was standing next to Ballard (boning up on such things as facial mannerisms for future emergencies) when someone rushed in. 'Burroughs has arrived!' Beside me, Ballard heaved an audible sigh of relief. 'Now we can all relax,' he said.[192]

Burroughs, who had apparently planned to capture the atmosphere of Phun City through the tape-recording of 'found sounds' for later use in composite works, overdosed on drugs and spent most of his time in the medical tent.

The posturing excesses of the counterculture that became part of the landscape adjacent to *New Worlds* were as counterproductive for Ballard as they were for Chris. Ballard later insisted that as 'an old-fashioned storyteller at heart', writing that 'fails to engage the reader's emotions' and in which 'technique becomes the real subject of the novel' is effectively 'a dead end'.[193] Part of his frustration with B. S. Johnson stemmed from what he saw as Johnson's 'modest concern for his readers'.[194]

While Ballard did not abandon the language and imagery that characterize *The Atrocity Exhibition*, his handling of them altered. As the old-fashioned storyteller he professed to be, Ballard would soon prove that there is nothing old-fashioned about story. His next book would be still more radical, and equally misunderstood, both within science fiction and by the literary mainstream.

EIGHTEEN

'THE HOUSE OF WOMEN'

The months following the death of Mary were lonely ones for Ballard, months in which he found himself resenting the sight of other couples, ostensibly happy, going normally about their business.[195] The pressure was relieved by alcohol, and eventually by resuming his sex life. 'I remember embracing my first lover – the estranged wife of a friend – like a survivor at sea clinging to a rescuer.'[196]

According to Fay Ballard, her father's first serious girlfriend after Mary was Helen Baz. 'She worked at London Zoo,' Fay remembers. 'She was slender, with red hair, which she did in a beehive hairstyle. She had a daughter, Yasmin, a couple of years older than me. Helen was warm, and fun to be with. We used to play all kinds of practical jokes on her, but she never minded. She would come and stay for the weekend in Shepperton, or sometimes we would go to her flat in London. I remember once she threw a big Hallowe'en party, with lots of dry ice.'

During the summer of 1966, Ballard and Helen would holiday in Valencia with Jim junior – Ballard's first return to Spain since Mary's death – while Fay and Bea stayed behind in Wales with Granny Matthews, a summer made memorable by the England World Cup victory at Wembley in July. Both sisters remember having to come to terms with the idea of their father making new relationships. 'When we were younger it was harder, as we were all quite possessive of him,' Bea says. 'At the same time, we wanted him to be happy, and the idea of sharing him became easier as we grew older and developed our own love lives.'

But Ballard seemed actively to reject the idea of settling down into a steady relationship of the kind he had enjoyed with Mary. Mike

Moorcock remembers Ballard 'trawling' the *New Worlds* parties and the Brunners' Friday soirées for suitable girlfriends – it was at the Brunners' that he had met Helen Baz. Elizabeth Blethen, who handled publicity for *New Worlds*, was an early companion, as was the American science fiction writer and editor Judith Merril, who came to London in the summer of 1966 lured by the excitement around the writers of the British New Wave, many of whom she would go on to publish in her 1968 anthology *England Swings SF*.

Fay Ballard remembers Judy as 'a charismatic, warm, energetic and determined spirit' who wore 'tight black slacks that were designed with a zip at the back'. Ballard, who later described Merril as 'strong-willed and combative, sensitive and astute ... capable of surprising shifts into a positively feline femininity that could be quite disorienting'[197] seems to have been consistent in liking the company of powerful, intelligent women who enjoyed robust debate in the way that he himself did. Certainly this was true of Claire Walsh, who Ballard met at a party at Michael Moorcock's in the spring of 1967.

Born in 1941 in Guildford, Claire Churchill grew up in London, where she attended the Burlington Danes Grammar School in Hammersmith (the same school attended, coincidentally, by the playwright Dennis Potter). While she was in the sixth form, Claire became pregnant with her daughter Jenny and left school without taking her 'A' Levels.

Her relationship with her parents had not been easy – her father Herbert was violent towards both her and her mother Eileen[198] – and Claire was thrown back on her own resources, living with her young daughter in a succession of temporary bedsits and shared houses. In 1959, she married Michael Walsh, who she had met through CND. The marriage was a failure – according to Mike Moorcock, Walsh was abusive – and they divorced in 1962. Claire escaped with Jenny to a two-bedroomed flat above a newsagents at 166 Goldhawk Road, Shepherd's Bush, the place that would become her home for the rest of her life.

Keenly interested in literature and music, she found work as a receptionist for Penguin Books, soon moving into secretarial work and then publicity, working for a series of publishers including Gollancz and Allen Lane. She was radical in her politics, a union woman, and her attempts to get better pay for women in the industry did not always go down well with her (male) bosses. Eventually she was made redundant. She always claimed it had been her union activities that lost her her job. She later turned to freelance work, editing the nautical journal *Seaways*, for which she was granted honorary membership of the Nautical Institute, and forming friendships with several sea captains. Her intellectual curiosity and love of learning were defining characteristics of a woman who – like so many of her time – seemed insufficiently rewarded for her abilities.

When she and Ballard met, Claire was working as publicity manager for Studio Vista. She was twenty-five, and beginning to find her own identity within the circles frequented by Michael Moorcock and other writers associated with *New Worlds* and *Ambit*. Moorcock, who had been briefly involved with Claire himself, invited her to the party specifically to introduce her to Ballard. He had told Claire in advance he thought they would be well suited.

'I knew it was a blind date,' Walsh recalled, 'but Jimmy didn't.'[199] As Moorcock had predicted, the attraction was mutual, and instantaneous. 'We were so excited by each other; for a long time in Shepperton, he didn't like it if I left the room even.' Claire's younger brother John, who studied art and design at Hammersmith College, remembers the first time he met Ballard, when Claire brought him home to the flat where they had lived as children:

> We were brought up in a dark, damp basement flat in Carlisle Place opposite a convent for Westminster Cathedral. Our mother took us to the convent primary school because it was 'just across the road'. Big mistake! We were both picked on for being Protestants, and having the surname Churchill made matters worse as the Irish nuns and schoolchildren had no love of the man, despite the war. It was in this dark basement flat that I first met Jim. Claire had brought him in to meet my mother. As chance would have it I was playing a record by Edgard Varèse called *Arcana*. Great blocks of dissonance and rhythm ... American new world music. When he came into the room I turned the music down. But J. G. was fascinated, and wanted to hear it again at full volume. This is not the usual line about Jim's dislike of music![200]

Bea Ballard, who maintained close connections with Claire after her father died, has clear memories of her from the time when she and Ballard began their relationship. 'She was very beautiful, very smart. She was a strong personality, which is probably what my father needed. He liked women with strong minds, who were intellectual, and Claire was all those things. She was well read, very knowledgeable. She was a natural researcher, she loved information, and my father was the same.'

Bea was also close to Claire's daughter Jenny, at least for a time. 'We got on well, even though as people we were quite different. I was an extrovert, sociable child, she was much quieter. She read serious books, even from a young age. She was a thoughtful, sensitive person. I liked her a lot.'

Claire quickly became central to Ballard's life and writing. As soon as she finished work on a Friday, she and Jenny would take the train to Richmond, where Ballard would pick them up and drive them over to Shepperton. They would stay for the weekend, Jenny sleeping on a camp bed in Bea and Fay's room. Holidays would see all four children packed into the back of the car for the journey south to Spain, Greece or Provence. These holidays – games on the beach and in the water, walks into town in the evening as the light faded and the heat dispersed – were a fixed point of Ballard's life, his one luxury and the only time he truly enjoyed travelling beyond Shepperton.

'We would always spend two or three days driving down,' Bea said, 'and stay in interesting places along the way. I remember Daddy taking us to see the cathedral in Chartres, pointing out the amazing stained-glass windows.'

Ballard's feelings for Claire were clearly significant, with a lasting mutual attraction that had been absent from his life since Mary died. But the emotional temperature of their relationship was more fraught. Ballard quickly became possessive of Claire, resenting anything he perceived as untoward attention from other male admirers. This situation was not helped by his drinking.

Before Mary's death, Ballard's consumption of alcohol was largely restricted to a couple of glasses of wine with the evening meal. 'We did have the odd heavy session of course, but nothing like on the scale of

Brian Aldiss or Harry Harrison for instance,' Michael Moorcock said. Things were to change dramatically after Mary died. Ballard began drinking as soon as he had taken the children to school and continued through the day until they returned home in the late afternoon. On those occasions when he went out in the evening, more alcohol would inevitably follow.

Both Fay and Beatrice were conscious of Ballard's drinking, though they do not remember feeling concerned by what they saw. They never saw him drunk, and accepted the ubiquitous tumbler of whisky on their father's desk as part of his daily routine. As he grew older, Ballard made conscious efforts to cut back, congratulating himself when he was able to delay the first drink of the day until after six o'clock and gradually tapering off his consumption as he grew older. In the final years of his life, Fay remembers, he went off alcohol completely and much preferred tea.

For a period of about ten years though, Ballard was alcohol dependent. The effect this had on his personal life varies according to who is speaking, though no one who drank as Ballard did could expect not to pay a price for it in some form. The worst effects came out in the evening, when in the company of friends and colleagues from *New Worlds* who would also be downing copious quantities of alcohol.

'He got into physical fights occasionally,' insists Michael Moorcock, 'almost with a kind of glee – deliberately baiting others. But only when pretty drunk.' Chris was always reluctant to place much value on such stories. In all the times he encountered Ballard socially, he never saw in his behaviour anything other than courtesy and restraint, especially when compared with others in the Moorcock circle, though he did occasionally hear rumours of his drunkenness from other people.

If anyone suffered for Ballard's drinking, it was Claire. The first period of their time together, though powerfully creative, was marred by jealousy, emotional turbulence and violent arguments.

'During those weekends when Claire stayed over, they would both be drinking quite a lot and sometimes they would argue,' Fay Ballard told us, their robust political disagreements quickly spiralling into more personal territory. 'I remember Daddy shouting "Kustow – Michael Kustow!", because Michael [the then director of the ICA] had made a move on Claire – it was not just Daddy who found her attractive. I used to find it quite frightening. I would call out "Please don't fight!" and Daddy would call back "We're not fighting, we're having an argument." The atmosphere in the house could be quite hard work when you were a child.'

There have been suggestions that these frequent shouting matches would occasionally boil over into physical fights,[201] fuelled on Claire's side by her anger and distress over Ballard's frequent infidelities. The final straw for Claire was Ballard's involvement with Emma Tennant, the novelist and travel writer who had begun her writing career as an editor at *Vogue*.

According to those who knew her, Emma was funny, sexy, spontaneous, a natural party animal. 'I remember that period when he and Emma Tennant were an item,' says the artist and *New Worlds* writer Pamela Zoline, who was herself involved with Ballard in the late sixties. 'She was hilarious. And when they were together that plummy aspect of Jimmy became more emphasized. Emma had this big flat, full of kids and artists. She was such a madcap, such an outrageous person.'

She was also deeply interested in science fiction, gothic fiction and avant-garde literature. Drawn to the writers and artists who made up the Moorcock circle, the failing fortunes of *New Worlds* inspired Tennant to set up a magazine of her own, *Bananas*, which ran for twenty-six issues from January 1975 until April 1981. The magazine, formatted to resemble a tabloid newspaper, was named after Woody Allen's 1971 movie and founded with the express purpose of providing an antidote to the 'literature of manners' that still dominated British book publishing. (It also managed to fulfil that brief with a considerable advance on *New Worlds* in terms of gender parity among its contributors.)

Through the course of its run, *Bananas* featured contributions from Angela Carter ('The Company of Wolves'), Heathcote Williams, Peter Redgrove, Sara Maitland (her first published story) and Ted Hughes, with whom Tennant later had an affair. A designated 'Russian Issue' (No 11, Summer 1978) featured the work of Osip Mandelstam, Joseph Brodsky and Andrei Platonov as well as poems by Marina Tsvetayeva in their brilliant new translations by Elaine Feinstein. *New Worlds* stalwarts Tom

Disch and John Sladek often featured, along with Ballard himself, whose stories for Tennant included 'The Air Disaster', 'Low-Flying Aircraft', 'Notes Towards a Mental Breakdown' and 'The Smile'.

'At that point,' Ballard recalled, 'I had not written any short stories at all for something like four years, largely because there was nowhere to publish. If Emma had not started *Bananas* it's probably not an exaggeration to say that none of those ten stories would have been written.'[202]

Ballard and Tennant began their affair sometime in 1974. Tennant's partial account of her involvement with Ballard appears in the opening chapters of her memoir *Burnt Diaries*, in which she describes how 'all night I dreamt of brown, muddy water, as if the Yangtze, the river of his captivity in the Shanghai concentration camp, surrounds him and anyone in his vicinity when sleep comes. His tales of the camp haunt the atmosphere long after he has gone ... I begin to realize how far he is from being a conventional Englishman, despite the brisk and slightly alarming air – of family doctor or solicitor – which he presents to the outside world.'[203] Speaking to the *Sunday Times* after Ballard's death, Tennant described Ballard as 'always extremely affectionate and old-fashioned in his ways. Never any hint of any violence.'[204]

In his 1982 interview with the editor, publisher and committed Ballardian V. Vale, Ballard describes how he and Tennant had to fit in their assignations around the needs of their young families:

> She said, 'Jim, I've never seen you before dark!' And I said, 'Christ, I am like a vampire!' Because she had children, I had children, and we met only in the evenings. Then she had to get the kids off to school and I had to get back to make sure my kids were disentangling themselves from early morning television or whatever they'd be doing ... This was a curious convention: intimacy of a very specialized kind, with absurd reversals where sex would take place followed by an extended wooing, rather than the other way around, with the wooing coming first.[205]

Tennant invited Claire to tea, supposedly so she could get to know her better. Claire was happy to accept her hospitality, until Tennant's persistent questions about Ballard made her suspect that there was something more to it. The fact that Tennant was far from the only 'other woman' in Ballard's life at that time is made clear by Tennant herself, who describes an encounter with a poet she identifies only by her initials – 'small, wiry-haired, hugely enlarged eyes glittering behind horn-rimmed glasses' – who calls at the *Bananas* office at 2 Blenheim Crescent bearing a jiffy bag containing one of Ballard's striped ties.[206]

Ballard's cavalier attitude towards their relationship had become impossible for Claire to live with, or ignore. At some point during the summer of 1974 she decided she would not be returning to Shepperton. When the Ballards left on their annual holiday that July, for the first time in some years, Claire and Jenny did not go with them.

'Women adored him,' Bea Ballard says of her father. 'Women liked him because he was likeable.'

Few of the women who knew and liked Jim Ballard in the early days are still living. Mary is dead, and so is Claire. So are Emma Tennant, Hilary Bailey and Judith Merril. Pamela Zoline, however, is still very much alive. Like Ballard, she was in science fiction but never entirely of it, an independent-minded, radical artist who was at the same time intimately acquainted with the Moorcock circle.

Her story 'The Heat Death of the Universe', first published in *New Worlds 173* in July 1967, is a landmark of the New Wave and an important piece of feminist SF. It describes in forensic detail a day in the life of Sarah Boyle, an intelligent, educated woman whose life has become defined by her role as wife and mother. Her home is its own universe, a 'closed system', for which 'the time must finally come when [it] "unwinds" itself, no energy being available for use.' Smashing together gritty, quotidian reality with the laws of thermodynamics, Zoline's story is as powerfully emotive as it is innovative, a timeless piece of work that remains as important now as when it was written.

I talk with Pam via Zoom early in the April of 2024. We begin by comparing the colours and atmosphere of our respective surroundings: the strident, glacial blue of the Colorado sky, the misty, grey-green tones of the Firth of Clyde. As with so many of these Zoom conversations, the common currency of our post-COVID era, the physical distance between us is both a source of wonder and barely there.

Pam is now in her eighties, as interested in ideas, as committed to her art and the life of the mind as she was during the time we would mainly be talking about. She is still writing, her most recent pieces of work are contributions to the sixtieth anniversary edition of *New Worlds*, which is being edited as we speak. Pam tells me that she has always been someone who prefers to focus on the future rather than the past, how it is only recently that she has begun digging down into her memories of London in the sixties and seventies and of Jimmy Ballard in particular. 'It has been valuable,' she says, 'but rather strange.'

I have a photograph of Pam from that period, an unaffectedly beautiful young woman petting a Newfoundland dog. She is wearing a baggy smock dress, typical for the period, a pattern of yellow flowers against a leaf-green background; her wavy brown hair frames strong features and a concentrated expression. She reminds me of Sandy Denny. The photograph was taken after her marriage to the artist John Lifton, who she met in London and with whom she helped to set up the New Arts Lab in Camden. Together they renovated a derelict rectory near Sherborne, which became their family home until the end of the eighties.

'We lived back and forth between the two places, between London and Dorset. John was teaching at the Royal College of Art. We would stay in London during the week, then we would go back to Sherborne at the weekend to work on the rectory.'

Their base in London was a tottering maisonette above a shop just off Camden High Street, not far from where Margaret and Tony Richardson now live and the same flat that would eventually become the permanent home of the science fiction critic and writer John Clute and his wife Judith, a fellow artist. The house was occupied initially by Zoline and two other writers, Thomas M. Disch and John Sladek, and quickly became a social hub for other North American SF writers who found themselves drawn to Swinging London and the British New Wave. It was in this same house, an intimate, convivial space bursting with books, that I met Zoline briefly in 2012, when I was there with Chris visiting the Clutes and Pam happened to be passing through.

Zoline came to London initially to study at the Slade School of Art, still dominated by the conservative values of William Coldstream and with the practice of drawing at the heart of its ethos. Zoline describes Coldstream as an arch-traditionalist, 'someone out of central casting'. But the mood was changing. Among the teachers at the Slade who energized the atmosphere and inspired Pam personally were R. B. Kitaj, Eduardo Paolozzi and Andrew Forge. Across the quadrangle in the philosophy department she attended lectures and seminars by Richard Wollheim, Gerald Cohen and Ted Honderich.

Pam had come to London fresh from Barnard College, part of Columbia University in New York City. 'I'd not had a particularly good time there,' she tells me, 'but when I got to London, and the Slade, it felt just right, even though I was a rogue student, and did not get a degree. I had been a young artist living in New York, where things were extremely intense, and in a sense so savage that London, by comparison, was comprehensible, and that was intoxicating for me. It relieved me finally of the last encumberments of being a kid from the suburbs, and gave me a mechanism for understanding the larger enterprise.'

It was this coexistence of disciplines, the bleeding of art into philosophy into writing, that encouraged Zoline to expand her focus.

> My practice as a writer only really began when I moved to London, and it began because I was part of this gang that turned out to be the New Wave. John Clute and I had been best and dearest friends since high school. Clute, Tom Disch and I had been living together while I was at Barnard, so when I got to London I was already part of that family. Then Clute and Tom became involved with Michael Moorcock. The most important thing for me about that time, about the work we were doing, is that it was in some ways a communal activity. *New Worlds* was such a nexus, such a nest, such a community – I think it was one of the best times, one of the most interesting times for the people who happened to be a part of it, a kind of skew-whiff Bloomsbury.

Adopted into the New Wave, it was not long before Pam encountered Ballard, whose work she was already aware of, though had not yet read. Their first meeting took place in the summer of 1967, in a Camden pub regularly patronized by the artists, film makers and writers who would later perform and exhibit their work at the Institute for Research into

Art and Technology – popularly known as the New Arts Lab – on nearby Robert Street. This centre of the artistic avant-garde was established in 1969 and housed in a former pharmaceuticals factory, a building Zoline describes as being so difficult to heat it was 'like giving artificial respiration to an elephant'. Spending time in the pub was almost a necessity.

Pam clearly remembers the moment when she first encountered Ballard.

> I was sitting at the bar, drinking Madeira and there was Jimmy, suddenly at my side. He introduced himself, told me he had read my story 'The Heat Death of the Universe' and that he liked it very much. He asked me – I remember quite clearly that he asked me several times during that conversation – what of his I'd read. I had to confess that I hadn't read him yet, which was awful because I knew what a big deal he was. He actually couldn't believe it – he thought I had to have been in some way influenced by him, and it was a funny, amazing moment, because I was still so American back then that I must have appeared to him like someone from out of the future, a creature from that 'next five minutes' that he wanted to write about.

If Zoline seemed exotic to Ballard, he was equally drawn to her innovative approach to making and thinking about art. If a trio of wrecked cars displayed (without explanatory notes) in a gallery setting was seen as either unnervingly provocative or deliberately obscure to many within the science fiction community, for an artist working in the post-Duchamp era, they made much more sense.

In her essay for the sixtieth anniversary edition of *New Worlds*, 'Crashing Cars',[207] Zoline gives an account of her collaboration with Ballard on another art installation, a 'portrait box' inspired by funerary artefacts in the British Museum and in particular the mummified body of the philosopher Jeremy Bentham, whose mortal remains were put on display in a glass-fronted wooden vitrine at UCL. Zoline's wooden, kiosk-like portrait boxes offer a radical alternative to the conventional painted likeness, gathering together documents, photographs and material possessions particular to the subject in a multi-sensory 'portrait' that the viewer can literally step inside.

A series of photographs showing the inside of J. G. Ballard's portrait box reveal a multitude of such artefacts: his own novels in multiple translations, a London telephone directory ('Postal Area S-Z'), its cover scribbled with personal memoranda, the *Advertiser's Announcement* 'Homage to Claire Churchill', an army of empty drinks bottles, a hamster cage complete with hamster (loaned for the opening of the exhibition by the Ballard children), a plethora of photographs, including one of Ballard at his desk, piled with papers, brightened by the light from the French windows opening on to the garden of his house in Shepperton.

On a shelf above the books, next to what looks like a pine cone is a blue rubber flipper, brought back from a summer holiday, its partner permanently missing in action.

'I knew it belonged to his son,' Pam says. 'And I always had to wonder: was it from *that* holiday, the one where Mary died?'

I am able to tell Pam that I know about the flipper because I have a picture of it, a print taken from one of the finely detailed drawings in Fay Ballard's 'House Clearance' series. These were shown at an exhibition staged in 2014, at a gallery called Eleven Spitalfields, in Whitechapel. I remember the day Chris and I travelled up from Hastings to see it. We had lunch with our friend, the writer Matt Hill at a pub on Charing Cross Road, the first time we'd met him in person, which is strange to think about now. Afterwards we took the tube across to Liverpool Street to meet with Fay. The three of us sat together in one of the rooms of the gallery and Fay asked Chris about the times he had met and corresponded with her father.

I feel sad looking back on that day, which carried so many hidden intimations of the present moment. We wanted to buy one of the prints and Chris chose the flipper. He liked the shape of it, and the fact that the Ballard children had used the real one as a doorstop. Fay's drawing is composed so that the flipper is standing upright, the fin pointing down. At first glance, it appears to represent a cowled woman, gliding towards you, hands folded in front of her. As a piece of graphic artistry, it is exquisite. We called it 'The Nun'. She used to hang in Chris's office; now she hangs in mine. I catch sight of her every time I look up from my desk.

When Zoline first started seeing Ballard, he did not tell her he was already in a relationship. 'He told me what had happened to Mary and said it was something he preferred not to talk about, so we didn't. He never particularly wanted me to meet his children. He kept a space between me and them. There was a layer around that whole part of their lives that still seemed extremely deep and private and sensitive.'

Pam only learned of Claire's existence later on, when eventually Ballard told her she had found out about their relationship and that they would have to stop seeing each other. Zoline insists she took the breakup lightly. 'Those were the times we lived in,' she says. She had always assumed he was probably involved with other people.

> Jimmy was a one-off, an impressive and fascinating person. His whole presentation of self was striking and unusual. Partly it was the cadences he used when he spoke – he had an accent which was still straight from if not the top drawer then the second drawer of colonial life. He had the habit of command, but in a really self-deprecating manner. So often there was a layer of laughter and self-critique. I remember the way in which he would hold a conversation, put forward a kind of thesis, add to it, add to it, add to it, then come to a conclusion, and all the stress and energy contained in that argument would be released in that gleam of illumination that he was sharing with you. He was a compelling conversationalist, fascinated by ideas. There was never much small talk. His work was his play.

When I ask her if she ever experienced any aggression from Ballard, she is categorical in her denial.

> I never saw Jimmy aggressive at any time. He liked a drink – most of us did at that point – but I never saw him drunk. He seemed to be someone very much in charge of himself. Operating under a certain amount of pressure, but not somebody at the mercy of his emotions. He was older than the rest of us and he'd been through the wringer. He seemed to have more of a grip on the way the world worked. I didn't perceive him as troubled or unsettled, especially when

compared with some of the other people I was hanging out with. Tom Disch was magnificent, but also, always, hugely troubled – that was part of who he was. Jimmy seemed to think the world was pretty intense and fucked up, but that those of us who knew that were better off than those who didn't.

The word she uses to describe him, more than once, is gallant.

I am also keen to talk to Pam about her experience of the New Wave as a female artist. There was no shortage of women on the fringes of the Moorcock circle, though they have tended to be viewed as a supporting cast. Girlfriends and wives, lovers and muses, as in Antonioni's 1966 film set in Swinging London, *Blow-Up*, it was the men who produced art, the women who were its subject, or its facilitators. The number of women who feature in the pages of *New Worlds* is shamefully low.

In a letter sent to Fay not long after Ballard's death, Hilary Bailey describes a typical Sunday during the closest period of Ballard and Moorcock's friendship, when Mary Ballard was still alive and she and Jimmy would come over for lunch at Ladbroke Grove. 'The two men separated from the women and children,' she writes, 'so the menfolk were upstairs, talking about writing and planning strategies, while the women and children were downstairs – this could be seen as segregation but quite what discussions could take place with the addition of two women and five children is hard to imagine. And we were happy where we were.'[208]

The idea that the men might take their turn in looking after the children clearly never occurred to them. Hilary remembers Mary as 'content, unassuming, loving, the light of the family', and the Ballards' marriage as 'a marriage of its time, and theirs'. Though she theorizes that with the children reaching school age, Mary might have 'had the opportunity to expand her horizons', what comes across most forcefully is the rigidity of the intellectual pecking order, even within the British New Wave, which was supposed to be progressive.

'Definitely in that period, women all across the board were fighting with one hand tied behind their back,' Zoline tells me. 'It seemed normal to us, that there were fewer women published in *New Worlds* – that was the state of things we were working to overcome. Most of the arts had the same statistics. For me, a good part of what I drew on in writing "The Heat Death of the Universe" were observations that I gathered from the couples I saw around me.'

Mike and Hilary Moorcock would have been one of those couples. 'Mike was so giant, in his whole presence. He was so funny, he was so reckless. The energy with which he lived his life was hard on his intimate circle, Hilary for instance. The intensity of that life, the intensity of what it was like for Hilary to keep that life going. Mike was like the pirate captain, for sure.'

For Hilary Bailey as for so many, it was impossible to maintain an even balance between providing the family with emotional security and trying to maintain her own life as a writer.

> Hilary was as bright as Mike, and arguably funnier. She had an amazing, ironic take on life. Emma Tennant had enough money to buffer her, but Hilary was saddled with those beautiful kids, pretty much while the boys' club was going on upstairs. Hilary was a writer – she would have loved to be a part of that. Mike was a philanderer, a romantic who fell in love over and over again, and that was all on Hilary. There was comedy, tragedy, romance, farce – every genre packed into what was going on in that amazing household.

There is a troubling echo of this particular aspect of the *New Worlds* ambience in an account reported by John Baxter in his 2011 biography of Ballard, *The Inner Man*, of evenings out at Ballard's favourite Chinese restaurant many years later: 'If the party was large enough to fill two tables, the women sat at one, the men at another, allowing Jim to hold court. It was made clear that the men were for talk, women for fun. Female attempts to enter the conversation were laughed off or ignored.'[209] Baxter's book has proved controversial in some quarters – Beatrice Ballard has pointed to numerous factual inaccuracies within the text[210] – and as this description is unattributed it should be treated with caution; nonetheless there is a depressing ring of truth about it when taken in the context of certain other of Ballard's unguarded comments about women.

'Men can drink alone, but I don't think women should. They go downhill very rapidly,' he said in an interview with Jeannette Kupfermann in 1988.²¹¹ Still more problematic is his dismissive attitude to the mothers of Fay and Bea's schoolfriends. Those who show concern for their daughters' personal safety while in the company of boys 'simply could not cope with the growing evidence that their daughters were younger, more womanly and more sexually attractive than they were'.²¹² Ballard blithely insists that he is far more concerned about his daughters being involved in a car accident than anything they might get up to at a party. How he might have felt about Fay and Bea's safety in the age of Andrew Tate and Wayne Couzens we can only speculate; Ballard being Ballard, he would most likely have written about incels and MRAs as contemporary monsters: ghastly, but above all *interesting*.

It is perhaps inevitable that Ballard's own life experience as a sexually active male with a good deal of cultural capital tends to dominate his attitudes and preconceptions, especially given that he was born in 1930. None of this is to deny that Ballard was genuinely interested in women, and enjoyed their company. He needed them in his life and he often valued their input and opinions. As for the women in his novels and stories, while it is true that Ballard's fiction serves up its fair share of neurasthenic goddesses and lumpy harridans, his novels do also feature independent, capable women who are every bit the intellectual equal of the doctor antiheroes.

The writer and long-time Ballard enthusiast Deborah Levy sums up Ballard's women best: 'The great thing about them is that they do not want the male lead to marry them and are never about to roast a chicken.'²¹³

Ballard's married life with Mary lasted only a decade, but those years were crucial, forming him both as a person and as a writer. The Ballard mythos would have his personal life divided rigidly in two: the contented father and monogamous husband of the years with Mary, the tormented, borderline alcoholic of the years following her death. Michael Moorcock still insists that Ballard never stopped loving Mary, or blaming himself, however wrongheadedly, for her death. The brutal suddenness of Mary's passing encourages such an analysis, which in fact is a kind of airbrushing, a simplification. What we can never know is how Ballard's marriage might have fared had Mary survived.

Success as a writer pushed Ballard into a higher orbit; within a year or so of Mary's death, his situation was very different from what it had been when he first married her. His increased visibility was beginning to take him away from the family home, bringing him into contact with more women of the type he liked: strong, fascinating, sexually confident and with their own ideas.

Would Ballard have remained the devoted family man we have been taught to recognize from the 'before' period, happily going home to Mary and the children in Shepperton without being tempted by the creative, outspoken women circling around him? Or would the same problems, the volatility and jealousies that beset the first period of his relationship with Claire have arisen soon enough?

That his increasing success as a writer and the public exposure that accompanied it followed so soon after Mary's death must have been shattering for Ballard. Mary had been keenly supportive of his work, not just in helping to provide an environment in which his writing could flourish, but also in understanding and believing in the kind of stories he wanted to develop. It is clear from her letters that she felt a deep personal commitment to her husband's career.

Even without the children to consider, to lose such an active partner would have been catastrophic. Michael Moorcock believes that Ballard 'never fully confronted the pain or indeed the "unfairness" of losing Mary and gaining professional success'. This, Moorcock suggests, 'put a strain on relationships'.

John Baxter argues that Mary's death 'freed' Ballard, not only to pursue a more adventurous and emancipated sexual life, but also to explore themes in his writing that Mary would have disapproved of.[214] But while Ballard acknowledged that Mary had occasionally been 'outraged'[215] by the negative depiction of marriage in his stories, this is to ignore the fact that Ballard had begun experimenting with modernist techniques several years before Mary died, and that themes of violence and trauma had been present in his work from the beginning. As Ballard's first reader and sounding board, Mary was undoubtedly in tune with how her husband's mind worked and aware of the ideas he wanted to pursue, even when his portrayal of women threw up questions.[216]

Mike Moorcock told Chris in an email that girlfriends of Ballard had seen Mary's clothes still hanging in the wardrobe in Shepperton years after her death. Though it is tempting to infer from this the image of a man still haunted by the ghosts of his past, forever frozen in time, it is equally likely that Mary's clothes remained untouched through simple inertia. Clearing away the belongings of the dead is an act of will, the saddest of tasks, and we know already how much Ballard disdained housework. In all likelihood, he found it easier to leave these things alone, and return to his desk.

19

'THE BURNING CAR'

In February 1969 the Institute of Contemporary Arts in London (ICA) published their monthly events sheet, which included on one side a section of text by J. G. Ballard. This was called 'Crash!' and it later re-appeared as one of the six short prose satires appended to the nine main 'condensed novels' in *The Atrocity Exhibition*. These pieces were written as parodies of scientific papers, satires of a dead-pan kind that aimed to show up the pornography of science.[217] The text of 'Crash!' adumbrates what can be seen as the central tenet of Ballard's later novel *Crash*, published in 1973.

In 1970 Ballard sponsored an exhibition of three cars damaged in accidents, at the New Arts Laboratory in London. It was the sort of confrontational 'happening' that was often mounted during that hectic period of the visual and performing arts at the end of the 1960s. Ballard had obtained the vehicles from car breakers' yards around London.

The result was more of a media event than a responsibly curated exhibition, and featured a topless female model and various then current celebrities. It received a critical drubbing from the press. Several of the cars were further damaged by members of the public, who overturned them and splashed them with white paint.

The following year Ballard appeared in a short BBC film directed by Harley Cokeliss[218] called *Crash!* Although the car used in the film remained undamaged, much was made of the alleged sexual similarities between the styling of the vehicle and the body of a young woman, played by Gabrielle Drake.

When Ballard completed and sent in *Crash*, he received an initially hostile reaction from staff at his publisher, Jonathan Cape. Though the company's chairman Tom Maschler was enthusiastic, a widely reported but unattributed remark was attached to a copy of the typescript by one of Cape's senior readers: 'This author is beyond psychiatric help. Do not publish.' Ballard was delighted: he instantly considered it to be confirmation of artistic success. (The reader in question was Catherine Storr, née Peters, the second wife of the psychiatrist Anthony Storr, herself a writer, and the daughter of a leading literary agent. Her advice was ignored by both publisher and author.[219])

Cape published the novel in hardcover with a cover painting by Bill Botten. It featured an immense and jutting gear stick, presumably deliberately phallic, in front of a towering three-dimensional title piece that occupied most of the cover. This rankled with Ballard, who described it as 'monstrously bad, one of the worst book jackets ever – for sheer ugliness and crudity it would be impossible to beat.'[220]

The book received a mixed critical press. Anthony Burgess wrote: 'A work of very powerful originality. Ballard is amongst our finest writers of fiction.' The *Guardian* said, 'One of the few genuine surrealists this country has produced, the possessor of a terrifying and exhilarating imagination,' but added: 'As with earlier texts by Ballard, I could grasp why he sees a need to create a modern mythology out of technology gone mad, but I have to say that the tone strikes me as hellish.'

In the *Oxford Mail*, Martin Seymour-Smith said, 'J. G. Ballard's latest and by far best novel is nothing if not powerful in its impact. It is one of the more outstanding of recent warnings against the dehumanized eroticism and the brutality that are part and parcel of the new technology. An impressive book.'

When the book appeared in America, The *New York Times* wrote, '*Crash* is, hands-down, the most repulsive book I've yet to come across. *Sports Illustrated* coverage of the Round-Robin eliminations at Ravensbruck would be somewhat less freakish.'

The presumption of all Ballard's writings and artistic activities in this area is that there is an inherent sexual attractiveness to a car crash.

Ballard avers that the body shape of a modern car is an erotic one, partly modelled on the fantasies of the designers and advertised as something that would add lifestyle allure to whoever drove the car.

He extended this to suggest that the victims of a crash are transformed into sexual objects by their injuries or deaths, that when a celebrity is killed or injured the crash is of extra interest to the public at large, and that there is a substantial number of car crash adherents who haunt the clover-leaf crossings, flyovers and embankments of motorways waiting for accidents to happen and who then rush to the scene. Others patrol the freeways in fast cars hoping to witness or perhaps provoke a new accident. These are images central to *Crash*.

In his annotation to 'Crash!' in *The Atrocity Exhibition* Ballard says, 'Aside from the fact that we generally own or are at the controls of the crashing vehicle, the car crash differs from other disasters in that it involves the most powerfully advertised commercial product of this century, an iconic entity that combines the elements of speed, power, dream and freedom within a highly stylized format that defuses any fears we may have of the inherent dangers of these violent and unstable machines.'[221]

In the same piece, Ballard reminds us that Filippo Tommaso Marinetti, author of the *Futurist Manifesto*, announced the dictum in 1909 that a racing car is more beautiful than the Winged Victory of Samothrace, mounted on the main staircase of the Louvre in Paris. (Marinetti also helped draft *The Fascist Manifesto* – one wonders what he or anyone else actually knew about racing cars in 1909.)

Thus, J. G. Ballard set out the stall for his most extraordinary and controversial novel.

To read *Crash* as a novel is an undoubtedly unusual experience. In terms of written style, use of English, attention to character and detail, ability to create plausible descriptions and establish a sense of place, it is exemplary. It is a *well-written* novel by any standards. It stands, in fact, above the rest of Ballard's work in this respect. It has few of the nervous or characteristic tics one sometimes notices elsewhere in his work: the jarring bursts of exposition or narrative dialogue, for instance, which breaks in from time to time in his more conventional SF stories. *Crash* is smoothly told, professionally expert. This expertise tends unexpectedly to minimize the unique flavour found in Ballard's best work elsewhere – *Crash* is perhaps the least 'Ballardian' book he wrote.

The narrative voice is in the first person from the point of view of one 'James Ballard', although arguably one could accept that a more active and intriguing character is Dr Robert Vaughan, a flagrant sex addict with a voyeuristic and interventionist streak. Vaughan sets up and creates many of the sexual incidents he obsessively seeks, as well as taking advantage of happenstance. However, the 'Ballard' character does take part in a full share of the action.

The book is written with close focus: there is no doubt about the subject matter. This is a pornographic novel of the first rank, full of sexual coupling with dozens of pages of details about body parts, genitalia, glandular secretions, smells, smears and more. Those who are curious about sexual technique will possibly find answers; those who find pornography dull will probably be able to skim-read many of the more densely packed descriptive paragraphs. Those who are readily shocked will receive a delirious dose of shock.

It is therefore obsessively subject driven, and the author's intent appears to be arousing or stimulating the reader's interest in the sexual possibilities of the theory about crashed motor vehicles and the victims inside them.

It is this purpose which ultimately moves *Crash* away from straightforward obscenity (often defined as *something offensive to accepted behaviour or morality, especially sexual morality, or which is indecent or disgusting* – there is a great deal of this sort of thing in the novel) into the more intellectually defensible realm of pornography (*art or literature which is designed to stimulate sexual excitement in the viewer* or, in this case, reader).

The difference between obscenity and pornography is often seen as a fine one, and it has rarely been finer than in this novel.

Ballard himself said, '... I like to think that *Crash* is the first pornographic novel based on technology. In a sense, pornography is the most political form of fiction, dealing with how we use and exploit each other in the most urgent and ruthless way. Needless to say, the ultimate role of *Crash* is cautionary, a warning against that brutal, erotic and overlit realm that beckons more and more persuasively to us from the margins of the technological landscape.'[222]

He also said, 'I admit my own motives when I wrote the book were confused. I remember when I read the printed proofs nine months after

I had last read the manuscript I had to hang on to my chair. My first reaction was, "The guy who wrote this must be nuts".' He added that in terms of subject matter it had not been hard to write. He found that he had to will himself into a deliberate psychosis, the psychopathic two-plus-two-equals-five. It was a tremendous ordeal. He was bringing up three children, he said, and he was aware how vulnerable their lives were: any one of them might be killed in a car crash. He was morally exhausted because he appeared to be saying that bad is good and good is bad, inverting all the common assumptions of life. But maybe, he thought, readers' assumptions needed to be looked at in a new light. The light thrown by *Crash* was a baleful glare but at least it was a light which one did not get from fellow writers.[223]

The first time I read *Crash* I found myself half-smiling at some of the passages. In an early scene the 'James Ballard' character is taken to hospital after a car crash. He is X-rayed by a young female technician. As she arranges his body beneath the generator she chats about the state of the film industry. 'Ballard' is more interested in her close physical proximity and her sexual attributes:

> Unaware of my curiosity about her body she walked to the remote control switch. How could I bring her to life – by ramming one of these massive steel plugs into a socket at the base of her spine? Perhaps she would then leap into life, talk to me in animated tones about the latest Hitchcock retrospective, launch an aggressive discussion about women's rights …?[224]

It seemed to me the author was just as aware of the ludic quality of the scene as I was – it was black comedy.

A much later scene invoked the same feeling: 'Ballard' is making love to a young woman called Gabrielle. She has already suffered many injuries and her scarred body is held together by numerous calipers, clamps and splints. With Gabrielle's consent 'Ballard' painstakingly removes one by one these bars to sexual activity. Finally he is confronted by a nipple on a naked breast. He examines it carefully. 'For some reason I had expected it to be a detachable latex structure, fitted on each morning along with her spinal brace and leg supports.'[225]

Black comedy depends for effect on the collusion of the reader – we are in on the joke. But collusion in pornography? It casts into question the whole apparatus, the roles of author vs. reader, for instance. This is just small extra complexity in an already challenging novel. And are we expected to accept and believe the central theory, that car crashes provide a real sexual stimulant?

Ballard makes much of the alleged fact that we, as ordinary members of the public, have the same fascination with a crash scene as his characters. He points out that when a traffic accident occurs drivers of cars invariably slow down to take a look at the scene of horror. This is true, but anyone who drives in the modern world knows that delays around crash sites are inevitable: they are caused by recovery vehicles blocking the carriageway, police or ambulance activity, wreckage on the road surface, and so on. Passers-by will take a look at what has happened as they drive slowly past, but their reaction is more likely to be a feeling of horror or pity than a surge of uncontrollable erotic passion.

In other words, the entire substructure of *Crash* is based on a fantasy – or worse, to quote a distinction made by the author Anthony Burgess, a fancy. The fact that it is persuasively and imaginatively argued, consistently explored and has helped create one of the greatest novels of Ballard's career, does not diminish this. A fancy is unworkable and untestable, and when pursued ruthlessly to the end it becomes a presumption too far.

A film adaptation of *Crash* was released in 1996. It was directed by David Cronenberg, and starred James Spader, Holly Hunter, Elias Koteas, Deborah Kara Unger and Rosanna Arquette. The film is of interest for several reasons, not all of them good.

Writing here of the film at this stage is a disjoint from the natural sequence of Ballard works, as the film was made late. The novel was more than twenty years old by the time the film was completed, and because of extra delays in release caused by concerns about pornography it was a quarter century late in the USA.

Significantly, the film of *Crash* followed the Steven Spielberg adaptation of *Empire of the Sun* by nearly ten years. *Empire*, both as a novel and as a film, had been a big hit. As a book alone it elevated J. G. Ballard from the status of fringe or avant-garde writer, and made him a bestselling and widely respected author around the world. The novel was shortlisted for that year's Booker Prize. Ballard was interviewed many times, accepted into the literary culture, appeared on television; he was frequently asked by the press to review or recommend other writers' books. When the Spielberg film was successfully released in 1987 (box-office earnings were greater than $66 million) his reputation was secure.

Cronenberg's film of *Crash*, honourably intended and made with obvious skill and commitment, was a harking back to an earlier manifestation: the Ballard who was writing before *Empire of the Sun*, book or film. Perhaps most people who had simply enjoyed *Empire* cared nothing for Ballard's past books, while the readers and critics who took Ballard seriously as a writer saw *Crash* as an extra insight into his complex career.

Even so, the release of the film opened up the forces of conservatism and repression, and their attempts to make viewing the film as difficult as possible by seeking to encourage authorities to ban it.

David Cronenberg himself, a stout defender of his film on release, had gone through serious doubts about the project. The novel was sent to him by Jeremy Thomas, the producer, but he managed to read only about the first third of it. He said he found it disturbing: repellent, coldly sinister, non-human and clinical in its prose. He felt it misunderstood technological man.

After a period he went back to the book – on a second reading he saw it differently. He believed its particular message had been absorbed by the culture. There was clearly something in that, but in doing so he had also started to accept the central fantasy about the alleged connection between car crashes and sex.[226]

Although the film was professionally made, using well-known actors and an experienced technical crew, it has a 'flat' appearance: scenes are mounted at a slow pace, the actors whisper to each other, there are many lingering close-ups of their faces apparently responding to physical or sexual feeling caused by some sort of unseen contact out of frame. Many scenes contain nudity and sexual grappling, but the film is almost entirely devoid of erotic content. In this respect it often looks absurd. There is little narrative consistency: several scenes consist only of stunt driving, with no narrative to establish why or how the sequence is taking place. Predominantly, the film lacks irony or any sense that the central premise is unworkable: J. G. Ballard's obsession is taken at face value.

The scene from the novel described above, where 'Ballard' tries to make love to Gabrielle, is mounted as standard 'kinky' sex without a moment of questioning or distance. Black humour does not exist in Cronenberg's depressing and implausible world of car-wreck enthusiasts.

In 1999, Iain Sinclair produced a book on the film, lumberingly called *Crash – David Cronenberg's Post-Mortem on J. G. Ballard's 'Trajectory of Fate'*, published by the British Film Institute. This is about as fine an impressionistic rendering of the film as you will find, illustrated throughout not only with stills from the film but also with interviews with people closely associated with Ballard or the film industry.

Sinclair delivers this accurate verdict: 'The value of *Crash* the film is easy to overlook. It belongs to its own time, not to Ballard's 1960s. It belongs to a climate of pre-millennial boredom. It's a novella of the last days. It has to run for ever, hours and hours of road footage, centuries of sex without fertility or climax. It's a chamber work from the era of Clintonian telephone adultery (where the participants fall asleep). I want to see all the out-takes, the wet dawn motorways, the yawning, shivering actors. That's the vision that has been tapped. Post surveillance anti-drama.'[227]

Alexander Walker writing in the *Evening Standard*, headlined the film, more succinctly but much less defensibly, as 'being beyond the bounds of depravity'. In his review he said, '[It contains] some of the most perverted acts and theories of sexual deviance I have ever seen propagated in mainline cinema.'

Christopher Tookey, for the *Daily Mail*, wrote, '[This is] the point at which even a liberal society must draw the line.'

Ballard himself liked the film. 'The movie is actually better than the book,' he said to the audience at the Cannes Film Festival, where it was awarded a Jury Prize. 'It goes further than the book, and is much more powerful and dynamic. It's terrific.'

* * *

Not long after coming out of hospital, Chris sent an email to Harley Cokeliss, the documentary film maker who collaborated with Ballard in the making of the 1971 short film *Crash!* He was eager to learn more about Cokeliss's impressions of Ballard and the time they spent working together. Chris soon heard back from Harley's son Barney, who is also a film director. He had made a short video interview with his father, putting to him some of the questions Chris had outlined in his email.

Harley is being interviewed in Barney's living room. He seems a delightful man – still spry, his lively sense of humour immediately evident. Dressed in a checked open-neck shirt, with his curly hair and glasses he reminds me a little of Kurt Vonnegut. Behind him on a wooden sideboard are two lamps, a selection of family photographs, a glass vase of cut flowers. On the wall there are various artworks. Though the background details are blurred, one of them catches my attention immediately because it seems familiar. With a sense of incredulity, I pull out my magnifying glass to get a closer look and I see that I am right: the image is the same as the one that is now hanging beside my desk, the print from Fay Ballard's 'House Clearance' series – the same upended flipper, aka 'The Nun'.

Cokeliss first encountered the work of Ballard in his early twenties – he had come to London to study at the London Film School, and never left.

> I was reading a lot of science fiction then, but Ballard's stories had a voice that was unique. The sound of a J. G. Ballard story is unlike anybody else's story. His attitude to the world was very engaging and when I started making arts documentaries for the BBC, Jim was very high up on the list of people I wanted to make films about. There was a very dynamic executive producer there, and he would give some of the young directors working with him a pretty free hand.
>
> I started making regular trips to see Jim. We'd sit in the kitchen in Shepperton. Jim would more often than not have a whisky. I did not join him in that – I was driving, so I wasn't drinking. I'd have a cup of tea or coffee. I knew I was dealing with someone of serious intellect, but he was also a lovely guy, an open-hearted, generous man. I miss him.

The making of *Crash!* – and the ideas expressed in it – seemed to follow on directly from the 'Crashed Cars' exhibition at the New Arts Lab the year before. 'There was always going to be a book,' Cokeliss was sure, 'though it was never stated that baldly.' Ballard was involved with the making of *Crash!* from the beginning.

> He was really interested in parking structures. There was this one near Watford[228] that was a spiral – we featured that in the film. Jim loved American cars, those kind of exaggerated design features. American cars had fins, and grilles, and chrome, and decorations – Jim liked that. There are visual clues in these cars that are reminiscent of human body parts – Jim would bring out those ideas, that what we were looking at was some kind of psychological sales pitch, to make us want to buy the car because it was connected to our animal nature. His ideas were very visual, but also quite abstract.

Barney Cokeliss later tells me that his father's short-term memory has started to become a little erratic, though watching him in the video you would never know it. When Cokeliss talks about film especially he becomes immediately alive, focused, recalling in photographic detail what was said and done. It is easy to imagine him sitting across from Ballard, the two of them talking excitedly about the relationship between image and idea.

Ballard was interested in the films made by the Road Research Laboratory and in particular those that showed the possible effects of car crashes using crash test dummies. When Barney Cokeliss asks his father if he thinks Ballard believed his own thesis in *Crash*, that car crashes were sexy, Cokeliss is certain the interest was purely intellectual.

> I would say that Jim was looking at pathology. Just like the Vaughan character in *Crash*, watching the shape of the shadows move across a wall. Because this character had a disordered sensibility, they also would find something erotic about a wound that would be inflicted – an aperture of some kind, created by the chrome decorations on an American car, maybe, some kind of sexual connotation. That's the kind of fantasy ideas that would go through Jim's head – but that's Jim's character of Dr Vaughan. Not Jim.

In the annotations made to *The Atrocity Exhibition* in 1990, Ballard describes how during his first visit to the US in 1955 it seemed to him as if 'all the optimism of Eisenhower's postwar America was expressed in the baroque vehicles that soared along its highways, as if an advanced interstellar race had touched down on a recreational visit.'[229] The 'Crash!' section was originally written in 1968 and is presented in the form of a scientific paper whose section headings perform their own Ballardian elegy:

> Each afternoon in the deserted cinema/Tallis was increasingly distressed/by the images of colliding motor cars./Celebrations of his wife's death,/the slow-motion newsreels/recapitulated all his memories of childhood,/the realization of dreams/which even during the safe immobility of sleep/would develop into nightmares of anxiety.

Ballard cites these five short pages as 'the gene from which my novel *Crash* was to spring'.[230] In the 1971 film, Cokeliss's own documentary-style script, intercut with sections from 'You, Me and the Continuum', is relayed alongside a procession of prosaic yet subtly disturbing images, creating a similarly unnerving disjuncture to that played out between the section headings and the pseudo-scientific text in *The Atrocity Exhibition*.

'As an engineering structure, the car is totally uninteresting to me,' Ballard says in the film, offering us through Cokeliss's words an uncannily succinct description of the novel he was preparing to write. 'I'm interested in the exact way in which it brings together the visual codes for expressing our ordinary perceptions about reality, for example, that the future is something with a fin on it, and the whole system of expectations contained in the design of the car, expectations about our freedom to move through time and space, about the identities of our own bodies, our own musculatures, the complex relationships between ourselves and the world of objects around us.'

Ballard is shown at the wheel of a car, intercut with footage of vehicles being driven at speed around a loop of dual carriageway; next we see him looking around a car showroom – Cokeliss remembers one turquoise-blue Cadillac in particular that drew his attention – then walking amongst car wrecks in a scrapyard. He climbs into the driver's seat of one of the damaged vehicles, grasping the wheel as if trying to imagine himself as the car's last driver.

Playing opposite him is Gabrielle Drake, sister of the cult folk musician Nick Drake, who was to die in 1974 from an accidental drugs overdose at the age of twenty-six.²³¹ Drake, who went on to have a long and successful television acting career, is by turns aloof, sexually provocative and demonstrably fragile, and Ballard was sufficiently impressed by her performance to lend her name to one of the central characters in *Crash* the novel.

The film is economical, strange, compelling. This seventeen-minute broadcast – *Crash!* was first shown on BBC Two at 8:30 pm on Friday 12 February 1971 as a segment of the arts programme *Review* – was the first time Ballard's most provocative ideas and imagery had been unleashed on a wider public. It would be fascinating to discover what the casual viewer made of what they saw. That the film also offers a curious microcosm of seventies Britain – with Ballard's luxurious sideburns completing the picture – is part of its attraction. Both Fay and Bea Ballard vividly remember being taken to watch the filming taking place. Bea particularly recalls the experience as important in cementing her growing interest in the medium of television.

In his interview with the art critic and curator Hans Ulrich Obrist in 2003, Ballard spoke of the 'Crashed Cars' exhibition as 'an art show designed to carry out a psychological test, so that I could decide whether to write my novel *Crash*. I wanted to test my own hypothesis about our unconscious fascination with car crashes and their latent sexuality.'²³² Ballard spoke frequently of *Crash* the novel as an experiment, the stress-testing of an idea to its ultimate implications, and in the introduction to the French edition of *Crash* he explores the novel's relationship with science fiction and how in fact it 'takes up its position as a cataclysmic novel of the present day' in the same way as his earlier disaster novels investigated aspects of a possible near-future.

> Do we see, in the car crash, a sinister portent of a nightmare marriage between sex and technology? Will modern technology provide us with hitherto undreamed-of means for tapping our own psychopathologies? Is this harnessing of our innate perversity conceivably of benefit to us? Is there some deviant logic unfolding more powerful than that provided by reason?²³³

Though Ballard rowed back on this position in later interviews[234] I have always found it useful to think about *Crash* in terms of its relationship to science fiction, which is closer than many might believe. Even those of Ballard's novels that contain no immediately identifiable speculative materials are written with a science fictional sensibility, and when viewed through this particular lens – as a document from a future gone rogue – the effect of *Crash* on the reader is more powerful still.

Perhaps the darkest aspect of *Crash* is how close it came to becoming a prediction of Ballard's own future. Towards the end of February 1972 and just two weeks after the novel was completed, Ballard was driving along the A316 between Chiswick and Mortlake when his car, a Ford Zephyr, crossed the central reservation and overturned:

> After finishing the book and delivering the manuscript to my agent I was driving back from London in the rain about two in the morning, and the car skidded and swerved across the central reservation, smashed down a steel sign then rolled on to its back and was carried down the oncoming lane ... Thank god I didn't hit anything, otherwise everyone would have been dead. And I ended up with the roof crushed down upside down in my harness. There was petrol everywhere. People were standing around in the darkness bellowing, 'Petrol, petrol.' They couldn't open the doors because the roof was down. Of all things, the window-winder fell off. I must have knocked it off with my elbow. So I wasn't able to wind down the window. I suppose somebody could've kicked it in. I was lucky the thing didn't ignite.[235]

Together with the crowd of onlookers, Ballard attempted to set his vehicle upright and drive away. He was prevented from doing so by the police, who wanted Ballard to take a breathalyser test. When Ballard refused, he was arrested, then taken to hospital to be checked for internal bleeding and possible concussion:

> I got my head X-rayed and I must have been undergoing euphoria or something because I got into a fierce argument with this girl, the radiographer, about who owned the copyright of these photographs. I was looking at these photographs of my skull – front and side. And

the doctor was saying, 'Well, there's nothing there but the long-term effects take a long time to show.' I thought, 'That's great. Who owns the copyright?' 'We own the copyright.' I was saying, 'No. That's my head. I own the copyright. You own the plates, not the copyright. This is an important distinction.' Anyway, I got home by taxi. I was ill. I must've had concussion.[236]

Fay Ballard remembers coming home from school to find her father in bed, suffering from nausea and a powerful headache. The aftermath of the accident took on its own mythology. Ballard spent three days recovering, then hired a car from a local garage and drove out to the police car pound in Richmond where the Zephyr was being held hostage. He took a series of photographs of the stricken vehicle – 'I'd developed exactly the obsession I'd described in *The Atrocity Exhibition*.'[237] – which show heavy denting to the roof, to the rear and front bumpers, a smashed windscreen and buckled boot.

He eventually made arrangements to have the car repaired. Mike Moorcock remembers accompanying Ballard when he went to collect it: 'The car's not running, it's rumbling along. It stinks of death. It reeks of damp and mould. We're doing about ten miles an hour, everything steaming and banging. And he's insisting it's all right.'[238]

Ballard claimed that Moorcock had over-dramatized the situation and that the car was basically sound, though his own account of the crash was to change in later years, with him putting down the cause of the accident to a tyre blow-out, a detail that has become enshrined in the official narrative.

Blow-out or no, Ballard's refusal to take a breathalyser test earned him a one-year driving ban. Ballard rarely if ever used public transport and so felt he had been punished unduly, forcibly confined to Shepperton as to a desert island. This feeling of alienation – as well as its inciting incident – was to feed directly into his next novel, *Concrete Island*.

20

'THE CAUSEWAYS OF THE SUN'

'Vermilion Sands is a place where I would be happy to live,' Ballard wrote in the preface to the collection of short stories with this title. It is a playground resort that exists in neither the future nor the past. It depicts what was probably for Ballard a kind of idealized present: a tourist destination where the tourists come and go but no longer swarm, a strip of desert-like sand and scrub, unoccupied apartment blocks, motels and bars buried in ever-encroaching dunes, small galleries or studios run by failed artists where you can buy living sculpture or huge specimen plants whose vulgar flowers will serenade you while you sleep.

In the resort of Vermilion Sands former astronauts, fading Hollywood queens, beachcombers, body-builders, remittance men, opera singers, retired impresarios, wannabe playwrights and poets gather in a sort of timeless *danse macabre*, or pass through on their way to some other colony of misfits and chancers.

The ambience is somewhere between the French Riviera of the 1920s, Ipanema Beach, the Greek islands of the present, and the putative future of coastal east Florida where the freeways and strip malls that once serviced Cape Canaveral have been abandoned to slowly filling swamps and drifting sands. Deadly sand rays soar and hover above the villas and beach houses, realtors try to sell you a house that will reshape itself to your will, and beautiful women, obsessed with poetry or song, will tempt and seduce for the chance to make use of a studio space where they might perform.

Vermilion Sands is a short book, comprising nine stories written between 1956 and 1967. Included is the very first story Ballard sold for publication

('Prima Belladonna'); the last one ('The Cloud-Sculptors of Coral D') was written in the period between the death of his wife and the publication of *The Atrocity Exhibition*. With hindsight the overall effect, should one be needed, is that these stories are antidotes to the dark impression that might well have been created by books like *Crash* and *The Atrocity Exhibition*. The collection was first published as a whole in 1973, and has not been amended since. In this sense the stories belong to his early period, and are typical of the best fantasy work he was doing at that time. For many of his readers, *Vermilion Sands* represents peak Ballard.

There is an unusual lightness to the style, almost at times self-mocking. The descriptive language is rich and colourful, but never oppressively so. The narrators or central characters run shops or studios in a desultory way, or they are habitual loungers or regular drinkers, and have names like Tony and Harry and Raymond – the unearthly and glamorous women who pass strikingly through Vermilion Sands are sometimes described as having insects or jewels for eyes, and have names like Aurora Day, Leonora Chanel, Hope Cunard and Jane Ciracylides. They often appear in dreamy white gowns, and are protected or accompanied by silent bodyguards, brothers or chauffeurs who stand and wait, their impenetrable mirrorshades glittering in the rays of the lowering sun. This ambience alone sets the stories in a never-never land that sometimes seems part of a wish fulfilment period of the past, but it is an intriguing one where the reader accepts the make-believe because of the sheer novelty of the stories.

All the stories have a fantastic element: in 'Prima Belladonna' the narrator is the keeper of a shop that sells huge flowers that can be trained to sing. In 'Studio 5, The Stars' Aurora Day is a would-be poet who uses an AI verse machine that turns out an unstoppable flow of derivative lines. In 'Cry Hope, Cry Fury!' the narrator accidentally shoots and kills a gigantic sand ray flying above him, which throws him unwittingly into the role of the Ancient Mariner. In 'The Thousand Dreams of Stellavista' we learn of intelligent architecture, where mobile, mood-sensitive houses have memories and motives of revenge.

J. G. Ballard famously declared the space age had come to an end, that it lasted no more than about fifteen years between the mid-1960s and mid-1970s. He said he felt disappointed by this, but that his work was concerned with *inner* space, not outer space.

He did not disparage the urge to explore space. He followed NASA's Mercury program with interest, and when the Apollo missions began in 1968 he and his three children invariably stayed up late to watch the spectacular launches live on television.[239] They named their beloved dog, a Golden Retriever, Apollo ... a.k.a. Polly.

Ballard sometimes related the story of how one night he was standing in his garden and saw a fast-moving point of light crossing the sky. He realized it was the Skylab space station. He remembered thinking how fantastic it was that there were men up there, and was really quite moved by watching it. Then his neighbour came out into his garden to get something and Ballard said, 'Look, there's Skylab,' and the man looked up and said, 'Sky-what?' Ballard realized that he didn't know about it, and wasn't interested.[240]

'What happened to the space age?' he wrote in 1994. 'Is it still unfolding above our heads, or did it end ... with the first Skylab splashdown not shown live on television because the American networks knew that the public was bored?'[241]

Charles Platt, the graphic designer of *New Worlds*, encouraged Ballard to attend a certain party in London. He thought he might be interested in talking to a real-life aerospace engineer who was expected to be there. 'No, I have nothing to say to people like that,' he told Platt, sounding angry about it. 'To my mind, NASA completely missed the point. They should have put some schizophrenics up there in a space capsule with a tape recorder. Then we might have learned something interesting.'[242]

In 2003, Ballard told Stuart Wavell: 'NASA should be closed down. They've served their purpose. They're just going to go on killing astronauts.' NASA, he added, relied on the wrong hardware – brute force ballistic missiles of the kind that Verne had written about in the nineteenth century. 'It was quite obvious that those monsters could never launch enough men and equipment into space to maintain large space stations, either in orbit or on the moon's surface.' The human race should have waited for a more advanced technology to come along. NASA lost its audience.

They thought in terms of jut-jawed heroes out of SF comics. If you think of the navigators of the fourteenth and fifteenth centuries, they were a collection of fanatics, eccentrics and dreamers. But there were no madmen on the early spacecraft. NASA's astronauts were completely unpoetic. Space is a totally alien environment. It's probably a waste of time going. People now realize that the moon is about as interesting as an old gravel quarry. There's nothing there.'[243]

As for the longer-term prospect of inhabitable colonies on other planets or in permanent orbit above us, a persistent dream of space-age enthusiasts, Ballard was discouraging: 'A warning glimpse of what life would be like ... can already be seen around us – in rundown motorway cafés, in vandalized municipal high-rises, in the once ultra-modern elevators and miles of scuffed circular corridor at the BBC Television Centre. Will we find, when we at last leave our planet, not a series of Corbusier radiant cities in the sky, but seedy housing estates and third-rate airports?'[244]

He did not live long enough to witness the era of billionaires and oligarchs funding their own private space races. It's tempting to guess what he might say or think.

Once he became established as a writer Ballard was recognized as a leading exponent of science fiction. Throughout that traditional SF genre the likelihood of space travel in the future was unquestioned. Yet he maintained these dissident views about the brevity of the space age for most of his career – predictably, many of the older SF writers, especially in the USA, saw him in a negative light. What he said was dismissed because they thought he was a technophobe, an extremist, a radical who liked stirring up argument.

There are hardly any spaceships in Ballard's work. An early story, 'Thirteen to Centaurus', is about the moral effect on the participants of being confined in a multi-generational starship, travelling comparatively slowly to another star. None of the people on board will be alive when and if it arrives at its destination. But there's a twist: is the starship a real one or a simulation that never left Earth? The moral dilemma remains the same, and that is what Ballard explores.[245]

Another early story was 'Passport to Eternity', written during the long wasted hours of his time in the RAF. It was not published until 1962, after he had revised it. This story implies futuristic technology which might include space travel, but in fact it was written as a spoof of a kind of American SF that at the time Ballard found entertaining.[246] And there's a story from 1963 called 'The Time-Tombs' which is set on an unnamed planet, and which sketches in a few hints of settlements on other planets in the solar system, suggesting the use of space travel.[247]

In 1982 he wrote a story called 'Report on an Unidentified Space Station'. An expedition of some kind finds safe haven in an uninhabited space station, not marked on any charts. It is about five hundred metres in diameter. The travellers go aboard, find it deserted but in full working order. They explore the interior and discover the station is much larger than they assumed at first: they now estimate it must be at least a mile in diameter. The more they explore the more they learn about the sheer size of the station, which grows ever larger as they continue to investigate it. By the end of the story they have guessed it must be at least 15 million light years in size.[248]

But there are no conventionally described spaceships, nor space travel nor actual astronauts in any of these stories.

Elderly, disillusioned, fake or dead astronauts are a different matter. In 1988, the independent American publisher Arkham House brought out a collection of Ballard's short stories which took an adjacent interest in the after-effects of what he saw as the short-lived space adventure. *Memories of the Space Age*, which brings together eight substantial stories published between 1962 and 1985, might almost be seen as a darker counterpoint to *Vermilion Sands*. Former astronauts feature in both collections.

'The Cage of Sand' is probably the most remarkable of these stories. It is set on a deserted future Florida coastline. The promontory of Cape Canaveral, long abandoned as a rocket launching area, is smothered by Martian sand. This was brought back from Mars as ballast, but it was found that the microbiological analysis of the sand had been inadequate. It contained a residue of ancient organic matter. The sand began to spread rapidly and soon the entire peninsula of Florida had been turned to red Martian desert. Now Cape Canaveral is a ruin, where 'the old launching gantries and landing ramps reared up into the sky like derelict pieces of giant sculpture.'

To this zone come three people, occupying an empty hotel that is half-buried in the dunes. One of them is Bridgman, former architect of a big space development company, obsessed by the sense of failure of not achieving his ambitions for the design of a new spaceport. With him is Louise Woodward, the widow of an astronaut killed during a mission in space and whose body is now endlessly orbiting in his capsule; finally, Travis, trained as an astronaut but whose nerve failed him, making him hit the abort button seconds before the engines ignited. He has been haunted by guilt ever since. The three have been drawn to this stretch of coastline because Woodward's capsule regularly passes overhead, and is expected to make a landfall soon. Meanwhile, wardens who protect the ecologically sensitive zone and keep people out of it are hunting for them.

Written with a superb sense of the strange, using evocative language that is a reminder of his own depiction of Vermilion Sands, Ballard produced in 'The Cage of Sand' one of his finest stories. It was still early in his career.[249]

The same book contains the not dissimilar story, 'The Dead Astronaut'. This is shorter, less floridly written, but set in the same general place. For instance, of Cape Canaveral (still at the time of writing being called Cape Kennedy), Ballard writes, 'The launching towers rose into the evening air like the rusting ciphers of some forgotten algebra of the sky.'[250]

The longest story in the book, 'Memories of the Space Age' itself, is another vision of a future abandoned space centre. The Cape Kennedy gantries remain in ruins, with a brief descriptive passage comparable with the other two: 'A threatening aura emanated from these ancient towers, as old in their way as the great temple columns of Karnak, bearers of a different cosmic order, symbols of a view of the universe that had been abandoned along with the state of Florida that had given them birth.'

But this future Florida is covered in dense jungle, where cheetahs and zebras roam, and in the skies above fly rickety biplanes and triplanes from the era of the first world war. Time is freezing, perhaps moving in reverse. A doctor and his wife are in an abandoned hotel in Titusville, pursuing their obsession with the images of the space age – familiar Ballardian themes, but enhanced by a sort of mystical glow, a reference back to the first iteration of the 'illuminated man' in a Florida jungle? Ballard reworks his themes constantly, but invariably invests them with something strange, something new.[251]

'A Question of Re-entry' invokes the mood or ambience of Conrad's *Heart of Darkness*, with a Lieutenant Connolly leading a search mission up a tributary of the Orinoco River. Colonel Francis Spender, an astronaut who not only managed to land on the moon but also heroically made a successful return journey to Earth, has not been found after his capsule deviated from the planned touchdown. He has come down somewhere in the Amazon rainforest along a line linking Lake Maracaibo with Brasilia.

Many astronauts have died in similar attempts at moon landings. Ballard asks rhetorically of the space race: 'If the sea was a symbol of the unconscious, was space perhaps an image of unfettered time, and the inability to penetrate it a tragic exile to one of the limbos of eternity, a symbolic death in life?' The searchers meet a man called Ryker, rumoured to have gone native with the tribal people. Ryker throws doubt on the hope that either Spender or his capsule survived re-entry, but the behaviour of the tribal people seems to indicate that they revere the astronaut as a deity. The story revolves around the clash between civilization-based knowledge and native belief.[252]

Writing about the two key stories in this book, 'Myths of the Near Future' and what Ballard called its companion piece, 'News from the Sun', he said:

> I can remember when people throughout the world were intensely interested in the future, and convinced that it would change their lives for the better. In the years after the second world war the future was the air that everyone breathed. Looking back, we can see that the blueprint of the world we inhabit today was then being drawn – television and the consumer society, computers, jet travel and the newest wonder drugs transformed our lives and gave us a powerful

sense of what the twentieth century could do for us once we freed ourselves from war and economic depression. These two stories are attempts to free us from the tyranny of time where we will spend the rest of our lives.[253]

Memories of the Space Age is that unusual thing: a book of separate short stories with consistent themes, in this case written over a period of two decades. Ballard displays a real faith in science and technology, but also questions its actual value.

21

'A DECLINE IN PROPERTY VALUES'

Two novels followed *Crash* in relatively quick succession. The three taken together can be thought of as comprising a loose trilogy, because there are themes detectably in common, but each is a standalone book. Neither the publisher nor the author ever made any attempt to force a common link. The two titles that follow *Crash* are *Concrete Island* (1974) and *High-Rise* (1975).

Concrete Island is a Robinsonade, a story defined as being of someone marooned and separated from the rest of the world by circumstance – according to Ballard his novel should more correctly be termed 'inverted Crusoeism', his name for a story of someone marooned and separated from the rest of the world *by choice*.[254] In fact, *Concrete Island* is both. The story begins with the central character involved in a serious accident that leads to his being marooned, and it ends – well, it is a novel by J. G. Ballard.

Robert Maitland, a well-off architect (another Ballardian archetype), is driving his Jaguar at high speed down the exit lane of an elevated freeway in west London when the front nearside tyre bursts. Out of control the car snakes from side to side, crashes through a temporary barrier made of wooden trestles and plunges violently down a grass-covered embankment. It comes to rest against the rusting chassis of an overturned taxi. Maitland is knocked unconscious, and is badly injured.

When Maitland recovers consciousness the next morning he realizes he is in effect trapped on an island. He staggers around, still half concussed, dragging an injured leg, desperate to find help and rescue. He discovers he is not on a concrete island, as the title of the book has it, but is in an area of long grass and other wild-growing scrub surrounded by the concrete architecture of the road system. He is between steep embankments and grey pillars, beneath flyovers, hard against high walls: an abandoned desert where the broken remains of vehicle parts, litter thrown from cars and general filth have accumulated, and where the London traffic roars by continuously along the overhead road system. There is no escape. For a few days he makes increasingly desperate attempts to draw attention to his plight, but he is consumed by pain, thirst and hunger.

He comes across traces that suggest there are other people already existing on the island, and finally meets them: Jane Sheppard, a part-time prostitute, who uses the night times to pick up the drivers of passing cars, and Proctor, a semi-insensible former circus acrobat who is dangerously violent. Maitland discovers that they live in underground remains: the area was crudely constructed over the site of former houses, an old cinema, a car breaker's yard, all now covered over by the rough terrain. Although terrified of Proctor, Maitland starts a tentative relationship with Jane, hoping she will help him escape. The pathways she uses to leave the area are too steep for him to clamber up.

His injuries slowly turn out to be less serious than he thought, so Maitland renews his efforts to escape, but he has become embroiled in the rough lifestyle of the other two. He is partly master of them, partly their slave. He fights and intimidates Proctor, but is forced to be carried bodily by him when moving about the zone. He has a physical relationship with Jane, but she continues to serve as a sex worker every night. As a return to his old life becomes increasingly difficult to achieve or even imagine, Maitland abandons his efforts and seems resigned to staying on the island indefinitely.

Somewhere in the middle of these transactional developments, the nature of the book undergoes a change. The original Robinsonade situation, set up by what has every appearance of an unpredictable traffic accident, shifts slowly into Ballard's more familiar territory: desperation followed by a modicum of ingenious survivalism, leading to acceptance, nihilism, anomie. The book becomes inverted Crusoeism. Regular readers of Ballard's work will anyway be expecting this. If a squad of rescue workers had suddenly appeared on the traffic island with ladders, lifting gear and stretchers, roughly analogous to Defoe's description of the mutineers' ship that releases Robinson Crusoe, there would be widespread disappointment. Maitland was doomed from the start. Ballard's protagonists invariably head south into the torrid heat, welcome the entropic end of the universe, or in this case live on in squalor by choice.

Concrete Island is an interesting novel for its blend of realism and obsessive behaviour, but it is overall a minor addition to Ballard's work. *Robinson Crusoe* depended for its effect on a solid base of realism: it was a real island, the protagonist was there because his ship had foundered, his life was threatened by the arrival of cannibals, and so on.

The thread of realism in *Concrete Island* is often tentative. It is true that in the real world these massive road constructions blight and desertify the land they cross, and that the zones beneath the dark, rain-soaked arches become a sort of undefined territory. In many cases, especially in or near big cities, they have become temporary refuges for the homeless, areas of crime or drug dealing, places where people skateboard or drive cars recklessly. Ballard, though, takes it to an illogical extreme, where the confined area is almost impossible to leave, but at the same time has the convenience of liveability. Jane Shepherd, for instance, has an identifiably 'normal' life as a casual prostitute. She has constructed a home for herself. She buys groceries at a local store, she cooks meals, she even has a telephone landline fitted. Yet Robert Maitland feels existentially trapped, marooned, in despair.

So the contrast the reader instinctively makes with imagined reality is not consistently possible. A similar comment could be made about, for example, the flooding of London in *The Drowned World*, where a penthouse suite at the Ritz is somehow not only still usable but has a working air conditioner. The difference is that in the earlier novel Ballard's outlandish imagination was otherwise given free rein, stimulating in the reader one fabulous concession after another. In *Concrete Island* the appeal to known reality is disconcertingly at odds with sordidity.

Kirkus Reviews said of *Concrete Island*, 'Escape becomes problematical: from where? to what? and on what terms? The "conspiracy of the grotesque" that traps him is more than Maitland's trial — it's his only destiny, and perhaps no more than technological man deserves. Ballard handles this kind of reductive moral fable with incomparable finesse, investing the narrative with savage horror that eats away at banal appearance and reveals the skeleton beneath the skin.'

The *Sunday Times* said, 'Ballard writes with taut and precise economy, and the moral of his brilliantly original fable is plain: the interstices of our concrete jungle are filled with neglected people, and one day those people could be ourselves.'

The third novel in this immediate post *Atrocity* group was *High-Rise*. The influence thrown by *The Atrocity Exhibition* was still detectable, but it progressively lessened with each new novel. *High-Rise* even showed traces of black comedy once again, something absent from *Concrete Island*.

It's difficult to generalize about the 'type' of book *High-Rise* might be. It is not in fact at all a conventional novel, but in structure more of a saga. It's a sequence of overlapping scenes that do not follow one from another to create a story or plot — we move from one incident to the next. Throughout it is written carefully, with the sense of background oddness that is distinctively Ballardian. Each new scene is usually more of the same as the preceding ones, or slightly more extreme. A huge number of people (as characters) are mentioned in the book, but few are named or fully described.

The scenario is set almost entirely within one building: a forty-storey skyscraper or condominium, which is said to house an array of a thousand luxury apartments. The standards of luxury are of course described from a 1970s' point of view, but Ballard draws an ambitious picture: some of the building's spacious levels include a supermarket, restaurants, a bank, hairdressers, a junior school, shops, swimming pools, play areas for children, a sculpture park and so on.

The building is occupied on a general class or income basis, in a semi-allegorical way: the lower levels are for well-paid workers, such as flight crews for airliners. The central area is where true professionals live: doctors, lawyers, accountants. The top floors are for the enviably wealthy or super-rich. The penthouse is occupied by one man, the architect who designed the building and who is described oddly as the first tenant — one would assume he would possess the freehold to the building. In fact we never discover who actually is the landowner, but we are told this building is only one of five such towers placed fairly close to each other in an area of former dockland. The place they are in appears to be London, or some other large British city.

The three main characters are:

Richard Wilder, who lives on the second floor. He is a working man, a television producer, a pugnacious former rugby player, recognized by many of the other tenants because of the noisy parties he often throws. Dr Robert Laing has only recently moved in. He is a consultant at a teaching hospital, and lives on the twenty-fifth floor. The reader discovers the state of affairs inside the building as Laing does. The architect who designed the entire edifice, and who now occupies the penthouse, is called Anthony Royal.

Apart from a few minor named characters who appear from time to time, most of the residents are identified by the floor on which they live, or by their job title. We hear briefly about a gynaecologist, a market analyst, a film editor, a cost accountant, a choreographer, a sound man, an account executive, a radiologist and many more mid-range professionals. What female characters there are — lovers and wives — are identified in most cases by their first names only.

Chaos and anarchy are present in the building from the first pages. The elevators work only intermittently, children's areas have been arbitrarily closed, the power and water supplies go off and on, the supermarket runs out of food, the waste chutes are blocked, adultery and rivalry seem to be normal social behaviour not only between neighbours but across the invisible lines of class and income. People throw waste and other rubbish off the balconies, so that the cars parked below are always being damaged.

The situation steadily or unsteadily worsens. Some of the residents who have jobs do still leave the building during the day, but this becomes increasingly difficult. Parties are thrown every night, and these almost always end in orgiastic scrums of half-naked people or drunken and violent conflict. Corridors and shared areas quickly fill up with plastic bin bags, loose rubbish and broken glass, and the more affluent residents put up barricades.

The story, such as it is, and only of vague interest or purpose, involves Richard Wilder setting out to film a documentary of life in the building, moving slowly upwards through the social strata. His activities with a camera neither aggravate nor lessen the other tensions, and anyway he seems half-hearted about the project. He is a clearly unpopular figure. He is envious of Robert Laing, who becomes known to Anthony Royal and part of the architect's charmed circle, if only temporarily. Sexual relationships multiply but become increasingly casual. One man commits suicide by leaping from a balcony.

Gradually the chaos subsides, but as the novel ends it is clear to Laing that the other four high-rise stacks will soon head down the same chaotic route.

Much of *High-Rise* is descriptive narrative, but there is almost no sense of relationships between the various middle-class characters, except conflict, threats, fear, anger and sexual dalliance. Dialogue is at a minimum, and what there is serves the particular moment.

For the early part of the book the reader senses a situation arising that will be not dissimilar to that in William Golding's *Lord of the Flies*, in which a mini-society evolves while cut off from the rest of the world. In practice this turns out to be only one narrative strand of *High-Rise*, never explored properly for its allegorical possibilities. The content of the novel is made up of the events it describes, so it is to be taken as actual rather than symbolic, the underlying meaning being a vague one that might include economic and class differences, sexual rivalry, violent instincts released.

Thus Ballard is implying social criticism in a microcosm, the reader left to make of it whatever seems relevant. The abiding shadow of the author's detention with hundreds of expatriate Brits in a Japanese prison camp? His frustration with the dull reality of British social mores after his release? His discontent with the contemporary world (the mid-1970s)? All are possible.

The film of *High-Rise* was released in 2015, no longer contemporary but depicting an historical period four decades in its past. The men have long sideburns, moustaches and flared trousers, while most of the women have relaxed sexual attitudes and are willing handmaids to the wishes of men. To a modern audience this at first gives the film an appearance of being dated, rather than an historical reconstruction. That impression soon fades.

Written by Amy Jump and directed by Ben Wheatley, the film improves in some ways on the novel, while actually reproducing it

Right: Ballard and his 1958 collage. At twenty-eight years of age Ballard was already working with the material that would form the basis of his most experimental works of fiction.

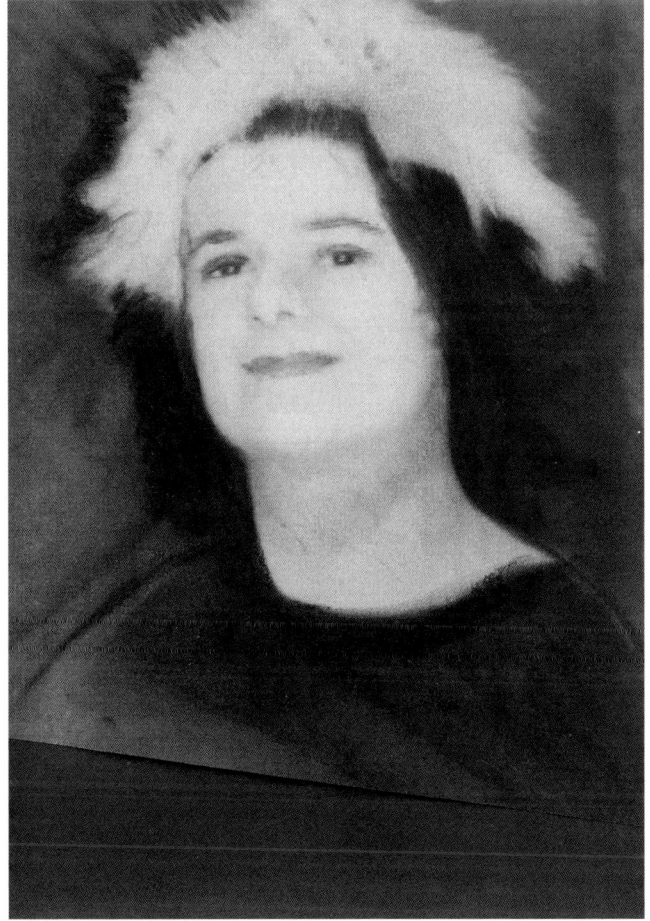

'Mother Reinstated', drawing by Fay Ballard made from a photograph of Mary Ballard, discovered in Ballard's desk after his death. First shown as part of House Clearance, Eleven Spitalfields, London 2014.

Ballard with Fay, Beatrice and Jim junior at Old Charlton Road, Shepperton, 1965.

Michael Moorcock, 2009.

Christopher Priest (left), Brian Aldiss (right) with their editor Charles Monteith of Faber & Faber, London, 1970.

Christopher Priest (centre) at the 'Phun City' music festival, Patching, West Sussex, 1970.

Martin Bax looks on as Ballard presents Ann Quin with first prize in Ambit's 1968 competition for 'stories written under the influence'. Quin's drug of choice was the contraceptive pill Orthonovin 2.

'Homage to Claire Churchill', the first of Ballard's Advertiser's Announcements, published in Ambit 32, summer 1967.

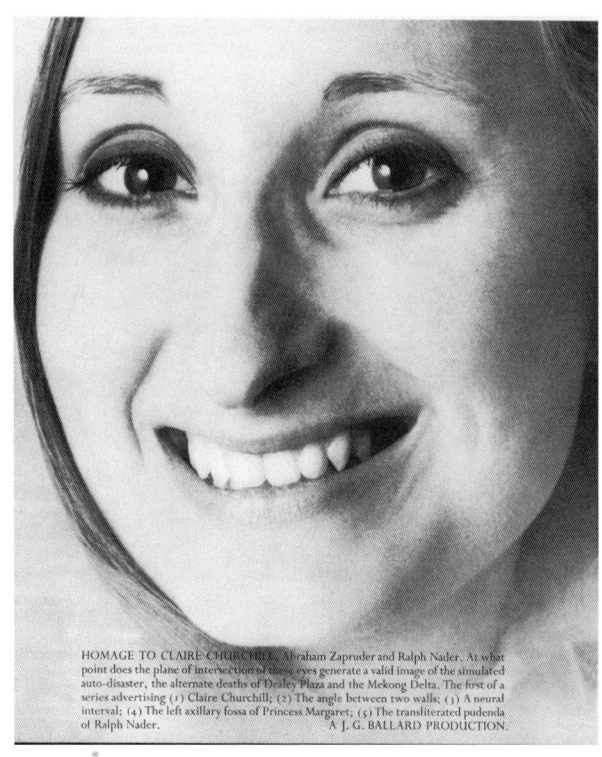

Lindsay Fulcher in 1984.

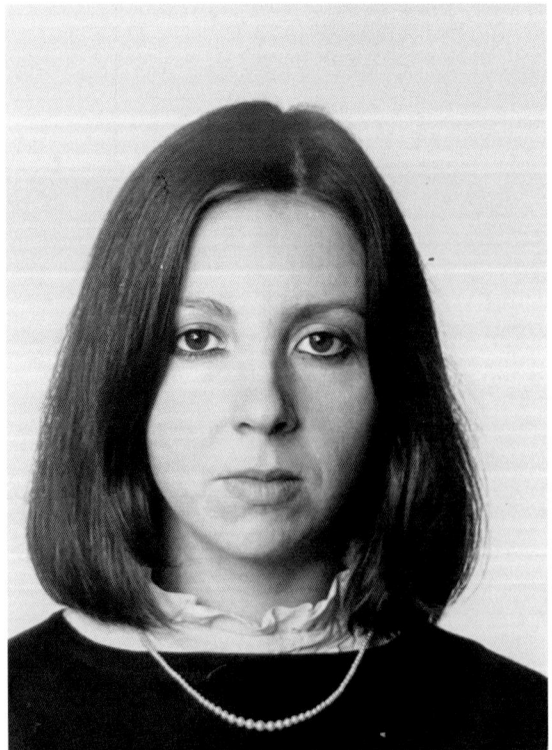

J. G. Ballard, 1987.

Ballard looks out for the final time on the garden at Old Charlton Road, May 2008.

Beatrice Ballard at her father's memorial event in 2009.

Film director Solveig Nordlund, 2009.

Above left: Christopher Priest and Fay Ballard, Eleven Spitalfields, London, 2014.
Above right: David Pringle at the Kelpies, Falkirk, Scotland, 2016.

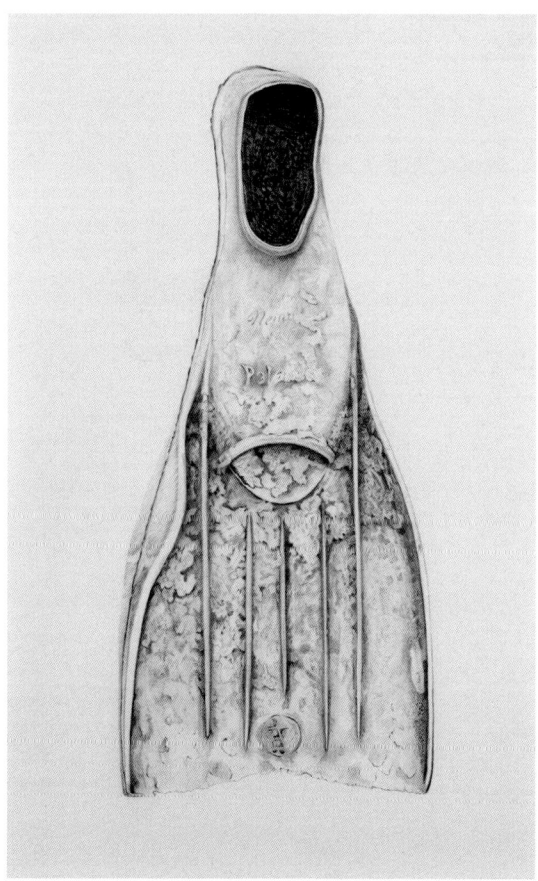

'Flipper 3', drawing by Fay Ballard first shown as part of House Clearance, Eleven Spitalfields, London, 2014.

Above: Ballard in 1988, pictured with Brigid Marlin's reconstruction of 'The Violation' by Paul Delvaux (1936).
Below: Christopher Priest and Nina Allan, Straad, Isle of Bute, 2018.

recognizably. There is a definite narrative thread, and the actors are given many scenes of dialogue to speak. The physical chaos of the disintegrating tower community is captured by production designer Mark Tildesley, and photographed brilliantly by Laurie Rose. The actors do well with the parts they play: Tom Hiddleston is a suit-wearing Dr Laing, Luke Evans is threatening and egocentric as Richard Wilder and Jeremy Irons plays Anthony Royal as a smoothie with painful sensitivity. Love/sexual interest is provided by Keeley Hawes and Sienna Miller, both in under-written roles.

None of these parts has the capacity to introduce any thematic material that would extend the shapelessness of the novel. The film, in common with the originating book, is about male needs, priorities and ego.

Like nearly all of Ballard's novels and the films based on them, *High-Rise* is a unique experience, both to read and to view.

* * *

The violence enshrined in the urban trilogy is at least partly an expression of the turbulent dichotomy of Ballard's own life. The split identity he carried was its own generative impulse, and if his relationships with women were frequently volatile, the 1970s coincided equally with some of Ballard's most creative and mutually productive friendships with men. We have already met one of them – or at least his fictional avatar. Dr Robert Vaughan, the 'hoodlum scientist' at the wheel of *Crash*, was based at least in part on a real scientist, though his degree was in psychology rather than medicine, and so far as we can know he did not harbour any secret fantasies about dying in a head-on collision with Elizabeth Taylor.

Ballard first met Christopher Evans in the spring of 1967. 'I remember talking to Chris Evans at some kind of a lunch place (probably a pub) on the corner of Portobello Road and Westbourne Grove,' Charles Platt recalled. 'Evans had met Mike Moorcock earlier that day at Mike's house. I don't remember who else was there, but when we first met Christopher Evans I remember afterward, everyone unanimously agreed that we had to introduce him to Jimmy.'[255]

The two hit it off more or less immediately, and it was not long before Evans took Ballard to see his workspace at the National Physical

Laboratory in Teddington. Ballard was especially curious about the large quantities of printed material Evans had in his office – magazines, scientific papers, advertising brochures for new products – and Evans began to send him weekly consignments of what Ballard came to refer to as 'the contents of his waste-paper basket'. Ballard was energized by this 'invisible literature', not only as a source of ideas but as a source of language. Ballard did not study the material in exhaustive detail; what he wanted was to gain a general sense of what was currently going on in science, the direction of thinking and imagining at the cutting edge.

'When they were together there was such excitement, there was such rapport between them,' Fay Ballard remembers. 'Chris would turn up in his leathers and his souped-up Mini. He was glamorous and handsome, warm, extrovert, friendly, a bit like a hurricane arriving. He and Daddy were always thrilled to see each other. Daddy would climb into the car and they'd shoot off to the pub, nought to fifty in the space of seconds. They would talk for hours. Daddy would return full of energy, full of beans from the conversation they'd had. Watching them together, you could see their friendship was a rare thing, a real coming-together of similar minds.'

Christopher Riche Evans was born in Aberdyfi, Gwynedd on 29 May 1931. He spent his childhood in Wales, a fact that would for Ballard almost certainly have carried echoes of Mary. Like Ballard, Evans spent two years in the RAF, not because he had any intention of following a military career but because he wanted to fly aeroplanes. He left the RAF in 1952, taking up work as a science journalist on various publications, though significantly and unlike Ballard, he remained a keen pilot, noting his touchdowns at rural airfields in an annual diary. In 1957, Evans began his studies at UCL, gaining his degree in psychology in 1960.

A year's fellowship at Duke University in North Carolina offered him the opportunity to further his interest in parapsychology – the study of so-called psi phenomena such as telepathy and telekinesis – working under the botanist J. B. Rhine, who had founded the discipline. While there, Evans met fellow parapsychology enthusiast Nancy Fullmer; the couple would go on to marry and have two children together, Sam and Victoria. On his return from America, Evans furthered his studies at the Physics Laboratory, University of Reading, where he worked on eye movements under the tutelage of Professor R. Ditchburn, eventually completing his PhD. It was then that he landed a job at the National Physical Laboratory, where Barnes Wallis had tested and perfected the 'bouncing bomb' used in the Dambusters raids, and where Evans went on to become Chief Scientific Officer.

A writer himself, Evans was keenly interested in science fiction and the literature of the uncanny, the kind of writing that could shed a light on the inner workings of the human mind. He edited two anthologies of science fiction and horror stories – *Mind in Chains* and *Mind at Bay*, which included older ghost stories by M. R. James and May Sinclair alongside contemporary work by John Sladek, Brian Aldiss and Ballard himself – and wrote *Landscapes of the Night*, an exploration of the nature and meaning of dreams. His 1973 study of Scientology and other systems of mind control, *Cults of Unreason*, was widely praised. (It also happened to be a favourite book of Chris's – his copy is here beside me in my office.)

Most of all, Evans was interested in the advance of computer technology, and the ways in which artificial intelligence might change and enhance human thinking. Evans, like Ballard, was attracted most to the art and literature that embodied such ideas, that expressed change. He was naturally charismatic, often appearing on popular science programmes for TV and radio, the Brian Cox of his day.

'Chris was the first "hoodlum scientist" I had met, and he became the closest friend I have made in my life,' Ballard said. 'He raced around his laboratory in American sneakers, jeans and a denim shirt open to reveal an Iron Cross on a gold chain.... a young Olivier with a degree in computer science.'[256] Evans's love of all things American, naturally, was a point of attraction. He hung California licence plates above his desk, and 'liked nothing better than flying into Phoenix or Houston, hiring a convertible and setting off on the long drive to LA or San Francisco'.[257] As early as 1968, the two were planning a stage play based around the ideas that eventually manifested as *Crash* the novel. The play was to be presented at the ICA, and would explore the 'hidden meaning of car crashes'.[258] Eduardo Paolozzi was to make the crash test dummies. The idea was diverted into other avenues before the play was written.

Evans's own admiration for Ballard was never in doubt. In an interview for *SF Digest* in 1976, he praises Ballard for his depth of understanding of sociology and psychology which, he insists, 'is much more profound than I find in colleagues who are psychologists and sociologists'. Describing him as a close friend, he adds that he will read anything that Ballard writes. 'He's the only writer of whom I can say that. I get constant surprises from his writing and see that he's right on the nail.'[259]

Ballard and Evans appeared together on an episode of BBC2's *The Book Programme*, hosted by Robert Robinson.[260] They discuss the end of the space age, the relevance of science fiction, and Ballard's own work. The back and forth between the two of them appears natural and spontaneous, relaxed yet engaged. Evans expresses his admiration for *The Drowned World* and clearly knows Ballard's oeuvre inside out.

Moorcock and Evans didn't really get on. Moorcock thought privately that there was something fraudulent about both the man and his science, though there may well have been an element of jealousy in Moorcock's dismissal. He knew that Ballard was moving on, that his affections had shifted. There is also a good chance that certain aspects of their personalities – both charismatic, both liking an audience – were so similar as to make it difficult for them to be friends.

Ballard always insisted that in private, Evans was different from his TV persona, that he was 'quiet, thoughtful and even rather shy, a good listener and an excellent drinking companion. Some of the happiest hours of my life have been spent with him in the riverside pubs between Teddington and Shepperton.'[261]

Tragically, their friendship was to be cut short by Evans's untimely death from cancer in 1979. In August of that year he attended Seacon, the World Science Fiction Convention in Brighton, where Evans had been invited to speak about his forthcoming book and TV series, *The Mighty Micro*. He was looking very thin, but was suntanned and in good spirits. There were hopes that his health might be improving but the Brighton Worldcon turned out to be his last public engagement. Christopher Evans died on 10 October, two weeks before the first broadcast of his new TV series. The suddenness of his passing at the age of just forty-eight was a profound shock to everyone around him.

Chris Evans inspired a second fictional self after his death. In *The Kindness of Women*, Ballard describes the young Cambridge academic

Dick Sutherland, 'the rising star of the Psychology department', as being 'more like a film actor than a Cambridge don ... He wore basketball sneakers, tartan shirt and jeans, clothes only seen in Cambridge on off-duty American servicemen.'[262] When Sutherland learns he has terminal cancer, he becomes determined to make one last TV programme, a sequence of films centred upon his own approaching death.

'Do I walk around all day with a feeling of terror, like a victim in a horror film?' Sutherland says to camera. 'Surprisingly, the answer is no. If anything, I feel cool and detached, as if all this is happening to someone else. The brain seems to have developed a way of standing back from itself, like a locomotive uncoupling the carriages behind it. To tell the truth, the biggest problem faced by the dying is how other people feel, especially their friends. There's a real sense in which the dying have to die twice, once for themselves and once for their friends.'[263]

As he drives home from the TV studio, Jim finds himself reflecting that 'Dick had many acquaintances but virtually no close friends apart from myself.'[264] Dick Sutherland's final weeks are presented with great tenderness and in unsparing detail, passages that are all the more poignant for the real experience of friendship and mortality that lies behind them.

Chris Evans's own final TV project, a six-part series exploring the development and potential of computer intelligence, aired its first episode on Monday 29 October 1979, the broadcast having been delayed for over a month due to a technicians' strike at ITV. *The Mighty Micro*'s opening titles show a sequence of images that form a visual shorthand for advancing technology. The colours – over-exposed, leached-out – are the shallow greens and oranges of Polaroid photographs.

In his opening voiceover, Evans describes how humans have risen to rule the planet via the development of tools and machines: a series of photographs offer a more detailed exposition of the opening credits, ending in an image of the then newly-constructed World Trade Center, now freighted with meaning that would have been absent when the programme was made. Evans predicts that we will use computers to increase the power of our brains as we once used machines to amplify the power of our muscles.

As the camera finally zooms in on Evans, we see a skinny, tautly alert man, with dark hair, thick dark eyebrows that meet in the middle and intense, deep-set dark eyes. He is at ease in front of the camera, his voice gentle and slightly diffident, but you can sense beneath his seventies-orange, open-necked shirt and easy manner the tightly wound energy of a coiled spring. In the intensity of his focus and slight edginess you can, if you are looking for it, definitely catch a glimpse of Robert Vaughan.

The friendship between Ballard and Evans was important to both of them because their interests overlapped to a remarkable degree – that particular combination of psychology and hard science, literature and technology. That they were part of different disciplines and to an extent different worlds was for Ballard a distinct advantage, providing the distance he needed in order to be frank and open.

Ballard said on numerous occasions how difficult he found the society of other novelists, that he actively avoided their company. The reason he gave was the stuffiness of the British literary establishment, though there was almost bound to have been an element of rivalry, a dislike of having others in his own creative space. He preferred the company of visual artists, sculptors, film makers, people who conceptualized – as Evans so successfully did.

With his attractive personality, his love of fast cars and piloting skills, his ease in front of the camera, Evans symbolized also a kind of wish fulfilment for Ballard, the epitome of the dashing man of action he felt that he himself could never be.

The sense of identification Ballard always found with visual artists drew him naturally to Eduardo Paolozzi, and the thirty-year friendship that grew out of their first meeting was a source of inspiration to them both. Ballard had been fascinated by Paolozzi's work since first seeing his 'nuclear man' installation at the Whitechapel in 1956. He continued to follow his career through subsequent exhibitions at the ICA, and having read about Paolozzi's interest in the art of the American pulp magazines, suggested to Michael Moorcock that they commission him to design artwork for *New Worlds*.

Ballard made contact with Paolozzi, who invited him and Moorcock to visit him at his studio in Chelsea. 'We got on famously from the start,' Ballard remembers. 'His mind was light and flexible, he was a good listener and adept conversationalist with a keen and well-stocked mind.

... He was always pushing at the edges of some notion that intrigued him, exploring its possibilities before filing it away.'[265] For Ballard, Paolozzi's interest in technology, his manner of 'teasing out the visual connections between Egyptian architecture and modern refrigerator design' was a vital reflection of his own imaginative lexicon and 'closer to science fiction, in my eyes, than the tired images of spacecraft and planetary landscapes in SF magazines'.[266]

As part of a conversation with Frank Whitford for *Studio International*[267] Ballard finds parallels between his own incessant hunger for information and Paolozzi's, while Paolozzi expresses a distinctly Ballardian apprehension of reality as a stage set: 'You know, in the crowded underground train everyone's reading the *Standard* with headlines like "20,000 dead". Any of these large human disasters, Pakistan, Ireland, but Dad, Dad still comes home and Mum's still fussing because he's fifteen minutes late. And that's what I mean by the insulating against experience.'

Eduardo Paolozzi was born in Edinburgh on 7 March 1924, the eldest son of an Italian family who had first come to Britain at the turn of the century. Eduardo's parents, Rodolfo and Carmela, ran an ice-cream parlour at 12 Albert Street, Leith. As a boy, Eduardo was expected to help out in the shop after school, as his own father had before him, though in the winter when business was less intense, his father – 'a wonderful man ... a great maker'[268] – would turn his skills to constructing radio sets, a pastime that stimulated the young Paolozzi's interest in technology. Like many of the boys at his school, Paolozzi was also obsessed with collecting cigarette cards. He pasted whole albums full of them, together with other printed material – magazine illustrations and postcards – that caught his eye, an early indication of his prodigious talent.

Rodolfo was keen for his son to maintain his links with his Italian heritage, and from the age of ten, Paolozzi spent his summers in Montecassino, at a summer camp run by Mussolini's fascist party – 'specially built futuristic buildings on the Adriatic – it was every boy's dream!'[269] He grew up bilingual, slipping between languages as easily as between countries, but Paolozzi's secure and nurturing childhood within the established Italian community of Edinburgh was brought to an abrupt end in 1940, when Mussolini declared war on Britain. Winston

Churchill signed an executive order for all Italian and German men to be apprehended and interned.

Paolozzi, who was just sixteen years old at the time, spent three months incarcerated in Saughton Prison (now HMP Edinburgh) while his father, grandfather and one of his uncles were put on board a ship together with more than a thousand other Italian and German (some of whom were Jewish) internees to be deported to Canada. The *Arandora Star*, an ex-cruise liner repurposed as a POW ship, set sail from Liverpool on 2 July 1940. She was unescorted, and had not been properly registered as a civilian vessel. In the early hours of the morning she was struck by a single torpedo from a German U-boat. She sank rapidly, with several of the lifeboats damaged and unusable and many of the Italians fearful of leaving the ship.

Eight hundred and sixty-five people perished. The three Paolozzi men were among the drowned.

Paolozzi's experience of war bears marked similarities with Ballard's, most of all the sense that what was accepted as ordinary reality could be overturned and destroyed at any time. He acquired much of the same personal resilience and determination. A short but unpleasant interlude at an army training camp in Slough saw Paolozzi invalided out as 'mentally unfit', a turn of events that entirely suited his purpose, which was to study art.

He went first to the Slade, but the traditional values that still held sway there were antipathetical to his own growing interest in a more avant-garde approach. He quickly decamped to Paris, where he immediately found the sense of excitement and disruption he had been looking for. Speaking on *Desert Island Discs* in 1990, Paolozzi describes how in those immediate postwar years, Braque, Brâncuși, Léger, Giacometti were all in the telephone book.

'I just rang them up and asked if I could come and see them ... You were immediately shown into their studio as if you were an American millionaire.'[270] He felt that the general sense of postwar optimism helped him gain an entrée – he was young, British, immature but bold. 'I felt absolutely at home, because it was such an absolutely different world from this grey London. London after the war had that grey depressive feel of London before the war. Paris was the opposite – exuberant, rustic, fun-loving, sensual, everything open on Sunday ... All the bookshops were full of books on surrealism and a lot of surrealism was erotic and decadent.'[271]

In his studio on the rue Visconti, Paolozzi began the lifelong habit of gathering found objects, ready-made illustrative material, 'throwaway materials' from which 'wonderful objects' might be made. His love of Dada, of surrealism and especially of Picasso is immediately seen reflected in his groundbreaking early collage.

His life in London in the fifties and sixties quickly took on many of the attributes of Ballard's own. In 1955 he married Freda Madge Elliott, an artist and textile designer, and moved with her to the rural Essex village of Thorpe-Le-Soken. The photographer Nigel Henderson, who had been with Paolozzi in Paris and later exhibited alongside him at *This is Tomorrow*, had already relocated to Thorpe with his wife Judith, an anthropologist, and was keen for the Paolozzis to join them.

They moved into the cottage directly adjoining the Hendersons', where Freda in due course gave birth to three daughters – Louise, Anna and Emma – and quickly found herself isolated in the country à la Sylvia Plath while Paolozzi spent most of the week in London, working at his Chelsea studio. Like Ballard, he was attractive to women and liberally played the field. (When Freda finally filed for divorce in 1988, Paolozzi had the gall to express himself shocked. Freda died in 2023 at the age of ninety-eight.)

In a short BBC profile of Paolozzi from 1971[272] there is brief and unexpectedly moving footage of Paolozzi and Ballard together, wandering around a hangar-sized display of first world war weaponry and artifacts in the Imperial War Museum. They seem particularly interested in a pair of aerial bombs, the product of the German steel and armaments manufacturer Krupp. (JGB: I think they're too heavy for any aircraft of the day. EP: That's what I've felt. JGB: They're massively built. EP: Well, the bombers were getting very big by 1918, German and English.) Listening to Paolozzi talk – 'I don't think society's that geared up to completely functional life. I'm just trying to recreate that whole kind of normal twentieth-century schizophrenia.' – is so like listening to Ballard it is uncanny: the same disruptive imagination and deadpan delivery, the same ability to link unlikely images in the creation of something startling and new.

Paolozzi shared with Ballard a similar dislike of technology within his own environment, refusing to use an answering machine or a fax in much the same way as Ballard declined to own a computer. 'Eduardo and Daddy had a huge amount in common,' Fay Ballard remembers. 'They both saw themselves as observers of life in Britain.' When Fay was working at the Royal Academy in the 1980s, she came to know Paolozzi quite well. 'The three of us would go and have lunch together sometimes, and Daddy and Eduardo would spend the whole time talking about the insides of the latest Boeing jet, in real detail, as if they were both engineers.'

Harley Cokeliss, who made a film about Paolozzi for the BBC, has fond memories of a particular Chinese restaurant in South Kensington where he, Paolozzi and Ballard sometimes had dinner. 'Jim and Eduardo were very harmonious in terms of their attitude to the modern world. There was a sensibility and sensitivity between them. It's not surprising that they were friends.'

But there were differences between them also. Paolozzi loved and knew music, both jazz and classical: Stravinsky (his dearest love) and Britten alongside Lennie Niehaus and Django Reinhardt, the lightly woven, intricate neoclassicism of Poulenc and Ravel. In music as in art, he favoured strong, graphic lines as opposed to the murky impasto of Romantic orchestration, though his temperament was more volatile than Ballard's, his natural generosity often morphing into something darker. He had a tendency to take offence and to perpetuate feuds, and when he fell out with the Smithsons, the architects who had collaborated with him on the Whitechapel installation, he went round to their garden after dark and tried to dig up the sculpture he had given them. He took himself seriously and – unlike Ballard, whose graceful irony was a social equalizer as well as a deflecting shield – did not care who knew it.

More significantly, Paolozzi, whose background had been much less financially secure than Ballard's, went out of his way to cultivate and enhance his rising status within the British art establishment. He was proud to accept his knighthood when he was offered it in 1989 – Fay

Ballard suggests that he saw the honour as in some way reparative, a form of compensation for the harm that had been done to his family by the British state. He openly enjoyed his fame and financial success in a way that was alien to Ballard, and that eventually opened a distance between them.

'To what extent did Eduardo's very busy social life influence his work, possibly for the worse?' Ballard found himself asking. 'I greatly admire his early sculptures, those gaunt and eroded figures cast from machine parts who resemble the survivors from a nuclear war ... It's difficult to imagine the Paolozzi of the 1980s, who dined most evenings at the Caprice, producing those haunted and traumatized images of mankind at its most desperate ... Eventually, by the late 1980s, I had to retreat gently from this competitive circus.'[273]

By the time Ballard began gaining wider recognition with *Empire of the Sun*, Chris Evans was dead, Mike Moorcock had relocated to Texas with his third wife Linda Steele, and Eduardo Paolozzi was moving in different circles. Though his crowd of admirers and acquaintances was large and growing larger, the number of Ballard's close friends – those who inspired him creatively and with whom he had considered himself on an equal footing – was gradually shrinking. A strange incident in the summer of 1993 would reduce it still further.

On 13 August, Martin Bax, the editor of *Ambit* and Ballard's ardent supporter since the 1960s, celebrated his sixtieth birthday. His wife Judy, a head teacher and Labour councillor, had organized a dinner for him at the Chelsea Arts Club. Many of the writers and artists who had contributed to *Ambit* were in attendance, including Ballard and Paolozzi, and Ballard had made himself useful to Judy in helping to draw up the guest list.

The day after the celebrations, Ballard sent a letter to the Baxes, complaining about the behaviour of one of their sons, who had been seated at the same table as him and Claire. As to the nature of the supposed offence, the Baxes had no idea. But that was the last they heard from Ballard, who never spoke to them again.

Bax and Ballard had been close friends and associates for more than thirty years. Their shared background in medicine, their similar interest in the intersection of science and the arts, as with Chris Evans, made them natural collaborators. Ballard had been a keen advocate for Bax's own writing, describing his 1976 novel *The Hospital Ship* in a cover blurb as 'the most exciting, stimulating and brilliantly conceived book I have read since Burroughs' novels.'

In a strange twist of fate it had also transpired that Judy Bax, whose maiden name was Osborn, was the daughter of the Reverend George Osborn, the headmaster of the Lunghua camp school who had been such a positive presence in the life of the young Ballard, as well as instrumental in getting him into The Leys. Ballard would regularly take the children for Sunday lunch with Martin and Judy at their home in Highgate, where they would enjoy Judy's excellent cooking, the families taking a walk together afterwards on Hampstead Heath. 'Judy was always quite maternal towards us, she was a very warm person,' Fay Ballard remembers. 'Martin was more cerebral, more reserved than Chris Evans but highly intelligent. He and Daddy were on the phone together a lot.'

For Martin Bax, this overnight cooling of affections must have been inexplicable. It was almost as if, creatively estranged from Paolozzi and physically distanced from Moorcock, Ballard had decided to deliberately sever the remaining tie with a part of his life he wanted to leave behind.

He did form new friendships with men in later years: Iain Sinclair was one, Will Self another. Self first discovered Ballard as a young teenager in the early seventies, stumbling across his work in the science fiction section of his local library in East Finchley. 'It's hard to say how it was that I divined something different about his work at that impressionable age,' Self confided to Radio 4 in 2009. 'But when I came to reread Ballard in my late teens and early twenties, I saw that he was one of the handful of English-language writers who dared to assay the bigger picture.'[274] Self met Ballard in person for the first time in 1994, when he made the pilgrimage to Shepperton to interview him for the *Evening Standard*. 'He had read and approved of my work, and although I ventured to suggest we might meet up again, he told me, gently, that the real commerce between us was at a textual level.'[275] The two continued to correspond, but it was not until a couple of years before Ballard's death that they began meeting regularly for conversation over dinner at one of Ballard's favourite Thai restaurants. Ballard, it seems, had missed the younger writer's company and was delighted to see him again. The two were regularly in contact until the end of Ballard's life, and Self's friendship with Claire lasted until her own death in 2014. Self has regularly cited Ballard as the central influence upon his own writing. 'If I were in search of an antiheroic hero it would be him,' Self told the *Guardian* just months after Ballard's death in 2009. 'Over fifteen years I got to know this intensely private man – a little. It was difficult for me not to look to him for advice – and he showed me the respect of never providing any, save by omission, the real advice being: think for yourself.'[276]

Fay Ballard points to her father's association with the writer and philosopher John Gray as being significant also, as it was a relationship Ballard himself had initiated. Praising it as 'a deeply provocative and unsettling book', Ballard named Gray's 2002 exploration of human and animal consciousness, *Straw Dogs* as one of his books of the year in both the *Daily Telegraph* and the *New Statesman* – he later told Gray he had read it twice in one sitting. The two would lunch together at Joe Allen's, a New York-style bar and brasserie in Covent Garden, every couple of months.

Ballard was initially put in touch with Gray by Jason Cowley, the then literary editor of the *New Statesman*, after Ballard had read and enjoyed one of Gray's reviews. 'When I met Ballard for the first time, I found that he embodied everything I admired in his work,' Gray remembered. 'Unlike many others, it wasn't his dystopian vision that gripped my imagination. For me his work was lyrical, an evocation of the beauty that can be gleaned from landscapes of desolation.'[277]

Gray first read Ballard as a teenager in the 1960s. He came upon *The Drowned World*, completely by chance, in his local library. Though he had read and enjoyed the stories of H. G. Wells, he would never have described himself as a science fiction fan. 'I was drawn to *The Drowned World* initially because I liked the title,' he told me. 'I had read Richard Jefferies's *After London*, but I realised straight away that this was something very different.'

Born in 1948 in South Shields, Gray remembers his own childhood as a time of huge change. With many of Britain's cities damaged by bombs, postwar redevelopment of the urban environment tended to involve destruction on a scale not dreamed of even by the Luftwaffe. The established working-class community he grew up in was swept away, leaving many families divided, removed to vast estates and high-rise developments with few facilities and insufficient infrastructure. Alienation and social deprivation were swift to follow, a legacy that continues into the present day.

Though he had not experienced war directly as Ballard had, Gray found in Ballard's fiction a persuasive and disturbing reflection of his own environment, the sense that familiarity does not mean permanence, that known reality might be altered overnight. He was already a fan of Conrad, and found similarities there also, especially in *The Crystal World*, which he went on to read soon afterwards. For Ballard as for Conrad, the experience of a journey is as much psychological as it is physical, a means of catharsis.

'There is always a glimmer of light in Ballard's stories,' Gray insists. 'People re-emerge from the chaos and violence. Life goes on in another way.'

Gray has long believed that Ballard healed his war trauma himself through the practice of writing, transforming stark moments of ephemeral reality into lasting visions. Far more difficult to overcome was the loss of Mary, which Ballard spoke about to Gray only in the broadest outline of what had happened. He was lucky to have met Claire, who was able to accommodate his need for solitude whilst still providing the background of security and deep affection he needed to maintain his stability.

Gray confirms the view that Ballard read little fiction, and that the novels he returned to tended to be one-offs – Herman Melville's *Moby-Dick*, Anthony Burgess's novels, Lawrence Durrell's *The Alexandria Quartet* – books that do not belong to the literary mainstream but that provide glimpses of a world that has already vanished. He draws an intriguing parallel between the works of Ballard and the final novel especially of Mervyn Peake, who had also grown up in China and who, as a war artist, was one of the first outside witnesses to be confronted by the nightmare of Belsen. Peake, like Ballard, was influenced by surrealism and though his use of a multi-layered, often ornate language differs significantly from Ballard's more direct manner of expression, there are intimations of a shared sensibility.

'We did not meet often, but when we did, our conversations would always be long ones,' Gray says. 'Jim had a unique mind, a unique way of thinking and speaking. I valued and cherished our friendship and still miss it.'

Of all Ballard's works, it is the short stories that Gray returns to most often. He admires *Vermilion Sands* especially, and the loose collective of stories that deal with the twilight of space exploration. 'Memories of the Space Age' and 'The Cage of Sand', with their painterly qualities, their galleries of brilliant images, are as close to perfect as any work of fiction can be.

'My father loved those lunches with John,' Fay said. 'They were important to him. Intellectually, he and John were on the same page.'

Things were different now, nonetheless. Ballard was a well-known writer. People wanted to hear what he had to say, and the friendships he would make from now on would inevitably be affected by his literary status as well as the distance he instinctively put between himself and others. The years of energized, hours-long telephone conversations in the hallway in Shepperton were all in the past.

I met Martin Bax once. It was in the late 2000s, at the Owl Bookshop in Kentish Town, where a friend of mine was giving a reading at the launch event for the latest edition of *Ambit*. I was still living in London then, and Martin Bax was still editor of *Ambit*. Focused, energetic, engaged, he seemed as committed to the magazine as ever – and as interested in science fiction. There were plenty of people at the launch. There was the usual jockeying for position that accompanies all small press events. It was an interesting evening.

Martin Bax died in March 2024. I learned the news more or less exactly as I began working on this book. I felt so sad, that it was now too late for me to speak with him: one more link broken, another opportunity lost.

22

'THE EVENING'S ENTERTAINMENT'

This chapter is in part a personal interlude – I do not presume a special knowledge of or close friendship with J. G. Ballard, but we did meet several times and we worked together occasionally. As an independent novelist I chose to keep a professional distance from him – I was reluctant to allow there was any influence on me from his work. I rarely wrote or spoke about him and, I believe, only ever reviewed one of his novels.

However, as I approach the culmination of my own career as a novelist, and because of writing this book, I have at last paid detailed attention to what is known of Ballard's life and thought. I see and understand from a fellow writer's point of view several things about him with which I identify closely.

My interest in Ballard's writing has lasted for practically all my adult life. I discovered what he was doing soon after his first few stories were published, and from the outset I knew I had found a writer whose work spoke to me, not only for the quality of his writing and thinking but also because of some intangible extra that I did not fully grasp. I have in fact never unravelled or exactly understood the 'Ballardian' feeling that his writing uniquely induces.

I have already described how Ballard, trapped on an airbase in winter in a remote part of Canada, discovered science fiction. I learned about this with deep interest. My own experience directly mirrored his. Although I was nowhere near the RAF I too discovered American science fiction almost by chance. I was young, in my very early twenties, the same sort of age Ballard had been when he impulsively joined the Air Force.

I had to overcome the familiar prejudice against SF because it usually looked awful: the books and magazines were traditionally packaged in colourful, lurid or catchpenny artwork, predominately illustrated with spaceships, half-naked young women and bizarre alien monsters. Once past those I discovered that the actual writing inside was generally more serious or seriously intended than I had expected, that SF contained intriguing ideas and a questioning and often sceptical approach. On the whole it was written somewhat better than the packaging suggested.

Like Ballard, I did not confuse it with mainstream literary fiction but I did feel that the genre was underrated and to a large extent misunderstood. Although SF has traditionally been bracketed with other forms of commercial writing – detective stories, Westerns, romances, etc. – I knew there was a discernible difference. I became an enthusiast for it in the way adolescents often do. For a year or so I read almost nothing else.

However, after a few months of intensive reading I realized that there was some kind of heart missing. Like Ballard, I became aware of the endless belief many of the established SF writers had in the alleged wonders of technology, or the way they almost invariably came up with engineering solutions to social or political problems. They accepted as natural many subjects in which I had little interest. They described empires and kingdoms and emperors and kings (admittedly in outer space), they loved weaponry, in their stories there was an abundance of soldiers and military pilots who were heroes or at least leading figures, the writers' political assumptions were obviously different from my own ... and I was picking up an awful lot of American jargon.

I could understand and enjoy the stories they told but they did not match my outlook in the real world. I had already read all of H. G. Wells's short stories and his scientific romances, and Orwell's *Nineteen Eighty-Four*. I had also discovered a handful of good modern British writers – notably John Wyndham and Brian Aldiss – who seemed more in step with me. I liked their sense of irony, the familiarity of a British or European outlook, the way they used the English language, the interest in but slight mistrust of science and technology. Also, the packaging was subtly different: many of the book covers used surrealist or abstract designs from established artists. I began to take notice of other British writers, and shortly discovered the stories of J. G. Ballard.

He, while in Canada, had discerned for himself the attractions and shortcomings of genre science fiction. I reached a similar conclusion – but for me there was a guide. Unlike him, I had the benefit of the example of Ballard's work as a totem, a clarifying shortcut.

I was thirteen years behind him and he was already writing and publishing prolifically. Once I had read some of his *Vermilion Sands* stories, and after I had read 'The Voices of Time', 'The Waiting Grounds' and 'The Terminal Beach', I knew that never again could I take seriously the work of the leading American SF writers, such as Robert A. Heinlein or Isaac Asimov. They were interested in things that did not really concern me, except at the edges – Ballard wrote about art, memory, cinema, imagination, evolution, sex, identity, truth, the mind. Everything of his came as a stimulating reminder of the things that mattered to me, emotionally, intellectually and personally.

When Ballard wrote occasionally about his sources of inspiration he mentioned films he had watched, artwork he admired, the work of painters like Salvador Dalí, Max Ernst and Gustave Moreau. These were artists whose work I had seen but hardly appreciated. (Heinlein declared his own major influence was a magazine editor called John W. Campbell Jnr, of whom I knew even less.) I was instinctively with Ballard: the surrealists and symbolists sounded more interesting, and anyway Ballard said he liked the same French films as me. It was a clear divide, and I set out to explore it.

I was impressionable and open to new things. I learned quickly but quietly.

Ballard worked hard. From the point of view of a biographer, the latter part of his life, which is to say the many years following the death of his wife, is relatively free of external incident. He spent a great deal of time at home, writing. Once a year he and his children, and sometimes his long-term partner Claire, would rent a villa somewhere in the south of France, or in Spain or on the Aegean, and bask in the sunshine for a month. But he was otherwise not a regular traveller: he visited the USA a couple of times, he went to a film festival in Rio de Janeiro, and towards the end of his life he was taken back to Shanghai by the BBC to try to connect with the places he had known as a child. The rest of the time he stayed at home and worked hard.

He lived nearly all his life in a small semi-detached house in Shepperton, not far from the western motorways and London Heathrow Airport. A large system of reservoirs was close at hand, although because of high banking the waters would rarely be seen; the River Thames flowed by, always visible. Shepperton Film Studios were one of the biggest local employers, of technicians and extras.

Ballard's house was often described by journalists and interviewers who went there to meet him, sometimes in terms of surprise. Presumably they had expected something they might identify as the grand residence of a famous author. Instead they found a narrow driveway semi-blocked by a car parked at a lazy angle, and a 1930s house similar to dozens more built at the same time. The paint on the front door was blistered and peeling.

Inside, a sense of chaos and cheerful untidiness reigned. There were only two main rooms on the ground floor: one was a general sitting room, where there was a television and which had been for years used by the children as their play area. The family called this the Nursery. The other room, smaller and at the back, was where Ballard had a desk, typewriter, fax machine, books and piles of the sort of stationery materials you find in any office: boxes of paper, files, unsorted documents and so on. He always used a typewriter, and never tried word processing software. He did graduate to an electric typewriter, though.

Two large paintings that Ballard commissioned from the American artist, Brigid Marlin, dominated the downstairs rooms. Two aluminium palm trees, a present from Emma Tennant, half-blocked the hallway. 'A bicycle saddle, two expired telephones and a cricket ball stand on a sideboard, like a Dadaist art exhibit. Ballard negotiates his way to the dining table, all but hidden under the peeling trunk of a huge yucca plant. It appears to be dead. "It's not dead!" Ballard almost shouts. (Indeed, closer inspection reveals its furthest shoots snaking behind the net curtains in a desperate search for light.) "It's trying to escape!"'[278]

Fay Ballard said, 'Some objects have not moved for twenty years. There is still a revolting rose ornament on the stairs, a blue flipper from an old summer holiday holds a door open, a peeled orange on the mantelpiece in the nursery has been there for at least fifteen years.'[279] Ballard himself said, 'It's still there – and it isn't a peeled orange, it's a lemon that's all dried up. I just never saw any point in moving it and then it became quite a nice ornament. I'm all for leaving things untouched and unmoved for fifteen years.'[280]

In the J. G. Ballard papers, archived in the British Library in London, there are several examples of his working methods in the shape of early drafts. Not all his novels are included, but there are enough papers for a logical reconstruction to be possible of how in general he must have worked; he was anyway willing to describe his methods to interviewers. They are important to know about, because in terms of literary craft they are fairly unusual.

Essentially a writer in the narrative mode, in almost every case Ballard began his work with a plot synopsis. He said:

Whether I'm writing a novel or a short story, I always write a synopsis. In the case of a short story it'll be about a page long; in the case of a novel about twenty-five pages. And I try to give it the shape and flavour of the final short story or novel. If I'm satisfied with that, I'll then go ahead and write it. If I'm not satisfied with it, if it doesn't work for me as a story, as the sort of story you would tell somebody sitting next to you in an aircraft, there's something wrong with it. So that's the first stage, and then I write the short story or the novel.[281]

He also said, 'The detailed synopsis for a novel will sometimes be anything up to thirty thousand words in length. It's just me working out my story and my cast. I once did one for a book called *The Unlimited Dream Company*, where the synopsis was longer than the book.'[282] The papers of this particular novel have been lodged at the Harry Ransom Humanities Research Center, University of Texas at Austin. It comprises three hundred and five pages of 'composite typewritten and handwritten manuscript with extensive changes and additions', and he had commenced writing it in May 1976.

Ballard followed the synopsis by writing a first draft: 'I try to write about one thousand words a day in longhand and then edit it very carefully later before I type it out. I have been known to stop in the middle of a sentence sometimes when I've reached my limit.'[283]

The 'typing out' amounts to the creation of a second draft. An author transferring a handwritten original to typescript will never slavishly copy: amendments, improvements and deletions will almost inevitably occur during the process. The result will be a sequentially typewritten improvement on the longhand draft, but in most cases it still could not be read as a book.

A final typescript, ready for submission to the publisher, would then be prepared, meaning the whole book would be typed again, using the second draft as the basis. More minor adjustments would inevitably take place.

In these days when writers almost universally use word processors, which make text endlessly manipulable, where deletions are invisible and cut-and-paste techniques allow second thoughts about emphasis and sequence of action, the temptations for authors to take a piecemeal approach to revisions is almost irresistible. Certainly, among many writers with whom I have discussed this, once they have struggled through a first draft the idea of the 'hard graft' of actually retyping everything from beginning to end (good, bad or indifferent) is unthinkable. They are saved from that by the ease of working on a computer. It can be a satisfying and rewarding process, looking at existing work on a computer monitor, and picking at it, sometimes one word at a time.

Ballard said:

> They say you can already tell the difference between a novel that is written on a word processor and a novel written on a conventional typewriter. You'll notice this particularly in commercial fiction – what you have is excellent paragraph-by-paragraph editing, grammar, structure and all the rest of it, but very loose overall chapter-by-chapter construction, and this is because you can't flip through a hundred pages on a word processor the way you can with a pile of typescript. So the detailed structure is very tight and elegant, but the overall structure is weak.[284]

Retyping and rethinking in a holistic way was Ballard's method. It offered a level of re-imagining. By retyping the entire text, the best of what had already been written could be simply typed again, but everything else would inevitably be re-examined. I believe this through-going method made his work coherent.

And it is another area of similarity between myself and Ballard. All my own early novels and stories were drafted direct on to a typewriter – I never wrote in longhand. Many mistakes and corrections occurred. I discovered that a first draft usually turned out to be an imperfect attempt at the book that was planned: there were slow passages, repetitions, patched-up plot events, long rows of xxxxx, and so on.

I have always disliked the thought of anyone seeing my first drafts, and think of them as rough-hewn. I can hardly bear to read them myself. So for a novel I would embark on a second draft, which involved beginning-to-end retyping, which at least produced a closer semblance of what I had hoped originally it might become. Again, no one was expected to see it, but it was never hard graft: I saw it as a chance to re-imagine, and incidentally to anticipate. One of the hidden advantages arose because I already knew what lay ahead in the story. This provided the opportunity to anticipate events or scenes or character revelations that were to come later, and so prepare subtly and even silently for what might seem to a reader to be a logical but unexpected development.

Then, because the second draft was still a working paper, after a period of checking and making piecemeal revisions by hand I would type out a third version, which went to the publisher. This became my normal working method.

When after the first decade and a half I transferred to writing on a computer I was at first tempted by the thought of piecemeal revisions only. I was new to computers and my fellow writers who were computer literate ahead of me were already relishing the freedom to pick endlessly at their texts. But by this time my retyping method had become habitual. I therefore continued to work on multiple drafts and redrafts, and still do. A lot of retyping, but it isn't such a bad thing to have to do. All writers of course develop their own quirky habits, but I am encouraged by the knowledge that Ballard worked in much the same way.

For Ballard, though, it was not an invariable practice, as he told Peter Linnett in February 1973: 'About ten of my short stories I've written straight on to the machine. That was the final draft. What I wrote was put in an envelope and sent to the editor. I did that with a story called "End-Game", a long short story, written in two days, straight on to the machine. No revision whatever, except for the odd word here and there. I was in the right mood, my mind was working the right way.'[285]

We know Ballard was a conscientious and hard-working writer – he wrote the whole of *The Wind from Nowhere* in two weeks, and a few years later wrote the expansion of 'The Illuminated Man' into 'Equinox' at short notice and to a tight deadline. But the care he put into his drafting work was habitual, and goes a long way towards explaining the unusually high quality of so much of his work.

Reading some of the many interviews Ballard gave, and from the autobiography he wrote shortly before he died, we know that he was a devoted family man, a view totally endorsed in adulthood by his daughters, Fay and Beatrice.

He felt keenly the fact that he had never had a loving relationship with his own parents. This had been partly caused by the circumstances: long-held middle-class social attitudes in an expatriate society that expected and valued them, Chinese servants wordlessly replacing the roles of father and mother, a series of White Russian governesses, then the years of too-close confinement in a cramped room in the Japanese camp – but mostly he blamed himself. He said, 'I know how much physical affection is the cement that holds a life together in later years. My own father was a physically affectionate man, but in my adolescence I won't say I had a very close relationship, and in my late teens we actually fell out.'[286] Later he said, 'By the time I saw my father [when James senior returned belatedly from China] it was the early fifties and I'd made a lot of important decisions in my life. Coping with England for a start. I didn't have any help from him there. When I saw him in the 1950s it was too late. I'd made all these decisions – to become a doctor or whatever – and as soon as I left school I knew I wanted to become a writer. These are decisions I never talked over with him.'[287]

In compensation he later built his working life around the needs of his children.

Bea described a typical day:

> Daddy would wake us up, or if we were up before him he'd make us turn off the TV and get dressed. After breakfast he would drive us to school. He went home and started work more or less straight away – we never saw this but I know he would pour himself a glass of scotch, which he sipped while working. He broke off for lunch, which he ate standing up – usually paté on toast or a sandwich. Then it was time to take Polly the Golden Retriever for a walk. When he was back, he poured another scotch and worked through until it was time for us to be picked up and brought home from school. If he was slightly drunk we never noticed: he was always the same to us. We would help him make dinner, which we usually ate sitting down with the television on.[288]

Bea also said:

> I remember when we were children growing up in Shepperton our excitement the day that our first colour television set arrived. It was as if we were stepping into a whole new world. No more black and white! Everything seemed different, more real. My father was particularly excited by the US space program, and I remember watching with him the Apollo rocket launches from Cape Canaveral. It was deeply exciting to see these events beamed live into our living room.[289]

Ballard became a self-confessed television junkie, at least during the years in which he was bringing up the children alone. He said:

> My kids loved *Doctor Who*, and because of that I liked it too when I watched it with them. I also had a soft spot for *Blake's 7*. It wasn't quite camp, but it was almost on the way to being camp. I can't remember what it was, but there was a strange sort of space station that looked like a nightclub marooned on a beach. I thought it was rather good in its way.[290]

He added, though, 'I think the best things on British TV are American programmes – like *Kojak*, *The Rockford Files*, *The Streets of San Francisco*,

Hill Street Blues, Hawaii Five-0.' It was pointed out to him that writing a book like *Hello America* would require input from actually being in the USA and travelling around to meet people. 'No,' Ballard said. 'I got that from *Kojak* and *Vegas* and *The Rockford Files*! If you watch those with the sound turned down you can pick up an enormous amount of information, because *Vegas* was certainly filmed in Las Vegas. And I take it *The Rockford Files* was filmed in Los Angeles.'[291]

'Television does my travelling for me,' he said in 1987. The coming of satellite and cable TV was something that fascinated him:

> It's going to be a problem, because television produced a set of sustaining myths which kept this nation going. I think there will be a kind of inward collapse. But that's when things might start to get interesting. It's quite possible that deregulation of the airwaves will lead to a deregulation of the imagination.[292] It's here in Britain that television is a dangerous medium. A large number of the ills that beset British life can be laid at the door of television – the vast repertory of myths and national delusions that it creates.[293]

A brief note about most of the chapter headings I have used in this present book. They have of course been chosen to represent in summary, or indirectly, or in reflection, the content of the chapter. But they have another purpose too.

Chapter headings are only briefly noticed by most readers – if we see them it is usually before we read the actual chapter, and in most cases soon forget whatever it was that appeared at the beginning. Why then do authors make them up and put them in their books? Most modern writers seem not to: half titles appear less and less often these days, normally replaced by stolid numbering in Arabic notation (1, 2, 3, etc.) or by something like 'Part I' or 'Chapter One', and so on. Fashions in book design change – it is hardly worth mentioning.

As in many things, J. G. Ballard was slightly different and therefore what he did was, I believe, in fact worth mentioning. Practically all his novels carry chapter headings, many of them seemingly eccentric and out of key with the main text. That is why I started noticing them. The only books of his without chapter headings are *The Atrocity Exhibition* (never described as a novel on first publication, and the individual components only get labelled as 'chapters' in later editions), the novella *Running Wild* (which takes the form of a forensic diary), and notably *Crash* (unusually this novel has only numbered chapters).

Many of his chapter headings have an over-dramatic or even sensationalist quality. They seem out of key with the main text, which I always took seriously. I soon grew to like them. When opening for the first time one of his later novels I always made a pleasurable and intrigued scan of the Contents page, trying to imagine what lay ahead. Maybe that was Ballard's purpose?

In discussing some of his earlier stories and novels I said that sometimes there was a quality of adventure fiction, sitting oddly in stories of cosmic awareness such as 'The Waiting Grounds', and even in *The Drowned World*. This was an impression enhanced by Ballard's use of chapter headings.

In *The Wind from Nowhere* we find 'The Corridors of Pain', 'Death in a Bunker' and 'The Gateways of the Whirlwind'. Perhaps this is a special case, as it is easily Ballard's most commercially orientated novel. But *The Drowned World* has chapters headed 'Carnival of Alligators', 'The Man with the White Smile', 'The Pool of Thanatos', 'The Ballad of Mistah Bones' and 'The Feast of Skulls'.

The Drought has, among others, 'The Coming of the Desert', 'The Fire Sermon', 'The Drowned Aquarium' and 'The Burning Altar'. *The Crystal World* includes chapters headed 'Mulatto on the Catwalks', 'Duel with A Crocodile' and 'Saraband for Lepers'.

There are many more of like approach in *Concrete Island* and *High-Rise*. The point is not that these are misleading (in fact in most instances they are literal summaries of scenes or narrative events), but that the adopted tone and the choice of words are often discordant.

In producing this book I decided to replace the obvious, descriptive chapter headings with roughly appropriate borrowings from some of his novels. Thus, Chapter 3, which might properly be headed with something exact and uncontestable like 'Internment in Lunghua Camp', has become 'A Landscape of Airfields' from *Empire of the Sun*.

The Appendix at the end of this book includes a list of the sources of all the chapter half titles used here.

* * *

In a 1986 interview for Swedish TV with the film maker Solveig Nordlund, Ballard speaks about his anonymous life in Shepperton, how the place's appeal for him lies in its distinction of being 'nowhere'.

> I like to think of myself a bit like the surrealist painter Magritte, who led a very bourgeois life in a quiet suburb of Brussels, took his Pomeranian dog for a walk at the same time every afternoon, drank a little coffee in the local café and played a game of chess, and then went back to this very bourgeois house ... I think that's the perfect background for certain kinds of imagination.[294]

Shepperton provided a blank canvas for his surrealistic visions, and of all Ballard's novels, it is his 1979 work *The Unlimited Dream Company* that comes closest to evoking the queasily heightened strangeness of a surrealist painting. Originally to be entitled *The Stunt Pilot*, *Dream Company* – like William Golding's 1956 novel *Pincher Martin* – takes place entirely within the mind of its protagonist, who is probably dying or already dead at the start of the novel.

Blake calls himself a stunt pilot, though in fact he is an aircraft cleaner at the old London Airport. Obsessed with the concept of man-powered flight, he finds himself stealing a Cessna and shortly afterwards crash-landing, like some home-grown Icarus, in the Thames at Shepperton. The marvellously uncanny book jacket created for Cape by Bill Botten precisely depicts the vision Blake sees – or believes he sees – as he fights free of his burning aircraft and surfaces from the water.

What follows can only be described as a visual artwork conveyed through the unlikely medium of the written word. Though the narrative is broadly sequential, *Dream Company* is in its own way as experimental as *The Atrocity Exhibition*. In an interview for the science fiction quarterly *Vector* to tie in with the novel's publication, Ballard further expands upon his intimate creative relationship with surrealist painting, repeating his frequent assertion that he wished he had been a painter instead of a writer. 'That was my real ambition for many years ... I sometimes think that my entire output as a writer has been the substitute work of a frustrated painter, and that if I could be given the gift of technical facility I'd stop writing. That probably isn't true, but I do still feel that my imagination would express itself much more directly, more easily, through visual imagery than prose narrative.'²⁹⁵

It is a measure of how seriously Ballard took the fantastical flights of *Dream Company* that he referred to it as an encoded autobiography. 'If for flying you substitute writing fiction, or using the imagination, the book has all the elements.'²⁹⁶ Though he claims there are 'no correspondences' between himself and Blake, there are in fact many. Disowned by his successful father, Blake finds himself thrown out of medical school and embarking on 'an erratic and increasingly steep slalom' of short-lived and unsuitable jobs, 'a messiah as yet without a message who would one day assemble a unique identity out of this defective jigsaw'.²⁹⁷

It has been suggested that Ballard's initial inspiration for *Dream Company* was drawn from William Blake's 1810 phantasmagorical poetic odyssey *Milton*. Ballard would neither confirm nor deny this, and though it is at least conceivable that the novel's plot, such as it is, was taken from Blake's epic poem, there is no strong evidence that Ballard ever read the work. The protagonist's name notwithstanding, what is not in doubt is that *Dream Company* draws as much from Ballard's own imaginative lexicon as from William Blake's. The vision of Shepperton transformed into 'some corner of a forgotten Amazon city'²⁹⁸ with rainforest vegetation and flocks of exotic birds is an instant reminder of the primeval landscapes of *The Drowned World*, just as the recently abandoned shopping malls and petrol stations, the overgrown gardens pointlessly tended by still-spinning water sprinklers might be a direct quotation from *The Drought*.

The length and detail of Ballard's synopsis for the novel, as well as the unusually long gap between books suggest that Ballard found the material difficult to mould into shape. He later referred to *Dream Company* as 'imaginatively exhausting, a real set of balancing acts'.²⁹⁹ Yet even as the novel arrived in bookshops, Ballard was already beginning to think about what would come next.

The first public notice of the novel that is widely considered the most significant milestone in Ballard's writing life came in the latter quarter of 1982. 'No hint as to what it's about yet,' wrote David Pringle in his J. G. Ballard newsletter, 'since he does not like to discuss work in progress.'³⁰⁰

Early in 1983, the science fiction writer Colin Greenland published *The Entropy Exhibition*, the first book-length study of the British New Wave and adapted from Greenland's doctoral thesis. The author's foreword acknowledges Ballard as a first reader, though there is no published record of what he thought of the book. Greenland's study is heavily reliant on Michael Moorcock's account of the *New Worlds* era and insufficiently distanced from its academic origins to provide much in the way of personal insight, which I think is a shame. Though still widely discussed and argued over in science fiction circles, the definitive account of the New Wave remains to be written. I was forever encouraging Chris to take on the challenge, but he refused to be drawn.

In the aftermath of the Falklands conflict, Margaret Thatcher's Conservative government was returned to power on a substantial majority. Meanwhile, many thousands of protestors marched on the US air base at Greenham Common, where American cruise missiles were scheduled to be stationed later in the year – not exactly in Ballard's back garden, but still uncomfortably close.[301]

In the June of 1983, David Pringle was able to report that Ballard's next novel would be a semi-autobiographical novel set in the Shanghai of Ballard's own childhood. 'It is not SF, nor even a fantasy, though he says the events have been heightened somewhat.'[302] Pringle added that the novel was provisionally scheduled for publication in 1984.

Ballard would later describe to Pringle how 'writing about and describing the camp in detail brought back other memories that I'd completely forgotten: the terrible smell of the place, and the heat and terrific humidity in the summer and the fierce cold in the winter, all those things I'd completely forgotten, the texture of everyday life in the camp. The particularly awful taste of sweet potatoes – not, I may say, the golden sweet potato that Americans eat, but the grey sweet potato that was a cattle-feed in China, particularly small foul things. All that came back.'[303]

By now, news of the novel and its purported contents had begun to circle in the world of publishing. At a dinner given by the Book Marketing Council in October, the publishing director at Gollancz,

Victoria Petrie-Hay, strongly hinted to Ballard that Gollancz were interested in acquiring the book, which already had the provisional title *The Empire of the Sun*. The rights were being handled by Maggie Hanbury, marking the beginning of an association that would endure until Ballard's death.

Hanbury had originally trained as a nurse at Guy's Hospital, but soon realized she was in the wrong profession. She worked as a secretary for a firm of architects, and then as an assistant to Eva Neurath, joint founder of the art book publishers Thames & Hudson. Hanbury was later introduced to Ballard's long-time agent John Wolfers, who invited her to come and work for him. When Wolfers retired in 1982, it was Ballard who encouraged Hanbury to relaunch the agency under her own name.

'I was completely taken aback by his suggestion as the idea had never occurred to me. But gradually I came to the conclusion that I must do it,' Hanbury told me by telephone. Just a few months later, Ballard delivered the typescript of his new novel. 'I read it sitting at the kitchen table. I could feel the hairs on my forearms standing up. I knew immediately that it would be a bestseller.'

Hanbury sent the manuscript to Ballard's regular publisher, Jonathan Cape. After waiting several weeks with no response, Hanbury eventually received an offer that was roughly in line with what her client had been paid previously. At Ballard's suggestion, Hanbury then approached Gollancz. They responded swiftly with an offer that was substantially in excess of Cape's and that Ballard was delighted to accept. It was then down to Hanbury to inform Cape's head of publishing that Ballard would be leaving them.

'Tom Maschler was furious,' Hanbury remembers. 'He could be pretty scary when he didn't get his own way.' But neither Hanbury nor Ballard were in any doubt that they had done the right thing. The acquisition was officially announced in December, with the definite article dropped from the book's title and Malcolm Edwards assigned as editor. If this was a turning point in Ballard's life, so it was in Hanbury's. Little more than a year after setting up on her own, she found herself seated across from Ballard at one of the top tables at the Booker Prize dinner in the Old Library at London's Guildhall. 'I bought a knee-length, sequinned cocktail coat for the occasion,' she said. 'I reckoned it was worth splashing out.'

She remembers Ballard as visionary, humorous and intellectually brilliant. 'He had beautiful manners. Working for Jim was an absolute delight.' She is especially proud to have eventually brought all of Ballard's work under one publishing roof at HarperCollins, and to have masterminded the publication of *The Complete Short Stories of J. G. Ballard* in 2001. Ballard never gave her any clues about his work in progress, and they rarely saw each other in the period between books, when he was writing. The first Hanbury would know about the contents of a new novel would be when Ballard delivered the typescript and they would have lunch. 'He only ever wanted something simple,' she says. 'Bread, cheese, salami. We would talk for an hour or so and then he would go home.'

The one time they pushed the boat out was when Steven Spielberg bought the rights to *Empire of the Sun*. 'Jim drove over to the office on Lambeth Road with a jeroboam of champagne. There was no way we could drink it all. When he left to drive home I was terribly worried, as I knew he would have been well over the limit.'

She retains a boundless admiration for *Empire of the Sun*, and a special fondness for *Miracles of Life*, which she counts among her favourites of all Ballard's works.

23

'GIVING HIMSELF TO THE SUN'

Empire of the Sun established Ballard with a worldwide reputation, outsold all his earlier novels and story collections put together, and introduced his writing to hundreds of thousands of readers who previously would have been mostly unaware of his body of work. To these people the book would represent a fresh and intriguingly written account of an important event in the second world war, one not widely publicized and only described in a few little known or poorly distributed accounts by some of the people it had happened to.

Empire of the Sun was treated as a major work, written in an expert way by an author with a long list of other books already in print. It has historical importance because of its subject matter and its literary place is that of being one of the final books to be written about the second world war by someone who lived through the events described.

Aside from the mass market there was another kind of readership keenly waiting to get hold of a copy — this was the relatively small but dedicated group of readers who had followed Ballard's career from the outset. They — or to be accurate, as I would have to include myself — *we* were impatient. We knew three general biographical facts about Ballard, not in detail but sufficiently that we anticipated the new book with immense interest.

The first was that it was an open secret that he had spent a long period of the war years in a Japanese internment camp in China. Ballard often mentioned it but without going into detail. In the postwar years it had become known that captured British, Australian and American troops, held as prisoners of war in harshly run Japanese labour camps in the Straits Settlements, Malaya and Thailand, had been treated at best neglectfully but at worst brutally and torturously. There were several books about survivors' experiences: notably those written by Russell Braddon, *The Naked Island* (1952) and *End of a Hate* (1958), and Laurens van der Post, *The Seed and the Sower* (1963). The success of the film *The Bridge on the River Kwai* (1957), based on the 1952 novel by Pierre Boulle (later the author of *Monkey Planet*, the novel upon which the *Planet of the Apes* films were based), had dramatized some of the cruelty of these camps, and for many people might represent the bulk of knowledge on the subject. These accounts described immense deprivation, lack of medical care and frequent physical beatings. We were naturally curious about J. G. Ballard's experiences – had he suffered anything similar to that?

We, his most invested readers, also realized that Ballard had a unique mind and imagination, was intellectually unpredictable and that he frequently hinted at dark experiences in his past. We assumed that at last he might reveal in this new book some of the matters that for several decades had been deep and unstated in his writing and general outlook. This was the man, after all, who had written extraordinary works like 'The Voices of Time', and *Crash* and *The Atrocity Exhibition*!

Finally, we knew that before *Empire of the Sun* he had already written a short story called 'The Dead Time', which was published in *Bananas* in 1977. (It was later included in the collection *Myths of the Near Future* in 1982, two years before *Empire* was published.) This dealt explicitly with the experience of leaving the camp at the end of the war, but left undescribed what had happened during the period of internment.

'The Dead Time' is a decidedly odd story, a first-person account by a twenty-year-old man, who is released from a Japanese prison camp near Shanghai at the end of the war. He has been locked up for three years. He sets out across the paddy fields to try to reach his parents, who had been interned in a separate camp. After several adventures, including a long drive in a Japanese military truck laden with Chinese corpses, he reaches the other camp, and although by now wounded and suffering hallucinations he is reunited with his parents.

This story provided a tantalizing glimpse into Ballard's possible past, but the hallucinatory material suggested a streak of fantasy. We had to wait for the novel to learn more.

'The Dead Time' and *Empire of the Sun* seemed at the time to be a definitive Ballard break with writing science fiction. They are not SF, and no amount of careful argument can slot them into the more narrow genre – although one certainly could argue that the narrowness of SF had become slightly wider as a consequence of Ballard's recent work. He never disputed the term 'science fiction writer' when it was used about him, sometimes in a misjudged attempt to categorize him away from the mainstream of literary writing, but he would argue that while genre SF remained restrictive on writers, the sensibility of the fantastic was a resource that was underused by most current novelists. That sensibility was to re-appear regularly in the work that followed Ballard's novels about his China experiences, but it seems odd that almost none of his later writing was recognized by the genre awards listings. He was still often referred to as 'one of the greatest SF writers of all'.

Meanwhile, let us concentrate on *Empire of the Sun*.

The novel opens on the eve of the Japanese assault on Pearl Harbor, but because of the International Date Line Shanghai is already in the morning of the next day. The protagonist is an eleven-year-old boy called Jim. (In the film he is scripted as Jim Graham, Ballard's own first two names.) The events and experiences of British expatriates in Shanghai's International Settlement are filtered through Jim's juvenile perspective. He is depicted as an intelligent, observant, energetic and resourceful boy, eager to please.

A series of adventures (and misadventures) ensue. In the chaos that follows Pearl Harbor the Japanese take control of Shanghai. Jim is separated from his parents – he believes them to have been taken by the Japanese to an internment camp. He hides from the Japanese in a series of houses abandoned by the wealthy expats from the International Settlement, surviving on scraps of leftover food. He tries to locate his parents. He teams up with two American former civilian sailors, named Basie and Frank, who are attempting to run a racket. Jim decides his only hope is to surrender to the Japanese, whom he admires for their military skills. After several failed attempts, he and the two Americans are rounded up and taken to Lunghua Camp. Here Jim at last feels safe.

This extended passage takes us to approximately halfway through the novel.

Four years pass. This passage of time is described briefly as one Jim thoroughly enjoys, sheltered from the worst effects of the war by the presence and activities of the adults: amateur theatricals, lectures, schooling and so on. This period in the camp slowly becomes impossible to maintain: food and other supplies start to dwindle.

It is now the summer of 1945 and the war appears to the internees to be coming to an end. The airfield next to the camp is regularly attacked by American aircraft, and because he is a close witness to some of the raids, Jim's admiration switches to the American pilots.

Jim has formed an alliance with a Dr Ransome, who both controls and educates Jim, but also helps him survive. The Japanese guards are still armed. The countryside around the camp is full of hazards, with bands of Japanese and Chinese soldiers roaming without restraint. Jim feels secure within the bounds of the camp, but he and many other internees are forced by the Japanese to march to Nantao. Here they are made to spend several days in a disused Olympic sports stadium, where many of the weaker people die. Jim knows several of them. The married couple, Mr and Mrs Vincent, with whom Jim had spent many months sharing a room in Lunghua Camp as substitute parents, die during the forced march. Jim witnesses the flash of the atomic bomb that destroys Nagasaki.

He manages to return to Lunghua, where Dr Ransome informs him the war is definitively over. The Americans have begun parachuting essential supplies to the camp, and Jim relishes chocolate, Spam, powdered milk and a huge range of American magazines. Later, Dr Ransome takes Jim to the camp where his parents have been interned. Reunited, the family move back into their former home in Shanghai, but soon Jim and his mother board a ship back to England. His father stays behind. Jim fears that in the future China will become resurgent and take its revenge on the West.

The first thing to say about *Empire of the Sun* is to repeat the warning Ballard himself made several times: that the book is only semi-autobiographical and that details have been changed and many other elements of the story invented. It is not therefore a reliable account of what 'really' happened.

In particular, Ballard found during the writing of the early part of the book that the presence of the young Jim's parents made the narrative flow difficult to maintain. He said the book felt 'wrong': the boy who grew up to become the writer J. G. Ballard was essentially alone in the camp.[304] He therefore decided that the protagonist would be separated from his parents for the whole period of internment. There are consistent references throughout the book of this young teenager eager to find and reunite with his parents. In reality, as later explicitly described in his autobiography *Miracles of Life*, Ballard was with his parents the whole time.

Described by several reviewers as a kind of Robert Louis Stevenson boy protagonist, Jim in the novel comes across as a frequently appealing, observant, brave, resilient and thoughtful child. His perspective, as related, is consistent: he harmlessly misunderstands many of the events or developments during the war, and often ascribes teenage motives to some of the adult characters. He assumes they have the same drives as himself. For instance, Jim develops a liking for the sweet potatoes that were a staple of the diet, and often saves up a spare one or two to offer to a friendly adult. In fact, the vegetable provided by the Japanese guards was a strong-tasting tuber normally used as animal fodder. This sort of thing gives the narrative a wistful feeling of innocence.

Further deviations from the assumed reality occur in the first half of the book – the whole of Part One, in fact. This long passage depicts public chaos in Shanghai and Jim's attempts to survive it: crowds milling, soldiers marching, roads blocked. In the real world it was different. After the attack on Pearl Harbor in December 1941, the Japanese certainly took control of Shanghai and declared the International Settlement closed, but the Ballard family continued to live in their house in Amherst Avenue. Ballard himself was attending school, and even pedalling around Shanghai on his bicycle. All expatriates had to surrender their cars, and adults had to wear red armbands with numbers on them. The cinemas were closed, there were no more gymkhanas or military tattoos or drinking sessions at the country club. Children on the way to school had to pass through checkpoints. But life remained relatively comfortable.[305]

The rounding up of expatriate males began at the end of 1942, when about three hundred and sixty of them were moved to a camp in the Haiphong Road, in the west of the city. Neither Ballard nor his father was included in this.[306] The Ballard family was finally interned in April 1943, but it was an orderly procedure. The internees had sufficient warning that they could pack personal belongings, including winter and summer clothes, school books for the children, supplies of food. Some people even arranged for their own beds to be moved to the camp ahead of them.[307]

None of this is reflected in the novel, nor in the Steven Spielberg film adaptation three years later. The impact of Pearl Harbor is depicted as creating confusion and panic in the city, young Jim borne away by events. From the point of view of a novelist this is an entirely defensible decision. Attention to correct detail and obedience to the real events of the past is optional. Ballard considered he was writing fiction, freeing himself to describe the feelings or worries he perhaps went through during the period, rather than the actual events as they happened.

As Ballard himself predicted in the weeks before publication, some of his fellow internees complained in public that the novel exaggerated the horrors of camp life. They maintained that in spite of the occasional shortage of food there was no neglect by the Japanese and the camp was largely self-governed by the internees. The BRA (British Residents' Association) was the organizing body, which makes it sound as if Lunghua modelled itself on middle-class English country towns like Dorking or Guildford. Mains electricity was supplied and drinking water was trucked in. A school was opened, there was a small hospital run by medics, a theatre space gave the opportunity of amateur dramatics, and so on.

In fact, in Ballard's novel the details of life in Lunghua are mentioned only synoptically, so the almost instant negative response (from a handful of people) tends to indicate that it was something of a sore subject, with a ready defence of some kind. From everything that is known, from other memoirs and not just Ballard's, there seems to be no secret shame to hide. No one died violently in the camp, the inmates were often cold in winter, their clothes became shabby, the food wasn't attractive and was sometimes in short supply, but no one suffered malnutrition or brutality.

Possibly, there was confusion in the minds of some of the other surviving internees, because a few of the names Ballard gave to fictitious characters were based on remembered real people: there was in fact a Dr Ranson in the camp, for instance, although nothing he did even faintly resembles the actions undertaken by his near-namesake in the book.

In September 1984, Ballard appeared before a live audience at the ICA in London. He was asked by the interviewer, Matthew Hoffman, about his naming of real or known people. He said he based Jim's experiences partly on his own, but more on those of a boy who had been a close friend of his in the camp. Bobby[308] had lived a few rooms away from the Ballard family in G Block, but he had been separated from his parents, who were trapped in North China. Bobby was in effect virtually orphaned by the war. He spent the internment in a room with a family — husband, wife and a young child, a couple named in the novel as Mr and Mrs Vincent — in circumstances rather like Jim's. So it was an amalgam of experiences but it was still basically a fiction.[309]

The negative response is a reminder that many readers seek the 'reality' behind novels. An invented story intrigues and interests them, but they continue to believe that the story must at its heart be *true*. Curiosity leads them to false assumptions about why and how a novel is written, especially one that is clearly semi-autobiographical.

If there is a fault with *Empire of the Sun* it concerns the extent and nature of the fiction Ballard created. It is a good novel in many ways: it's told well, it is always highly readable, the characters are for the most part sympathetic and believable, the events described probably do have true correlatives even if we never find out what they were, Jim the protagonist is credible, both as a child and later as an adolescent.

The book was popular and the forty years' wait for it to be written was necessary, at least for the author. What Ballard often said was that it took him twenty years to forget what had happened in the camp, followed by another twenty years working out how to remember and write about it.

Looking at Ballard's published work as a whole, especially including his short stories, it seems that in most of his fiction the power of the imagination is deployed with greater force than that of accurate journalism. He is not inaccurate, though — we know that he loved reading scientific papers and advertisements for new processes and ideas, but these inspired his vivid imagination rather than supplied him with facts or plots. Some of the dreamlike imagery he conjured is still, more than half a century after its creation, unparalleled.

Graham Greene wrote interestingly about the use of memory when writing fiction. In his autobiography *A Sort of Life* (1971) he said that the use of experience has a place in a novel, but it is an unimportant one. It can fill in a gap, provide an anecdote. He suggested that it was better for a novelist to forget – that which is forgotten becomes what Greene described as the compost of the imagination. Greene was one of the writers Ballard admired. It's possible he read this.

Empire of the Sun is excellent fiction and it deserved the success it received, but others of his novels have a more satisfactory feeling, a literary wholeness, a shape, a feeling of metaphorical purpose. Maybe if he had written *Empire* after the first twenty years of forgetting it would have been a rather different book?

The novel was popular with critics:

John Sutherland said in a long review, 'I believe that this work, which has evidently risen like a slow bruise from Ballard's childhood, will exercise a claim to be considered the best British novel of the second world war.'[310]

Allan Prior reviewed it on the day of publication. He wrote, 'This wonderfully well-written book is not a bitter novel, it is a brilliant one. It should win the Booker Prize.'[311]

Nicholas Shrimpton said, 'I have never read a novel which gave me a stronger sense of the blind helplessness of war. Its atmosphere is unforgettable.'[312]

Robert Nye said, 'A very considerable achievement, a novel of clear moral purpose and power, excellently designed and beautifully written.'[313]

Philip Howard said, 'In its expression of the heart of darkness in the human condition, experienced by a small boy, the book explores the same dark jungle as *Lord of the Flies*.'[314]

As for the Booker Prize: *Empire of the Sun* was shortlisted for the award and immediately became the bookmakers' hot favourite to win, at 6/4 on.

Ballard attended the dinner and the ceremony, which was broadcast live on Channel 4's *Book 4 Special: The Booker Prize*, presented by Melvyn Bragg. The programme also featured a pre-recorded interview with Ballard by Hermione Lee.

So clearly was Ballard's novel the leader in the shortlist that when the prize was announced it came as something of a shock. The surprise winner was Anita Brookner, a Reader in art history at the Courtauld Institute, for her fourth novel *Hotel du Lac*. The bookies had rated her a 6/1 outsider, and the day before the ceremony Ladbrokes stopped taking bets on Ballard.

The Booker judges' chairman, Professor Richard Cobb, said Brookner's novel was 'written with dry humour, minutely observed and always at a very low key'. This gave it the 'elegance and apparent simplicity of the eighteenth century'. Cobb was an historian whose life was spent exploring the French Revolution. He created a minor sensation when he announced at the prize dinner that he had read neither Joyce nor Proust.

Nearly two decades later a collection of Cobb's letters appeared: *My Dear Hugh: Letters from Richard Cobb to Hugh Trevor-Roper and others* (2011) edited by Tim Heald. Usually indiscreet and written from a position of unquestioning self-importance, one of the letters revealed a crowing delight in having had the power to influence the Booker result. 'I have managed to keep Martin Amis and Angela Carter and something-something de Terán off the shortlist and manoeuvred so that BALLARD did not get the prize to the FURY of the media, the critics and Ladbrokes. So I have done a little NEGATIVE good.'[315]

Ballard's editor Malcolm Edwards later reported that one of the judges, the Labour MP Ted Rowlands, had informed him after the dinner that he had been Ballard's only supporter on the panel.[316]

By the beginning of 1985 *Empire* was an established bestselling book in Britain, with more than 45,000 copies sold. After the temporary excitement and controversy of the Booker Prize, it had been awarded both the *Guardian* Fiction Prize and the James Tait Black Memorial Prize for Fiction. It had been published in the USA with several admiring reviews. Media interest was growing.

In October, Ballard told a long-time admirer, Peter Brigg, that he had received a phone call from Robert Shapiro, a producer at the Warner Bros film studio. Shapiro was in Shanghai with mooted director Harold Becker and the playwright Tom Stoppard, recceing locations. There was some success: they told him the Bund and Nanking Road were much as he had remembered and described them. The team had visited the Lunghua Pagoda, but so far they had been kept away from the site of the camp itself, and the airfield next to it. Ballard asked Shapiro if they were planning to film there, and he said, 'Oh, no – we will film the camp scenes in England.' Ballard said he immediately thought, 'Oh my God, Shepperton studios! My neighbours will be recruited to play the internees, the wheel will have come full circle.'[317]

In the event, *Empire of the Sun* was filmed at Elstree Studios to the north of London, and on location in Shanghai and Spain. As often happens in the build-up towards actual filming there were many changes of plan. Harold Becker dropped out and David Lean came in to direct, with Steven Spielberg as a producer for Lean. Spielberg was attracted to directing the film himself because of a personal interest in Lean's films and second world war topics in general. Lean eventually moved to another project, explaining, 'I worked on it for about a year and in the end I gave it up because I thought it was too similar to a diary. It was well written and interesting, but I gave it to Steve.' Spielberg later said, 'From the moment I read J. G. Ballard's novel I secretly wanted to direct it myself.'[318]

Tom Stoppard wrote the first draft of the screenplay, on which Ballard briefly collaborated. An uncredited script re-write occurred before Stoppard was brought back to write the shooting script.

Principal photography began in March 1987, and lasted for sixteen weeks. The filmmakers had searched across Asia in an attempt to find locations that resembled 1941 Shanghai. Failing that they entered negotiations with Shanghai Film Studios and China Film Co-Production Corporation in 1985. After a year of negotiations, permission was granted for a three-week shoot. It was the first American film shot in Shanghai since the 1940s.

Over five thousand local extras were used, some old enough to remember the Japanese occupation of Shanghai forty years earlier.

Ballard made a cameo appearance in the costume party scene at the beginning, dressed as John Bull, but did not make the final cut. He can be briefly glimpsed in the director's cut of the film.[319]

In December 1987, Ballard flew with Claire to the USA for the film's promotion, first to Los Angeles and then New York. A huge number of interviews had been arranged.

> We were picked up in this limo, sailing down Santa Monica Boulevard on the way to the Beverly Hilton Hotel, and I was looking out at this landscape and thinking this is just what I expected, it's like *The Rockford Files*. But then I thought, 'Wait a minute – there's something wrong here!' I looked up and there was a gigantic billboard about the size of two tennis courts, with *Empire of the Sun* and Steven Spielberg, and there was my name in the same size letters. I thought, 'Good God, this is the one unexpected element.' A couple of miles further along Wilshire Boulevard or Santa Monica Boulevard there was another of these things. They were all over the Beverly Hills and Hollywood skyline. I got into the hotel, switched on the TV and out came the *Empire of the Sun* commercial. Opened a newspaper – full-page advertisements for the film. It was rather like one of those Hollywood monster movies where some creature has escaped and is clambering over the rooftops of the city. In this case it was the movie based on my own book – my own book, as it were, broken loose from inside my head and scrambling over Beverly Hills![320]

The official premiere of *Empire of the Sun* took place on 8 December. The cast included Christian Bale, John Malkovich, Miranda Richardson, Nigel Havers, Joe Pantoliano, Leslie Phillips, Emily Richard and Rupert Frazer. Ballard attended the event.

> The American premiere of *Empire of the Sun* was a wonderful night, a reminder of the limits of the printed word. Sitting with the sober British contingent, surrounded by everyone from Dolly Parton to Sean Connery, I thought Spielberg's film would be drowned by the shimmer of mink and the diamond glitter. But once the curtains parted the audience was gripped. Chevy Chase, sitting next to me, seemed

to think he was watching a newsreel, crying: 'Oh, oh ...!' and leaping out of his seat as if ready to rush the screen in defence of young Bale. I was deeply moved by the film but, like every novelist, couldn't help feeling that my memories had been hijacked by someone else's. As the Battle of Britain fighter ace Douglas Bader said when introduced to the cast of *Reach for the Sky*: 'But they're actors.'[321]

After the premiere, Ballard went on a tour of the USA. He discovered that there was widespread hostility aimed at Steven Spielberg, nowhere more intense than in Los Angeles itself.

As I sat in the Beverly Hilton, a journalist asked me with genuine indignation: 'How could you allow Spielberg to film your novel?' Looking out at the countless Porsches that Steven had helped to pay for, I mumbled that he was, after all, the greatest film maker in the world. 'The most successful,' the journalist snapped with a sneer, the only time in America when I have heard anyone deride mere success.[322]

Ballard added:

I have often thought that Spielberg is the Puccini of cinema. That's the highest compliment I can pay him. There are people who feel queasy at the thought of *Madame Butterfly* or *Tosca*. I have a woman friend who won't allow me to go to Puccini operas – they are not intellectually respectable enough. But he is, nonetheless, one of the greatest composers who ever lived. You can say that Spielberg, like Puccini, is a little sweet to some people's taste, but what melodies, what orchestrations, what cathedrals of emotion unmatched by anyone else.[323]

Roger Ebert reviewed *Empire of the Sun* in the most positive of terms:

Spielberg's story is based on the autobiographical novel by J. G. Ballard, who lived through a similar experience as an adolescent. But if Ballard had not written his novel Spielberg might have been forced to, because the story is so close to his heart. Not only do we have the familiar

Spielberg theme of a child searching for his parents, but we also have the motif of the magic above reality – the escape mechanism into a more perfect world, a world that may be represented by visitors from another planet, or time travel, or hidden treasure. This time, it is the world of the air – and airplanes.[324]

An ex-internee named Stella Sollars, however, raised what was becoming a familiar complaint. She had been held in the camp with her family, and had launched a crusade to tell people that *Empire of the Sun* may be good drama, but it was not historically accurate.

She told the *Montreal Gazette*, 'It's a very beautiful film. It really stirs up the emotions. That's why I want people to know it really wasn't that way. I don't want everyone to run out and sell their Hondas in a backlash against the Japanese.'

Sollars said she read Ballard's book when it came out and considered it to be 'a novel loosely based on fact'. Spielberg's movie had rekindled her ire. She was twelve when she and her family were sent to Lunghua. 'We had dignity and courage,' Sollars said of the camp's residents. She went on:

> We were clean. We bathed every day, even if it was ice-cold water. Spielberg portrayed a bunch of snivelling people fighting over bad potatoes and rice. That's not true. Food was scarce. We rationed. But we didn't fight over it. He dresses the British like poverty-stricken Appalachians. We were never that dirty. We may have dressed in old clothes but most of us were prepared and packed well. We had winter clothes. We ran our own hospital in the camp with about twenty-five physicians, not just one doctor in a dirty coat. The camp was run according to the rules of the Geneva Convention. We were visited every six months by the Swiss consul, who received an accounting of all civilians, and families were not separated.

Daniel Bays, a professor of East Asian history at the University of Kansas, said Sollars' recollections seem to be historically correct, but that was not the point. 'This is clearly a work of fiction,' Bays said. 'Ballard obviously used literary devices to put his young hero in the position of observer. And, too, observations are not an objective thing.'[325]

The following March, Ballard took part in a newspaper discussion of the descriptions of camp life in the book, and also in the film. He said:

> I am fed up with this. I can't go on and on explaining that the book, and therefore the film, is semi-autobiographical. Most, and I stress most, of the events I depicted came directly from my own experiences but the film is based on a novel, therefore it uses fiction. Why won't they understand this? Let them write their own novels and films. These people resent any notion of their lives in Shanghai which might suggest that it was a place where servants were paid ten pounds a year. They have an amazingly rosy view of life in that camp. They make it sound like paradise. They are concerned that I paint an uncomplimentary picture of the British at the time. They reject any criticism of the British because by implication it is a criticism of them. The film is an imaginative recreation of the period based on my own experiences.[326]

It is also worth mentioning at this point that the experience of other British internees, confined in other camps, differed wildly from that of the Ballards and of Stella Sollars. The Kendal-Wards, Ballard's friends from Amherst Avenue, spent the final fifteen months of the war interned at the Lincoln Avenue camp, based around a former housing compound for employees of the Bank of China. The concrete buildings had been severely damaged during the 1937 battle for control of the city, and the camp ground in general was more cramped and inhospitable even than the rough ground at Lunghua. Much worse though was the treatment meted out to the internees. Speaking to the *Gloucestershire Echo* to mark the fiftieth anniversary of VJ Day,[327] Grace Kendal-Ward recalled the brutality of the camp guards, who branded her arms with a red hot poker for the 'crime' of scavenging scraps to feed her children. Food and water were perilously scarce, and the whole family witnessed violence and torture on a daily basis. Any sense of camaraderie among the camp's inmates had been largely eroded by the struggle to survive. Even fifty years later, Grace Kendal-Ward still had nightmares about the camp, as well as suffering the effects of the beriberi she contracted there.

The controversy over the facts behind *Empire of the Sun*, though, soon died down. The novel is now a recognized classic, which has entertained and informed thousands of readers around the world. The Spielberg film, popular in its day and sometimes compared with *The Bridge on the River Kwai* because of its subject matter, has less enduring qualities. Notable for an energetic and attractive performance from thirteen-year-old Christian Bale, the constant scenes of crowds, chaos and wreckage tend to draw the audience away from the essentially sympathetic and occasionally touching story of young Jim Graham, which for regular Ballard readers was probably the rationale for the whole thing.

A journalist phoned Ballard to tell him about a Spielberg plan to return to his roots and do sci-fi, but in the unlikely company of a mad cult writer. (The film was *Minority Report*, the mad cult writer Philip K. Dick.) Ballard was upbeat. 'I like the idea of someone having to investigate their own crime before it happens,' he observed acidly. 'Maybe Jack Straw should be sent a ticket.'

Ballard was vehement that Spielberg is misunderstood. 'Don't imagine that he's a suburban fantasist, he's not. He's interested in panic, fear and what it is to dream: is reality a conspiracy, are we who we think we are? Those are the same themes that you find in Dick's writing.'[328]

24

'THE GREAT AMERICAN DESERT'

In Los Angeles for the premiere of *Empire of the Sun*, Ballard had a day free. Since childhood he had always admired the biggest gas-guzzling American cars, with their chrome trim, bright paint jobs, soft suspension, hordes of options and accessories – now he wanted to drive one around for a day. He approached the Avis concession at the Beverly Hills Hilton Hotel. Finding the car he wanted was a more difficult task than he expected:

> I tried to rent a Buick but the Avis man was appalled. 'Sir, we have Porsche, we have Mercedes, we have Jag-U-R.'[329] He tried instead for a Chevrolet. 'Sir, we have Mercedes, we have BMW ...'
> 'Thanks, but I'd like a Chevvy.
> This was not their usual line of business, but of course it was the USA, where the customer is king. I got a Chevvy in the end, probably smuggled in from a blue-collar suburb, and spent the day exploring a familiar universe of palm trees, car lots and pleasant middle-class housing, a tribute to the enduring qualities of painted glue. Later, describing to my hosts an immense drive from Venice Beach to Silver Lake, I met an appalled response. 'My God! You were in the ghetto.' Bearing in mind that Beverly Hills is a tiny enclave on the rim of the vast metropolis I had criss-crossed, I wondered who was in the ghetto and who was outside it.[330]

This was in 1987, during what turned out to be Ballard's first long visit to the USA. I came across the anecdote shortly after I read his 1981 novel, *Hello America*, which I assumed then had been based on an earlier visit. His book had reminded me of a one-act play by Tom Stoppard called

New-Found-Land (1976). This was a political comedy involving two Home Office officials, one very junior, the other very senior. For some reason the junior abruptly bursts into a long and detailed soliloquy describing his recent journey across the USA – his memories consist almost entirely of a string of clichés: the Fall colours of New England, a choo-choo train to Chattanooga, the dead Western heroes buried in Boot Hill, the dustbowl of Oklahoma, and notably a glimpse of Las Vegas: 'a nightmare of acrylic lights, against a magenta sky, huge electric horseshoes, dice, roulette wheels and giant Amazons with tasselled breasts.'[331]

I did not suppose that Ballard was aware of this little-known play, but it seemed at least to respond to the same wish to satirize, or celebrate, the familiar popular symbols of America.

In fact, Ballard had passed briefly through the north-eastern United States on his way to his RAF posting in Canada, but that journey left no apparent trace on his imagination. His only source of inspiration for *Hello America* was from watching American TV shows at home.

The book had begun with a commission from an independent British publisher to write a novella for young readers, to be illustrated by the artist Jim Burns. Similar illustrated books were being commissioned from Brian Aldiss (*Brothers of the Head*, 1977) and Harry Harrison (*Planet Story*, 1979). Concerns arose about the publisher, and the book never appeared in that form. He resold it to his regular publisher Jonathan Cape, and expanded it to a regular length.

Hello America is probably Ballard's weakest novel, at least of this middle part of his career. It is not plausible in terms of character, plot or background. To accept its conceits even at a surface level is to make the reader impatient and to argue rationally if internally against what has been written. It is commendable only because it is so different from his other books, an attempt to try something new. It's sheer fantasy throughout, but it is random, erratic, inconsistent, quirky, with not even a semblance of logic.

A shipload of explorers arrive unconvincingly in the ruins of New York City, which appears to be abandoned. They then set off on a long journey to the west, already squabbling and seeking power over each other. Throughout their travels they pass by or notice or try to destroy the various assumed symbols of Americana. They encounter 'Indian tribes' with names like Xerox, Divorcees, Heinz and GM. There is a squad of robotic past presidents, armed to the teeth. One cliché follows another. Part of the journey is a madcap race through the deserts in the centre of the ruined country, a sequence which is obviously a close cousin to the events in George Miller's film *Mad Max 2* (one of Ballard's personal favourites). Eventually they arrive in Las Vegas where they encounter the president of the USA, named Charles Manson. Other cities are attacked with nuclear weapons launched by Manson, but somehow most of the irritating characters survive.

It is a tiresome book, justifiable to the modern adult reader only by the knowledge that while he was putting the book together Ballard must already have been engaging with the major effort required to write *Empire of the Sun,* which was to follow three years later.

He said of it:

> It was meant to be illustrated, so it's full of visual imagery. Sadly the publisher went bust, so I thought I'd expand it and make it into an extravaganza. It's an out-and-out entertainment, a children's book for grown-ups, but I think it makes a few points about modern America. It takes all those images that Americans have exported to the world – gangsters, Buicks, Marilyn Monroe, blue jeans, Coca-Cola, Hollywood, etc – and reconstructs America using just those images. I hope it's fun.[332]

Hello America was reviewed by Martin Amis: 'Ballard's talent is one of the most mysterious and distempered in modern English fiction – and it is by far the hardest to classify.' He described the novel at length, finding it in some respects to be 'a simple adventure story, Buchan or Henty adrift in the time machine', and concluded: 'It is futile to have expectations of Ballard: he will inevitably subvert them. All we know for certain is that the novels he will write could not be written, could not even be guessed at, by anyone else.'[333]

Writing from New York Charles Platt said:

> Re. the unfortunately titled *Hello America* (to which editors here have replied, 'Goodbye, J. G. Ballard'): I spoke to Don Hutter, editor-in-chief at Holt, Rinehart & Winston, a year or so ago about this book, and again this last summer. Don is not the sort of editor to shy away from

'controversial' material. Rather, he seemed to feel simply that the book is lightweight and lacks a first-hand understanding of what America is all about. I agree to the extent that I think it would have been better, ideally, if J. G. B. could have visited the USA. It's not that the book is factually incorrect; simply that it lacks a sense of authenticity which matters to an American audience. Americans are actually very tolerant of outsiders satirizing their culture – in fact they have invited it, over the years. But only if the outsider meets them on their own terms, which is fair enough. Personally I like the book, but I doubt it will sell here.[334]

Hello America was finally published in America in 1988 – no doubt a side-effect of the success of *Empire of the Sun*. It was reviewed by the US science fiction writer Gregory Benford:

As the most widely known representative of the British New Wave in science fiction in the 1960s, J. G. Ballard enjoyed some publishing success in the United States. In the '70s and early '80s, however, American publishers seem not to have been enthusiastic about his work, so some books of that period, such as *Hello America*, went begging. Now that novel has finally been given its first American edition, with a few amendments to update its futuristic landscape. It forcefully reminds us of Mr Ballard's middle period, when he ruthlessly used the icons of pop America for bizarre effects. Why did Mr Ballard's audience in this country fade when he turned to these interests? We seem to care a lot about what others think of us. But Mr Ballard's pictures simply bored. Perhaps we, who live inside the landscape and who invented its imagery, think it is merely amusing, not the stuff of myth. Certainly the comic-book shallowness of this novel doesn't intrigue or illuminate. Nonetheless, *Hello America* has charm if it is read as a comic book tour of imaginary landscapes.[335]

In 1994 Ballard contributed a two-page introduction to a new Vintage paperback edition of *Hello America*:

Whenever I visit the United States I often feel that the real America lies not in the streets of Manhattan and Chicago, or the farm towns of the mid-west, but in the imaginary America created by Hollywood and the media landscape. Far from being real, the sidewalks and filling stations and office blocks seem to imitate the images of themselves in countless movies and TV commercials. Even the American people one meets in hotel lobbies and department stores seem like actors in a huge televised sit-com. 'USA' might well be the title of a 24-hours-a-day virtual reality channel, broadcast into the streets and shopping malls and, perhaps, the White House itself …

* * *

Ballard's affair with Emma Tennant came to an end in the latter half of the seventies, as Tennant became more seriously infatuated with the poet Ted Hughes. It was around 1980 that Ballard met Lindsay Fulcher, a friend of Fay's.

'I have a very vivid memory of walking under an umbrella with her in the rain, and her saying she thought I'd get on very well with her father. I hadn't quite clocked who her father was, particularly. I hadn't read any of his books.'

Fulcher was born in 1951. She was brought up in a small village in rural Suffolk. 'It was very gossipy,' she says, 'and I disliked it intensely. As soon as I turned eighteen I hitchhiked to London with £5 in my pocket and took my chances.' After leaving university she became a librarian, eventually landing a job at the Museum of London, which was where she met Fay.

At seventy-three, Lindsay is still striking, her straight, shoulder-length hair parted in the middle and set off by the bold ultramarine of the top she has on. She wears black-framed spectacles and a gold cuff bracelet on her right wrist. She is clearly determined, imaginative, strongly independent.

She tells me the boyfriend she had before she met Ballard was 'a total Ballard-worshipper', which probably put her off reading him. On first meeting Ballard, she found him 'a funny sort of bloke. He had a Ford Capri, which I thought was rather vulgar.' She remembers feeling bemused and vaguely insulted, that a friend would try to set her up with her father. Fay's instincts had been correct, however. The two found they got on very well, and began seeing each other regularly.

'He wasn't interested in marriage, in having a wife. We would meet for dinner every three weeks or so. It was not a passionate love affair. For me, it was the friendship – I liked him, and I was interested in him. For him it was probably the romance. He did call me a muse at one point, but I felt uncomfortable with that. It was a civilized friendship, with sex.'

She visited the house in Shepperton only twice. Normally he would come to her in Hackney. They found many interests in common – Lewis Carroll, the surrealists, Alfred Jarry. 'I've never met anyone else like him. He was strange, unknowable, probing – always wanting to know about you, whilst keeping himself a secret.'

The love of her life, the passionate admirer of Ballard with whom she'd been at university and who she'd wanted to marry, was Orlando Mark Lobanov-Rostovsky, a Russian prince more usually known as Mark. The name takes me back instantly to the time I was at Oxford, writing about Nabokov and where displaced Russian aristocrats floated within the orbit of the department: Tolstoys, Pasternaks, Obolenskys fleeing the post-Soviet twilight of their vanished empire. The relationship did not come off. Bored with being a librarian, Lindsay left the Museum of London in the mid-to-late eighties and retrained as a journalist. She worked for various magazines, eventually and incongruously winding up at *The Lady*. 'Finally I'd come as close to being a lady as I possibly could, which wasn't very.' She stayed for seventeen years.

Fulcher also featured in the pages of *Ambit* magazine. In Issue 96, published in the spring of 1984, there is a set of photographs taken by Dan Goldstein in 1978. The images are a record of a piece of performance art by the abstract painter John Blackburn called 'The Earthworks', in which Fulcher and Blackburn alternately bury each other in a shallow grave. Fulcher is clothed in a white shroud before being covered with earth; Blackburn is buried naked, and face-down. 'I was stupid enough to agree to it, and it was very, very unpleasant. It was in March, in Kent.'

Blackburn, who died in 2022 aged 90, later revisited the photographs and made paintings from them. When I ask Lindsay if she became part of the group of writers and artists associated with *Ambit*, she says no. 'I tended to skirt around the edges. I have never liked being sucked into anybody's circle.'

Ambit 96 also contains Ballard's short fiction 'The Secret Autobiography of J. G. B******'.

Ballard and Fulcher continued to meet occasionally even after Ballard reconciled with Claire. For Ballard, the sense of risk inherent in maintaining the relationship was repaid by the pleasure he obviously found in Lindsay's company, the feeling of being young again, adventurous. The fact that she was not particularly interested in his work was probably part of the attraction. Though Ballard's taste for more esoteric entertainment was long in the past – Lindsay's suggestion that they take in a show at the famous Soho strip club Raymond's Revue was firmly dismissed – they both enjoyed evenings out at the French pub and other sixties haunts.

'Our relationship was interesting, it was amusing, it was lively, it was attractive. He would always bring a bottle of champagne, and he would always drive home in the early hours. We both liked going out to restaurants, but there were certain places he would not go, in case Claire found out.'

Eventually he stopped coming to see her because driving became too painful – Ballard was seriously ill, but did not yet know it. The final conversation Fulcher had with him was by telephone, not long after he was diagnosed with cancer. Fulcher was deeply upset by the news, but Ballard, she says, was very matter-of-fact about it. '"Well, my dear, no one lasts for ever," he said. That was the last time we spoke. I wouldn't say that I knew him very well – but maybe nobody did.'

By another strange coincidence, Fulcher was also painted by the American artist Brigid Marlin, who she had known for some years even before meeting Ballard. Marlin has depicted Fulcher as the goddess Circe, who turned Odysseus's sailors into beasts. The men, clad in striped, pyjama-like garments, many of them unshaven – are they prisoners, Holocaust survivors? – can be seen standing stiffly together in the painting's upper left. Some have already begun their metamorphosis, the pyjama stripes morphing to zebra stripes, while two gryphons – half-man, half-bird – fight with flaming torches. Tigers, dogs and swine look on. Circe herself is just a girl, and recognizably Fulcher. A plume of opiate steam rising from the bowl she carries cloaks the painting in an aura of shimmering blue.

Fulcher does not particularly care for the painting, but I rather admire it. There is a disarming innocence about this Circe, an ambivalence or lack of knowledge about the power she carries.

In 1992, Ballard would inscribe a copy of the 1970s Panther paperback edition of *Crash* with the words 'Dearest Lindsay, the one I most want to crash with! Love, Jimmy.' An appropriate inscription, given that Fulcher describes herself as a bit of a petrolhead.

'Sex and cars – the sexualization of cars – went together in the sixties. Especially if you lived in a little village, that's where you'd have your early sexual experiences, the car would become a kind of sexual arena. I had a boyfriend who had a Marque 2 cream-and-white Jaguar with red leather seats.' But funnily enough, she says, Ballard was never keen on sex in cars. 'He was too nervous! He was afraid the police would come along. You can imagine the headline – author of *Crash* found "in flagrante" in a Ford Capri in Islington. Somewhere in the East End, anyway. It was pretty rough around there back then.'

But the success or failure of a relationship is often in the timing, and when Claire unexpectedly made contact again towards the end of 1983, Ballard discovered that he was ready to pick up where they had left off. He was now over fifty. His children had all left home. The turbulent years were at an end. 'One begins to apply the principles of cost accountancy to one's social life. Do I want to drive twenty miles to make small talk at a publisher's party? Well, the answer is no – why bother, when I can go on with my work instead?'[336]

'I nearly married two other people on the rebound,' Claire said, speaking about their nine-year separation. 'For a long time we were not in touch. Then out of the blue I rang him because I had seen a car going down the road that reminded me of his. He just said, "I was waiting for you to ring" and from then on we got back together ... It just happened that little by little we melded down into a terrific contentment.'[337]

It seems significant that this steadying of the ship occurred in the months immediately after Ballard finished writing *Empire of the Sun*. It was almost twenty years since the death of Mary, and just as that crisis precipitated a period of deep unsettlement in his personal life, so his opening up about the memories of Shanghai and his reunion with Claire seem deeply psychologically linked.

Like Mary, Claire had a substantial involvement in Ballard's work. In the early, more volatile period of their relationship, Ballard used Claire –

and his attraction to her – as active inspiration for his collages, 'Advertiser's Announcements' and even in his novels. Throughout the longer, more settled period of their partnership, Claire acted to an extent as Ballard's eyes and ears on the wider world, undertaking online research and sourcing material as background for his fiction he may never have come across otherwise.

'Claire came along to readings, performances in ways Jimmy never would,' Iain Sinclair remembers. 'She was bright and driven, and prepared to take Jimmy out and about in those emerging downriver landscapes – as well as the galleries.'

In *Miracles of Life*, Ballard describes Claire as 'passionate, principled, argumentative and highly loyal ... a staunch supporter of my writing and the best friend I have had.'[338] At a dinner to celebrate their fortieth anniversary, Fay Ballard remembers how her father said that in all their years together, they had never been bored with one another.

From the time of their reunion until less than a year before Ballard's death, Ballard and Claire maintained the same pattern that had defined their relationship through the early years, with Ballard in Shepperton during the week and spending the weekends with Claire in the flat on Goldhawk Road.

'He would drive up on a Friday and even after all these years I couldn't help waiting at the window, and going out to meet his car in the street. And whenever he went back to Shepperton, we would always part as if we were leaving each other for a very long time – and then he would be back again along the Westway the week after.'[339] On those days they were not together, they would speak on the phone.

Claire would have welcomed a more permanent arrangement: 'I would have loved us to live in a nice house with a nice garden and live the bourgeois dream. But Jimmy was amazingly unmaterialistic. That was one of the great and attractive things about him. The thought of going to an estate agent would really appal him.'[340] For Ballard, the solitary routine he had established for himself had become essential to his work and to his wellbeing, and Claire, who understood him better than most, acknowledged his need for independence.

Though the precarity of the arrangement must have been difficult for Claire, especially given that she probably suspected that Ballard still occasionally indulged his outside interests, there is little doubt the relationship was a defining one for both of them. Claire particularly enjoyed their summer holidays in southern Europe, when they were able to spend time alone together free of the distractions of London and in a kinder climate. In an interview for the *Observer* not long after Ballard's death, Claire describes the excitement she would always feel as they set off on their travels. 'I would always wait for him in the terminal at Heathrow. He liked me to be there first because he would worry. And seeing him arrive with his suitcase, always smiling, ready for anything, that was wonderful. Jimmy was very special in that way.'[341]

TWENTY-FIVE

'THE THIRD NILE'

The years leading up to what many would read as Ballard's return to the apocalyptic mindset of his early disaster novels were characterized by disasters in the real world, both at home and abroad: street riots in Brixton, Toxteth and Tottenham, the murder of PC Keith Blakelock, the now notorious TV advertising campaign warning against HIV, the explosion, soon after take-off, of the space shuttle *Challenger*, the meltdown at the Chernobyl nuclear reactor and the bombing of Libya by American warplanes stationed in Britain. On this latter, Ballard was typically provocative.

'My reaction to Libya was *three cheers*,' he said in a 1987 interview with the performance artist Mark Pauline. 'I'm all for bombing Gaddafi. But I was practically alone – Thatcher and I are the only two people who supported the action! The British reaction, on the whole, was hostile, and I thought this was deplorable and showed the country in its weakest light.'[342]

As with his earlier comments about cruise missiles it is difficult to gauge what he really believed. Ballard tended to see politics as either spectacle or material and frequently both – Thatcher herself might easily have been a character from one of his own novels, and indeed was to become one, albeit in disguise. While Britain struggled with the evolving social and political reality of the 1980s, Ballard was experiencing the increased visibility and financial rewards that come with having written a bestseller. He now had money he could spend, if he wanted to, and in the summer of 1986 he met with the American artist Brigid Marlin and commissioned her to recreate two lost paintings by his favourite surrealist artist Paul Delvaux.

Ballard had first come across Marlin's work some years earlier, when he happened to see a reproduction of one of her paintings in a magazine. 'The sense of a clearly realized poetic universe, in which every detail, however modest, was accorded equal attention, was what most gripped my imagination.'[343] Ballard wrote Marlin a letter of appreciation, and the two eventually connected in person.

Delvaux's *The Violation* and *The Mirror* had both been destroyed in the London Blitz in 1940. Marlin recreated them using black-and-white pre-war reproductions. Ballard was delighted with the results, which were duly installed in Ballard's study in Shepperton. Frequently remarked on by journalists, they dominated and in some sense defined Ballard's home environment until the end of his life. 'I think that, in a way, I've already entered the painting and gone to live with these magnificent women,'[344] Ballard told the *Independent* in 1994.

Marlin, who had no particular affection for Delvaux – she disliked the way he deadened colours by mixing them with black, as well as his habit of painting women to look like dolls – had agreed to Ballard's commission on the condition that she could afterwards paint his portrait, a work that now forms part of the contemporary collection at the National Portrait Gallery. Ballard, not at all enthused by the idea of having to remain immobile for hours in someone else's creative space, took some persuading, and Marlin, interviewed in 2010 by Andrew Bishop, suggests that the relationship that developed between them during Ballard's sittings at her studio in Hemel Hempstead was good-natured but quite combative on occasion.

'It was like trying to paint a caged animal,' Marlin remembers. 'All the time I was trying to paint him he was supposed to be sitting still. He wouldn't stay in his chair, and his mind wouldn't stay still. All the time he was sitting there and I was trying to paint, his mind was going all the time.'[345] Marlin, who had lost a son to suicide, was not enamoured by the harsher aspects of Ballard's worldview. A powerful creative personality in her own right, she described Ballard as 'full of unsorted-out complexes. He'd seen too much as a little boy, his parents gave him no direction, no feeling of anything. He escaped from this strange world we live in. He was a good father to his children, but I think he took refuge in having as many women as he could ... I think women fell like ninepins ...

He wasn't handsome – you wouldn't rush towards him because he was so beautiful or alluring. But there was a profound animal magnetism. It was like being in the presence of a temporarily tame tiger.'[346]

Though they spent many hours in each other's company while Marlin worked on the portrait, Marlin found that 'he didn't give much of himself, so it was extremely difficult to extract him. The fact was all the time I was trying to paint Ballard he was trying to write me. In other words, we were each trying to suck the other one into our own fantasy worlds. I was trying to do a surrealist one of him and he wouldn't be sucked in. At the same time he was trying to write me in one of his bloody books, and I wouldn't be sucked in. The two of us were at an impasse. It was very funny. He criticized the portrait all the time.'[347]

Ballard also questioned Marlin repeatedly about how she had learned to paint, but when she offered to give him some basic instruction, he quickly took fright, asking if she could teach him by telephone instead. Marlin tersely observed that 'Ballard would not have been a good painter because he couldn't even make himself draw an apple.' And Ballard being Ballard, he was unable to resist making a play for Marlin, an overture she rebuffed, albeit with good humour. 'Let's say he grabbed at life's pleasures greedily rather than trying to lift himself. It was one of the things we argued over. I was divorced but I wasn't going to be promiscuous. He was a naughty man. We had a few ding-dong battles, but we were friends. I liked him, after all.'[348]

Marlin likened Ballard's genius and dedication to his work with that of Stanley Kubrick, who she knew through her friendship with his wife, fellow artist Christiane Harlan. Her portrait of Ballard is a strange one, and not altogether successful. Marlin paints in tempera, which gives a refined, luminous, but untextured surface. Ballard in the picture appears younger than he should, the skin of his cheeks unlined, his mouth almost prim. In contrast with what Marlin has said about Ballard's inability to stay still, the man in the portrait appears oddly static, watchful but in an incurious way, the only clue to the restlessness of his mind the heavily corrected manuscript on the table in front of him. There is value in the portrait – the association between artist and sitter makes it interesting in and of itself – but it would have been fascinating, all the same, to see a more robust portrait commissioned, something more penetrating and more wayward. A J. G. Ballard by Tom Wood, for example, or even Maggi Hambling.

At the time of his sitting for Marlin, Ballard was already preoccupied with writing the second draft of his next book, a task he said he hoped to complete by the end of November.[349] *The Day of Creation* was among Chris's favourites of Ballard's novels, perhaps the one he had most looked forward to revisiting and writing about. Though time ran out on him in this as in so many other matters, we are lucky at least to have the review he wrote for the *New Statesman* at the time the book was published:

> One of the familiar smaller pleasures of a J. G. Ballard novel is the way in which the chapters are named, a surreal blend of fanciful Freud and boys' action/adventure stuff. For example, five consecutive chapters in *The Day of Creation* are called 'Piracy', 'Out of the Night and into the Dream', 'The Naming of New Things', 'The Helicopter Attack' and 'Escape'. Readers who discovered Ballard's work through his 1984 novel *Empire of the Sun* might have been slightly disconcerted there by the same kind of thing ('The Refrigerator in the Sky' and 'The Bandits'), but Ballard veterans usually turn to the contents page first for a quick preview of the happy and fruitful madness to come.
>
> *Empire of the Sun* was the anomaly in Mr Ballard's career.
>
> Because it had autobiographical content it seemed to reveal the source of practically everything else the author had written, but the earlier novel was of a familiar *type*, and was enjoyed by more people, probably, than had read all his other books put together. *Empire of the Sun* was a World War II novel, perhaps the last great one to be written by a participant in the war. But it was not like his other novels (which I preferred): *Crash*, *The Unlimited Dream Company* and so on. The new novel returns to this mainstream of Ballard's work.
>
> It has no plot in the conventional sense, but then Ballard novels rarely do. Plenty of events, though ... in fact, the pace of things happening hardly slackens from beginning to end. The story opens with the narrator being clubbed with a rifle barrel, and from this moment the action is thick and fast, acted out by a cast of oddly-named Ballardian henchmen: two separate bandit groups (one of them led by a General

Harare), a German television documentary filmmaker (Sanger) and his Indian associate (Mr Pal), a Japanese photographer (Miss Matsuoka), a boatload of whores (led by a widow named Nora Warrender), a child-woman called Noon who communicates by tapping her teeth. The narrator is a doctor called Mallory who works for the WHO, but the central character (arguably) is a *river* called Mallory, which comes into miraculous existence, witnessed by the doctor, named after the doctor by the TV man (the National Geographical Society register it as such), and purchased by the doctor from the police captain for a thousand of WHO's dollars ... The doctor now sets off up-river in a stolen car ferry, pursued by bandits (the police captain's Mercedes is strapped to the deck). I hope all this makes sense so far.

All of Ballard's best novels contain an obsessive quest. In this one the doctor is searching for the source of the new river, but for reasons which are not altogether clear. Certainly not to the reader, and perhaps not even to himself: sometimes Dr Mallory wishes to revive the weakening flow of water so that the desert may be irrigated, at other times he seeks to strangle it at source. Both impulses merge. The two competing guerrilla groups are in hot pursuit, the widows trail behind, the filmmaker provides a topographical commentary, the child-woman takes refuge inside the police captain's car, endlessly playing tapes of Marxist travelogues ... and from time to time a helicopter zooms in to attack. Everyone is ill, wounded, dying or insane. Every physical object, no matter whose it is or what it is being used for, is decrepit. The new river, after a few days in existence, is littered with beer coolers, air conditioners and condoms.

But for all this superficial detail, and for all the explanations and incidents, and the ceaseless narrative tone of the writing, the novel is virtually static in form. The real journey described in the book is an inward one. This is not *Heart of Darkness* at all ... *Aguirre, the Wrath of God* or *Fitzcarraldo* would be closer. Werner Herzog once described himself as someone who shouldn't be allowed to make films, presumably because he endangered other people's lives; novelists endanger only themselves, but perhaps J. G. Ballard feels the same way about himself.

He is a unique writer with a distinctive vision unmatched by any other living novelist, and in *The Day of Creation* Ballard is at the height of his powers. Like those of surrealist paintings, the images are not only appalling and sometimes beautiful, but their juxtapositions are frequently comic and are drawn with great technical skill. The book is original throughout, and induces a feeling of crazed credulity. It will undoubtedly sell as well as Empire of the Sun, but it is not at all the same kind of thing. To those of us who have been feeling psychically endangered by Mr Ballard's writing since the early 1960s, this feels like a triumphant return to form.[350]

Although Chris, like many of Ballard's earliest fans, celebrated The Day of Creation as a return to his source, Ballard himself believed the novel flowed naturally out of Empire of the Sun, from his memories of the 'huge riverine world of Shanghai', and that writing about that period in his life 'had opened a lot of interior doors and windows'.[351]

More than any other of his renegade doctors, Dr Mallory's backstory recalls Ballard's own: a childhood in Hong Kong, a failed relationship with a successful father and subsequent disenchantment with the medical establishment. The novel's images of wanton destruction, scenes in which a bursting dam leaves the surrounding landscape churned and poisoned, 'a dangerous slide of charred earth, knife-sharp debris and the still-smouldering skeins of the retention nets'[352] are a practical demonstration of reality as a stage set, immediately reducible to its grubby components, while the welters of rubbish and destroyed consumer goods that clog the riverbanks might as well be symbolic of the whole of Western civilization: corrosive, misguided and ultimately ephemeral.

And yet The Day of Creation is also awash with reminders of Ballard's earlier disaster novels: the widowed Nora Warrender with her rescued macaques and marmosets recalls coolly resilient Catherine Austin, trying desperately to save the zoo animals in The Drought. Captain Kagwa's attack helicopter reveals the shadow of Strangman's speedboat, with crocodiles, in The Drowned World, just as Mallory's quixotic journey upriver reprises that of Edward Sanders, heading inland towards the leper colony in The Crystal World.

In his not uncritical but typically insightful review for the New York Times, the science fiction writer and academic Samuel R. Delany points especially to Ballard's language, what he calls his 'stylistic signature' as being 'particularly effective for evoking the archetypal Ballardian objects: draining lakes, dried-up swimming pools, empty rivers, dusty streets, ruined machinery, beached boats, wrecked cars – or the obsessed men and women haunting them.'[353]

The idea of the River Mallory as a literal time-stream, returning the land and the people who inhabit it to a state of prehistory is familiar from *The Drowned World*, just as Dr Mallory's brute insistence on pushing northwards into the mountainous interior is a reiteration of Dr Kerans's self-annihilating journey south.

Ballard is as obsessed with inner space as ever, but there are differences. Where Ballard's earlier doctor-heroes are largely passive, observing the chaos even as they allow it to wash over them, Dr Mallory stands out as being aggressively involved in the action to the point of madness. He repeatedly refers to his conflict with the river as 'a duel'. Where Kerans, Ransom and Sanders are morally centrist, Mallory appears to be driven more by the 'hard core of misanthropy, often masked by a professional dedication to good works, that is more common among physicians than their patients realize'.[354]

The work of an older, more experienced writer, *The Day of Creation* feels much angrier about the world than the earlier disaster novels. While the pointless destruction of nascent industry by squabbling warlords is condemned for its violent upending of the lives of ordinary people, so is the clueless intrusion of Westerners into a country they do not understand. Sanger's charitable mission – his pointless delivery of aid supplies that are effectively useless – is unmasked as a licence to pursue his own obsessions and self-aggrandisement. Ballard – who makes direct reference to 'famine in Ethiopia'[355] as one of the West's stock images of African lives – would have been more finely tuned to First-World arrogance than many.

Whilst Ballard was keen to downplay the work of Joseph Conrad and in particular *Heart of Darkness* as a direct influence – 'Conrad in *Heart of Darkness* is not the least bit interested in the river. The river could be a superhighway ... Whereas the river is all-important in my novel.'[356] – he did at other times speak of the admiration he felt for both Conrad and Greene, whose writing similarly reflected their 'foreign' status in an England where neither had felt entirely at home.

Interviewed by Philip Dodd for the Radio 3 programme *Night Waves* in 2003, Ballard spoke of his attachment to Conrad in a way that directly contradicted his usual reticence: 'I admire him enormously and always have done. I mean, there's something about that almost narcotic prose, those great rhythms that flow like a tide, and his higher romanticism, and the sense, of course, of dark forces below the surface exerting a tremendous pull, so that the world of reason – of some late, high Edwardian world of reason – is constantly being threatened by this sort of madness just below the surface. You know, it got me straight away.'[357]

The Day of Creation is arguably the closest Ballard ever came to writing a love story. The approach is far from conventional, and this would not be a Ballard novel without some element of moral controversy. Though his beloved, the child-woman Noon, is just twelve years of age, Mallory is at pains to justify his attraction to her by portraying her as age-less, or even age-fluid, a tributary of the Mallory itself.

'Unlike the others, Sanger and Captain Kagwa and Nora Warrender, she accepted that the river and I were one,' Mallory insists. 'I knew now why I liked her to bathe naked in the river, to immerse herself in that larger dream that sustained our journey.'[358] Mallory finds himself hypnotized by 'the sleek, swollen surface of the river, like the fleshy body of a sleeping woman'.[359] The novel's final chapter, entitled 'Memory and Desire', ends with Mallory 'waiting for a strong-shouldered young woman, with a caustic eye, walking along the drained bed of the Mallory with a familiar jaunty stride'.[360] Lost to the world of his past, Mallory's dreams are of the river, and the girl who is its spirit.

Though Ballard's many fans within the science fiction community rejoiced in what they saw as Ballard's return to the genre, *The Day of Creation*, for all its heightened atmosphere, is a novel that contains no speculative elements and that has no science fictional rationale. In this it differs radically from the early disaster novels, though as the story is told with an identical sensibility – what might be called hallucinatory realism – the fans either did not notice, or did not care.

In the autumn of 1984, the British science fiction magazine *Interzone* had published a new story by Ballard entitled 'The Object of the Attack'. The story purports to be an extract from the 'forensic diaries' of a

Dr Richard Greville, Chief Psychiatric Adviser to the Home Office, who is involved with examining the case of a convicted terrorist.

Some five years before the story opens, Matthew Young strapped two dozen sticks of gelignite to his chest before launching himself in a hang glider upon Windsor Castle. The glider becomes tangled in the trees before hitting its target, but the would-be assassin has been the subject of official consternation and public outrage ever since. Now held in the Home Office Special Custody Unit at Daventry, Young's motives for the failed suicide bombing are still unclear. It is Greville's task to get through to Young, to determine, if he can, the object of the attack.

Greville forms a strange and unlikely bond with Young, whom he calls 'the Boy', through the visionary art of Samuel Palmer, the nineteenth-century English landscape painter whose ecstatic interpretations of pastoral landscapes are held by many to embody the idea of God in nature. Young, who has been heard repeating the Islamic mantra 'Allahu akbar', believes himself to be in service of the divine, but Greville is astounded to discover that his intended target was not Ronald Reagan, Princess Diana or even the Queen – all present at Windsor Castle at the time – but Colonel Thomas Jefferson Stamford (his name most likely borrowed from Thomas Stamford Raffles, the governor of the Dutch East Indies who secured British control over Singapore in 1819) a former Apollo astronaut who later becomes the founder of the 'first space-based religion':

> Without thinking, I drew the last photograph from the dossier: Colonel Stamford in his white space suit floating free above a space craft during an orbital flight.
>
> The chanting stopped. I heard Young's heels strike the metal legs of his chair as he drew back involuntarily ... As his head hammered the warders' feet I realized that he had been chanting not 'Allahu akbar' but 'Astro-naut ...'[361]

'Who better than a pioneer aeronaut to kill a pioneer astronaut, to turn the clock of space exploration back to zero?'[362] Greville concludes. 'The Object of the Attack' channels much of the background hum of current news events: the IRA mainland bombing campaign (uncannily, their closest attempt upon the life of Margaret Thatcher took place in Brighton more or less at the same time the story was published), the 'Star Wars' strategic defence initiative, the mass rallies held by US evangelist Billy Graham in British cities. It reiterates also Ballard's by-now-familiar disenchantment with the manned space program and with the idea of space exploration in general.

'Will NASA one day evolve into a religious organization,' Greville wonders as more former astronauts rush to join Stamford's movement. It is telling that the doctor does not report the escaped Young's whereabouts to the police, and thus enables his second assassination attempt upon 'the Astro-Messiah'.

'The Object of the Attack' seems likely to have drawn also on more personal material. In an interview with Jon Savage for the San Francisco-published punk paper *Search & Destroy,* Ballard had spoken about his son Jim junior's conversion to Christianity and how this had surprised him:

> He was brought up in a (say, agnostic) humane, intelligent and loving home atmosphere. The first thing he did when he went to Warwick University three years ago was join a Christian Union – he became a devout Christian! At Warwick, and at most universities I think these days, the largest student society now is the CU I noticed that my son ... has also become, although he's a very engaging, pleasant character, he's become surprisingly dogmatic and moralistic.[363]

He went on to tell V. Vale in 1982 how Jim junior had come to regard his degree in History as 'a complete waste of time ... a terrible error'. Ballard describes how after leaving university, Jim junior became unemployed for three years before taking a six-month course in computer programming and finding a job with a software company. It is clear that Ballard is unimpressed by the choices his son has made, by his aspiration to what Ballard calls 'the bourgeois life ... a house in the suburbs and a BMW and a boat in the drive. His soul is carpeted wall-to-wall with the best Acro-Pad. It's a terrible prospect!'[364]

According to Beatrice, father and son were particularly close during Jim junior's teenage years. On the many evenings when Fay and Bea were out in London with friends or boyfriends, the two Jims would often stay at home, cooking a meal together and playing chess. Jim junior loved making model aircraft – his bedroom ceiling swarmed with dozens of perfectly executed Airfix construction kits – and would enthusiastically discuss engineering, history and other mutual interests with his father.

It was only after Jim junior left home for university that a distancing occurred. He began to reject the family and in particular his father, who he would harangue in unpleasant letters and late-night phone calls, the latter often fuelled by excessive alcohol consumption. Ballard tried talking with him and did his best to find common ground but the younger Ballard remained hostile and the two were still not fully reconciled by the time of Ballard's death.

Fay Ballard describes her adult brother as 'intellectually bright, fascinated by current affairs, and very informed, someone who could have a conversation about the end of liberal democracy as much as the industrial revolution'. Jim junior, who during his working life was employed by the Birmingham branch of the US tech firm Kalamazoo, writing software for Ford, maintains his interest in history and is a keen photographer. He has a lively sense of humour, and enjoys a walk along the Grand Union Canal, a drink in the local pub with friends.

'He would usually come home for Christmas,' Fay said. 'And he would make occasional visits to London during the year. Daddy was always pleased to see him when he did.'

The death of Mary aside, Ballard's estrangement from his son seems likely to have been one of the greatest sadnesses of his life. It is possible that Jim junior, who was almost nine years old when his mother died and whose memories of her would have been stronger and more detailed than those of his sisters, resented the silence around the subject of Mary and never fully processed his loss. He formed a strong bond with Mary's sisters, Peggy and Betty. With the onset of adolescence, it would have been easy and even natural for his anger and grief to become focused around his father, as indeed Ballard's own frustration and unhappiness in the years immediately after the war became linked with his emotional distancing from James senior.

'The Object of the Attack' lays bare Ballard's concerns about the disillusionment of youth and where it might lead, ideas that would soon resurface in *Running Wild*, published by Hutchinson as one of a series of original novellas in November 1988. Ballard wrote the story between publicity trips to the USA in the spring of the same year. The work sees the return of Dr Richard Greville, who on this occasion has been called to the scene of a mass murder and assumed kidnapping at an exclusive gated development, Pangbourne Village. Pangbourne Village is a law unto itself, an enclave for high-earning lawyers, stockbrokers, businessmen and, of course, doctors and architects.

In spite of being heavily protected by surveillance cameras and security guards, all the homeowners as well as any staff who were on the premises at the time – some thirty-two adults in all – have been found murdered. All lines of communication to the outside world were severed shortly before the killings. By examining what remains of the security footage, the police have concluded that the murders all took place within the same ten-minute window. All thirteen children of the various households have disappeared.

It does not take Greville and his police sidekick Sergeant Payne long to work out that the children themselves are the culprits. In essence, *Running Wild* is a Ballardian take on the locked room mystery, though for Ballard the solving of the mystery has less allure than the construction of the locked room, in this case Pangbourne Village itself, a pristine version of hell in which everything runs so smoothly and so *reasonably* it represents a form of madness.

The external trigger for *Running Wild* was undoubtedly the spree killing that took place in the Berkshire market town of Hungerford in August of the previous year and a mere half an hour's drive away from the real village of Pangbourne. When 27-year-old Michael Ryan shot and killed sixteen people before turning the gun on himself, he became responsible for one of the worst crimes of gun violence the UK has ever seen. Ryan is referenced several times in *Running Wild*, and Greville identifies himself as the author of 'an unpopular minority report on the Hungerford killings'.[365] A stash of gun-related magazines – *Guns and Ammo*, *Commando Small Arms*, *Combat Weapons of the Waffen SS* – is discovered hidden in the bedroom of the oldest of the Pangbourne children, seventeen-year-old Jeremy Maxted.

The Hungerford tragedy was a shocking and disturbing incident, whose social and cultural ramifications, at least in Britain, have been profound. Chris was in the close vicinity of Hungerford on the day of the shootings — he had been driving from where he then lived in Pewsey to visit his friend David Langford in Reading. The massacre, and the questions it inevitably raised about gun control and youthful disaffection, were the central inspiration behind his 1997 novel *The Extremes*.

Chris was particularly interested in the differing attitudes to guns in the US and the UK, and used many of the same magazines hoarded by Jeremy Maxted for research. Normally he would have retained such materials as part of his archive but in the case of the gun magazines, he told me, he threw them away as soon as the manuscript had been delivered. He did not feel comfortable having them in the house.

Ballard's response to Hungerford is less specific: 'In a totally sane society, madness is the only freedom.' [366] Bea Ballard has also suggested that the novella was at least partly inspired by an incident concerning a young music scholar, the son of friends in London, who felt under such enormous parental pressure to succeed that he ended up setting fire to his piano. *Running Wild* represents a microcosm of Ballardian themes and developing interests, and the poisonous perfection of Pangbourne Village, its well-tended avenues and neatly-clipped trees are a flash-forward to the gated communities that would become the defining landscape of Ballard's late novels.

'There is no such thing as society,' said Margaret Thatcher, or words to that effect. But as Ballard entered his sixth decade, his sights became even more keenly focused upon society and how it operated. As always, his gaze was critical, iconoclastic. Unsurprisingly, what he saw he did not find pretty.

26

'THROUGH THE CRASH BARRIER'

In June 1992 Ballard travelled to the Italian seaside resort of Viareggio, where for the next six days he served on the jury of a film festival. Small festivals like this one, the annual *MystFest*, are mounted in towns and cities all over Europe during the summer months. They are usually stimulating events to seek out if you love movies, but they have an attractive extra quality if your background is the world of books in Britain. Film festivals don't have much in common with the rather inhibited and wordy tradition of British literary festivals – the film world is of course all about image and careers and money (invariably excess of, or lack of, at opposite ends with no median), and the audiences are actively involved.

A typical screening of almost anything new will provoke a knowledgeable festival audience to noisy applause – the initial appearance on the screen of a renowned actor usually provokes loud cheers and clapping, sometimes hisses and boos. Known trademarks of certain directors will get a murmur of informed appreciation, while every re-used cinematic cliché or pretentious camera angle will get a scorning response. Love scenes make everyone happy. Outside the theatres, the terraces and pavement cafés are busy with earnest-looking people, arguing and laughing. The town's hotels and bars are crammed with journalists, fans, television crews, aspiring directors and hopeful young actors.

A typical festival jury will be headed by a film world dignitary: a senior actor, director, producer or even a festival organizer from another part of Europe. The rest of the jurors will be a polyglot selection of younger actors, technicians, upcoming directors, critics, cineastes, journalists … and a writer.

At the festival in which Ballard served as juror, the veteran director Jules Dassin was in the chair. Alongside Ballard were Suzanne Cloutier (who years before had played Desdemona in *Othello*, directed by and starring Orson Welles), Bob Swaim (director of *La Balance*) and two Italian cineastes. The first meeting of the jury went well: they all seemed to like the same kind of film, and agreed on the qualities that would make a winner. This unanimity broke down as soon as they started viewing the films: perhaps because of the noisy influence of the rows of responsive audience amongst whom they sat, every juror began picking a favourite.

After the jury had viewed a few of the films in competition, the intolerance or assumed superior experience of the senior member showed itself. This is a phenomenon known to festival juries everywhere. There is thought to be no argument with someone who has an encyclopaedic knowledge and years of experience. According to Ballard, Dassin was one such. He called another meeting. 'These films are all rubbish,' he said. 'Let's just give it to Nicolas Roeg.' Roeg's new film, *Cold Heaven*, was in contention but had not yet been shown. Ballard pointed out that they had so far only seen five films and they ought to watch the rest. 'They're going to be rubbish too,' Dassin said magisterially.

They went back to viewing and at the end held a vote: the winner was a film made in Germany about a Turkish detective, which they had had to watch without subtitles. Roeg received a Special Jury Mention.[367]

Ballard's involvement with film was as a lifelong moviegoer, a regular reviewer and essayist on the world of cinema, and also, from time to time, the creator behind several film projects.

He said that his moviegoing began in 1946 after he arrived in England from China, recoiling mentally and spiritually from what he saw as the grey and distracted social conditions. There were few things anyone in Britain could do with their leisure time, so a huge number of people went to the cinema two or three times a week. Ballard joined them. He said, 'In gigantic art deco Odeons, like smoke-filled cathedrals, I saw the postwar films of Alfred Hitchcock, Howard Hawks, John Ford and Roberto Rossellini when they first came out. Even more exhilarating, I saw Robert Mitchum, Marlon Brando and James Dean before they became stars. On dull afternoons, when I should have been dissecting cadavers, I watched *Sunset Boulevard* (1950), *Orpheus* (1950) and *Rome, Open City* (1945). A completely new culture and social climate were being created, international in spirit and more urgent than almost any novel.'[368]

Sunset Boulevard made a tremendous impact on him. He was twenty years old. 'I knew that I was going to become a writer, and the sort of writer I wanted to be was Joe Gillis. The idea of dying face down in the pool of a great mansion in Beverly Hills struck me as something worthy of Puccini. For years after seeing *Sunset Boulevard*, whenever I found myself in a pool I dipped my hat to Joe Gillis by lying face down for a few seconds, imagining myself in a pool in Beverly Hills.'[369]

He was particularly interested, for perhaps understandable reasons, in contemporary Japanese cinema. 'The first Kurosawa film I saw was *Rashomon* (1950). Quite apart from its very subtle and complex story, it had a level of elegance and visual sophistication that few contemporary American or European films had. The richness of the film and the themes it tackled, the moral relativities that underpinned or undermined the truth, were quite remarkable.'[370]

'A brilliant film, a masterpiece,' he said of Godard's *Alphaville* (1965). 'The sense of interior space was wonderful. I wish I could say that had influenced me. I hope it did. I loved all those chrome hotels – and the great Akim Tamiroff, in his overcoat, sitting sadly on his bed. Eddie Constantine, the glamorous super-hunk. I think originally Godard was going to call it *Tarzan vs IBM*. I loved that film.'[371]

Ballard regarded Jean-Luc Godard as an important director, of equal stature to Stanley Kubrick, albeit in a different way. He also greatly liked the work of Michelangelo Antonioni. 'I wrote a script from my novel *Concrete Island*, that a French director wanted to film. That was last summer. I don't know if he'll actually make the film. I once also wrote a script from my early novel *The Drought*, which was bought for television by David Frost, but he's never used it. I found Kubrick's film *Dr Strangelove* (1964) outstanding, a masterpiece, absolutely overwhelming. Recently I saw again Fellini's *La Dolce Vita* (1960) on television, and again this film made a great impression on me.'[372]

Ballard's interest in film lasted all his life. Bea Ballard remembers how in the days of video cassettes, and video stores on the high street, her father's favourite thing to do in the evenings was to walk down to the local video shop and rent a movie. 'He saw a vast number of films that way, both American and European, and kept very up to date with cinema, even from the suburbs of Shepperton.' Ballard also continued to enjoy his visits to the cinema.

> It's funny, but I'm probably the last person in this country who's still going to the movies in his fifties. Nobody here over the age of forty goes to the movies. For a man of fifty-six to be going to the movies is practically a social crime. It's unseemly behaviour in the elderly. When the lights come on at the end of the evening, I always feel vaguely guilty looking around, like some middle-aged man hanging around the school playground. But I've recently seen a remarkable new kind of film: films like *Blue Velvet* (1986), *Raising Arizona* (1987) and *Blood Simple* (1984).[373]

Ballard made other attempts at writing screenplays, with variable success. He was commissioned by Hammer Films to write an original treatment for the sequel they planned to make to their version of *One Million Years BC*. Aida Young, the producer, had read Ballard's novel *The Drowned World* and was very taken with it. 'In 1970 they brought out this sequel, *When Dinosaurs Ruled the Earth* [later changed to ...*World*], and I wrote the original treatment for it, for which I got a screen credit. It was a film without dialogue and the script was credited to Val Guest, the director; I would say that of what you see on the screen, many of the basic elements and the overall storyline are mine, and much of the detailed narrative is his.'[374]

In 1973 the film critic David Pirie added this explanatory note about the Hammer film: 'Most of Ballard's material was subsequently lost in Val Guest's clumsy screenplay, but enough of it remained to make *When Dinosaurs Ruled the Earth* a far less predictable and boring film than others in the series. Ballard had conceived an account of early life on this planet which would illustrate Hanns Hörbiger's theories about violent cosmic upheaval and the creation of the moon.'[375]

In 1978 Ballard was given the chance to write the novelization of a film then being made by Ridley Scott. He turned it down. 'The script outlined a hackneyed story about a malevolent stowaway, with dialogue that rarely rose above: "Chow-time." "Where's Dallas?" "Topside." "Uh-huh." What amazed me was not that someone had decided to film this script, but that he had been able to form any idea of the finished movie from these empty lines. Yet the film was *Alien* (1979), one of the most original horror movies ever made, and the throwaway dialogue perfectly set off the terrifying vacuum that expanded around the characters.'[376]

Ballard was not against the idea of novelizing someone else's screenplay. Nor was he entirely unmoved by science fiction movies as such. 'My father did enjoy SF movies if they were beautifully directed, stylish and imaginative,' Bea Ballard remembers. 'He loved *Mad Max 2*, and also *Blade Runner* — he found the visuals incredibly arresting and exciting, taking you into a world of the future that felt possible. When we were children he took us to see Stanley Kubrick's *2001: A Space Odyssey* at the local cinema in Walton-on-Thames. I remember being blown away by that movie, even though I was only about nine years old.' Ballard also enjoyed thrillers and classic noir. 'I like stylized narratives where there's a great deal of form and flow, like a good Raymond Chandler or a good B movie, a hard-driving thriller in fact where you know there's a plot, you know there's a story, but you don't need to follow the detailed ramifications. Like *Vanishing Point* (1971), which I loved. I thought that was a colossal film.'[377]

Ballard, in spite of his many insightful essays on cinema, remained essentially a writer of books. He became detached and sceptical of the film world, while continuing to be fascinated by its products. 'Thirty years ago, after first bruising myself against the silver screen, it occurred to me that the experience of bringing up young children was the best possible training for dealing with people in the film world. Those passionate enthusiasms which could evaporate like the mist on a margarita, the life-long friendships virtually signed in blood that never outlasted a lunch, the sudden treacheries and wounded innocence, reminded me that I was dealing with a tribe of likeable but unreliable four-year-olds.'[378]

27

'I GIVE MYSELF AWAY'

It was seven years since the successful publication of Ballard's 'break-out' novel *Empire of the Sun*, and four years since Spielberg's film adaptation of it. Ballard clearly considered the time was right for a continuation of Jim's story. Presumably he felt he should respond to the interest the novel and film had aroused with its details of the physical circumstances of the Japanese internment camp, but also with the obsessive effect the original narrative offered. It had been something of a revelation to almost everyone who read it.

Part of its appeal was the distancing effect of writing it as semi-autobiography, sliding almost undetectably between true reminiscence and fictionalization that was based on events either Ballard remembered happening to others, or in which he could imagine himself being involved. It was a remarkable way of handling some recognizably difficult psychological material.

The new book was a conscious return to the same approach, so anyone seeking after the 'reality' should be on their guard. Most of *The Kindness of Women* (1991) is fictionalized, which is to say it is probably true in one sense, but unreliably so. From the point of view of this present book, the ascertainable facts of the life of J. G. Ballard have mostly been covered, or will be, and much of the novel deals with the life and experiences of 'Jim Graham' as an adult. Treating it as a *roman à clef* allows us to clear this up, enabling discussion of it as a novel without distraction.

Soon after first publication my colleague David Pringle closely compared the various named or repeating characters with the real people known to have had an influence on or presence in Ballard's life. The author later confirmed that 'most of the characters in *The Kindness of Women* are complete inventions. Sally Mumford, Peggy Gardner and David Hunter are wholly imaginary.' At different parts of the novel these names were deployed, often fulfilling various roles. For instance, David Hunter (who Jim knew as a boy in Shanghai), is said to be present at the RAF pilot training camp in Canada – in reality very little is known about Ballard's fellow cadets at the base in Moose Jaw. Later we see David Hunter as a possible avatar of the character Vaughan, in *Crash*.

Ballard also noted that Charles Platt's speculation[379] that Sally Mumford was based on the writer Emma Tennant was not correct, 'though there were lots of scatty young women like her in London in the '60s'.[380]

Other names were easier to place on real people, but the caveat remains: it is interesting to pursue but in the end unreliable. Fiction is made up for a reason!

We won't dwell on all the acts of fiction in this brief description of the novel, but the very first page contains material that must be at least partly invented. Jim describes how as a seven-year-old he would ride his bike down to the Bund in Shanghai to see how the war was progressing. He reports the bombing of citizens sheltering in The Great World Amusement Park, a public bazaar, with a greater tally of innocent victims than ever before. In fact, he believes it is still the worst atrocity of its kind.

The incident was a real one, and the casualties not exaggerated, but in August 1937 the real Jim Ballard was six, and the Battle of Shanghai had been going on for some time. There were artillery exchanges every day. It is impossible to believe that this English boy would have been allowed to venture out alone on a bicycle. So this is obviously one of the events in which he could only imagine himself being involved.

Many sequences are described, some of them taking place before the beginning of the story as told in *Empire of the Sun*. We are introduced to Olga, his White Russian governess, his friend David Hunter, the camp commandant Mr Hyashi, and a girl a year older than Jim called Peggy Gardner.

* * *

This partial summary of *The Kindness of Women* is the last thing Chris wrote. He had been anxious to cover this novel, because of its close connection with *Empire of the Sun*. But his strength was failing. I have an abiding and painful memory of him at his desk at this time, trying to summon the energy to write but merely sitting, leaning slightly forward, clearly exhausted. His mind was as active as ever but his body was reaching the limit of its endurance.

He told me he had finished writing the chapter, and it was only when I came to examine the manuscript after his death that I discovered he had in fact been able to complete only a small section of it, which he had entitled 'Chapter Z'. Immediately following his own text he had cut and pasted a section of the plot summary from Wikipedia (clearly labelled as such) as an aide memoire. I felt deeply upset when I saw this, because it was so untypical of him: a grabbing at words, a kind of panic-buying, a final attempt to shore up a dam that was about to break.

'I've always stressed that both *Empire* and *Kindness of Women* were novels,' Ballard wrote to David Pringle in the October of 1993, 'though based on my own life without which they could never have been written at all. They represent my own life seen through the body of fiction that was prompted by that life.'

The publisher's synopsis on the inside flap of the first edition presents *The Kindness of Women* as a direct successor to *Empire of the Sun*, 'one of the most important and popular novels of the postwar years'. *The Kindness of Women*, the blurb insists, is 'truthful in its self-portrayal, fictional in its other characters and incidents ... the warmest and most passionate novel Ballard has ever written.'

As with his later and less mitigated exercise in autobiography *Miracles of Life*, one gets the sense that *The Kindness of Women* was a book Ballard wanted to write, that he was anxious to set certain facts definitively on the record. There is a great deal of warmth in evidence, both for the women who offer Jim their 'kindness' following the accidental death of his wife Miriam, and most notably for his children – Henry, Alice and Lucy in the novel – whose daily needs and normal affections form the grounded centre of a world that might otherwise have spiralled out of control.

None of this is sufficient to hide the fact that *The Kindness of Women* is a very odd book indeed. While Ballard insists that his two autobiographical novels are works of fiction, *The Kindness of Women* does not really work as a novel unless the reader has some prior knowledge of the life on which it is based. Ballard offers no explanation of how or why the fictional Jim became a writer, the struggles he experienced in doing so, the kind of books he writes – clearly he is assuming we know all this already, that this is in fact why we are reading the book in the first place. Were *Kindness* blatant autobiography that would not matter, or at least not as much; as things stand, it is a lack that amounts to dishonesty, effectively robbing the 'novel' we are supposed to be reading of its reason for being.

Though the publisher is careful to insist on the fictional nature of 'other characters and incidents', much of the reality of Ballard's life and friendships through the 1960s are all present and correct: the 'Crashed Cars' exhibition, the Phun City rock festival, the bad LSD trip, the alcohol-fuelled debaucheries of the film festival in Rio are all rehashed at length and in some detail. There are some notable absences, however: there is no character correspondent with Michael Moorcock, no Ladbroke Grove, no *New Worlds*, no science fiction. Following the success of *Empire of the Sun*, Ballard's ambivalence about his literary origins becomes more pronounced, and as with *Miracles of Life* later on, *Kindness* is as much a deliberate curation of the facts as it is a laying bare.

Ironically it is in those portions of the novel that can be read purely as fiction – surreal, hallucinatory, powerfully original – that *The Kindness of Women* is most successful. In the scenes set on the Moose Jaw RAF base, both Jim and David Hunter are driven to become pilots by an obsession with nuclear warfare born out of the rubble of the second world war. Both saw the flash of the explosion over Hiroshima, both dwell endlessly upon the intimate and sinister presence of nuclear weaponry secretly stored at US air bases close to where they went to school.

For Jim, the obsession is ultimately a dead end, a piece of stray trauma made literal in the unexplained disappearance of a rogue Turkish pilot beneath the iced-over waters of a forbidden lake. His salvation, we are told, comes through his writing. For David Hunter, the nuclear obsession becomes all consuming, made manifest in a dark and uneasy fetish for crashed cars and leading ultimately to a fatal accident and a nervous breakdown.

The chapters set in Spain – 'a dream more lurid than any of Dalí's paintings, a vision of the world's end seen in terms of polluted sand, the stench of sun-oil and terraces of over-exposed flesh'[381] – recall for me my own childhood experience of Porto and Estartit in the early years of the British holiday boom. Here is a photo of my brother on the beach, a tiny blond urchin, frowning, in a purple T-shirt; the scents of Ambre Solaire and Johnson's baby oil, the scratchy ubiquity of too-hot sand; squabbles over spilled orange juice and lost binoculars amidst the ribald games and laughter of the adults, unsettling through being incomprehensible, part of a set of codes we are secretly debarred from. My dad is drunk and thinks he's hilarious; my mum is taciturn, permanently on edge. Whether you realize they're listening or not, kids know what's going on. Are these minor duplicities harmful? If they are anything they are corrosive, a betrayal of what is being advertised.

Ballard's bullfighting sequence in particular is profoundly disturbing and all the more effective as a result.

In terms of narrative structure, Jim's supposedly unremarkable existence in Shepperton (heating up baked beans for the kids and taking the dog for walks) serves little purpose and sits oddly against the bestiality going down in Rio; once again, if we didn't know who the author was, we would probably be asking ourselves why it is included. As for the women, kind they may be, but they are very much a supporting cast. They all have jobs – mainly 'something in publishing' – but none of them are allowed to *do* anything, to ultimately become anything except, of course and blessedly, mothers. Peggy Gardner succeeds as a doctor but in spite of her many affairs her career supposedly renders her 'spinsterish' and seems to preclude her from having any permanent attachments. No woman in *The Kindness of Women* is allowed to make art.

They are invariably described as 'strong', these women – 'strong hips', 'strong legs', 'strong wrists', 'strong bones', 'strong outlines' – but real intimacy is rare, almost off-limits. Even Miriam, Jim recalls, took care to keep a portion of herself secret from him.

As in so much of autobiography, the author's deeper self is revealed as a by-product, almost by chance.

The press reaction to *The Kindness of Women* was mostly positive, though in some quarters less ecstatic than to *Empire of the Sun*. For William Boyd in the *Weekend Telegraph*[382] the book 'is full of mesmerizing writing, classic examples of the Ballard style, paragraphs and pages that disturb and enthral'. For Peter Kemp in the *TLS* though[383] the 'hectic glamour' of a disintegrating Shanghai as conveyed in the opening chapters is muddied and weakened by 'a muddled bunch of notions about dehumanization'.

Nicholas Wollaston in the *Observer*[384] insists that 'this is autobiography taken to the highest reaches of fiction, another wonderful novel of scorching power, shot with honesty and a matter-of-fact lyricism that seems to catch even the author by surprise.' Reviewing the novel a week later in the *Sunday Times*,[385] Nick Hornby, though suitably impressed by Ballard's 'cool, glassy, almost eerily unengaged' prose, makes the insightful remark that in the chapters detailing Jim's escapades in the 1960s, 'readers might find their energy flagging and irritation setting in, not because of the material, but because of Ballard's attempts to summarize in one-liners the abstruse messages of the fiction he produced at the time.'

The Kindness of Women tells us little about Ballard we do not already know; at the same time, it is more readily deciphered – more explicable and thereby less powerful – than either *Crash* or *The Atrocity Exhibition*, the novels that form its largely unspoken subject matter.

In the final chapter of *The Kindness of Women*, 'Dream's Ransom', Jim reflects upon how, with the making of the Hollywood film based upon his boyhood experiences in wartime Shanghai, 'the clock of [his] life had come full circle, in all sorts of unexpected ways.' The simulacrum of Amherst Avenue constructed by the film crew at Shepperton Studios is so effective in recalling the past that it may as well be the real thing: 'This is the right way to go back to Shanghai, inside a film. In a sense they started shooting it fifty years ago…'[386]

As he brought his thirteenth novel to a close, Ballard had made no firm plans to revisit the city that had cast such a profound spell upon both his real self and the fictional version. But the lure of the real Shanghai would ultimately prove impossible to resist.

TWENTY-EIGHT

'THE ROAD TO SHANGHAI'

The hour-long TV documentary *Shanghai Jim* was made by the BBC as part of its *Bookmark* series and timed to coincide with the publication of *The Kindness of Women*. Produced by James Runcie, the son of the then Archbishop of Canterbury, Robert Runcie, and first broadcast on 25 September 1991, the programme marked Ballard's first return to China in forty-five years and was an indication of how substantially Ballard's media profile had increased. The assistant producer, Randall Wright, visited David Pringle in Brighton in advance of filming both to discuss Ballard's work and to take copies of David's interviews and other papers.

Shanghai Jim opens with a voiceover reading from near the end of Part One of *Kindness*, the moment when Jim Graham is leaving Shanghai with his mother on board the *Arawa*. As the ship pulls away from the harbourside, Jim spots his father looking up at him from the crowd below. His father is waving him goodbye but Jim finds he cannot wave back, a piece of inexplicable callousness we already know had happened in real life. 'Perhaps I blamed him,' Ballard writes in *Kindness*, 'for sending me away from this mysterious and exhilarating city.'[387]

The programme shows us Ballard packing his suitcase and leaving Shepperton, driving along a busy dual carriageway towards the airport. In the next sequence, we see him strolling around a Chinese wet market, then listening to live jazz in a harbourside bar. His former home at 31 Amherst Avenue is still there and still intact, dilapidated but still faintly glamorous, its elegant gables and multi-paned windows hemmed in by a wealth of tropical vegetation. 'My bedroom still has its original blue paintwork, and I recognized the little bookshelves, where I kept my copies of *Chums* annual, and *Boy's Own Paper* and all my American comics.

It was like a sort of time capsule, really, that I'd stepped into after all these years.'

The air is vibrant with the songs of cicadas and other insects. Ballard speculates about what his life might have been like, had the war not taken place. In all probability he would have gone on living in Shanghai, sleeping in that same bedroom in Amherst Avenue. 'I see around me here a kind of alternate life that I never managed to live because of the war.'

On the day Ballard returns to the Lunghua internment camp, the sun is shining. Ballard stands on what was once the roof of the commandant's office and points out familiar landmarks: the water tower, the married couples' quarters, the camp offices. G Block, where he and his family were kept prisoner for almost three years. The room the Ballards occupied is very small, furnished with a set of bunk beds and not much else. Ballard describes how during the day his father would stand his mattress upright against the wall so they would have enough space for a table to play cards on and eat their meals. 'This little room is as close as I will ever come to home,' Ballard insists, 'the most important place in my life.'

With its dingy paintwork and concrete flooring, the building is easily recognizable as the school it has returned to being, its corridors standing silent and eerily empty through the summer vacation. Ballard describes the camp's inmates as 'a very large nuclear family of some two thousand people'. He speaks once again of the closeness, the sense of community that grew up among the internees, how many of them found security in the camp, a place of safety amidst the chaos of war.

The images of Lunghua are arresting, significant. They make Ballard's account of his strangely static war years all the more compelling. Yet the idea of being forcibly confined here is sobering and more than a little chilling. Seeing the concrete, barrack-like structures, the dusty and arid expanse of the surrounding scrubland, I cannot help wondering how Ballard's feelings about Lunghua might have differed had he been an adult: James Ballard senior for example, his own life derailed in moments, his home and possessions requisitioned, two young children to protect and care for and no idea how the war might eventually pan out. John Gray said to me that Ballard had told him his parents were 'demolished' by the experience, though this is something Ballard rarely touched on in his many interviews.

Unsurprisingly, the idea of revisiting Shanghai had been on Ballard's mind more or less since the writing and publication of *Empire of the Sun*. While on a publicity tour of the US for *The Day of Creation* in 1988, Ballard described in an interview with Richard Kadrey how he had been approached by a woman who as a child had been in the same accommodation block as him at Lunghua: 'She had a school photograph taken in something like 1938 that showed me as a little seven-year-old. It was rather touching.'

He went on to recount how as a guest on a local radio programme in Chicago he had spoken to the wife of his erstwhile friend from Amherst Avenue, Malcolm Kendal-Ward. 'The last time I saw Malcolm was a few days after Pearl Harbor. He was my closest childhood friend. It was all quite strange.'[388]

Through the winter of 1984–5, Ballard had exchanged a number of letters with the Canadian English Literature professor Peter Brigg, who Ballard had first encountered through the pages of David Pringle's semi-regular Ballard newsletter *JGB News*. Brigg was in the process of writing a short monograph on Ballard's life and work,[389] a book that aimed to bring Ballard to the attention of American scholars and that Ballard would later compliment as 'a superb piece of work, a remarkable effort altogether, brilliantly written and with an extremely wide range, both imaginatively and in terms of the ideas discussed.'[390]

Though based at the University of Guelph in Ontario, Brigg at the time happened to be living in Shanghai, teaching English at the Shanghai Institute of International Economic Management. Ballard wrote to him in the first instance asking whether he thought it would be possible for a private Western citizen to travel within communist China. 'The notion of going back to Shanghai is a bit of a pipe-dream,' Ballard conceded, 'an ambition for the long term which I mean to fulfil one day, but not yet. A certain amount of mental preparation is needed – for some reason the whole thing is a bit of a daunting prospect.'[391]

Brigg and his wife subsequently took the bus into the western suburbs of the city, where they were able to confirm that 31 Amherst Avenue was still standing and if somewhat neglected was largely intact and currently being used as offices and – appropriately enough – a book depository. Brigg's photographs of the house show it largely as it appears in the BBC documentary some six years later. 'When I left China in 1946 I virtually repressed all memory of my childhood, for all sorts of reasons,' Ballard says in the film. 'Gradually I think I realized by the end of the seventies that so many of the moments in my novels and short stories only made sense if they were seen in terms of an attempt to recreate Shanghai.'

On camera, he describes his journey to Shanghai as 'a settling of account, a coming to terms with the past'. The making of the BBC documentary presented Ballard with the ideal opportunity to revisit his childhood within the secure framework of a business trip: being in Shanghai to work on the film not only facilitated the practical arrangements, it also provided an emotional safety net, a rationale for what otherwise might have been a lonely and traumatic encounter with an earlier self.

To some extent he was aware of this, even leaned into it a little. Writing for the *Daily Telegraph*, Ballard describes landing at Shanghai International, once the site of the old aerodrome where he had climbed inside the cockpits of crashed Japanese aircraft. 'James Runcie, the *Bookmark* film's director, was waiting for me. I greeted him with the line I had rehearsed all the way from London, suggested by Conrad's novel about a European trader driven mad by an impenetrable Africa: "Hello, James. Mr Kurtz returns to the *Heart of Darkness*."'[392]

Speaking to Sue Lawley on *Desert Island Discs* just a couple of months later, Ballard describes how it took the film crew two days to find the camp, because the landscape was no longer recognizable from what it had been. During the war, the Lunghua camp stood isolated among abandoned paddy fields; now the entire area south of Shanghai had become a built environment of 'massive industrial estates, cement works, huge blocks of workers' flats that completely screened the camp from sight'.[393]

Stepping inside the room where he and his family had been interned, Ballard said, 'wasn't traumatic at all, it was like going home – that was the strange thing. In a sense I was expecting the worst, but in fact it was a wonderfully fulfilling experience.'[394] Writing a postcard to his daughter Fay while he was still in Shanghai,[395] Ballard described the trip as an 'exciting 2 days so far – found our old house & filmed inside my bedroom, then tracked down the camp, & our family room. Very strange.' A couple of days later he sent another postcard, this time to Mike and Linda Moorcock. 'Finally got back to square 1. Very strange – I haven't changed but Shanghai has – tracked down the camp & stood in our old room, waiting for an avalanche of memories, but none came.'[396]

This stark personal admission seems to suggest that to an extent at least, the Ballard we see in the *Bookmark* documentary is a construct, the version of himself the film makers had wanted to record and had, in a sense, paid for. The journey had been necessary and important – in an interview for CBC Radio in 1993, Ballard would describe how after returning to England he felt 'enormously elated for about three months, walking on air'[397] – but the impossibility of a permanent resolution must have been apparent. 'Shanghai had forgotten us, as it had forgotten me, and the shabby Art Deco houses in the French concession were part of a discarded stage set that was slowly being dismantled.'[398] The past is irrecoverable; the Shanghai he had known was gone, and the alternate self that had lived out his life there an unreachable stranger.

'All my characters spend their time constructing personal mythologies, which can sustain their inner lives,' Ballard says in the *Bookmark* documentary, and his return to Shanghai proved to be most fruitful as a literary experience, a coming to terms with 'the sort of dreams that to some extent have sustained me during the past forty-five years in England, which has never really felt like home'.

In 2007, the Canadian journalist, independent publisher and Ballard devotee Rick McGrath travelled to China to visit the Ballard house, now an upmarket Shanghai restaurant named SH508. Presented with photographs of his erstwhile home in its new incarnation, Ballard pronounced it virtually unrecognizable, the new owners having extended the house and substantially altered the layout. 'In an odd way it's quite reassuring that everything has changed so much,' he added in an email. 'The Shanghai I knew, along with 31 Amherst Avenue and Lunghua camp, only survive inside my head.'[399]

The restaurant changed hands in 2009, when it underwent a second major refurbishment, though the distinctive gables and roof outline remain.

A year or so after Ballard returned from filming *Shanghai Jim*, he spoke about the experience in front of a live audience at Blackwell's bookshop in Oxford. The event was written up for the student newspaper *Cherwell* by the future academic and film maker Richard Misek. The photographs taken to accompany the article are by Barney Cokeliss, who was then a student at Magdalen, reading English. The black-and-white images show Ballard wearing his customary tweed blazer, a shirt in a wide pinstripe, a defiantly spotted tie. His gaze is direct, assessing. The merest trace of a smile. Here is Ballard, if we dare say so, at the height of his powers.

Barney Cokeliss looks uncannily like his father. He tells me that the Oxford photographs were taken 'in some windowless room' above the main bookshop, also that he had photographed Ballard before, in 1990, not long after finishing his 'A' Levels. He recalls:

> He was very kind, very welcoming. He was enthusiastic about the fact that I was Harley's son. He invited me to come out to Shepperton and photograph him at home. I was struggling for the first time to use a proper camera. Being nineteen, I thought I'd better make sure I had the best possible equipment, so I rented an enormous medium-format camera that I didn't quite know how to use. I ended up with a series of slightly forlorn-looking, underexposed gloomy pictures, which were quite atmospheric but not particularly accomplished.

I have one of them in front of me. Ballard reclines in an armchair, and because Barney has told me the photographs were taken in Ballard's study I find myself wondering if it is the same armchair Bea would sometimes sit in as a child, studying with fascination the illustrations in Jacob Kulowski's *Crash Injuries* while her father worked at his desk alongside her. Probably it is. Although the photograph is quite dark, just as Barney has described it, there is a candidness about it, a vulnerability almost, that makes it different from so many of the other images of Ballard I have seen. There is more of the private man here. His eyes distant, focused inward, it is almost as if he has forgotten he is being photographed.

Fay later told Barney he may have been one of the last to have visited Ballard in Shepperton. 'I had no idea at the time, how rare it was for people to go to his house, how few were invited in,' he says. 'When I met Jim the second time, in Oxford, he remembered me and was delighted to see me. His real personality was so far from anything you might deduce from the books. I think of him as a gregarious introvert. He had an extraordinarily warm, affable, generous spirit.'

Barney grew up surrounded by Paolozzi collages, and sees his art very much as a corollary to Ballard's. 'They have such a similar way of looking at things. Ballard seemed to have a really clear eye about what modernity actually was – which included living in the suburbs at Shepperton.' As a postgraduate Fellow at Princeton, Barney was awarded $1,500 to make a short film, for which he chose to adapt Ballard's short story 'Love in a Colder Climate'. Ballard, he remembers, raised no objections and was fully behind the project. Barney feels sure that his father remained important to Ballard because of when they met. They were both young still, and hungry for success, both beginning to make their way. Barney's favourite work by Ballard is *Vermilion Sands*. Like Chris, he is able to recount the stories in filmic detail.

'He didn't want me to photograph his desk,' Barney says of Ballard at their first meeting. I think it must be because of this – the lack of tangible photographic evidence – that Barney remembers Ballard owning a big-box, cathode-ray computer, which of course he never did.

I discover that Barney went to school with the SF writer China Miéville, that he is also a friend of Ophelia Field, daughter of Nabokov's beleaguered biographer Andrew Field, whose work I read when I was at Corpus, just a year or two before Barney began his studies at Magdalen. Michelle Field is Nabokov's goddaughter. Nabokov, apparently, gifted her a lacy, rather saucy Babygro as a christening present, which she still has.

29

'THE PREDATORY BIRDS'

One sometimes hears of writers who are settling down in what might be called literary comfort zones, those areas of their work in which it seems the author is trading on or extending the ease of familiarity. It can be tempting for both writer and reader – also for many publishers, who will usually welcome the chance to avoid a certain kind of risk brought on by authorial restlessness. But writers sometimes are thought by readers and critics to return to their comforts too often or for too long – also if an author decides to venture out, put the real or illusory comfort behind and try something else, they worry they may be criticized for that.

It is remarkable that J. G. Ballard has several times turned his back on what must have been a familiar approach to his fiction and tried something new, while at the same time somehow managing a continuity of effect with what has gone before. In most of his work, the indefinable Ballardian quality remains, sometimes manifesting itself in a different way but usually subtly present.

It's fair to say that the stories of *Vermilion Sands* come close to the home territory of Ballard's work – he after all said that he would live there if he could. Many readers feel the same way too: it is a created ambience sufficiently strange and alienating to cast an imaginative spell, yet most of the stories feature shopkeepers or semi-retired artists forming relationships with beautiful people of the opposite sex. The physical environment of Vermilion Sands can be readily understood: cars, motels, abandoned holiday apartments, sand dunes, warm weather, a distant glimpse of ocean.

Most of these stories were written close to the beginning of Ballard's career (the last one was published in 1970), and although I suspect that readers would have relished a novel set in Vermilion Sands he never wrote one. Ballard was often willing to tackle his ideas in a different way — which should be considered a strength, an interesting wish to move on and expand his art. From this we received *The Atrocity Exhibition* and *Crash*, also, eventually, *Empire of the Sun* and *The Kindness of Women*. But the same instinct led him into more uncertain territory — *Hello America* is as second-rate as Ballard ever produced. Now, more recently, we have *Rushing to Paradise* (1994), certainly not of the second rank, but neither is it quite of the first. Not everyone agrees with that summary judgement, as we shall see.

Rushing to Paradise is a novel about a quarrelsome group of oddball characters, drawn to each other by external circumstances and differing personal motivations. It is also about a sexually alluring woman who charismatically attracts and controls those around her, even while acting repugnantly. There is a confrontation with a hostile but uncommunicative authority (in this case the French government and armed forces) who wish to exploit a harmless and beautiful place by using it as a test range for nuclear weapons. All of these may be thought of as core Ballardian subjects, certainly not from his early comfort zone, but topics that have memorably arisen before in his work.

The difference in *Rushing to Paradise* is that for probably the first time there is a commitment to the natural world, a concern about a species threatened with catastrophic culling or even extinction. The Pacific atoll of Saint-Esprit is the home and breeding ground of thousands of albatrosses. Dr Barbara Rafferty, a middle-aged radical feminist and conservationist, sets up a sanctuary to observe and protect them; she brings with her from Hawaii sixteen-year-old Neil Dempsey, who is along for the ride (they both find each other physically irresistible) but who in fact has an obsession with nuclear testing. Although they make a safe landfall on the island, the French attack them and Neil is shot in the foot. They return to Hawaii. As a result of this publicity, when they go back to the island after Neil has a spell in hospital they now attract many curious visitors, including wandering sailors, airline personnel, Club Med owners looking to build a resort, various hippies, mystics and esoteric scientists.

Eventually tiring of their attention, Dr Barbara resolves to rid herself and the sanctuary of all men. One by one they fall ill and die. She nominates Neil to the task of inseminating all the women, but another young sexually active male arrives on the atoll. Neil now falls ill with the same mysterious illness – he is in no doubt that Dr Barbara is responsible, and that he is being supplanted by his new rival. Her madness is plain to see. She suddenly turns on the colony of albatross, slaughtering as many of the birds as possible before wading into the sea, ostensibly to drown herself. At the last moment Neil and all those who remain alive are rescued by a French naval ship.

Although this is one of the most wide-ranging and knowledgeable of Ballard's novels, set in a landscape that's detailed, plausible, fresh to his work and has several novelties, it presents a central problem: the endless parade of minor characters who are given token descriptions and motivations. Much of the dialogue seems arbitrary, with non sequiturs adding an element of distracting surprise and irrelevance. Several characters assume a certain involvement to the action, then subside from view, or are killed. Things are started and not finished. Little is explained, or not satisfactorily. There is much action, but of the inconsistent, muddling sort. Events are summed up – the final chapter reads as if Ballard was exhausted by the whole thing and simply wrote a terse summary of the climactic actions and revelations.

'The human male sex is a sort of rust bowl,' Ballard said later, with what might just be relish. 'The feminist movement has meant that women have resexualised themselves and resexualised their imaginations. Dr Barbara is a very particular kind of feminist. She would endorse the pro-pornography lobby: that women have as much right as men to produce and consume pornographic imagery... She says somewhere that women were the first domestic animals, because they domesticated themselves. She wants a new kind of undomesticated woman, who can take the stage now that men have become obsolescent.'[400]

* * *

This is as far as Chris was able to come with writing about *Rushing to Paradise*, a novel he had wanted to experience because it was new to him, one of the very few of Ballard's works he had not read at the time of publication. He enjoyed it very much for around half its length and then – as so often happened with him and fiction – rapidly grew bored with it.

'The whole novel has a certain fascination, and at the outset one follows the story with interest,' he writes in his summing-up. 'But chaos breaks out soon, as the weird and unbelievable characters begin to react against one another, or, more often, ignore what the others are doing. It's a substantial disappointment after the promise of the opening pages.'

Immediately following his own final words on the novel, Chris had queued up two reviews from the time of publication, one from Scott Bradfield for the *Independent*, who broadly agrees with Chris that 'this motley crew never quite comes together', and that 'in *Rushing to Paradise* the satire feels awkward and the dialogue contrived'.[401] By way of a corrective, he had also singled out a quote from *Kirkus Reviews*, who pronounce *Rushing to Paradise* 'as fast-paced as a thriller, and always distinguished by Ballard's hallucinatory clarity and precise observations: a fiercely contrarian novel that's both Paradiso and Inferno ... Ballard's triumphant synthesis of the range of themes that have preoccupied him throughout his career.'[402]

In an interview with Pat Kane for BBC Radio Scotland broadcast in January 1996 and published in an abridged form in *The Scotsman*, Ballard talks at some length about his lack of sympathy for the CND, insisting that the idea of unilateral disarmament and the demonstrations at Aldermaston and Greenham Common seemed to him 'like a glorified Children's Crusade ... ignoring the realities of the world we lived in'. As on previous occasions, he advanced the view that the dropping of nuclear bombs on Hiroshima and Nagasaki saved more lives than they extinguished. 'And also of course they have a sort of apocalyptic significance that touches the mythic level of our imagination – this is primitive man inventing fire.'

In the same interview he refers to Greenpeace – the sinking of the *Rainbow Warrior* by French operatives in 1985 is spoken of repeatedly in *Rushing to Paradise* – as 'another branch of the Children's Crusade. I think it has very little to do with reality. It's rather dangerous in many ways, because single-issue fanatics are able to manipulate the mass media in very skilful ways, and they can set agendas that hide all sorts of obsessions of a rather dangerous character ... *Rushing to Paradise* is exactly about the hidden agendas that lie behind the extremist fringes of the ecological and feminist movements.'

One does not come to Ballard for his liberal politics, and we have travelled far enough on this journey to know that Ballard's ideas about feminism are – to put it most generously – muddled. He railed violently against Andrea Dworkin,[403] yet she was as much a maverick and as much the inspiration behind the psychotic and unstoppable Dr Barbara as Camille Paglia, whose views Ballard rather admired, at least when they fell suitably into alignment with his own.[404]

It would be a mistake to think that Ballard is even remotely interested in the fate of the albatross. If he had been, he would have done enough research to know that the Wandering Albatross of Coleridge's *Rime* – the species he is supposedly writing about – is a bird of the Southern Ocean, and does not live or breed at the latitudes in which his novel takes place. (The albatrosses of the North Pacific, the Laysan and the Black-Footed, are rather smaller, and sport distinctive black tails.)

Rushing to Paradise is a magnificent grandstanding exercise, everyday sexism and reactionary zeal scattered wantonly amidst the radical chaos. Perhaps the most wayward and bleakly funny of all Ballard's novels, it offers also a wry and original commentary on the Thatcher years. 'Dr Barbara is loosely based on one of my heroines, Margaret Thatcher,' Ballard tells Pat Kane in his interview for BBC Scotland. 'I try to convey something of the energy and shrill drive of the younger Margaret Thatcher, the Margaret Thatcher of the early eighties, in the way that Dr Barbara behaves.' And though one sighs at Ballard's use of the invariably gendered adjective 'shrill', there is undoubtedly something of Thatcher in Dr Barbara's obsessive pursuit of unpopular ideas, her immutable insistence on there being no alternative, her remorseless energy, even her blond hair, which Ballard references so often it becomes a leitmotif.

'Dr Barbara loathed the status quo, and thrived on tension and conflict. Yet he still admired her more than any woman he had ever met,'[405] Neil Dempsey reflects as he comes upon the evidence of one of Dr Barbara's first outrages against her own community. And while Ballard speaks of *Rushing to Paradise* as an attempt 'to answer the question of how David Koresh persuaded his Branch Davidian followers to die with him, or how the Reverend Jim Jones persuaded nearly a thousand followers to commit suicide in Guyana,'[406] we recognize equally in Dr Barbara's lethal acts of sabotage a uniquely Ballardian mindset, a new, still more perverse iteration of Dr Mallory's attempts to destroy the river that bears his name in *The Day of Creation*.

Here again is the 'ship of fools', the demented film mogul for whom reality is only accorded value when viewed through a lens, the affable middle classes enthusiastically descending into savagery. The same quixotic mission – a Children's Crusade, indeed – that goes viral before collapsing beneath the weight of its own madness. There is even an attack helicopter thrown in.

As a novel, *Rushing to Paradise* is taut, provocative, brilliantly made, as propulsively deranged, in its own way, as *Crash*. Above all, in Neil Dempsey's obsession with atomic testing, with the blighted, liminal landscapes of postwar détente – 'The towers on the high island ... swallowed by the advancing forest, ancient megaliths left behind by a race of warrior scientists obsessed with geometry and death'[407] – we are taken back to the nuclear flash that concludes *Empire of the Sun*, that continues to haunt the pages of *The Kindness of Women*.

Rushing To Paradise powerfully recalls the fascination with Hiroshima and its personal significance that characterizes so many of Ballard's finest short stories and that has been a presiding influence over his work from the beginning.

'A lot of people, myself included, when their children grow up, feel a huge vacuum,'[408] Ballard told the *Mail on Sunday* in 1988. 'Nature's contingency plan is death – it has provided no other. When you live alone, however many close friends or love affairs one has, you still feel a sense of emptiness.'

In November 1994, Fay Ballard married Jonathan Stokes, a clinical psychologist, at Chelsea Town Hall registry office. Her first child, Isabella – Ballard's first grandchild – was born two years later. In October 1995, Beatrice Ballard married fellow TV producer Nick Rossiter, who she had met while working at the BBC. Their wedding took place at the Jesuit Church of the Immaculate Conception in Farm Street, Mayfair. Bea gave birth to her first child, Pandora, in March 1997. Further grandchildren would follow: Fay's son Matthew arrived in July of the same year, with Bea giving birth to a second daughter, Alice, in February 1999.

With the departure of his children, Ballard's life swiftly settled into the routine that continued almost until his death. He wrote every day, shopped for provisions at the local supermarket, walked the dog by the river for exercise and for thinking time. Weekends were spent with Claire in Shepherd's Bush. His dislike of cooking and love of good food meant that he would usually eat out several nights during the week also, either with Claire or with other friends.

Though he was reasonably accommodating of interviewers, Ballard generally disliked people coming to Charlton Road and never entertained at home. Both Bea and Fay Ballard have said that during the last twenty years of his life they rarely if ever visited their father at the Shepperton house – either he would come to them, or they would meet at a restaurant. Tidying the house for visitors, making small talk, worst of all buying in and preparing food – for a writer of Ballard's temperament, such tasks can feel crushingly onerous, a waste of valuable time. Far more pleasurable to meet with friends on neutral ground, where one can enjoy their company for a few hours and then return to the necessary comforts of solitude, and home.

Nor did the increase in his bank balance make any discernible difference to his habits or lifestyle. Aside from the Delvaux copies he commissioned from Brigid Marlin, Ballard's only notable extravagances were his annual holiday – 'he would always rent a really beautiful villa', Bea told me – and his patronage of good restaurants. Indeed, Ballard's otherworldliness and complete lack of interest in material possessions became another aspect of his mythology, a trait Bea Ballard attributes to her father's time in Lunghua, where he and his family quickly learned to survive on very little. 'What became important was having enough to eat, warmth, shelter. Living from one day to the next. I don't think he ever really left that feeling behind.' The writer and film maker Chris Petit recounted how 'Ballard's money, since he started earning enough to put a bit aside, apparently just sits in an ordinary bank account, not even gaining interest, to the despair of his bank manager and accountant. The only change in Ballard's habits is that he has been known to take a boat across the Channel for the day so that he can eat lunch in France.'[409]

Ballard's editor at Gollancz, Malcolm Edwards, similarly described how Ballard, after receiving the first payment for the film rights to *Empire of the Sun*, 'decided he should celebrate, and went to his local supermarket to splash out. After wandering the aisles for a while he came home with a tin of salmon. His interest in wealth and its trappings was non-existent.'[410]

As Ballard's public presence became increasingly defined by the story of his childhood in Shanghai, his fame as the author of *Empire of the Sun* and his quasi-mythic status as the 'seer of Shepperton', so the divide between the persona Ballard projected – faintly eccentric but always gentlemanly – and the private man, whose energies were subsumed into his work and whose personal concerns and dilemmas remained a matter for himself alone became more entrenched.

'Talking to Ballard is like reading his fiction,' observes Jeannette Kupfermann, interviewing Ballard for the *Mail on Sunday*.[411] 'You're never quite sure of the ground you're on. The voice is plummy – the voice of an actor. He's both congenial and strangely guarded; he appears open and easy-going yet gives nothing away. He appears buoyant, but just occasionally the voice trails off into wistfulness.'

Though his reviews were frequently to be spotted in the broadsheet books sections, there were those who suspected he rarely read the novels he was asked to comment on,[412] or at least not in full.[413] He remained uninterested in the literary establishment or bookish gossip, though those moments when it was possible to glimpse a truer, tougher version of himself were invariably associated with his work, and his fierce protection of his position within a personal hierarchy.

Ballard was always ambitious – it is practically impossible to maintain a career in writing without a streak of ruthlessness – and although he came to shun deliberate confrontation or feuding as a waste of energy, there were definitely red lines. An early glimpse of Ballard's harsher side first surfaces in 1966, when Ballard was supposed to be taking over the editorship of *Impulse* magazine – formerly *Science Fantasy* – from Kyril Bonfiglioli, who was stepping down. His proposed editorship never got beyond the first meeting with the magazine's art director, the writer Keith Roberts.

Michael Moorcock describes the confrontation between the two as being like Palestine and Israel – that is, impossible to resolve: 'Jimmy was at his worst, raving, really raving, saying "if this bloody idiot can't get his act together, there's no point."'[414] Ballard took massive exception to Roberts's ethereal, Rackham-like drawing style, later describing Roberts in a postcard to Chris as 'an utterly 10th rate mediocrity' and making it clear that his 'appalling covers & general crudity & lack of imagination' were altogether too high a price to pay for any future involvement with the magazine.[415] Though admittedly a difficult personality, Roberts still stands as one of the most interesting and gifted writers of SF in Britain in the postwar era. But once Ballard decided to cut someone loose, he rarely changed his mind.

Letters written to Iain Sinclair in 1999 reveal an increasing defensiveness over Michael Moorcock's importance in his personal story arc. While lavishly praising Sinclair's own recently completed BFI monograph on Cronenberg's *Crash*, Ballard throws scorn on Moorcock's contributions, given in interview. 'I'm not sure why he's in the book at all,' Ballard writes, 'presumably he's there to provide anecdotal evidence of my life at the time I was writing *Atrocity Exhibition* and *Crash*. The problem is that his anecdotes are all wrong, but will be memorialized in your text.'

A second letter, written less than a week later, shows no reduction in his ferocity: 'It's not a matter of different takes on events so long ago, but of complete fictions – almost all Mike's anecdotes are simply untrue, and are there to serve his own re-invented past ... I think you've been misled by Mike into thinking that he and I formed any kind of imaginative partnership. *Crash* and the Moorcock novels you mention did not come out of what you call a shared background. There was no shared background. Mike and *New Worlds* under his editorship had no influence whatsoever on *Crash* or *The Atrocity Exhibition* ... My friendships with Paolozzi, Chris Evans and Dr Martin Bax were far closer than my friendship with Mike, and far longer-lasting ... Mike's *New Worlds* was a latecomer to a major shift in British SF that had begun years beforehand.'

Three months later, Ballard wrote to David Pringle, enclosing copies of the letters he had written to Sinclair and advising him to take Michael Moorcock's contributions to the *Crash* monograph – which Pringle had written to praise – with 'a huge pinch of salt'. He then makes it clear by way of a postscript that he does not want Pringle to publicly broadcast what he has said. What Ballard thought, felt or did in private was one thing, but he did not want the self he presented in public – sanguine, controlled and carefully curated – to be questioned or doubted.

Sometime in the winter of 1994, Claire was diagnosed with breast cancer. Though the disease would eventually return to claim her life two decades later, she was successfully treated and in 1995 entered a long period of remission.

On 9 September 1998, Ballard's mother Edna died at her home in Claygate, Surrey. 'My mother based her whole life as far as I know on playing bridge and drinking large martinis,' Ballard said to Robert McCrum in 2006.[416] 'She died at the age of 93, a wonderful advertisement for the misspent life. I mentioned the two-martini lunch to her and she said, "Two martinis? *Five* martinis."'

Even if Ballard and his mother had not been close, they had always maintained a connection and the death of Edna would undoubtedly have signalled the end of an era.

THIRTY

'TOO SOON, TOO LATE'

When Chris came out of hospital at the end of August, we were fully convinced he would live long enough to complete this book. At the very least, we believed he would have time to produce a full first draft, a working copy that I could pull together and polish if necessary, but that would in essence be the book as he had envisioned it.

The first days back at home were confusing, difficult in the main because we were suddenly at the centre of a whirlwind of medical attention, an unending stream of phone calls and visits from physiotherapists, occupational therapists, district nurses and outreach workers. NHS professionals with forms and clipboards, wanting to ensure that we were coping, both mentally and practically, with the new and brutal facts of our change in circumstance.

Even though Chris had worked hard to regain some basic mobility while he was in the Beatson, the physios were advising that Chris should discontinue his use of the walking frame, that he should confine himself to the wheelchair only, even indoors. They warned us that if he were to fall and injure himself, he might exacerbate his spinal compression and find himself paralysed.

We looked at each other in silent rebellion. We were determined that Chris would keep walking for as long as he could. His sanity and our freedom – to get out of the house, to visit friends, to manage hospital visits – depended upon it. We were to discover within a day or two that we had another ally – another good angel – within the medical profession, our Macmillan nurse Evelyn Glass, who came to the house to introduce herself and to explain her role. An expert in end-of-life care, she had a way of clearing aside the bullshit and letting us talk about what we were feeling. More even than that, she was able to cut through inflexible, one-size-fits-all NHS protocols and get us the help we actually needed, when we needed it. Chris was always reassured by her presence and her directness. I do not like to think about how I would have managed without her support.

I fielded the calls and kept track of the appointments. I was operating in crisis mode, as I had been for the past six weeks. I think I still am, to an extent, even as I write this. It is a habit that is difficult to shake.

Because Chris could not climb the stairs, or at least not without some risk involved, I had borrowed a bed from our friends, the writer Anne Charnock and her husband Garry, which Garry and I had set up in Chris's office. I had brought down his bedside lamp – the ancient green Anglepoise that has since become my bedside lamp – his bedside cabinet, his radio. Everything fitted and the space felt cosy, a bed surrounded by books, a place for settling down for the night after hours bent over the page, like the Oxford study of an eccentric don in an Iris Murdoch novel.

Chris found the bed comfortable and slept well. He was able to use his walking frame to get safely back and forth from our downstairs toilet. We discovered his wheelchair was ideal for him to sit in while eating and watching TV. We clutched at these small successes, delighted. What we wanted above all – words we repeated to one another again and again – was to establish a new form of what we referred to as our normality, a life we could live together without outside interference.

I asked Chris more than once if there was anything special he wanted to do, any places he wanted to go, the kind of 'bucket list' questions I felt I should ask but that we both agreed seemed pointless, almost a joke. Perhaps they brought home to us the truth of things, more than we were able or willing to accept. We both understood, in any case, that travel beyond our local area was more or less impossible. Chris was too frail.

At one point, I remember saying: 'I don't believe any of this.' 'Neither do I,' Chris replied. 'I'm in denial.'

We held each other. We even laughed. So long as we were together, so long as we could *talk*, we believed that we could make sense of things, that we would face what future we had on our own terms. We waited for the flurry of medics to leave us alone so Chris could get back to work. Writing, reading, the book, *this* – we had realized from Chris's first weeks in hospital that these were still the things that mattered most to us.

Two months after his death, I dreamed of Chris for what has so far been the only time since he died. Parts of his body and internal workings had been replaced with metal. I had to support him while walking almost entirely. He seemed fragile, but in a stiff, mechanistic way, as if his legs and spine had been reconstructed with Meccano struts, and when I saw him trying to eat or blow his nose I had to look away. But he was totally himself, nonetheless, and unafraid of these changes, which I intuited he saw as necessary to his survival.

He knew he was ill, that he was dying, but he was determined for us to stay together for as long as we could.

'Let's just keep going,' he said, and then I said, 'We can do this.'

This dream should have been a nightmare but it was not. The joy in being with Chris again – in us speaking and laughing together – was overpowering. It was *us*, that was the thing, that was what mattered. I felt enormously protective, but also triumphant. I could not stop touching him. We were back.

When I woke I knew I had dreamed of him and I felt happy, not sad, as if his whole way of being – our whole way of being – was there still, inside me, the way I had been imagining and telling others.

Not long after Chris came home, we set up our first Zoom interviews with Fay and Bea. I had written to them both about Chris's diagnosis; they were warm, supportive, concerned, eager for us to begin our work with them as soon as we were ready. I say 'our' and 'we' because already this book had become our book. Chris was writing alone, he was intending to complete the manuscript alone, but he wanted and needed me beside him in a way he had actively resisted before his illness.

From the time we first met, Chris had always discussed his work with me in detail, but he never liked me to become what he called 'too interested' in what he was working on, to pick up his ideas and play with them, to suggest things. He liked me to listen, not talk, not because he was uninterested in what I had to say, but because he didn't want to be influenced by it.

He needed to go it alone and although I sometimes found his reticence frustrating I understood it completely, just as I understood now that something had changed, a shift that would have been perceptible only to us.

When I watch back that first Zoom interview with Fay, what strikes me most forcibly is how much like himself Chris looks and sounds, how in charge of his material, how proactively engaged. It is still summer in the recording. We are sitting side by side at Chris's desk. I am wearing a pink T-shirt. Sun streams through the blinds. In the two-minute gap between one recording session and the next, we chat-bicker-laugh, the same as always.

Before leaving the Beatson, it had been agreed that Chris would continue with his chemotherapy treatment at the Inverclyde Royal Hospital, Branchton, just a fifteen-minute drive from the Wemyss Bay ferry terminal. His treatments would be administered at three-week intervals, under the supervision of our new oncology consultant, Dr Vivienne MacLaren. On Thursday 7 September, the day before what would be Chris's second dose of chemo, we were scheduled to meet with Vivienne in her office to discuss how things were going.

The oncology department was quiet, well ordered, welcoming. We found our way without difficulty and with a certain amount of merriment — this was our first trip over to the mainland since Chris had come home and we felt we had achieved something. With me unable to drive and Chris unable to walk, any trip out of the house had started to take on something of a Laurel and Hardy aspect: Chris would ease his way out to the car using his walking frame; I would fold up his wheelchair and stow it in the boot of our battered black Volkswagen, heaving and gasping at the weight of it, which was considerable.

Once behind the wheel, Chris felt as comfortable and at ease as he had always done while driving. Pushing him around the hospital compound after we arrived there, I was firmly in charge of getting us where we needed to go.

I liked and trusted Viv immediately, as I had trusted Ben Fulton. She was young, warm, approachable, someone I felt I would be able to talk to about anything. I wanted to know more about her, to ask her how she came to be involved in cancer diagnosis and treatment. I wished we could have met her under different circumstances. The three of us chatted about our journey over, about our lives since Chris had come out of hospital, about books. Vivienne congratulated Chris on looking as well as he did. Then she told us that she would be lowering the dose of carboplatin for the second treatment.

'The blood sample shows there's been damage to the kidneys,' she said. 'We don't want to risk any further damage without assessing how effective the chemo has been so far. You have to remember that this is quite a toxic treatment.' She said she would arrange for a further CT scan, to be carried out in advance of Chris's third chemo treatment on 29 September. 'That's the day before our wedding,' Chris said. We asked if the treatment could be scheduled for the morning again, so we could be back on the island in time to have supper with the Clutes, who would be travelling up from London.

Chris seemed to tolerate the second chemo treatment as well as the first – aside from one short period of extreme nausea, he suffered no discernible side-effects. Ten days later we headed to the Gartnavel Hospital in Hyndland for the CT scan, a journey that involved doing battle with Glasgow's convoluted system of motorways. Chris handled the driving without any hint of strain but he was nervous about the appointment. Although I reassured him that this scan would be quick and simple, nothing like what he had experienced with the biopsy, he was still wary of any further encounters with the MRI machine. He was seen quickly, and the scan passed off without incident.

The following Wednesday, Evelyn came to take Chris's blood sample in advance of his next chemo treatment on the Friday. But when Vivienne called us on the Thursday morning to discuss the results, it was with bad news.

The CT scan had shown mixed results: while some of Chris's tumours had shrunk, others had remained the same or actively increased in size. Just as worryingly, readings taken from the blood sample revealed that Chris's kidney function had decreased still further.

'We can't afford to let that drop below thirty per cent,' Viv warned us. 'The effect of that would be as detrimental as the cancer. With that in mind, and with the chemo not having been as effective as we would have liked, I would strongly advise you against continuing.'

She added that she would schedule a second radiotherapy treatment, to try and stabilize the tumours at the base of Chris's spine. 'This should help with the back pain you've been experiencing,' she said. Up until now, we had been successful in managing Chris's pain with paracetamol. The whole point of us being registered to Inverclyde and to Vivienne had been to minimize the disruption and difficulty of travelling to and from the mainland but the radiotherapy would be carried out at the Beatson, and would necessitate two trips into Glasgow, one for the pre-treatment scan and then another for the treatment itself. Chris did not seem deterred by this, but I was becoming increasingly concerned about him driving on the motorway again. His tiredness was becoming more noticeable, at least to me.

I remember it was this — the thought of these car journeys — that I found most troubling. The more far-reaching implications — that once the second dose of radiotherapy had been administered, Chris would in all likelihood not be offered any further treatment — were too serious to be fully acknowledged. Instead, I stepped around them, as one might step around a pothole or a particularly large puddle. Chris was still strong, still working, still *managing*. We would manage this, too.

We were together for twenty years, living under the same roof for thirteen of them. We slept thousands of nights side by side but we were never to share a bed as man and wife. This is a sadness I have not put into words until today.

We had spoken now and then about getting married, though the matter did not feel urgent, to either of us. Chris had already been married three times; I felt an instinctive caution about being legally bound. We both knew we were together for life. Neither of us felt the need for outside sanction. 'We're fine as we are,' each of us had said to the other on numerous occasions. Both of us meant it.

Chris's diagnosis changed everything. I'd heard too many horror stories about the partners of terminally ill people being shut out of the decision-making process – by family, by medical staff, by the legal profession. Suddenly it seemed dangerous for both of us, not to make things official. 'I think we should get married,' I said to Chris, the day we had it confirmed that he had cancer. I spoke the words almost without thinking about them. Chris looked momentarily surprised, then elated. 'Do you mean that?' he said. I did. His happiness and excitement were palpable. 'I hope I live long enough,' he said, 'I hope I get there.'

I told him not to be ridiculous, of course he would get there. Everyone we told was enthused by the news. A wedding is easier to talk about than cancer. For me the two will always be linked. Most marriage vows speak of the life that is being promised, that is still to come; ours were mostly about the life we had already lived.

I wanted the wedding to be in September. I have never liked October, the harbinger of winter, that feeling of encroaching darkness as the clocks go back. September is amber, translucent, the month of last chances. With Chris still in hospital I filed the necessary paperwork, spoke with the registrar. By the time Chris came home at the end of August everything was arranged. We would marry at Eaglesham House, Rothesay, on 30 September. Anne and Garry Charnock had offered to host the reception.

Before Chris went into hospital I had been in the tentative early stages of researching a new book. The story was based around a murder committed in Sussex, soon after the war. When I realized I would not be able to travel for research for the foreseeable future, I set that manuscript aside to work on something else, a novel set here on the island, but the story kept veering off into more personal territory.

I doubt I will ever go back to it, though there is a boy in the story who keeps resurfacing, perhaps I'll write about him. When I read through those pages now I can still feel the terrible effort that went into producing them, traces of story like traces of rust, dry streaks of broken thread.

How are you supposed to arrange your time when you know the person you are living with is dying?

There is a feeling you cannot escape, that your actions and even your thoughts are decomposing like compost, held to ransom.

Against this finality how can they have value, how can they have weight?

And so you float in an endless present that is really stasis.

And this:

Cancer is not a willing decline, said the retired doctor. It is a robbery. It is having your house burgled and trashed, your bank accounts emptied by thieves.

And then, this:

I just don't know if I will ever get over it, Kaja says. It is the evening before her wedding. I have never felt less present, less in charge of my life. Her face is like a ghost's face, a white lady that haunts the grange, hair piled high beneath a dusty veil. I can't explain what this is like, not to anyone, Kaja says. The words just aren't there.

There was more about Kaja's wedding, but I deleted it. The day before Chris and I got married was a kind of blankness. There were problems on the West Coast Main Line and the Clutes, whose train was left stranded at Oxenholme for more than three hours, only narrowly avoided missing the last ferry of the day. We met them at the quayside and drove them to their hotel. There was a vicious wind blowing. Chris wanted to go inside with them but the driveway was long and steep and he could not manage it. I was trembling with stress, terrified that Chris might fall, appalled that John and Judith had had no supper.

'We got some fish and chips,' Judith said, 'at Wemyss Bay. Don't worry about us.'

Lizzy and Simon at least were safely in Glasgow, eating Chinese.

30 September was warm and bright. The harsh wind had blown over, downgraded to a mellow breeze. Our guests greeted us as we arrived, then seated themselves in the function room of Eaglesham House, sunshine spilling in through the tall windows. I had chosen to read 'Waiting' by the Russian poet Yevtushenko, whose work I have known

and loved since the age of sixteen. Our friend Matt Hill read the closing pages of Chris's novel *The Adjacent*, the same pages I will end up reading myself the following August, at Chris's memorial.

Chris's witness was John Clute, mine was my mother, Monica. Monica is now in her eighties, and had been unwell for most of the summer. In the wedding photos she looks fragile, softly outlined as a ghost. She cried as we read our vows.

The scents of lilies and wood polish, the accumulation of memory, like a kind of soft dust. At the reception, Chris spoke about love, and what it meant to him. 'I enjoyed that day so much,' he said to me repeatedly in the months that followed. 'I wish we could do it all again.'

Our wedding was a gift, all the more precious because its meaning is still unfolding. Just a week ago as I write, Eaglesham House was put up for auction, the council offices having been relocated to the old Royal Bank of Scotland premises in the centre of town, which are cheaper to run. Our wedding was one of the last to be celebrated in the old building. That too feels like a gift, a gift of late summer.

'We made it,' Chris said. There is a photograph of us kissing, taken by our friend Janet Bentley as the registrar, Sandra Cobain, pronounced us husband and wife. I was going to write that we look as we did in the old days, but it wouldn't be true. What we look like are two people who have found what they were searching for. The fact of our marriage sustains me in ways I never imagined.

I have in front of me Chris's desk diary from 2023. I have fetched it from his office, where it has remained since his death in its usual place, to the front and to the right of his computer screen. Although I have been steadily dismantling our home for several months now, Chris's desk stands exempt from this putting-away, this setting-aside, an island of the past.

I brought the diary upstairs because I wanted to check the dates of Chris's hospital appointments. They are not in my own diary – I have the foolhardy and occasionally disastrous habit of carrying lists of scheduled appointments around in my head – but Chris always made a note of everything, and although I know it will not matter in the least to anyone reading this book if Chris's palliative radiotherapy session took place in the second or third week of October, it is important to me. It is important to me because details – facts – have always been important to me and I want to be sure I am remembering correctly. Remembering correctly gives me back the past, not as a block of malleable clay but as real time, passing.

I knew even before Chris died that I would have to complete the personal sections of this book as soon as I could. Not out of fear that I would forget things, but through knowing that the quality of my recall would change over time. From the recording of actual memories to the recounting of a story. Memory remembered. Already, the transplanting of Chris's diary from his office to mine feels like a wounding, a crumbling away of raw time into a kind of dry powder.

As with the notebook he brought out of the Beatson, I find it painful to read. The normality of the year's first weeks and months – an online writing course we taught in February, the twins' visit in March, Eastercon in April, trips to the cinema – sliding inevitably towards the disaster we did not know was coming. The journey to Stratford that never took place, the vast blank spaces of July and August when Chris was in hospital, the abrupt and terminal change of subject on the farther side of them. There are still bright glimpses of our life from before – a podcast interview Chris recorded, a meal with friends – but they are vastly outnumbered by blood tests, hospital appointments, phone consultations with Vivienne.

I come upon the date of the preparatory scan – Friday twentieth October, changed to the nineteenth. 'Moved because of bad weather forecast,' Chris has written, signalling the alteration with a circle and an arrow.

He is right of course, I remember now. I remember going into Chris's office and telling him there were high winds forecast for most of the twentieth and I was afraid the ferries would be suspended. I remember Chris was annoyed with me. He did not want to believe what I was saying about the weather because the appointment was important: if we missed the preparatory scan, his radiotherapy treatment would be delayed. I told him I was going to fix the problem and I did. I phoned the Beatson and explained about the weather and how it might prevent us from getting across to the mainland. The guy on reception in radiotherapy gave us an appointment for the Thursday instead. Lucky for us. On Friday the twentieth the winds blew in as forecast and the ferries were off from mid-morning for the rest of the day.

I had forgotten all about this until just now, until I looked in the diary and saw what Chris had written. Dark blue ink, the handwriting more spiky than usual, tapering off. I remember him telling me he was finding it difficult to hold the pen, how much this bothered him. By the following week, his handwriting has deteriorated still further and in places is impossible to read.

Chris had his second radiotherapy treatment on Tuesday the twenty-fourth. The radiology department is in the basement, a strange, lightless place that nonetheless thrums with the same quietly directed activity as the rest of the hospital. What I remember most clearly from that day is a guy I happened to speak to while I was waiting for Chris to be brought back to the reception area. He was using a wheelchair, and asked me if I would bring over one of the plastic stacking chairs for him to rest his leg on. His lower left leg was grossly swollen, the skin an angry red. The man looked to be in his forties, fifty perhaps, though with Glasgow men it is sometimes hard to tell. He was clearly a regular in the department, joking with the nurses and admin staff. He radiated good humour and a matter-of-fact courage that reminded me of John, from the Royal Alex, with the amputated leg.

I have often thought about him since, wondering about his case. The leg looked very bad. I hope he made it. I hope he is out there somewhere, enjoying this miserable excuse for a Scottish summer.

We reached a turning point much sooner than I had been prepared for. Chris was tired now, much of the time, and more frequently in pain. Time makes its escape so fast, even from me.

I am preparing someone for a journey they do not wish to go on. I am becoming increasingly aware that this – this bearing witness, this absorbing of existential terror and ordinary grief – will probably be the most important thing I ever do. To help him to die in peace, and surrounded by love.

The place we have reached is a place where really there is nothing but this love, sharp as a spear and robust, I believe, as a breakwater: barnacled, eroded, yet there still like the stump of a tooth refusing to detach. A castle for anemones and shrimp, for pale green crabs that scoot and scuttle in its crevices and hollows.

More beautiful than roses, those crabs, eternal and mysterious.

Or imagine a storm, the clouds thick and stuffy as army blankets, so opaque it barely gets light even when the sun does, eventually, come up. The most daunting wind and rain, and somehow there is a barn, a derelict outbuilding, a brick shithouse, and you manage to pull open the door and get him inside.

This love is like that.

I awake at around 4:30 and go out into the rain. I run gingerly at first because it is dark and the pavements are wet, streaked with the dropped-penny light of streetlamps. Late November, and my heels slamming the concrete. This running is the only thing in my life that is still normal and it is keeping me alive.

Lights in the water, flowing upward, the distant mer-kingdom. Slap-slap, slap-slap. And I am thinking I should write these things down while they are still going on, while they are actually happening. While I am running the writing-down seems possible, my thoughts fluid and supple as dreams. Once I am back inside the house the gap between thought and written word widens to a vast arch, cathedral-like. I gaze upwards into the vault, too tired to speak.

What I find most of all in my writing is the wonder and grounding sympathy of ordinary things. Streets, houses, signboards. A crappy parade of shops, steel shutters drawn down. The sound of a darts game spilling from the open door of a city pub. Someone buying a newspaper. A can kicked noisily down the road by a trio of youths.

And look, here is a ball of twine. The twine is a greenish-brown colour and stinks of creosote. The twine was previously kept in the top drawer of a tallboy in my grandmother's garage, a drawer that always sticks slightly when you pull it out. You have to wiggle it a certain way to get it back in. Forcing it does not do the trick – it only sticks harder. Can you hear the noise it makes, that woody squeak? Yes, you can. Inside the garage, my grandmother's car, a white Ford Escort, slumbers beneath an army blanket. If you listen carefully you can hear it muttering in its sleep.

The ball of twine is Ariadne's thread, which is a kind of anchor. When I enter the labyrinth, I must do it my way. The Minotaur is in there for sure, but so are other things: a lost umbrella and a missing sock, a stack of cardboard boxes stuffed with old newspapers. These are the things that will convince you the Minotaur is real.

I keep thinking about those godawful cancer memoirs, in which every detail of the diagnosis and treatment is rehashed, every feeling examined, every minor resentment exhumed and released into the wild. Why would I want to share the minutiae of these secret routines? My momentary frustrations, the sense that the present tense has expanded to fill the world.

What weight do these things have, when set against the fact that at some point I will recover my sense of myself and move into the future and you will not? That at some point, I will write this, and what I hate most about those memoirs of illness is the happy ending. Death as a sort of redemption, a literal closure, the well person regaining their life and moving on. A narrative pitfall that is impossible to avoid – the writer is, after all, still living – but what I am writing here has no value unless it remains *ours*. Unless I am able to make it clear that I accompanied you to the point of departure and you had to go on without me, though you did not want to.

But still I wonder if this going on without me might offer perhaps a kind of freedom? The expressly sanctioned permission to *let it all go*?

What I am writing here has no value unless I get somewhere close to the truth about how it feels to know you are losing someone, and to feel conflicted on every level about what you are going through.

The inability of certain people to respond. The sense, with some of them, that they are in wilful denial. That they are embarrassed, even. Hushed with a sense of horror at what must not be named. I understand, believe me. I don't blame anyone, not least because for me too there is a sense of impasse, an inability to put into words those things hardly anyone wishes to know about in any case. I find my earlier willingness to write upbeat, stress-the-positive emails has all but run out.

I step back, trying to see the horror of it from where they are standing, the bent-over, shrunken man, his wrists like sticks. The way he slurs his words slightly now, because of the morphine. The way it is actually a miracle that he can still stand or walk at all. Some are waiting for it to be over, for different words to be needed, words that are maybe easier to say. Death is something concrete at least, a thing that has happened. Dying is something awe-ful. Too intimate, terrible and personal for ordinary discourse.

They need space from us, from *it*. They have my sympathy. It feels like an abandonment, nonetheless. I hope I keep the part of me that cannot forget.

On the morning of 5 December I tell him the only way I can face this is if I pretend he is going to Mars. Once he is on the voyage, there will be no way for me to contact him and no way back. We will be on different trajectories, but he will still be out there, somewhere.

December 11

To see someone in that much pain, and to know it can only get worse, that the only way to escape it is through non-existence.

Pain is normally something you recover from, or move through. To move only towards the exit door is a non-compute. To watch it happen is an act of negation, of criminal negligence.

I have come increasingly to dread this time of year. My whole body becomes tense, waiting for the solstice, waiting for the physical release of the year as it turns, a moment that is supposedly intangible yet that for me is internally felt as a sigh of relief.

The only sanity is in the mornings, when I go out in the dark, the moon huge and lambent, the wet pavements, the vast, seismic calling of rooks as they flood from their roosts into the bruise-blue, magnificent emptiness of the lightening sky. The sun rises, the dog star burns. The miracle of the world, turning.

It turns not for thee.

14 December, and the last time we will watch a film together, Christian Petzold's new movie *Afire*, which has recently become available via streaming services. The film is about a young writer and his friend, a photography student, who leave the city for a holiday on the Baltic coast. The writer is humourless, priggish. He is so obsessed by the idea of himself as a writer that he fails to recognize the fact that life is passing him by. Then his friend gets killed in a forest fire and everything changes. His tutor drives in from the city and turns out to have cancer.

'Why is it always cancer?' you say, but still we manage to laugh about it, the idea of cancer as a cinematic cliché. I sit at your feet, as on so many other evenings, your fingers stroking my neck, and there are moments when I forget that any of this is happening and then remember again. I find I do not like *Afire*, which in German is called *Roter Himmel*, red sky, as much as I have loved Petzold's other movies. There is something too finished about it. The symbols – the diverging roads, the burned piglet – are too obvious. The writer character – Leon – seems more of a dick than others of his kind, whose stories have been told before and handled better. The moments of redemption at the end feel too easy, yet already I glimpse an evening in the future when I will watch this film again and cry and cry, missing you in a way that has no consolation.

This is the week I realize you are not going to come anywhere close to completing the work you set out to do. Your ideas, your ability to think is unimpaired; the will to compose a written argument is beginning to slide.

16 December, and you are able to write a paragraph, perhaps two. You sleep now for hours, sixteen out of twenty-four. When you go to bed at night you do not read. You do not read, and this is unheard of. Only a fortnight ago you would read for an hour, maybe more.

You are afraid of being unable to breathe. I hold your hand and promise you this will not happen.

17 December, and this is when you tell me you are finished with this book, that you cannot go on, that work is now beyond you.

You have spent the day trying to write about *The Kindness of Women*, a book you have told me you did not think much of the first time around and that you have not enjoyed any better on a second reading. As with *Empire of the Sun*, you seem unable to come to terms with what the book represents. Fiction, or memoir? Whichever way you look at it, you find the work unsatisfactory. As memoir, it bends the facts too far out of shape; as fiction, it does not go far enough. You call it *fictionalization*.

I suggest that you are letting your superior knowledge of Ballard's life intrude on your reading, that the book should be considered as text and text alone. You concede that this might be so, but each time we discuss it you slip back into the same arguments. This has nothing to do with the disease, though it is true your ability to mount your case articulately has come under strain. The words you use feel half-hearted, sliding over one another in the way they do now as you fall into sleep.

I am heartbroken. But we can still talk, thank God. We can still talk of the things that made our life together miraculous in the first place.

'I keep thinking: *this is what it's like*,' you say. 'I just wish this was an experience I could come through, and be changed by.'

19 December
We have talked about death a great deal even before now, though as we are increasingly faced with the practice, the theory we once found ourselves discussing seems a small, pale, paper thing, a confetti-strip of torn reality.

I have tried to imagine and think of death as falling asleep, though the idea has become oppressive rather than reassuring. A mind trapped in stale meat, gasping for release. A great wave, as sometimes in dreams such a wave has come for me, only now I cannot surface, gasping, into wakefulness.

And then as I am falling asleep I experience a shift in my thinking, an idea that rises towards me like a searched-for image or keepsake coming suddenly to light: the spirit, not held within the body but flying free. Like a moth, I see it – a moth, emerging from an earthenware pitcher in which it has been trapped. Its wings unfurl from around its fuzziness and now it can take flight, into the vast night scented with petrichor and sprinkled with stars.

The body – the earthenware pitcher – an empty chrysalis. A moth, patchy-pale and miraculous, fragile yet free.

As I fall back into sleep, I know that something has changed. There is a sense of something new that can be safely moved towards. When I test the idea again against the grey light of morning I find it still holds true.

'A moth, or a wren,' I say to you later. 'Or an oak tree.'

'An ash,' you say. 'I would always be an ash.'

I know that such images, such consolations are commonplace, and yet this new knowledge, as it is felt, seems profound. It also feels true, so simple in its obviousness, a thing I should have known all along but realize only now.

It feels important, to pass this thinking on to you.

'There is something of the numinous in human beings,' you say. 'I have always known this, and yet I've always resisted it. Up until now I have resisted it. Now I don't.'

For some days now I have been witnessing a change in you. As if you are moving away, becoming part of something else.

As if you are in touch with something that neither of us can see yet, but that we both know is there.

The shortest day.

The worst is knowing that really you are not capable of writing further, that your journey as a writer is come to an end.

You do not seem to know this, or not fully, and that at least is something.

I tell you that you do not need to worry about this book, even though in the moment of speaking I do not know if I can bring myself to complete it.

If I can bring myself to keep living through these moments, these hours, through the thought of the days to come.

If I have it in me to do what is necessary *to make something of them.*
My mind is a blank slate.
You must go on I can't go on I'll go on.
The words, like building blocks, like bricks securely slotted into place. Look, this sentence goes here, as in a well-made wall. And in the night I think of the moths, rising up into the darkness, the only image that comforts me because they are free.

The peppered moth, Biston betularia. Like a bride, her train floating behind her, festooned with flowers.

Her wings, pale triangles, flicker secretly in the moonlight.

These are the things that happen behind closed doors.

THIRTY-ONE

'THE UPHOLSTERED APOCALYPSE'

The summer of 1995 saw Ballard checking the proofs for his upcoming non-fiction collection, *A User's Guide to the Millennium*. David Pringle had undertaken the bulk of the preliminary work in sourcing and compiling an initial selection of suitable articles, with Ballard making the final choice and deciding the running order. The book was scheduled for publication early the following year. *User's Guide* was to include book and film reviews alongside more discursive pieces, and forms the first significant attempt to locate Ballard within the context of contemporary thought.

There are essays on science fiction and Walt Disney, inner space and Einstein, astronauts and Coca-Cola as well as several autobiographical sketches, pieces ranging from the early 'manifestos' written for *New Worlds* right up to the lengthier rumination on the end of the war in Shanghai published in the *Sunday Times* to mark the fiftieth anniversary of VJ Day in 1995.[417]

If *User's Guide* is a taking-stock, it must have seemed to Ballard that it was not before time. In the November of 1995 he would celebrate his sixty-fifth birthday. Brian Aldiss, a friend through the early years of Ballard's life in writing, had turned seventy on 18 August while just a week later John Brunner, whose Friday night soirées both Ballard and Chris had frequently attended during the *New Worlds* era, died of a stroke while attending the World Science Fiction Convention in Glasgow. He was sixty years old. In an interview with David Pringle that October,[418] Ballard spoke of his sorrow on hearing of Brunner's death, adding that he had 'got the impression that Brunner had been very unhappy ... As a novelist he'd found his particular market completely gone, hadn't he?'

Chris was at that Glasgow Worldcon – 'The Book on the Edge of Forever', his longform investigative essay about Harlan Ellison's ill-fated *Last Dangerous Visions* anthology had been nominated for a Hugo Award – and remembered how Brunner's death had cast a deep shadow over the proceedings. Chris had often spoken to me of just how depressed Brunner was in the years following the death of his first wife Marjorie, partly as the result of an unhappy second marriage, partly – as Ballard deduced – from the fall of his work from favour in science fiction circles. Brunner increasingly sought refuge in alcohol, a strategy which according to Chris made his repeated late-night telephone calls both painful and embarrassing.

If there was a feeling of stagnation in science fiction at the end of the nineties, of old orders coming to an end with no clear line of succession, for Ballard the sense of time's passing – of the world moving on without him – was equally acute. He had expressed his fear 'that everything has happened; nothing exciting or new or interesting is ever going to happen again ... The future is just going to be a vast, conforming suburb of the soul' as far back as 1982[419] and prefiguring Francis Fukuyama's *The End of History* by a decade. As 1995 came to a close, Ballard insisted that 'already we can see a realm dominated by invisible technologies. Smart cards and the modem will sub-contract many of the functions of the central nervous system, leaving us free to enjoy the pleasures of alienation and anomie. Psychopathy will form the only reliable basis for sainthood. Nothing will mean anything, and instant religions will flicker and fade like off-peak commercials. As always when visualizing the future, we find that we have merely described the present, and the 1990s hold almost all the patents on the day after tomorrow.'[420]

With so much of his own history now written, told and even filmed, for Ballard the need to break new ground as a writer would have been pressing, and how better to confront the complacency of the post-Cold-War equilibrium than by revealing it as a dangerous exercise in self-deception? Ballard had already made tentative mention of his work in progress in an interview with Andrew Asch for *Sci-Fi Universe* – 'It's a psychological study. Oh God, it sounds crazy. It's about the necessity of crime.'[421] – and *Cocaine Nights*, published in 1996, would prove to be his biggest-selling title after *Empire of the Sun* and *Crash*.

Cocaine Nights is a black comedy in the form of a crime novel. Ballard's enthusiasm for TV cop shows had discovered a new outlet, though fans of the police procedural would find themselves bemused by a scenario in which 'crime ... had become one of the performing arts'.[422] In *Cocaine Nights*, Ballard's petri dish for the cultivation of anarchy is the Spanish coastal resort of Estrella de Mar, a haven for tax exiles and other assorted expats presided over by a retired film mogul named Hollinger and his starlet wife Alice. Charles Prentice, a travel writer, heads to the resort on the trail of his brother Frank, the manager of Estrella de Mar's popular Club Nautico. Frank is in custody for murder – he has confessed to starting a fire at the Hollingers' villa, killing the couple together with their niece Anne, their Swedish au pair Bibi Jansen and Hollinger's personal assistant Roger Sansom.

Charles is in no doubt that Frank's confession is false, even though he perversely insists on sticking to his story. He moves into Frank's apartment, determined to discover the true identity of the arsonist and free his brother. As with the classic murder mystery *Cocaine Nights* nominally resembles, there are a number of equally plausible suspects – the novel even sports a *Murder-on-the-Orient-Express*-style denouement. In this case, however, the mechanics of the whodunnit are merely a convenient exoskeleton for what might be described as a queasy mash-up of the short-lived nineties TV soap opera *El Dorado* and David Cronenberg's *Shivers*.

As Charles arrives in Estrella de Mar, he is simultaneously lulled and discomfited by '[an] architecture dedicated to the abolition of time ... the apparent absence of any social structure, the timelessness of a world beyond boredom, with no past, no future and a diminishing present.'[423] An 'affectless realm' where 'nothing could ever happen ... where entropic drift calmed the surfaces of a thousand swimming pools.' But the more closely acquainted he becomes with individuals in Frank's circle – David Hennessy the lawyer-turned-club-treasurer, Irwin Sanger the rogue psychiatrist, Elizabeth Shand the steely entrepreneur, Paula Hamilton the resort's doctor and also Frank's lover, charismatic ex-army tennis coach Bobby Crawford – the more he begins to realize that the deadly, valium-induced stasis is an illusion.

Cars are wrecked and torched, yachts are set on fire in the harbour, porn films featuring some disturbingly familiar faces are left deliberately for Charles to find. There are spy cameras everywhere, but they seem to function mainly as another means of creating illicit images. No Ballard narrative would be complete without a mad doctor and in this one there are several. *Cocaine Nights* is the slippery underbelly of Vermilion Sands, a warped evocation of the déclassé, heat-hazed, concrete-and-palm-trees construct of the Mediterranean. The same landscape, ironically, that Ballard himself had returned to each summer for more than three decades and where, he had once declared, he would happily live full-time if he could properly afford to.

Bobby Crawford turns out to be one of Ballard's sainted psychopaths, the same kind of chaos-bringer we recognize from as far back as Strangman in *The Drowned World*, a close cousin of Robert Vaughan in *Crash*. Crawford's contention – that crime is a necessary catalyst for creativity – is the secret glue holding the community of Estrella de Mar together, and just as Neil Dempsey finds himself in thrall to Dr Barbara in *Rushing to Paradise*, so Charles Prentice falls spiritually in love with Bobby Crawford, aiding and abetting his lunatic schemes even as he fears their outcome may be fatal. He begins to see Crawford as his brother Frank saw him – as a passport to a more vital version of himself.

'This is Ballard's beach read,' declares James Lever in the introduction to the 2014 edition, 'designed to be picked up at an airport, consumed poolside and left, mottled with Ambre Solaire and disintegrating, its binding glue long-melted, on a shelf in the villa between the Dibdins and Rendells it is slyly constructed to resemble.' The larger-than-life characters, the expensive consumables, the sun-drenched ambience largely inure us to the outbursts of violence in *Cocaine Nights* – like Charles, we are prepared to turn a blind eye. And yet the concerns at the novel's heart are not dissimilar from those that drive *Crash*, a novel that just happened to be back in the news again owing to the storm of negative publicity surrounding the release of David Cronenberg's screen adaptation.

Crash had finished filming in December 1995, previewed in March 1996 and premiered at the Cannes film festival on 17 May. The film won a prize for its 'audacity, originality and daring', but was immediately controversial, causing audience walk-outs, jury abstentions and outrage in the print media. Ballard, who always enjoyed film festivals, seemed delighted by the attention – 'Cannes is a heady place for a novelist'[424] –

but a review in the *Evening Standard* on 3 June in which the critic Alexander Walker damned *Crash* as 'a movie beyond the bounds of depravity... that left many hardened film-goers at the Cannes preview feeling debased' generated a tidal wave of disapproval and active press campaigning against Cronenberg's film, most vociferously from the *Daily Mail*, whose front-page headlines exhorted the authorities to 'ban this car crash sex film'.[425]

While the movie opened in French cinemas in July as planned, *Crash* was not granted certification in the UK until the March of 1997, with cinematic release further delayed until June, three months behind the similarly delayed US release. The Tory Minister for National Heritage, Virginia Bottomley, urged local authorities to use what powers they had to stop the film being screened, a move that resulted in *Crash* being banned within the precincts of the City of Westminster, where it did not appear on a cinema screen until as late as 2020.

Ironically and predictably, the moral panic around *Crash* – much of the hand-wringing perpetrated by people who had not even seen the film – aroused increased interest in it, ensuring its enduring success as a cult classic. The discourse around the film was further intensified when in the early hours of Sunday 31 August, Princess Diana was killed in a car crash in Paris along with her lover Dodi Fayed and their driver Henri Paul.

The epitome of glamour and almost preternaturally photogenic, Diana was a Ballardian phenomenon even before her demise, a character who could have stepped out of a *Vermilion Sands* story or even from the pages of *Cocaine Nights* itself. Her recent association with the playboy son of a scurrilous Egyptian billionaire had done nothing to undermine the fascination felt for her not just in Britain but by the public worldwide. If anything it proved the opposite. Diana's untimely death in a Paris road tunnel with a drunk driver at the wheel was a human tragedy; alongside the Kennedy assassination, it was also a uniquely Ballardian moment.

I remember waking that Sunday morning, switching on my bedside radio at the precise moment the pips sounded for the seven o'clock news. I heard the headline with a sense of unreality, believing at least for a second that it must be some kind of joke. My feelings had nothing to do with the monarchy, pro or con. Diana had acquired the status of a modern myth; to see such an icon so casually destroyed – the attendant paparazzi jostling for images, like the Furies in pursuit of their victim – was profoundly shocking.

Neither were the Ballardian comparisons slow in coming. The science fiction editor Gordon van Gelder, attending the 1997 Worldcon in San Antonio, Texas, heard the breaking news. 'I remember I was sitting in the bar near Mike Moorcock when someone (I think it was K. W. Jeter) said, "Oh Ballard's gonna love this," and Moorcock agreed.'[426] Two weeks later Salman Rushdie, writing in *The New Yorker*, reflected on how 'it is one of the darker ironies of a dark event that the theme and ideas explored by Ballard and Cronenberg ... should have been lethally acted out in the car accident that killed Diana.'[427]

Speaking about the tragedy years later, Ballard speculated about how 'the outpouring of grief after her death was a collective mourning for the demise of the whole royal family. Perhaps we were grieving for the loss of our whole country because Diana was, in our eyes, the last perfect and wonderful thing.' He also recalled that 'some tabloid journalists seemed to think I'd orchestrated Diana's accident and planned the whole thing. I felt like saying, "Everything went nearly perfectly, but it should have been a Buick."'[428]

Four months before the death of Diana, Labour's landslide election victory on 1 May had done nothing to offset Ballard's conviction that the only future we had to look forward to would be one of political stagnation, moral nihilism and mind-numbing consumerism. Along with those of the rest of the country, Ballard's feelings about the New Labour project and Tony Blair in particular tended to veer between positive and negative in accordance with how successfully he appeared to be navigating the seismic political events that were to define his years in government. Certainly by the time Britain became joined with the Americans in their war with Iraq, Ballard felt critical enough of Blair to cast him as villain in his contribution to an end-of-year 'Heroes and Villains' piece in the *Independent*: 'He strikes me as a dangerous man, a would-be Messiah with a pocketful of nails, searching for a cross to die on.'[429]

If there was to be a response to the dangerous vacuity of Blairism it would have to be through art, maybe even Young British Art in particular. Less than a fortnight after Princess Diana's funeral, a new exhibition of contemporary artworks owned by the British–Iraqi businessman Charles Saatchi opened at the Royal Academy in Piccadilly. Featuring artists such as Damien Hirst, Sarah Lucas, Tracey Emin and Marc Quinn, 'Sensation' ran until the end of the year and attracted as much media and public controversy as Cronenberg's *Crash*. The tabloids seemed especially outraged by Marcus Harvey's *Myra*, a portrait of the convicted murderer Myra Hindley made up of thousands of photocopied images of a child's handprint.

Even if he was mostly unimpressed by the individual artworks on show at 'Sensation', Ballard was broadly in sympathy with what the YBAs were doing. 'Nothing is real, everything is fake. Bizarrely, most people like it that way. So in their installations and concept works the young artists are rebelling against this all-dominant adman's media-landscape.'[430]

Ballard maintained a keen interest in contemporary art and film making, with the works of Rebecca Horn[431] and Tacita Dean[432] coming in for particular approval. In February 1998, Jonathan Weiss's experimental film of *The Atrocity Exhibition* had its first public screening at the Rotterdam Film Festival. 'Weiss has drastically condensed and reconstructed the text,' writes Dennis Lim in the *Village Voice*, 'and yet somehow captured on film the essence of Ballard's writing, at once clinically precise and dreamily free-associative.'[433] The film's imagery is spare, stark, striking, repeatedly invoking the concrete, metal and smashed glass of the quintessentially Ballardian landscape. Weiss incorporates sections of news footage alongside original material, and uses as part of his soundtrack an extract from Henryk Górecki's Symphony No 3, a work that commemorates the victims of Auschwitz and that had recently brought this Polish post-modernist composer's work to worldwide attention.

The Atrocity Exhibition received its first British screening at the ICA in July 1998. Both Weiss and Ballard were present to answer audience questions.

Ballard would by then already have been at work on his next novel. In an essay first published in the *Guardian* in 1989, he describes how during their summer holiday in the south of France, he and Claire stumbled upon the site of what would eventually become Antibes-Les-Pins, the first 'intelligent' city of the riviera:

The 10,000 inhabitants in their hi-tech apartments and offices will serve as an 'ideas laboratory' for the cities of the future, where 'technology will be placed at the service of conviviality'. Fibre-optic cables and telemetric networks will transmit data banks and information services to each apartment, along with the most advanced fire, safety and security services. To cap it all, in case the physical and mental strain of actually living in this electronic paradise proves too much, there will be individual medical tele-surveillance in direct contact with the nearest hospital.[434]

'Claire couldn't wait to move in,' Ballard added. 'While I dozed on the balcony with Humphrey Carpenter's *Geniuses Together*, an enjoyable memoir of the 1920s Paris of Gertrude Stein, Joyce and Hemingway, Claire had discovered a piece of the twenty-first century under my nose.'

This chance encounter with what promised to be the ultimate gated community – a micro-society so complete unto itself that one need never venture outside – provided the germ of inspiration for what would eventually become Ballard's sixteenth novel, *Super-Cannes*.

Paul Sinclair meets his wife Jane at Guy's Hospital – she is a junior doctor, he is recovering from injuries sustained in a flying accident. They have been married just a few months when Jane is offered what seems to be the opportunity of a lifetime: a position as part of the medical team at Eden-Olympia, a gated community of elite researchers and captains of industry in the hills above Cannes.

The circumstances surrounding Jane's appointment are difficult enough – her predecessor, a young English doctor named David Greenwood, shot and killed eight people in a seemingly motiveless outburst of violence before turning the gun on himself. Matters are complicated still further when Paul and Jane arrive at Eden-Olympia to find they will be living in the villa where three of the murders supposedly took place.

Jane soon adjusts, quickly becoming engrossed in her work with the medical team. Paul, with little to do other than wander the manicured terraces and peculiarly empty recreational facilities of the Eden-Olympia campus, becomes increasingly obsessed with David Greenwood: why would this universally-liked English doctor have turned mass murderer, and was Jane's earlier acquaintance with the man, who trained with her at Guy's, closer than she admits?

As Paul begins to follow Greenwood's backtrail, he is tracked in his turn by Frank Halder, a security operative who reveals to him previously unreleased details about the murders. Wilder Penrose, the in-house psychiatrist, seems less interested in the murders themselves than in Paul's fascination with them. Violence, Penrose quietly insists, is a necessary release-valve for the unavoidable stress involved in working at the top of one's field.

When Paul happens to witness an incident in which security guards beat up a Senegalese immigrant, he begins to suspect that the attack was deliberately staged for the benefit of Eden-Olympia's overstretched executives. Frank Halder later confirms that the corporate ethos of Eden-Olympia not only allows for such unorthodox recreations, it actively encourages them. 'As long as they stay well outside the business park. In fact, it does everything it can to help...'[435]

The narrative trajectory of *Super-Cannes* closely shadows that of *Cocaine Nights*. Like Charles Prentice before him, Paul Sinclair sets out to unravel a mystery only to become a part of its deadly machinery. But if *Cocaine Nights*, with its unlikely murder plots and home-made porn movies, is blackly humorous, *Super-Cannes* feels simultaneously more focused and more vicious. 'Over the swimming pools and manicured lawns seemed to hover a dream of violence,'[436] Paul Sinclair observes. He has been told by Frank Halder that the bullets being stockpiled in the 'hunting lodges' set up by Eden-Olympia's part-time psychopaths 'have Ahmed and Mohammed written on them',[437] an insinuation that is even more shocking when we remember that *Super-Cannes* was published exactly a year to the day *before* 9/11.

In terms of how it functions as a thriller, *Super-Cannes* is a definite step up from *Cocaine Nights*. The plot is more fluently handled and for all the outlandishness of the central conceit there are fewer chasms of logic. The night-time street-scene of Cannes, where Paul prowls the bars on the hunt for clues, is as luridly threatening as Georg Grosz's Berlin. Anything might happen there, and does. Passages in which Paul tries to imagine David Greenwood's state of mind just prior to the killings –

'Had Greenwood felt the same clamour of the contingent? Had he seen the satellite dishes on the Merck building as they locked on to the sky, downloading Tokyo stock prices or Chicago pig-meat futures?'[438] – could be straight out of Don DeLillo. Yet still, *Super-Cannes* masquerades as a crime novel without properly becoming one. Ballard is not particularly interested in the solving of a murder; his interest in crime is in how it functions as an agent of chaos. As a background of derangement, both internal and external, against which the deliberately heightened action can play out.

Ballard spoke frequently of his first encounters with the British class system as of being forcibly immersed into a social construct he did not understand. But his obsession with gated communities and the super-privileged expatriates that live in them would seem to have less to do with the reality of contemporary Britain than with life in the International Settlement in pre-war Shanghai: the excessive drinking, the barely concealed affairs, the lawns of houses behind locked gates kept artificially green. In Shanghai as in *Super-Cannes*, money, status and race are a barrier and a protection against ordinary life – until the chaos outside the gates finally erupts into the violence of all-out war.

In 2001, Solveig Nordlund finally completed her movie *Aparelho Voador a Baixa Altitude*, based on Ballard's short story 'Low-Flying Aircraft'. It was filmed in Portuguese and stars Margarida Marinho, Miguel Guilherme, Rui Morrison and Rita Só. The film had its premiere at the Gothenburg Film Festival on 2 February 2002.

'Low-Flying Aircraft' was one of the stories originally published in Emma Tennant's magazine *Bananas* in 1975, quickly appearing again as the title story in a collection released by Jonathan Cape in 1976. The work is set in a world in the grip of a disastrous population crash brought about as the result of an epidemic of foetal abnormalities, cause unknown. In an abandoned resort on the Costa Brava – a classic early Ballardian landscape of crumbling concrete and encroaching sand dunes, though like Estrella de Mar (still twenty years in the future) it too has a Club Nautico – Richard Forrester and his pregnant wife Judith wait anxiously for the results of an amniocentesis test that will determine whether their baby will live or die.

Wandering aimlessly among the empty resort buildings, Forrester pursues a 'complicated rivalry' with Gould, a 'reclusive and standoffish doctor' who pilots a converted crop-sprayer and – in a clear reference to Chris Evans – 'looks less like a doctor than a middle-aged Hell's Angel'. Like many of Ballard's stories from this period, 'Low-Flying Aircraft' makes use of familiar science fictional material, rendered luminous and powerfully original through Ballard's inimitable deployment of a particular language. Gould's casual prescribing of Thalidomide to Judith Forrester may point towards the inspiration behind the story. (The Thalidomide scandal broke in 1961, with the British Thalidomide Children's Trust being set up in 1973.)

Nordlund shot her film on location in Tróia, a Portuguese coastal resort that was left only partially completed when investment in new building projects was brought to a standstill by the Carnation Revolution in 1974. A long-time champion of Ballard's work, Nordlund first visited the resort when her 1986 short film adaptation of 'Thirteen to Centaurus' (filmed as *Journey to Orion* and – appropriately enough – employing a disused car ferry as the generation starship) was screened at a cinema festival there. She immediately began to think of Tróia, with its abandoned hotels and beach facilities as the perfect setting for a new and more ambitious Ballard project.

Her original intention had been to shoot the film in English, with an English cast, but she was unable to raise the finance and with the resort scheduled for redevelopment she had to settle for a scaled-back version using a local cast and crew.

Nordlund firms up the dystopian undercurrent – in the film's opening, the Forresters (named Judith and Andre Ferreira in the film) are shown fleeing under cover of night from armed security forces – and makes the most of the ramshackle and faintly sinister atmosphere of the resort. An embittered collective of mostly elderly hotel guests spend their time playing cards, splashing about in the swimming pool and complaining about the frequent electricity outages. Strauss waltzes play on a loop in the hotel lobby. The women compare notes about their failed pregnancies and tease Judith cruelly about the likely outcome of her own. They talk in hushed voices of 'beachniks', deformed children that have survived and – like the forcibly sterilized mutants in John Wyndham's

The Chrysalids – been left to fend for themselves. Forrester is warned not to leave his wife alone on the beach.

The film's broader canvas allows Nordlund to give the characters more detailed backstories and to linger over the landscape she has created. Whilst the narrative is subtly different from that of the original story, the movie's atmosphere and visual imagery is wholly in sympathy with Ballard's vision. Judith's nightmares, involving outdated medical equipment, have a distinctly Cronenbergian vibe, and the film's scratchier surfaces and sharper edges make it more unnerving even than *Crash*. Nordlund's adaptation is intelligent and imaginative and deserves to be better known. Ballard himself admired the film, praising in particular its cinematography and Margarida Marinho's performance as Judith.[439]

'Low-Flying Aircraft' harks back to an earlier, inevitably more dynamic stage of Ballard's career; the turn of the millennium had seen Ballard regarding the future with a certain caution. In the November of 2000 he would turn seventy. Speaking to the *Daily Telegraph* the day after his birthday, he described this milestone as 'quite a frightening road sign. It's the biblical three score and ten,' he continued. 'I find strange warning lights I've never noticed before glowing red on my personal dashboard. I feel I can no longer pretend I'm not an old person. There are no dramatically new areas I want to explore in my writing. Most of my ideas circle inside my head like old luggage.'[440]

He had been ill for several weeks, brought down by a virus that forced him to cancel an appearance at the Book Now literary festival in Richmond and to put any birthday celebrations on hold. His health would continue to be affected into the following year. Writing to Rick McGrath in the April of 2001,[441] Ballard described his illness as 'a rogue virus, perhaps, dormant since childhood' and ascribed the delay to his next novel, which he had hoped would be finished in time for a 2002 publication date, to not being well enough to work.

This pattern of winter illnesses would continue, though Ballard had found himself unaffected by the millennium fever that had been sweeping the country twelve months earlier. As a symbol of the next thousand years, he found the newly inaugurated Millennium Dome singularly uninspiring. 'The Dome now stands and is open for business, the spiritual child of McDonald's and the Cape Kennedy Space Center,' as he described it to the *Telegraph*. 'Its interior, on the television screen, resembles Luton Airport in the year 2050, a timeless passenger concourse filled with electronic distractions, a Prozac palace creating the illusion that our boredom has been assuaged. For me, the Dome already seems to lie in its own past.'[442]

When asked by Tom Sutcliffe for the *Independent* if he felt any nostalgia for the simpler political reality of the Cold War, Ballard admitted that he probably did, 'because it did clarify the real conflicts between certain aspects of the human psyche'.[443] Speaking to Filippo de Porta for *Musica Repubblica*, Ballard feared that 'the suburbanization of the planet will produce an enormous boredom, the signs of which are around us today, and only acts of unpredictable violence are likely to give people a sense that they are free. A kind of therapeutic terrorism may come into being, which we already see in America in meaningless school shootings and other acts of violence.'[444]

The acts of violence that shocked the world and redefined all pre-existing political realities on 11 September 2001 were met by Ballard with horror, but with little surprise. Interviewed by Giles Whittell for *The Times* in the immediate aftermath, Ballard recalled how he was alerted to the terrorist attacks on the World Trade Center by Claire, who happened to be in the electronics department of Harrods at the time and saw the planes hit the towers on fifteen screens simultaneously. 'I think there's a clash of civilizations here,' Ballard said, 'We've got on the one hand this infantilized entertainment culture represented by America, and on the other... an Islamic race that feels itself threatened. We may also be watching the beginning of the end of the era of comparative peace and sanity created 200 years ago by the Enlightenment. It seems that the Enlightenment is being challenged and has nothing to answer.'[445]

Asked to comment on 9/11 a year later, Ballard damned the US for going to war with Iraq. He would go on to be highly critical of Tony Blair for allowing Britain to be drawn into the conflict under false pretences, with the Iraq war most often cited as the reason for his disenchantment with the Labour government. He believed the US was deeply mistaken in interpreting the motive for the attacks as one of envy.

'I think people have started to rethink their attitudes to America, conscious that US culture is swamping the planet ... The fact that

Americans are so puzzled that they're disliked is itself a sign that something is at fault.'[446] Speaking to Tom Sutcliffe in 2003, Ballard reflected that he had been 'as shocked as anybody' by what happened on 9/11. 'What was strange was the way in which the whole event seemed to be conjured out of the American popular imagination, straight out of Schwarzenegger movies and American comic books – they're full of planes crashing into skyscrapers and all that.'[447]

Ballard seemed to reject the widely held idea of 9/11 as an historical turning point. He saw it more as part of a pattern, an escalation in violence that was a symptom of a general malaise, the counterpoint to the endemic boredom, the 'suburbanization of the soul' that had been the subject of his previous two novels and would define his final ones. The attacks on the World Trade Center were on a different scale from the school shootings at Dunblane and Columbine, but they arose from the same impulse: an ambient psychopathy that could erupt anywhere at any time and be aimed at any target, 'the madness waiting to explode in the local hypermarket'.[448]

The politics behind the attacks, the shape of the 'new world order' they ushered in did not interest him so much as the 'latent psychosity lurking behind everyday life'[449] that had been his main preoccupation for much of the past decade.

Less than a year before 9/11, Ballard revealed to Edward Docx in the *Daily Express* that his next novel would be about urban terrorism. 'Things like the Soho bomb and the bombing of the MI6 building are very disturbing. Everywhere you look, you see meaningless acts of vandalism. The population feels to me to be peculiarly unsettled at the moment – waves of hysteria surge over the country and there is a tendency to over-react.'[450]

A piece in the *Guardian* six months later on the supposed 'dumbing down' of the BBC and the claim made by the then-chairman of the corporation, Gavyn Davies, that the only people complaining were 'white, middle-class southerners' saw Ballard floating the idea that 'the middle class is the new proletariat and in due course we will have to launch a revolution to free ourselves from the abuse we are now on the receiving end of. We are the new victims, exploited by society ...

There are beaters in the woods trying to flush out the middle classes and sooner or later we will revolt.'[451]

How tongue-in-cheek Ballard is being here is impossible to say, but he was clearly setting the stage for what would be his penultimate novel, now scheduled for publication in September 2003.

And it is another complicated rivalry with another man named Gould that comes to dominate *Millennium People*, this third of Ballard's increasingly strange, increasingly obsessive late quartet of novels. David Markham, an 'industrial psychologist' attached to the Adler Institute is on his way to Heathrow to board a flight to Florida when a bomb in the luggage hall brings the airport and its surrounding infrastructure to a standstill. A short while later, Markham learns that his first wife Laura, who also worked at the Adler Institute, has been killed in the blast. At Laura's funeral he encounters Major Tulloch, an ex-policeman now working for the Home Office. Tulloch is recruiting undercover operatives to infiltrate protest movements in an attempt to discover where the next act of seemingly random violence might be coming from.

Suspicious of Tulloch but determined to find out who was responsible for Laura's death, Markham mounts his own spying campaign, quickly becoming involved with a nascent revolutionary movement based around the fictional West London enclave of Chelsea Marina. Kay Churchill, a lecturer in film studies, Stephen Dexter, an agnostic vicar who rides around on a motorbike, and Vera Blackburn, an ex-MOD scientist and child murderer are led by Richard Gould, 'the Doctor Moreau of the Chelsea set',[452] a maverick paediatrician whose unorthodox approach to childcare has led to his dismissal from the hospital where he was previously working.

As the minor acts of vandalism perpetrated by Churchill and her associates begin their inevitable spiral into fatal violence, Markham begins to suspect that Gould may have still greater and more dangerous aims in view. But like Charles Prentice and Paul Sinclair before him, Markham finds himself increasingly drawn to this duplicitous renegade, unable to escape the vortex of his instability. 'I found myself liking him and drawn to his wayward ideas,' Markham admits. 'His threadbare suit and neglected body spoke of a certain kind of integrity that was rare in the corporate world of corridor politics taking over our lives.'[453]

Kay Churchill's tirade against the subjugation of the middle classes is as backhandedly true as it is hilarious – 'Professional qualifications are worth nothing – an arts degree is like a diploma in origami.'[454] – and indeed *Millennium People* contains some of Ballard's funniest lines. A taxi driver refuses to enter Chelsea Marina because it's 'far too dangerous ... a question of ethnic rivalries ... a dominance struggle between the traditional *Guardian* supporters and the new middle class from the financial services field.'[455] The showdown between police and the residents of Chelsea Marina is accompanied by Verdi's 'Chorus of the Hebrew Slaves'.

Ballard's late novels are usually described as satires. They have frequently been dismissed as too heavy-handed, a lessening of intensity from the surreal and terrifying visions of his earlier work. But as both Gould and Churchill repeatedly assert, though their acts of rebellion may seem childish and ridiculous, those who witness them will inevitably find themselves 'thinking about them later'. Ballard continued to see the novel as a radical form: the 'oral novel', with its realistic storylines, moral outcomes and relatable characters had always been anathema to him. In these late works as throughout his career, he is using the novel as a means of provocation, directly confronting the idea of literature as a safe space – a means of consolation – and presenting us with something that we will, like it or not, still be thinking about long after we have finished reading.

No novel by Ballard can be considered a safe space. In his revelation of Richard Gould as an abuser of children, Ballard is almost taunting us, daring us not to react, just as Gould's description of 9/11 as 'a brave attempt to free America from the twentieth century' is sufficient to explain why no American publisher would touch the novel.[456] 'The deaths were tragic, but otherwise it was a meaningless act, and that was its point,'[457] Gould insists. Ballard's frequent references throughout the novel to Gide's *acte gratuit*,[458] suitably updated as Gould's rhetorical injunction to 'fire a revolver into a McDonald's',[459] is the key to what this novel is really 'about'.

Reading *Millennium People* for the first time, I kept being reminded of Chris's insistence that *Crash* is actually a comedy. The more I came to realize I was being deliberately provoked, the more I began to suspect that early Ballard, with all its haunting beauty, has in a sense become my own literature of consolation; these late novels are a counterpoint to that, a new source of dis-ease. I began to wonder if the late books were for Ballard a form of self-questioning: after the seismic experiences of his youth, the tragic death of his wife, his 'redundancy' following the progress of his children into adulthood, is the deliberately warped worldview presented to us in *Millennium People* a reframing of the question *what is the point?*

David Markham's quest for meaning begins, after all, as a direct result of the 'meaningless' death of his first wife. Richard Gould cannily observes that 'divorce from a first wife is never complete. It's a process that lasts until death. Your own, that is, not hers.'[460] Speaking to Markham later about the disabled children in his care, Gould reflects that 'nature committed a crime against them'[461] — the exact words Ballard had used himself in lamenting the death of Mary.

'A terrorist bomb not only killed its victims, but forced a violent rift through time and space, and ruptured the logic that held the world together,' Markham reflects. 'For a few hours gravity turned traitor, overruling Newton's laws of motion, reversing rivers and toppling skyscrapers, stirring fears long dormant in our minds. The horror challenged the soft complacencies of day-to-day life, like a stranger stepping out of a crowd and punching one's face.'[462]

It is this idea that is at the core of the novel — of all the late novels but of *Millennium People* in particular — the sense that we live our lives on a knife-edge, a cosmic fissure we glimpse only occasionally, as the result of being knocked sideways by extreme events. 'A dream of violence had escaped from my head into the surrounding streets,'[463] Markham observes, in words identical to Paul Sinclair's as he surveys the too-perfect precincts of Eden-Olympia, and I find myself thinking of those weeks when Chris lay dying, when my sense of separation from ordinary life was more or less total. When I was confronted hourly with the sense of something monstrous bleeding through the backdrop, the knowledge that most of what we do stands irrelevant before the greater thing, the terrible mechanism of the universe, whose meaning we hide from ourselves for most of the time.

In the passages that describe the assault on the National Theatre there is an elegiac tone, a collage of imagery and memory and idea that is as heightened and as lustrous as any passage that might be chosen from Ballard's early disaster novels. Here, as everywhere, the quality of Ballard's writing is the proof of its seriousness. the outlandishness of the plot undermined momentarily by genuine feeling.

Writing in the 'Flyleaf' literary gossip column of the *Daily Telegraph*, Sam Leith grasps the essence of Ballard's achievement when he jokes that Ballard should have been awarded 'The Anita Brookner Prize for Writing the Same Novel Three Times ... *Super-Cannes* exposes the dark, atavistic forces that secretly underlie a seemingly idyllic gated community. Before that was *Cocaine Nights*, about a seemingly idyllic gated community that fell victim to the dark, atavistic forces which were secretly underlying it. That followed *Running Wild*, which took as its theme a seemingly ... need I go on? The irritating thing is that not only does he keep writing the same novel, it keeps being better than almost anything anyone else is writing.'[464]

From the evening of Monday 6 October 2003 and for the rest of the week, BBC4 ran a 'J. G. Ballard season' timed to coincide with the publication of *Millennium People*. Programmes broadcast included Solveig Nordlund's *Low-Flying Aircraft*, the 1965 'Out of the Unknown' TV adaptation of 'Thirteen to Centaurus' starring Donald Houston, Harley Cokeliss's *Towards Crash*, Spielberg's *Empire of the Sun* and the Bookmark documentary *Shanghai Jim* as well as the 2001 Profile interview with Tom Sutcliffe filmed beneath the Heathrow flight path at Shepperton reservoir. A new thirty-minute TV play *Home*, adapted from 'The Enormous Space' by Richard Curson Smith and starring Anthony Sher completed the line-up.

On 21 December, it was reported in the *Sunday Times* that Ballard had turned down the CBE that was to have been offered him in the new year's honours list for 2004. 'It was not for me,' Ballard was quoted as saying. 'I am opposed to the honours system. The whole thing is a preposterous charade. Thousands of medals are given out in the name of a non-existent empire. It makes us look a laughing stock and encourages deference to the crown. I think it is exploited by politicians and always has been. Half the honours are given to people in the armed forces and civil service as a way of keeping their loyalty. I can't take it seriously.' An interview in the *Guardian* the following day saw him expand on the topic: 'It uses snobbery and social self-consciousness to guarantee the loyalty of large numbers of citizens who should feel their loyalty is to fellow citizens and the nation as a whole. We are a deeply class-divided society. I think it's deplorable when leftwing playwrights like David Hare, who have worn their socialist colours on both sleeves for so many years, should accept a knighthood. God almighty, this man actually knelt down in front of the Queen. I'm in impressive company. Most of those who have refused are thoughtful people and people of spirit and independence ... It suggests there's quite a large number of people who reject the whole notion of honours in their present form. And it might do something towards bringing the whole system down.'[465]

'Now is it Tony or Cherie who is my biggest fan?' Ballard scrawled across the official letter offering him the honour. The spirit of Chelsea Marina was alive and well. A year later, Ballard's sister Margaret was pleased to accept an OBE for services to museums. Clearly, she was more forgiving of an imperfect system than her older brother.

THIRTY-TWO

'ABSOLUTE ZERO'

My time is past.
I am afraid that everything I do now will be a footnote.
I never thought that I would feel that
But I do.

I don't need things.
All I need now
Is a space to be quiet in and
A shore to walk along.
Sunlight, food and water and a lack of bombs,
Falling.

All I have – all I have ever had –
Is a way of remembering moments
And writing them down.

Chris's final saved version of this manuscript file is dated 21/12/23. In the early hours of Friday 22 December, he got out of bed to go to the toilet and found he could not walk. He still had feeling in his legs, but they would not support him; the effects of the spinal compression were finally making themselves felt. He fell heavily, helplessly, grazing his elbow against the bed frame. Later the following morning I found that his blood had soaked through the duvet and one of the pillow cases.

    I awoke to his cries, him calling out for me. He thought he was having a heart attack. He kept insisting I call for an ambulance, even though I tried to reassure him that what he was experiencing – unsurprisingly – was not cardiac arrest but a full-blown panic attack.

'You don't need an ambulance. What you need is to get warm and go back to sleep,' I said and said again, kept saying. I felt like a monster and the house seemed so dark. I managed to get him back into bed but still we were helpless now as we had never been, losing control of our lives in the way we had feared. After half an hour and more of pleas and demands his heart rate began to decrease and he grew calmer. 'The decisions you make have always been good ones,' he said. Conceded, really. Eventually he slept and I think I did too, I must have done. To be honest I can't remember. The hours passed.

When morning came we rallied, or at least we tried to. I got Chris dressed and into his wheelchair, so he was able to move around his office, to use the commode. He sat at his desk for a couple of hours. He could not work but he could read the *Guardian*, answer emails. In the afternoon he slept and then I made supper and we watched television, trying to be normal. The last message Chris read for himself from his own computer screen was sent by our friend the writer E. J. Swift, who had visited us on Bute the month before with her partner James Long.

I am so very glad I got to see you in November, Em writes. *And because I don't know when or if I will get to see you in person again, you're going to have to forgive a serious letter. Let's face it, there is no perfect time to send a Serious Letter. It's either too early or too late. So I'm going with early.*

Emma's letter is brave and true and honest and it is still unbearable for me to read, even all these months later, because it recalls a time so painful it should be left to its rest. The following morning is – what was it? Grey, I think. Raining, probably. I could look up the forecast on the internet – you can do that now – but I cannot face it. 'I can't last the day,' Chris said to me. 'Please will you get me into the Victoria?'

Some of the things I remember I won't write down. I cannot help feeling that to do so, even now, would be an invasion of privacy. Chris was a writer. He told his own stories. The fact that he can no longer speak for himself is one I must respect, accept, protect, keep in mind always. In any case, I did as he asked. I called the A&E department up at the Victoria and after I had answered some questions from the on-call doctor they agreed to send an ambulance. By the time I turned up at the hospital with Chris's things — his phone and notebook and Kindle — he was on a trolley, waiting to be assessed.

He was completely relaxed, and seemed more cheerful, joking with the nurses and with the duty doctor, when she arrived.

'He's nowhere near end-of-life,' I heard her whisper to one of the nurses. They took him on to the ward. The staff had made every effort to get as many patients as possible home for Christmas and by midday on the twenty-third there were only three or four unlucky or unwell enough not to have made it out. Chris had a room to himself, a privilege he had come to know through his various hospital experiences over the summer as something of a mixed blessing. It is blessedly quiet but it can feel lonely. Now that Chris is no longer capable of working, it can feel desolate.

I spend most of the afternoon there and some of the evening. Chris can still use his phone, thank goodness, he can still call me, still pick up. The next morning I arrive at the hospital just after nine. 'Thank God you're here,' Chris says when he sees me. He seems disorientated, no longer himself, unsure of what is real. The change in him is so dramatic it is terrifying. 'He was normal yesterday evening,' I say to the staff nurse. 'What's going on?'

I am told that it is the disease that is causing his confusion, but I cannot accept this. Eventually I discover that Chris has been given a form of morphine with a steroid component. As pain relief it is particularly effective, but for Chris even the small dose that he has been given is enough to make him hallucinate. I tell the staff nurse about Chris's sensitivity to steroids, about what happened to him in the Beatson. The difference now is that he is so weak he cannot recognize the hallucinations for what they are.

The staff nurse agrees to withdraw this particular medication. Over the next twenty-four hours, Chris gradually returns to himself, though his grasp of reality will never now be as steady or as consistent as it previously has been. When Evelyn comes back on duty later in the week, she puts a care package in place so that Chris can come home. He is desperate to be out of hospital. I know we are entering a new phase, the last one.

I am numb. I am running on autopilot. I cannot think or feel, I can only react. On the day before he is discharged — the Thursday — there is a torrential downpour, so heavy and so sudden the storm drains cannot cope. As I walk down the hill from the hospital towards the bus stop, I discover that the lower part of the town has flooded. The pedestrianized square opposite the ferry terminal has become a lake – there are actual waves, flickering across its surface in ripples of light. The vision is fantastical – Ballardian – and there is a part of me that refuses to accept that it is real.

I turn left towards Montague Street but the pavements are underwater. I head for higher ground, eventually arriving at the bus stop further along the front. The buses are still running, though the water, in places, is up to their wheel-hubs. They coast along, throwing up spray. Like Noah's Ark, I remember thinking, Noah's Ark with all the lights on, an image that seems to make sense, though only to me.

I speak to Evelyn early on the Friday morning. It is still dark. I had told her before Christmas that Leigh and the twins would be arriving on Bute on the fifteenth of January. When I ask her if I should tell them to bring their visit forward she says yes.

24 December
'I live and breathe you,' you said.

The worst, the worst, the worst is knowing you will never sit at your desk again, that you will never again open this file.

25 December 3:30 am
Ashes, ashes. You know how I have always hated this time of year, this colourless, leached-out interval between one year and the next, how I always long for it to be over, for the year to roll on its side so I can breathe again.

For now there is the dark, and rising from my bed I find some comfort in the view of what's outside: the roofs, the firth, the lights of the town across the bay where the ferries now lie, each close beside the other, resting today.

Always the water, the grey wet dawn. I put on my running shoes and go out into this darkness, this soft mist of rain. I cannot understand how things unravel so quickly. How just a week ago I was asking if you were sure you'd be able to make it up the stairs of the restaurant we'd booked for Christmas lunch.

Yes, definitely, you said, in what was totally your voice.
When we saw Evelyn before she went off-duty we both tacitly, without conferring, hid our plans from her. We both knew she would think we were crazy for even considering it.

Now I am running through this darkness, gazing out towards the lights – still there, still flickering – and wondering if you will recognize me when I get to the hospital, will you speak a word to me and know me, as you still did yesterday?

This is the only gift I want today. The only gift I want today is for you to know that I am there.

Yesterday you said, later: let me go.

You don't want my rage, my violence, my protest. Not my sadness even, not now. Only my love.

And this is it, the thing: we have each other. In every way and in the midst of every rage, we have belonged to each other and somehow realized it.
    I have realized over and again this belonging – *be careful what you wish for* – which is inescapable.

I am wondering: how did all of this happen so quickly?

I am wondering: how the hell do I hide my grief? Because that is what I have learned to do, what I have done now for so many, many years: until I have mastered my feelings, I keep them hidden.

I think this time the task is beyond me, though. Too big.

10:30 pm
And there could be nothing more to wish for, nothing more.

I am holding you in my arms. Though the bed is too small for both of us, I have managed somehow to squeeze on to it, to lie beside you. The nurses have put on Sinatra, because it is Christmas. You never liked Sinatra. He reminded you of your parents, you said, that whole generation

Forget all that and listen, I said. Sinatra is timeless, like Pavarotti, the voice of an age.

It was a very good year, he sings, and in the moment of his singing he is perfectly right.

Je t'aime, you said, mon ange, and peace is more precious than happiness, this I know.

30 December
And after that terrible week in the hospital you are home again. You are weak, and don't always want to talk, but you are lucid and most of the time at least you seem very peaceful.

On the evening before New Year's Eve you call me to you and we talk for almost two hours. I want you to know we will always have this, you say. This is our time, our hour.

Come tonight, you say. Take me into the dark corner.
It's not dark, I say. It's light. It's the universe. It's light.

I see again the peppered moth, its light-spattered wings fluttering upwards against the darkness, towards the moon.

Ever thine, ever mine, ever ours

1 January
Here comes a day I would normally celebrate. If Christmas is a taut holding of the breath, New Year is a shuddering exhale, a sigh of relief. The starred sky, the light on the water, the sense, finally, of something shifting, a coming back to life.

This year, the year comes in without a flicker. There is just one moment, around eight in the morning, when I glimpse it: those lights strung out along the harbour front, that opalescence. The smoky blue of storms that have worked themselves out.

EUMENIDES
They travel in threes. The first lot are fine. They remind me of the women I used to work with the summer I spent cleaning bedrooms in a hotel. There are others I quietly loathe, those blank-faced furies.
    They do not know my name
    They do not smile at me
    They touch you as if I am no one
    They make me feel like an intruder in my own domain
    The fact is that we have nothing to say to one another yet here we are.

Eumenides, three studies for figures at the base of a crucifixion. Aged twelve, those paintings terrified me. They were the first works of art that made me understand how art could horrify as well as be divine. That boldly-chosen orange. Those nameless, shrieking things.

The Eumenides are commonly associated with night and darkness.
    Knowing you will never know why I am so famished, that is the worst of it.
    The only way is down now.
    Down and through.

You, talking to yourself in your sleep as evening deepens its darkness into night. You sound happy, equanimical, engaged. I feel myself balanced on the abyss of parting. I fear I will not, after all, fully survive.

The devil is abroad. So early in the year, and already the devil is abroad.

3 January
When was the last time you woke, clear-minded, and whispered *hello you*?
You are quieter now, yet your dreams are plagued with cries

You trust me as a child trusts
When you wake you are different each time and I feel lonelier
Lonelier by the day

5 January
Bliss was it in that dawn to be alive
But to be young was very heaven

I'm in a state of bliss, you keep saying. I hope when you come to speak of this you will tell people that.

I am now an expert cancer sufferer, you say.
You can't win, but you can know.

You are travelling backwards through your life, examining every era from a new perspective.

You speak of bliss, and the transparent, washed-clean look of your face makes me think of the enlightened sanctity of the confessional.

You no longer want to talk about the book – this has happened quite suddenly – and yet your closeness to its source is more apparent to me than ever.

The divergence of our paths is grievously painful and yet it comforts me too.

You seem to know now, where you are going.

On Monday you asked me to bring you the Bible. The translation worked on by Edward Said, you said. You can no longer read – your eyes are giving you such trouble but it is not only that, it is more that you have lost the strength for it, lost the need – but simply holding the book in your hands (blue covers, silver lettering, silver sprayed edges) seems to give you satisfaction.

We talk about the language of the Bible and I wonder if you realize: you've never done this before.

It comforts me, that you do so now.

Choir practice, frost at midnight, the Sussex Carol. *A candle burned on the table*
>A candle burned
>Crossed arms
>Crossed knees
>Crossed fate

6 January
I still talk to you like you're going to live forever. My anger and my hurt, my desolation.

That you can still respond is both a miracle and a testament.

10 January
Like a great bird, a seafaring albatross, I am waiting for the wind to change.
>Salt eyes
>Salt seas
>Salt breath

I was trying to think up a story just now, you say to me, and there is nothing. I am bereft.

I tell you that the stories are still inside you, that they will never leave you, that if you were able to live for another ten years there would be more novels.

It is just that you are tired, I say. Too tired to follow the thread.

I tell you that it doesn't matter, that you have told enough stories already, that your work here is done.

'Norman Spinrad is irrelevant. Keith Roberts blew it. Tom Disch is like a cigarette lighter in a darkened room.'

11 January
Through the hours of night
You exist
In a kind of merciless, red-flecked twilight
Afraid you cannot breathe
Calling out in a voice not your own, searching for me, searching for anything you might yet recognize and I worry
About the (many, many) times I've spoken to you roughly
In case those moments return to harass you
Like barking dogs
The way such moments do in dreams

I feel the house shifting and reshaping itself about me
Becoming mine, becoming empty, becoming dead
A repository for things I no longer need

12 January (mostly)
You have lain quiet all night
And into this grey, stern morning
Of rooks,
Clouds –
This dress rehearsal –
I awake to the knowledge that when you are gone
There will be no summoning.

In the thought and in the dreaming you will be with me always
In the written word, perhaps,
Yes, sometimes
But in the things I will say to others there will be no trace of you
Just a construct
A carbon-copied
Facsimile, a
Made-up you that is really
   Mostly me

As in the past
That's how it was
Mostly
Anyway
The thing that was us a precious secret
A gift we managed to hold on to, regardless
And your own self a mysterious double
Hidden even (mostly) from me
And now slipping
Little by little
Into this rain-tipped
Pale-cheeked
Morning
And far from my sight

15 January
The last time we slept in the same bed
    10 July, the night before you fell
The last time you drove the car
    12 December, was it? Sometime around then
The last time we took a shower together
    21 December, the day before your legs went, the shortest day
The last time you sat at your desk
    22 December, though you could barely write a line
    The last
    The last
    The last
How many lasts before the last?

We are united, you said.
    The boy stood on the burning deck, whence all but he had fled.

17 January (Truly)
All this time

Since the last days began,
What you have liked to do most is talk.

People have come to see you and you have talked to them. Talked of your life and what you've made of it, the conclusions you have drawn from it, the wisdom you have to offer from it.

Sometimes for hours and past the point of tiredness you have talked, spoken your truth, the edges of words shorn off, blunted by dreams.

Most of what you say is true, or true enough. Some of it is grandiose, some might say deluded – if heard outside this situation it would be ridiculous. Some of it is funny, some wise; some – as has always been the case with you – extraordinarily insightful when you least expect it.

Some of it is playful, some of it shreds of the absolute, torn from the depths of a knowledge too brutal to countenance

Some spoken from the heart of loving kindness, so complete and so compassionate it hurts to listen and ach my love how truly you make the best of it, you are true beyond vision.

You want to know how you look, if you look a sight and I say no of course not, you look pale and very tired sometimes.

And sometimes, when the thoughts and words are rising in you and you gather them with all your strength you do
Truly
Look extraordinarily beautiful
Beautiful like a dying prince
Your hollow cheekbones and jutting brow
Carved in miraculous curves from some ancient grey marble
Some of the words you speak
Many of them, actually
Are only for me

I cannot imagine even for a moment that I would want to be saying – telling people – anything
Calling them to me to tell them things
Things about who they are and where they should be going and how
They should get there.

What would such words mean, coming from me?

I am erased
Not just by what is happening, but by those who watch.
Some of them,
Anyway.
In the end I have nothing to say
It is all in the work
The fitting-together of words
Like this, like that
Testing weight, testing heft, testing for size
The kind of work a bricklayer does
And the most I can hope,
The most I want is that someday
Someone will read them and hear their rhythm
Know they were deliberately chosen
That I tested their weight, and found it adequate
That I knew what I was doing

That magnificent rage of Plath's
In 'Lady Lazarus'
I salute it but I cannot summon it
I don't have the weight
Just a thunder of rooks, a storm of wings

And I hope that in my own
Last days I will lie quietly
Reading of Jane Eyre and Lucy Snowe
For the umpteenth time

Those strange grey girls with knowing eyes
Beloved mirrors
Locked in rooms they escaped through words
Walking some frozen path towards a crossroads in winter
The leaves yellowed and tired yet still ablaze
The blue rooks, calling

A bound trunk
Locked and hefted
Into the carriage.

19 January
Will there ever be a time when I can tell myself: this was just a few months?
    Will there ever be a time when I don't hear the thrumming and grating of the electric bed
    Thrumming and grating and shunting through the small hours
They're all about pain, the medics
    Managing your pain
    Alleviating your pain
    Ameliorating your awareness
    Dulling your responses
There are other kinds of pain, though
There are other losses
I, who live with you hourly, count the small things
Then I register the shock in the eyes of those who haven't seen you for a while now
And the whole thing washes over me again
The unstoppable tide of time
The slow inching forward
The place where we have found ourselves and where
Somehow
I must leave you
Find a way to retreat.

The world is still out there still moving but I am not allowed to touch it or only
Intermittently
Like a hand snatched back from flame
Or from extreme cold

I remember the first weeks of the first lockdown
That blue-swagged spring

Only this – this lockdown is different. The real thing.

21 January
Isha, Isha weht der Wind
Sag mir, wo die Blumen sind

22 January
I just want to get out of this place and go home, you say.

You keep calling me Renee. I'm not averse to it. I wonder if it's Renee Zellweger you're thinking of, her pile of blond hair. Or just some random mix-up. Either way, it does not matter. Nothing matters now. Our love for one another, it turns out, is stronger than any of it. Does that happen often, or are we as lucky as I think we are?

My understanding of life is zero today. I think of seabirds, ducking and diving amidst the storm winds, flipping from thermal to thermal their aloofness spins in their eyes. They must think us so dull, heavy, stupid.

Stupid as cattle, really.

I think of the albatross, coasting, her back like a shield and I think I have lived, and I have loved a person. We found each other in all the craziness and we made something of it

That is enough.

24 January (still)
The scab still on your elbow
From the night you fell;
Rust-coloured, crescent-shaped
The skin still knitting itself together
Imperfectly but with such purpose because
It can still do that, you see.

25 January (12:37 am)
My rage is a scream of denial
A negation of separation
A point-blank refusal of this scenario:
Something as appalling as this is
Should be disallowed

26 January (unlucky No 7)
I was once in love with a boy
Who loved Beethoven's Seventh
Forty years ago, give or take
You cannot be a writer because
You have nothing to write about, he told me
Deliberately

You know nothing about the world.
A bit of a dick I guess but
We were both so young.
I wonder where he is now.
I wonder if he can still play Mayerl's
'Evening Primrose'
The way he used to.

Send me out on the Seventh, you said.
    I have never told you that the Seventh is not one of my favourites and that
    Of the nine the one I love best is really the Third.

What was it Thomas Beecham said (he was so right)
About a herd of elephants?

But suddenly out of the ether they exploded:
Joana Mallwitz, Berliner Konzerthaus
Playing live

Modern tempi tending towards fast
Incredible energy in the string sections
Woodwind tender as night-owls
And I can only hope you heard it, love
I hope you heard

28 January
One month since you came home from the hospital, a geological age.

29 January
Everything begins and ends at exactly the right time.

30 January
Your breath moves, flickering in your neck like the dust-soft, purring movements of a moth in bracken.

31 January (At 3 am)
The cello carries the melody, a lament in the Byzantine mode. The higher strings, astringent, like open brackets. Music for small ensemble, 2 – 6 players. Music so true in this moment I think it is the only music I will ever need.

'I dreamed *The Hidden Treasure* in the form of twenty-five notes which I immediately saw as a Byzantine palindrome representing "Paradise",' John Tavener explains. '*The Hidden Treasure* was written in memory of Mother Katherine, who died on Christmas Day 1988, and of Sophie, a very dear friend who was tragically killed in Greece in January 1989.'

Chris was brought home from the hospital on Saturday 30 December. Aside from the electric bed, which was delivered on the Thursday, everything is as it was when he went in, though at the same time it is utterly different, as at the dawn of a new ice age.

Leigh and Lizzy and Simon arrived on Bute during the late afternoon. They came to the house the following morning, and for four more mornings after that. Chris was able to talk with them at length, to share memories, to tell stories, to say to them all the words he needed to say. He spoke incessantly in those days of family, of how he had loved being a family man, of 'our little family of five'. It was a time like no other and we all felt lucky to have had it – not everyone is that lucky. They departed at around midday on the Thursday. I had left the four of them that morning to be alone together, to share those final hours as the family they still were. When the time came for Leigh and the twins to leave, we clung together in the hallway, weeping. Chris said afterwards that the sight of us in each other's arms had brought to him a happiness that could not be equalled.

For another week, ten days or so he was still able to see and talk to people and to enjoy their company. Matt Hill visited, Anne and Garry Charnock, Lisa Tuttle and Colin Murray, Chris Johnstone the good doctor. Chris had words for them all.

Chris died in his sleep at around six-fifteen in the evening on Saturday, 2 February. I had noticed earlier in the afternoon that his breathing seemed different – small nips of air, like sips from a hot drink – and a prescience took me over, a foreknowledge I did not question. *Night was in the room.* I stood beside his bed, bent lower so I knew he would be able to hear me – they say hearing goes last – if he could still hear, and talked to him for an hour about our lives together.

'I'm going to feed the cats,' I said to him then, 'and then I'm coming back in here to sit with you and read.' I stroked his fingers, his narrow wrist, which first seduced me. I slipped my hand inside the sleeve of his vest, felt his warmth and smelled his skin, his scent, which had never altered, not even now.

I fed the cats and then I fed myself and returned to his side. He was so still and I thought at first he had already left. I rested my hand, my open palm against his breastbone. One breath, fluttering beneath my fingers, wings bright with dust. A ghost slips silently from the room. The moon-specked peppered moth flies softly free.

I called the district nurse, who certified Chris's death and then telephoned the undertaker. I sat beside him, waited with him, holding his hand until they came. After the undertakers had left, I posted the news of Chris's passing on my website, together with a poem by Robert Herrick, 'Ceremonies for Candlemas Eve'.

A day or two later, a friend reminded me that 2 February is also Groundhog Day, which in the USA and in parts of Germany, where the tradition originated, is used to predict the start of spring. The film of the same name, starring Bill Murray and directed by Harold Ramis, was one of Chris's favourites of all time.

14 February
Grief, like a bruise
It takes days to fully show

Only my rooks my clouds
Blue though they are, bring relief
Trace-memories of how we were
Beating the hour of eight
As they rise from the trees

The world without its hallowed centre
The unique set of two
I have my words but I don't have our laughter
My head on your knees, our talk –
Our little corner under the lamplight
Who knew?

My valentine, my valentine
Vale!

There is the text, and there is love, which is bigger than the stars, and that is all.

THIRTY-THREE

'A TASK COMPLETED'

'I do love writing about abandoned hotels and drained swimming pools. I wish I could write about nothing else. It's obviously something that happened during the war, when indeed I did see a great number of drained swimming pools and abandoned hotels, empty apartment blocks. I think the sense that one's returning to psychic zero, and that everything can start again, afresh, is what draws me to these images – because, after all, a drained swimming pool can be filled. It's pulling the sock of reality inside out. It's like walking through a deserted town – there's a mystery in the air. In fact, a deserted town has often more psychological presence than a town that is full of people ambling about doing their pointless shopping.' J. G. Ballard, April 1993.[466]

Towards the end of May 2024, I arrange to pay a visit to the Ballard archive at the British Library. Even before we knew how ill Chris was, we were coming to realize that he would not be able to make this journey himself; with the deterioration in his mobility, even the business of navigating King's Cross Underground would be impossible. I would have to go in his stead, which is what I am doing now.

London is where I was born, the only place I feel truly at home and that has not changed, though the pain of being here and in such circumstances is more severe and more destabilizing than I had anticipated. It is as if I have been cast adrift from the normal run of things. I keep thinking of Susan Kewley, from Chris's novel *The Glamour*, a woman rendered invisible through not being noticed. I talk about how I am feeling because I am expected to, because my friends are concerned, because that is what you are supposed to do in the wake of a bereavement. But no amount of talking can shift the weight of emptiness. This heavy-hearted feeling of being in a cul-de-sac, a dingy back alley of time, the cracked concrete green with moss, slippery with dripping water from a cracked overflow pipe.

The blue lights of Selbourne Road, Walthamstow, spread out below my twelfth-floor Travelodge window, the liquid flow of traffic, how you thrum on not regardless but despite; rivers of time, glittering, fluorescent stick-on stars fallen to earth.

London at least returns my gaze – knowing, constant, relentless – in a manner I can get on board with, with a truth that I can bear through being spoken plainly.

Yeah, babe, so it hurts. What did you think grief would be like?

The city has always been honest, at least with me. The hammering of rain on the roofs of taxi cabs, our togetherness flowing forever through the darkened streets.

When I arrive at the British Library it is still pouring with rain. I fill out a request form for the items I want to look at. Ballard professed not to care about his manuscripts – he even made some sort of joke about burning them in his back garden – though Chris Beckett, who catalogued the archive, confirms that Ballard's papers include material in draft form for all of his novels except for *The Wind From Nowhere* (presumed destroyed), and *The Unlimited Dream Company* (which as we already know resides in Texas).

There are three separate manuscripts of *Crash*, an intricate record of the novel's progress from first, heavily annotated handwritten draft to completed typescript. Beckett describes how he discovered, carefully wedged between the pages of the manuscript of *Millennium People*, a notebook containing Ballard's original outline for the novel. 'Several of Ballard's manuscripts were received as large tied bundles,' Beckett remembers, 'but the existence of the notepad for *Millennium People*, securely tucked away from view, was an unexpected surprise: it was evidence of a deliberate gathering by the author.'

The papers I want to see relate to unpublished material: a set of notebooks containing ideas for a novel that was never completed (Ballard referred to the project as *World Versus America* or *VUS1*), and in particular a file of notes for *Conversations with my Physician*, the book Ballard had intended to write about his illness in collaboration with his oncology consultant, Dr Jonathan Waxman.

There will be a ninety-minute wait, I am told. The manuscripts department is short-staffed at the moment and everything is taking longer in any case, because of the recent ransomware attack on the British Library. I sit in the downstairs café, waiting for my requested material to be retrieved from the stacks. I have not been inside the British Library since Chris and I attended the opening of the 'Out of This World' SF exhibition a decade ago. I remember we ran into Brian Aldiss, who was then still strong, still garrulous and amusing, still very much Brian. The building has grown unused to me in the meantime. I feel like a ghost here, a ghost of my former self. Poor, dowdy and alone, one of those crazy poets in their ugly hats and dripping raincoats who are turned away from their own performances because no one realizes who they are. Because they do not seem the part. Because they do not look how a poet is supposed to look.

When the papers are finally delivered to the reading room, my discomfort evaporates. The work restores me instantly. It is all I care about. The *VUS1* notebooks are a revelation, not only for what they contain but for what they are. Spiral-bound reporter's notebooks, wide feint, paper covers, the kind you might find on the intermittently stocked stationery shelf of your local supermarket. The kind you might use for making shopping lists, or taking down measurements – height, width, depth – when you are moving house. The kind of notebooks I remember from the 1970s, before the fetishization of stationery had properly started.

This lack of preciousness, this lack of ceremony is, or so it seems to me, pure Ballard. The way he uses the notebooks is equally informal, equally spontaneous. For some writers, the notebook is a recording device: scraps of dialogue overheard in a café, the colour and texture of clouds. For others, the notebook is a portable hard drive for the intricate, chapter-by-chapter working-out of plot.

Chris disdained notebooks as a working method. He owned a ton of them, and always carried one, but used them sparingly. Most of what they contain is facts: dates, places, book titles, films he had either seen or wanted to see. Though his memory for what he considered to be the spurious detail of life – the authors of books he had not read, stuff you told him yesterday, other people's birthdays – was often appalling, when it came to his own work, or any subject that interested him, his capacity for remembering was close to photographic. While he was working on them at least, he carried his books in his head from beginning to end.

Opening the first of Ballard's *VUS1* notebooks, I have the uncanny feeling of opening one of my own. There is the handwriting, for a start: the untidy scrawl that is meant for no eyes but his own. You can read it, just about, but you would never describe it as neat. More than that though, it is Ballard's use of the notebook as a sounding board, as devil's advocate. There is no landscape description here, no trying-out of dialogue. What there is, on every page, is a series of questions, ideas evolving, concepts in flux:

The more directly the war is presented, the more compelling the book will be.

I think there should be no neutral stance. The US is treated as Nazi Germany was in 1939–1945. There is nothing good to be said about the US, though the characters may remember a saner and more generous US of their earlier years.

Not bad – but what would the larger point be?

Ballard brings putative characters on stage – an English doctor, a CID cop, a female executive – arranges them in various attitudes, seeing if they might cohere as a group. He reminds himself to check the *Encyclopedia of Science Fiction* entry on 'War'. Then I turn the page and find myself staring at what might almost be an outtake from Chris's final novel, *Airside*.

Topics that interest me – AIRPORTS. Say that passengers caught in a terrorist outrage decide to stay put. They seize the airport, and establish a city-state…

As if a ghost had crept in, tapping me on the shoulder, and yet the feeling I get from handling these notebooks is less of being haunted than of returning to a conversation that was interrupted.

I never knew J. G. Ballard, but I might have done, it is only through a succession of unhappy accidents – near-misses in time – that I did not. He laid this notebook aside at some point, his fingerprints will still be on it. Now mine are, too, and so, in a way, are Chris's, though he was never here. The notebooks feel familiar because Ballard's way of using them is familiar – the same grappling for larger meaning, the same questions to self.

Whose story is this? What is it really about?

I set down my own current notebook on the table in front of me, side by side with Ballard's. Ballard's notebook has a shiny, holographic cover, a little flashy, a tiny bit kitsch, exactly the kind of notebook I would have chosen myself. I take out my phone and photograph them. I'm not sure I am allowed to do this, but I do it anyway.

According to Claire, Ballard's usual practice was to destroy his notebooks after each novel was published. 'Jimmy kept the early thoughts and false starts private. He wanted to keep his magic. In between delivering one book and starting another, he used to talk through ideas with me, thinking aloud about where he might go next. Reading the few notebooks in the archive is a moving reminder of this.'[467] Which suggests that if Ballard had had time to write *VUS1*, the three notebooks I am looking at now would no longer exist.

David Pringle mentions the *VUS1* notebooks in his Ballard chronology. He believes the notebooks probably date from 2003. He points up the comments Ballard made about the plot – 'A back story would describe the US imperial reach & attacks on other countries, its threats, use of force, etc. The events that have brought a sense of despair to its last allies, & the decision to attack the US before it is too late.' – and adds that on the inside back cover of a notepad, Ballard wrote what appeared to be a working title: *An Immodest Proposal or How the World Declared War on America*.

It is fascinating to see how fully in the mind of the older Ballard the USA has come to embody the forces of reaction: George W. Bush, the Iraq war, the skewed aftermath of 9/11, which is referenced directly.

You need not wonder what Ballard would have made of Trump, the 2020 election, the storming of the Capitol – it is all here, jotted down in these notebooks, not so much a novel-in-embryo as a tarot reading.

The file of notes for *Conversations with my Physician* is very thin, barely there, really. But what is there transports me. At the top of the first sheet of the unbound typed pages are some words of Fay's, handwritten in blue biro:

My notes to Daddy following our conversation about his ideas/thoughts for his book. He was in bed at Claire's, too ill to sit up, summer 08. However, a few days later he felt well enough to sit up and type a short note on his ideas.

It is not just Ballard I am with now, but Chris as well. Here, some fifteen years and more after these notes were set down, I find myself sitting before a ghost-image of our own book.

SECTION ONE, Fay types. *How this book came about. What purposes, clinical or otherwise, Professor Waxman and Ballard felt might be achieved by these weekly conversations, which began in November 2008, more than two years after W took charge of Ballard's case. Both men seem to have believed that a great deal lay unrevealed in their relationship, and that it was well worth exploring their very similar roles. Running throughout, chapter by chapter, is the thread of B's illness. Death still lies ahead, the end of the contest between the patient and his cancer, but to some extent it has been replaced by the sense of an indefinite half-time. The great paradox that presides over B's treatment is that this change of atmosphere is not achieved by Jonathan raising any false hopes. Quite the opposite. J is unfailingly frank about the end in store for B.*

Subsequent sections are outlined as chapter headings:

Patient and doctor backgrounds including medicine
Relationship to parents
Views on religion (life after death)
Cancer – attitudes to 'the big C'
Prostate cancer

Relationship between patient and doctor
Psychological state of patient and doctor

Various facts come to light in the brief notes for each: Jonathan Waxman read Ballard's early science fiction when he was a medical student; Waxman had been Claire's consultant when she was treated for breast cancer in the mid-1990s; Jenny Walsh – referred to in the notes as 'J. G. B.'s step-daughter' – had also been a cancer patient.

To some extent the impression we have of ourselves is a manufactured image created by our brains which makes possible our co-existence with ourselves, and with our families, spouses and children and with our colleagues in the work-place. How far does cancer replace this with a different image? Is this image more true to ourselves, or is it just another illusion? How far do serious illnesses in general reveal our true selves? Are there any ways in which we gain merit from a serious illness, even though we don't actually recover?

I wish this was something I could come through, and be changed by. I am brought up short by Ballard's momentary reference to Macmillan nurses ('superb') and by his pondering the effectiveness of art, literature and music as defences in reconciling the terminal patient to the prospect of death:

Or is there simply no defence against death, as nature demonstrates? Do we need a fresh approach to how we view our own mortality?

Ballard's thought process, his engagement with ideas appears as vital and as creative as ever. His fascination with science and with psychology as centrally present as in any of his novels.

It is sex to which we turn after bereavement, he notes finally under Section 11. *It is a door that is always open...*

Here the notes end. More even than the *VUS1* notebooks, I wish Chris could have seen them. I wish I could at least tell him about them because I think they would have mattered to him. I think – and even at a distance of months, it is still painful for me to know this, to have to write it down – I think they would have helped him feel less alone.

Writing to the film director Mike Hodges in the February of 2002, Ballard mentioned that his activities that winter had been curtailed by 'a really nasty virus, which I'm still recovering from – six months of fevers every afternoon & evening, two hospitals, three consultants & every test known to medical science. Answer – still a mystery.'[468] By the autumn of the same year, he was unwell again. Ballard's susceptibility to winter viruses appeared to be getting worse, though it seems that everyone put this down to his age, as I had done with Chris.

On 23 January 2004, the German photographer Helmut Newton died after suffering a heart attack while driving in Los Angeles. He was eighty-three years old, and a friend of Ballard's. The two had spoken by telephone just a few weeks previously. 'His death is a great loss,' Ballard said, 'but at least he lived to a great age and went with some style. He was a delightful companion, mischievous and forever young. I envied him enormously: he spent his life in the company of beautiful women and his own extraordinary dreams. Far from debasing his models, which Newton was sometimes accused of, he placed them at the heart of a deep and complex drama where they rule like errant queens, blissfully indifferent to the few men who dare to approach them. Newton's photography has endured for decades, as poetic and mysterious as when it first appeared in the 1960s.'[469]

Ballard spoke about Newton's art in the same way he spoke about Delvaux, and it is tempting to dream of the photographic accompaniments for *Crash* or *Super-Cannes* Newton might have created. Less than two months later on 11 March, Islamist bombers exploded devices on crowded commuter trains in Madrid, killing 191 people and injuring a thousand more. This latest act of terrorist violence was mentioned by Ballard in subsequent interviews, added to the catalogue of outrages that hover in the margins of his later fiction.

On 23 July a more personal tragedy struck the Ballard family when Bea's husband Nick Rossiter died suddenly of a heart attack at the age of forty-three. 'Daddy was the first person I called,' Bea said. 'There was a long pause on the other end of the line. "I'm so sorry, darling," he said, with a heaviness in his voice. I sensed he felt that history was repeating itself, and I knew he would understand, more than anyone, the struggle I would be facing.' The fact that Beatrice's two young daughters had been left without a father would undoubtedly have brought back Ballard's own feelings of devastation following the death of Mary. For Bea, his compassion and understanding in the immediate aftermath of her bereavement were a source of great comfort.

'What impressed me most about Nick was his complete integrity, his deep love for my daughter Beatrice, his idealism and his commitment to making the best possible programmes about the arts,' Ballard told the *Independent*. 'In many ways he was one of the last links to the great era of Huw Wheldon and *Monitor*.'[470]

Just over a year later, Beatrice discovered she had breast cancer. Her father, she said, continued to be a vital and supportive presence. 'I found it almost unbearable to have to call him and tell him the news,' Bea remembers, 'especially as it came so soon after losing my husband. The cancer was Stage 3, which meant I would be undergoing chemotherapy and radiotherapy as well as surgery. Knowing what my father had been through and survived in his life helped me to focus on staying strong, on believing that I too, for the sake of my children, would survive.'

Bea, who has won both Emmys and BAFTAs for her many high-profile entertainment and talk shows including the BBC's *Saturday Night Clive* and ITV's *Jonathan Ross Show*, credits her father not only with encouraging her early interest in TV but also with being a valued and trusted sounding board for new ideas. 'I always felt close to my father, as we shared many of the same interests, and often discussed what was going on in the world, be it politics or the latest advances in technology, new movies or TV shows. He was very amused by the advent of reality TV, a phenomenon he had predicted in his novels, along with YouTube and social media. My father once said he could imagine a TV show that featured celebrities fighting – which of course came to pass, with *Celebrity Big Brother* and *The Traitors*. He was always interested to hear about my work as a television producer. Not long before he died, he and I were working on an idea for a show that would feature his predictions for the 21st Century. He was keen to do it, and I had discussed the idea with the BBC. It is a shame the idea never came to fruition, as I know he would have been brilliant.'

Alongside the lively discussions, Ballard clearly relished spending time with his young grandchildren. 'He was amazing with my kids,' Bea says, 'thrilled to be a grandfather. He would come and have tea with me and the children every weekend. He would always bring them a big bag of sweets, and a pork pie for the dog.' Bea, like her father, has an affection for Golden Retrievers. 'Daddy loved to see the people around him enjoying themselves.'

Fay has similarly fond memories of the times Ballard spent with her own children. 'He would turn up with a dozen or more Kinder chocolate eggs. Within minutes, the floor of the living room would be knee-deep in silver paper, melting chocolate and small plastic toys. Daddy loved the sense of chaos that young children can bring. It appealed to his anarchic side. The kids remember those Kinder eggs even now.'

On 22 April 2005, Eduardo Paolozzi died at the age of eighty-one. He had suffered a stroke in 2000 that had almost killed him, and that left him partially paralysed. He spent his final years in a nursing home, a terrible reversal for this singularly talented artist, so full of life and opinions. Though Ballard had seen little of him in recent years, the death of his former friend would have marked a watershed.

Three months later on 7 July, the 7/7 bombings on London tube trains killed fifty-two people and injured 700. When asked for his reaction, Ballard spoke of the 'mistaken' ideals of multiculturalism and the need for Britain's Asian communities to properly assimilate. 'Blowing up bombs is their way of being modern ... The idea that large immigrant communities with ways of life unchanged since the Middle Ages should be encouraged to isolate themselves and make no attempt to join the host society has enormous dangers.'[471]

Writers as they grow older have to reckon with their changing relationship to the zeitgeist. And though he was always amused at my insistence on the word zeitgeist, this was a topic Chris discussed with me increasingly, both in relation to Ballard and to himself. Chris was an early adopter of digital technology – he wrote his novels on a word processor and then a computer from the 1980s onwards – but he disapproved of social media and never made use of it. Aside from a few cherished exceptions from his younger days – most notably the Beatles, Bob Dylan, *Monty Python* and *Fawlty Towers* – he was dismissive of popular culture and had no interest in it. He disliked most TV, and was happiest watching the news, though like Ballard he was an ardent, lifelong cinephile and – like Justin Farmer in his final novel, *Airside* – was able to recall every film he had seen in photographic detail.

During the last five years of his life Chris sometimes worried about falling out of touch, not so much with the world in general as with the world of science fiction. He found the increasing commercialization of SF – its decisive swing towards genre stereotypes and derivative forms – regressive and acutely disheartening. He feared that the open-ended, unpredictable, difficult-to-categorize speculative fiction he wrote – and to which he retained his allegiance – was not just under-represented, but actively rejected by the new 'new wave' writers of space opera, super-heroes and interplanetary adventurers, the same 'Buck Rogers stuff' Ballard had railed against in his *New Worlds* editorials of the early sixties.

Like Ballard, he found it difficult to sell his work in America – one US publisher, in rejecting Chris's 9/11 novel *An American Story*, accused him of 'trespassing on hallowed ground'.

Even before his cancer diagnosis, Chris was becoming increasingly aware of his own mortality, those same 'warning lights on the dashboard' that Ballard had intimated the year he turned seventy. In spite of these worries, his passion for the job of writing remained paramount, the thing we talked about, with undimmed enthusiasm, for hours every day. Like Ballard, Chris followed his own obsessions. His work still thrummed with power and energy, unique in its field.

Throughout the sixties and seventies, Ballard, in a sense, *was* the zeitgeist. He was now seventy-five. Although his capacity for intellectual engagement – with current affairs, with evolving technologies, with his own creative process – was undiminished, his relationship to the world had shifted, as was inevitable. Ballard never owned a computer or used the internet. He never had an email address. Aside from one brief, unsatisfactory experiment with a Dictaphone, he continued to write his manuscripts in longhand and type them up himself. Bea Ballard remembers undertaking a great deal of research into which computer might suit him best – many of her friends who were writers and journalists swore by the Apple Mac. Ballard said he would bear it in mind. Bea knew this was his way of telling her it was never going to happen. Claire, who was much more adept with digital technology than Ballard ever was or wanted to be, became his researcher. She surfed the web for stories she knew would interest him and then faxed them through to his office, the papers accumulating much like the scientific articles he had begged from Christopher Evans forty years earlier.

'I don't have any modern appliances,' Ballard admitted in an interview with the Australian journalist and writer Simon Sellars. 'I have a mobile phone but I hardly ever use it ... I used to see about three films a week. I was tremendously up with what was going on in the film world, but over the past couple of years, both my local video rental stores have closed down. And this means that I've stopped renting. So I've hardly seen any films at all for a long while. I mentioned this to someone recently, and she said, "Ah, this is because people are downloading films from ..." I couldn't make out what she was talking about, actually — from their mobile phones, it sounded like. Downloading from somewhere — they don't need to go to video stores any more.'[472]

Ballard regarded the world intently as he had always done, yet he sat at one remove from it. The feeling he had described on turning seventy, of having his ideas circling inside his head like old luggage, can only have intensified in the years since.

But for Ballard, as for Chris, the practice of writing was indivisible from the process of living; the idea of stopping would not have occurred to him. On 26 January 2006, the Canadian Rick McGrath emailed David Pringle to say he had received a postcard from Ballard with the news that he had just completed a new novel. *I will be fleeing south as soon as the Med warms up — then back in July/August for the PR treadmill.* A second postcard received on 8 February confirmed the novel's title — Kingdom Come — and a September release date. *It asks the question — 'will consumerism turn into fascism?' and argues that it might, if we aren't careful ...*

The M25 motorway runs through *Kingdom Come* as a unifying thread, an obsession that partly dates from and might well have been triggered by Ballard's participation in Iain Sinclair and Chris Petit's 2002 autofictional documentary *London Orbital*. The film is a visual companion to the book Sinclair had written, charting his walk around the 105-mile circumference of what Petit refers to in the film as 'the world's longest bypass'.

Sinclair first read *The Terminal Beach* as a student in Dublin, in 1964.

I liked the title. The stories were disconcerting, the prose efficient
and pared down. I didn't, at first bite, become a convinced disciple.
Ballard felt a bit too English, colonialist: I didn't immediately catch on
to the quality of his subversion, his edge, his well-mannered madness.
His dangerous surface. Or his slowburn humour. I was innocently
paddling across terminal shallows without noticing the nuclear power
station going critical on the horizon. The stories were like grey rooms
in an airport hotel. My key card didn't work.[473]

What shifted Sinclair's perspective was moving to London. Picking up on what was happening at *New Worlds* and the *International Times* allowed him to view Ballard through the filter of Burroughs. At this point something clicked. The US edition of *The Atrocity Exhibition* – with its introduction by Burroughs – was the first work by Ballard that Sinclair consciously 'collected', a copy that, as he later learned from Fay Ballard, had originally been inscribed to Monique and Andrew Rossabi, both close friends of Ballard through the *New Worlds* era.[474]

'That title became essential Ballard for me,' Sinclair remembers, 'a point of transit between early and subsequent texts.' In 1991, Sinclair appeared alongside Ballard in a fifteen-minute segment of BBC2's *The Late Show*, speaking about the redevelopment of Canary Wharf.[475] 'Jimmy and I were the contrasting witnesses. He was thoroughly in favour of the development, fruit of his *High-Rise* prophecy. I was being apocalyptic, in the afterglow of *Downriver*. I think now that this was a turning point for me, when I began to appreciate how much blade there was under the cool surface of Ballard's prose.'

Sinclair met Ballard properly at the end of the decade, when he interviewed him for his 1999 BFI monograph on Cronenberg's *Crash*. In his writing about *Crash*, Sinclair is preoccupied especially with the transplantation of the film's location from Ballard's London to Cronenberg's Toronto, a sleight of hand Ballard did not mind at all – indeed he embraced it – but that for Sinclair, a London writer by definition, constitutes a form of estrangement in and of itself.

The fiction grows out of this undisclosed, over-familiar urban landscape. Ballard's trick: to forge a poetic out of that which contains least poetry, the mundane, the scruffy, the band beneath language ... Perhaps the translation to Toronto was necessary, to free the film from the mess of biography, allowing Ballard's primary metaphors to reform in their essential chemical combinations.[476]

The interview took place at Claire's flat on Goldhawk Road. After that, the two saw each other regularly, usually together with Claire and Sinclair's wife Anna. 'He was good company, avuncular, taking charge, never discussing his books or work in progress. Ordering celebratory wine when books were done. I liked him, but didn't know him any better by our last meeting. There was a distinct feeling of the social, almost colonial again; exiles chatting in a foreign country. It was performative, genial and generous.'

Ballard had initially agreed to take part in an event to accompany the premier screening of *London Orbital* at the Barbican.[477] When he called to cancel, citing illness, Sinclair was not overly surprised. He ascribed Ballard's reticence to a general and growing dislike of public appearances, though in view of his increasingly poor health there was probably more to it. Ballard was replaced on the programme by his own blown-up photograph, with Sinclair and Petit reciting alternating sections of his poetic monologue 'What I Believe', as they do in the film.

London Orbital opens with footage of cars driving through fog that looks almost solid, a bank of wet dust. Streaming through the yellowish penumbra of the Dartford tunnel. Pixelated images of Margaret Thatcher, who for Sinclair has become the motorway's vampiric familiar spirit. A tower block being felled by a controlled explosion, a winter tree in the foreground, its delicate latticework of branches superimposed over the mushrooming dust cloud. Rooks take flight, screaming, and Chris Petit describes how in December of the year 2000 he was taken by Iain Sinclair to see a highpoint of his epic walk around the M25.

'Just east of where the motorway crosses the Thames stands a soap factory and a vast storage shed, with a Saxon church in between. It was in this bizarre location that Bram Stoker had set Count Dracula's

London estate, Carfax Abbey, whose only neighbouring buildings at the time were the old church, and a lunatic asylum.'

Sinclair warns him that by driving the route, he risks becoming one of Stoker's undead, a warning that of course Petit is bound to ignore. Film of the drive is shown alongside a sequence of snapshots taken by Sinclair during the course of his walk. Liminal spaces: tower blocks beside boarded-up cottages; uprooted road signs; cranes and masts and oil gantries, all those abandoned, outmoded ambitions, so last century. Modern highwaymen, Thatcher and Pinochet, Rainham Marshes. Here is the road, ceaselessly unfurling like a grey ribbon; cars spinning along like their own plastic replicas in a Scalextric set.

This is the new face of folk horror, the layers of decay and nostalgia that are all that remain of what the more right-wing psychogeographers call Deep England. Sinclair and Ballard share an interest in these landscapes, a set of overlapping imagery, though their angle of approach and sensibility are diametrically opposed. It is impossible to imagine J. G. Ballard writing about Count Dracula and Carfax Abbey; Ballard, whose science fictional sensibility is self-defining, would choose to focus instead upon the oil refinery now built on its site, its genetic link with the Exxon Valdez and Dubya Bush.

'On the M25, in this motorway zone there's no past, there's no future,' Ballard says in his voiceover. 'In the average science park or industrial estate, people sit in offices and there's no social hierarchy, because everybody really is classless. This is the world where, out on the M25, a new kind of transitory, transient England has come into being.' Near the end of the film you can hear him laughing: 'I want you to blow up the Bentall Centre, Iain. Bluewater. Your assignment is to destroy the M25!'

Of course it would be Ballard himself who would attempt that in *Kingdom Come*. 'Ballard was certainly one of the guides for *London Orbital*,' Sinclair agrees. 'I think *Kingdom Come*, to a degree, pays back the favour, lifting something from *Orbital* and conversations we had about motorways and off-highway super-stores.'

Ballard was already at work on *Kingdom Come* when in February 2005, a riot erupted at the opening of a new IKEA store in Tottenham. Some six thousand shoppers queuing for bargains caused a stampede that left a number of people in need of hospital treatment. 'At the beginning it was nice and calm, lots of staff hovering around,' one of the shoppers caught up in the frenzy told GMTV the morning after. 'Then, at around 10pm, the staff disappeared and slowly but steadily madness descended upon the crowd.'[478]

'People abandoned their cars and were fighting over sofas,' Ballard said. 'People think that the events in *Kingdom Come* are a bit extreme, but they actually aren't.'[479] The year before, two people had been killed in a similar stampede at an IKEA store in Jeddah, Saudi Arabia.

The retail outlet at the centre of *Kingdom Come* is the Metro-Centre, a labyrinthine shopping mall that dominates the landscape close to Brooklands, 'the town between Weybridge and Woking that had grown up around the motor-racing circuit of the 1930s.'[480] As the novel opens, Richard Pearson, a forty-two-year-old advertising executive, finds himself driving towards Brooklands through the apotheosis of the Ballardian landscape, 'a terrain of inter-urban sprawl, a geography of sensory deprivation, a zone of dual carriageways and petrol stations, business parks and signposts to Heathrow, disused farmland filled with butane tanks, warehouses clad in exotic metal sheeting ... the entire defensive landscape waiting for a crime to be committed.'[481]

And a crime has in fact already been committed. Richard's father Stuart, a retired airline pilot, has been murdered – shot dead by a lone gunman who fired at random into the crowds of lunchtime shoppers wandering the aisles and boutiques of the Metro-Centre. Largely absent from Richard's life, Stuart Pearson carried with him an aura of glamour and mystique that has exerted a powerful influence nonetheless. After flying millions of miles and navigating some of the world's most dangerous airports, his random death in a shopping mall seems meaningless and bizarre. Matters are further complicated when the prime suspect for the crime, Duncan Christie, a borderline psychotic with a personal grudge against the Metro-Centre, is released without charge.

Determined to discover the truth, Richard Pearson moves into his father's apartment and begins his own investigation into the murder. He quickly comes into contact with his father's solicitor Geoffrey Fairfax, 'on the outside a very pukka, old-fashioned solicitor. On the inside, a raving, right-wing nutter,'[482] Duncan Christie's old head teacher William Sangster, his therapist Tony Maxted, 'maverick psychiatrist, almost as odd as any of his patients',[483] and police sergeant Mary Falconer, 'a bundle of unease and disquiet wrapped inside an elegant blond package' who may inadvertently have supplied the murder weapon.

Driving around the town, Richard is unsettled by the racist behaviour of the local sports fans. He cannot help noticing that 'there were too many slogans and graffiti for comfort, too many BNP and KKK signs scrawled on cracked windows, too many St George's flags flying from suburban bungalows.'[484] The discovery of a stash of Nazi-related reading material in Stuart Pearson's flat does little to clarify matters.

If these witnesses have one thing in common, it is their hatred of the Metro-Centre. Geoffrey Fairfax keeps his curtains closed so as to block it from view, thereby revealing – in a vivid call-back to Ballard's 1961 story 'The Garden of Time' – 'a deep tribal loathing of the people of the plain who had settled around him'.[485] Dr Julia Goodwin, who fought in vain to save Stuart Pearson's life in the wake of the shooting, describes the Metro-Centre as 'a standing temptation to any madman with a grudge', while Mary Falconer, with her 'immaculate Rhine-Maiden hair', hints darkly that 'there are people who believe it's preparing us for a new world.'

The bemused narrator in their quest for the truth about the fate of an estranged relative, the suburbs dreaming of violence, the squeaky-clean surface hiding a darker reality, the cast of aberrant 'elective psychopaths' – the novel's likeness to its predecessors is almost parodic. The critical response to *Kingdom Come* was very mixed. The feeling that prevailed was that Ballard was getting old, that he had outplayed his hand. Negative comparisons were made with earlier books. Lionel Shriver in the *Telegraph* describes the novel as 'strained', insisting that 'for satire, there must be a rule that if you want to send up, say, consumerism, you do not use the word three times on every page ... This heavy-handed execution is especially disappointing because the premise is implicitly light.'[486]

Ursula Le Guin, who spent her whole life and career exploring the ways in which societies might become better integrated, complained that 'Ballard's narrator is inadequate: he has no access to work worth doing or any bond but sex; he is totally alienated. He can see the people of Brooklands only as parodies of himself. Work and family mean nothing to him, or to them ... The meanings of the words freedom, sanity and republic are here so compromised as to be meaningless.'[487]

Unsurprisingly, Le Guin found Ballard's portrayal of life in the new millennium distasteful to the point of loathing it. But to interpret Ballard's late work purely as satire is to misread him. From *Crash* onwards, readers and critics frequently found themselves running into the quagmire of taking him literally. Misled by the realist setting, the references to places they recognize and even live in, many have assumed that *Kingdom Come* is a political statement, a warning against the decadence of western lifestyles and the corrosive effects of consumerism.

While Phil Baker in the *Observer* insists that *Kingdom Come* 'remains implausible and unsympathetic as a full-length novel',[488] it is actually the very things that make some readers back away from it – its insouciance, its preposterousness – that are its keystones. As the Metro-Centre becomes its own sealed world, we are transported backwards to memories of *The Drowned World*, with its unnerving intimations of a regression to the Triassic. 'The Metro-Centre is dreaming you. It's dreaming all of us, Richard,'[489] insists William Sangster, and just like Kerans on the balcony of the partially submerged Ritz, Richard Pearson, 'inhaling the overripe air with its guarantee of yet another tropical day'[490] sits in his deckchair on the fake beach outside the Holiday Inn, drinking whisky and relishing his solitude:

> The silence was even more soothing, before the night patrols began to swear and stamp their way around the dome, torches searching the empty stores and cafés for any intruders. The artificial twilight lasted until the morning. During the long night hours, the ghost creatures of the dome, the thousands of cameras and kitchen appliances and cutlery canteens, began to emerge and glow like a watching congregation.[491]

The unshuttered shops, 'their interiors transformed into a street of caves crowded with treasure'[492] provide distorted echoes of the quayside stalls loaded with crystal artefacts described by Dr Sanders as he disembarks from the river steamer at the start of *The Crystal World*, and what could be a more potent metaphor for heading south than Maxted's final ordeal by fire, 'his hoarse cries lost in the fierce drumming of the inferno'.[493]

In its gradual slide from the quotidian towards the fantastic, *Kingdom Come* is a masterpiece of surrealism, to be understood most clearly when viewed through the same lens as the more directly signposted speculative novels of Ballard's early career. Ballard did not know when he was writing it that *Kingdom Come* would be his final novel, yet there is a recursiveness within its pages, a self-referentiality that is as poignant as it is uncanny.

'I loved her moods and bolshieness, the cigarette stubbed out in a slushy sorbet, the adversarial relationship with her car, the handsome black cat who slept beside her like a demon husband,' Richard says of Julia Goodwin not long after their first sexual encounter in Richard's father's bed. 'Everything between us inverted the usual rules. We had begun with sex of a fraught and desperate kind, followed by a long period of wooing.' More or less the exact words used by Ballard to describe the start of his affair with Emma Tennant in his 1982 interview with V. Vale.

There is a tenderness to Richard's words, a genuine affection that is more or less absent from most of the relationships described in Ballard's previous novels. This makes it tempting to believe that there is also something of Claire in Julia, just as Julia's laughingly reported description of Richard as 'beyond psychiatric help'[494] is a knowing glance backward at Catherine Storr's reportedly horrified response to the manuscript of *Crash*.

As a final, irrepressible piece of self-quotation, Ballard shows the Metro-Centre's exhausted hostages placing votive offerings of honey before the centre's furry mascots, the giant-sized Three Bears.[495] One of the hostages, 'a middle-aged woman in a St George's shirt, blond hair knotted behind her neck',[496] is singing something under her breath – what else but 'The Teddy Bears' Picnic', which Ballard famously chose as one of his eight records on *Desert Island Discs*.[497]

And still amidst the hyperreality that Ballardian prescience. On 1 October 2024, the BBC published a report detailing how a white supremacist organization has been setting up sports clubs nationwide as a cover for their racist activities.[498] 'Politics for the age of cable

TV. Fleeting impressions, an illusion of meaning floating over a sea of undefined emotions ... a virtual politics unconnected to any reality, one which redefines reality as itself'[499] is how Tony Maxted describes the rhetorical river in which Brooklands is swimming, and today as I write, almost two decades after the publication of *Kingdom Come* and with Hurricane Milton battering the Florida coastline I am listening to a report on Radio 4's *Today* programme of an elected representative of the Republican party in Georgia who has been using her official social media accounts to spread the latest conspiracy theory about the Biden government – that they have been deliberately directing the hurricanes against Trump territory.

'You're at a loss for words to describe how ridiculous this is,' says Brian Klaas, Associate Professor of Global Politics at UCL, 'but it could be enough to sway some people's opinions, because we do know that conspiracy theories do have sticking power in modern politics, because we know that people vote on perception rather than based on what is true.'[500]

I came late to Ballard's late novels. I was aware of the criticism that is frequently levelled at them, that they are clones of each other, the tedious carping of a writer who in his old age has taken on some of the attributes of a cracked record: at a loss for new material, he insists on endlessly repeating the same tired tunes. I read *Cocaine Nights* when it first came out and from what I can remember I did not like it much. For a long time I held off from reading the books that followed, afraid that I might be disappointed, in the novels themselves and also in Ballard, for failing to recognize the fact that he was stuck in a rut.

But the experience of reading these four late works back-to-back has transformed my understanding of their achievement. Who else dares to write like this, to give free rein to a single idea over more than a thousand pages? The more you are exposed to those endless repetitions and leitmotifs, the more you come to appreciate the final novels as a roman fleuve, a Gesamtkunstwerk, the Ring cycle of late capitalism: here we have the rising intimations and implications of *Cocaine Nights*; the night-ride of the weekend warriors in *Super-Cannes*; the appearance of a hero, doomed to be betrayed in *Millennium People*; conflagration, immolation and banishment in *Kingdom Come*. Even the novel's title plays along.

I find myself wishing I could run this idea past Ballard. I can see how it might have amused him, though I can imagine he hated Wagner even more than he hated shopping.⁵⁰¹

I heard Ballard speak only once, at the Institute for Education, not far from Russell Square. It was Thursday 14 September 2006, and Ballard was in conversation with Robert McCrum as part of the publicity tour for *Kingdom Come*. What I remember most about that evening was how excited I was to have the chance to see him, how impressed by his directness and keen intelligence, his seeming enjoyment of the occasion, the edge of glamour that hung around him, the silver hair straggling over his collar, worn longer than average for a man of his age.

He looked well, vigorous and engaged, full of life. Few people, if any, in the audience that evening would have known how ill he was. Just three months earlier, the lengthy uncertainty surrounding Ballard's health had been resolved, and the news was not good. Ballard describes the moment himself in *Miracles of Life*:

> In June 2006, after a year of pain and discomfort that I put down to arthritis, a specialist confirmed that I was suffering from advanced prostate cancer that had spread to my spine and ribs. Curiously, the only part of my anatomy that did not seem to be affected was my prostate, a common feature of the disease. But an MRI scan, a disagreeable affair that involves lying in a coffin wired for sound, left no doubt. Originating in my prostate, the cancer had invaded my bones.⁵⁰²

So eerily similar to what happened to Chris, a fact we spoke about often in the months before he died. Chris knew that I would write this, and yet now that the moment is here I find myself resisting it, as if by choosing not to set down the words I could make them less true. I am tired, I suppose, the words piled in drifts about my feet like fallen leaves.

Writing after Ballard's death, Martin Amis recalls the evening when he learned of Ballard's prognosis. He and his wife, the writer Isabel Fonseca were dining with Claire and Ballard, together with Will Self and his then wife Deborah Orr. This would have been sometime in the autumn of 2006, before the news of Ballard's illness became generally known. 'He revealed in the restaurant that he probably had "about two years to live." This was said with instinctive courage, but with all the melancholy to be expected from a man who loved life so passionately.'[503]

Those first weeks and even months, when you know the facts of what is occurring but they still seem distant, somewhere in the future and unconnected with the life you are still (mostly) living. The idea that you are dying does not seem real because you still feel (mostly) well. The business of your life is still ongoing. It is only gradually that the circle begins to close.

I remember the first time I read David Pringle's Ballard chronology through the late summer and early autumn of 2022. The idea of this book was just being born and Chris and I had no idea of what was to follow in the year ahead. Rereading the chronology now is like seeing one series of images superimposed over another: twin sequences of film, each the ghost of the other, inextricably entwined.

Sunday 29 October 2023, the last time Chris went across to the mainland. We drove to Gourock to have a curry with friends at Tulsi, on Kempock Place. The food was very good and Chris was happy, relaxed, glad to have made the effort. Carole and Iain drove back with us to Wemyss Bay, to have a last drink before the ferry left. Chris was very tired by then, and I so anxious to get him home we left his cushion behind on the ferry, the extra cushion we used to take with us to make sure he would be comfortable on the restaurant seating. We were both upset about losing it, ridiculously so, a small thing freighted with meaning it is difficult to parse.

Wednesday 16 November 2023, the French film director Cyril Leuthy came to our house to shoot some footage of Chris for the documentary he was making for German TV about *The War of the Worlds*. I remember us driving Cyril and his cinematographer Denis Gaubert all over the island, searching for a flock of sheep for them to film as background detail. The sheep would be weird, Cyril insisted, and they were fans of weird. Chris spoke about Wells for an hour, and then read from the novel, those first, famous lines about cold and distant minds. Our time with Cyril and Denis was a piece of enchantment, an episode snatched from the timeline of the encroaching finite and at the last moment of possibility. After they had left, Chris, utterly exhausted, slept for hours, barely moving, the light in the room slipping inexorably towards the dusk.

Friday 1 December, and lunch with Martin MacInnes, who had visited Chris several times while he was in the Beatson. I remember Chris was nervous about driving out to the restaurant at the south end of the island where I had booked a table. I remember how tender Martin was with Chris, how he helped him to the bathroom, how they came back laughing. How precious they were, those hours: our friendship, our talk, the business of our lives, in spite of everything, still going on.

Sunday 3 December, Chris wrote to Michael Moorcock. *Dear Mike, I simply want to say THANKS for the time and trouble you took, with my questions about Ballard. Probably still faintly annoying to you after all these years, but for me it was really helpful. I haven't finished the book. It was probably always insane to try within the known effects of this fucking cancer. I think I'm now approaching the terminal stage. A lot of pain all day, and general decline. I'm now on the palliative care register.*

Sometimes, writing costs. It costs to set these things down. I have to keep stopping. I keep pulling my hair through my fingers like one of those reclusive widows out of Henry James. I keep going because I know these memories are important and should be put on the record. I keep going because I know now also that once I have typed the words I can leave them to live their own lives, out in the world, wherever, independent of me.

There is a photograph of Ballard with Michael Moorcock, dated to September 2006. They are sitting in what looks to be the foyer of the Hilton hotel at 14 Woburn Place, Euston. There are small tables close by, with menus, but they do not appear to have ordered any food or drink. Ballard is wearing dark trousers and a grey tweed jacket with diagonal check. Moorcock is dressed in a cream linen suit and pale shoes, his right foot resting across his left knee. The photograph was taken by Linda Moorcock, at what would have been around the same time I saw

Ballard interviewed by Robert McCrum. There is a chance, I suppose, that it was later the same evening.

'Both of us were only in town for a short while,' Mike Moorcock remembers, 'and I was going back to Paris.' Moorcock has raised his hand slightly, he is looking at Linda, holding the camera; Ballard is gazing at Moorcock, his hands folded across his stomach. His lips are parted slightly, as if he has just finished saying something, or is about to speak. There is something in the way they are sitting – both slightly slouched, a relaxed attitude – that tells of long acquaintance and ease in one another's company.

In the March of 2007, some six months later, Ballard wrote to Michael Moorcock in the aftermath of a recent phone call:

> Yes, it was wonderful, & quite strange, too – I felt a huge affection for you – it still feels as if we'd stepped back 40 years to those great days when we started out – everything to play for, all the talent in the world and the sense that we were creating a new popular literature …
> I still think you ought to be back here, but there's something sour in the London air – money, probably, rotting in great heaps like piles of yesterday's fish – you'd find it fascinating, though, & completely changed. Ladbroke Grove, stamping ground of Jerry Cornelius, is now a super-rich enclave of bankers and TV execs …
>
> Things here are so-so, late-stage prostate cancer that's spread to my spine & ribs – I keep going care of Merck, Pfizer & Smith Kline – too many hospital car parks, waiting rooms, smiling nurses and friendly doctors whose lips say nothing but whose eyes say everything.

It seems it is only now, nine months after he was first diagnosed, that Ballard can bring himself to tell Moorcock about his illness. 'I don't know if their correspondence continued much after 2007,' says David Pringle, when I write to ask him whether he knows if there were any other letters, 'but I believe they kept in touch by telephone – or, at any rate, Mike and Linda kept in touch with Claire, and so they heard the sad news promptly when J. G. B. died and were able to announce it on the day.'

Writing to me about the hiatus in his friendship with Ballard towards the end of the *New Worlds* era, Mike Moorcock seems to believe that it was inevitable. 'In a sense, Jimmy and I were like brothers,' he says. 'I used to anticipate the falling-out of revolutionaries once the revolution has succeeded. Happily no ice-picks were involved, and we ended our friendship pretty much as it had begun.'

He describes to me how he still keeps Ballard's letters, tucked in between the pages of his books. 'It's the nearest thing to a filing system I have.'

'I've thought about writing a memoir,' Ballard said in an interview for *Time* magazine published that October, 'but I'm not sure I could. Various people have approached me about a biography. But that would require hundreds of hours of interviews about my parents and the like, which I don't necessarily want to consider. I might discover all sorts of horrible things about myself.'[504]

Even as he voiced his doubts about writing a memoir, Ballard would have known that he was seriously considering it. The timescales involved suggest it might already have been a work in progress. In August 2007, *The Bookseller* announced the acquisition of J. G. Ballard's autobiography *Miracles of Life* by Fourth Estate. 'J. G. Ballard has been a giant on the literary landscape for the last 40 years,' said the publisher's editorial director Clare Reihill, 'and his long-awaited autobiography will be a momentous publishing event. For fans of his work it will be a very insightful read. He has narrated his life exceptionally well, showing how events in his life have influenced his work.'[505]

Miracles of Life was scheduled for release in February 2008. No doubt the publishers were hoping that Ballard might still be well enough to undertake some publicity, though it was not to be. He had not felt able to attend a conference at the University of East Anglia in May 2007 – a two-day symposium dedicated to his work organized by the academic and Ballard specialist Jeannette Baxter – and a letter to David Pringle in June noted that he had had to pull out of several additional commitments in September. The coming months would see him increasingly reluctant to give interviews, and aside from Claire and members of his family he saw fewer people even than usual.

The launch event for *Miracles of Life* at the Southbank Centre, announced for 20 February, was cancelled soon after New Year. Chris and I had bought tickets. We were not yet living together but Chris had arranged to be in London on that day. I was deeply upset by the news. Chris had already heard via the science fiction grapevine that Ballard was unwell – Ballard had begun to tell friends and associates about his diagnosis through the latter part of 2007 – but the gravity of his illness was not made public until the book came out.

Miracles of Life was rapturously received. For many readers – those who knew his work mainly through *Empire of the Sun* as well as those who had followed Ballard's career from the beginning – this seemed to be the book they had been waiting for. Unlike *Empire of the Sun* and *The Kindness of Women*, *Miracles of Life* was real life as Ballard had experienced it, the truth unvarnished by fantasy or narrative sleight of hand. There was the sense that this was the book that would finally explain him.

'If this is to be his final book, it is a worthy one, as the story of both a remarkable life and an outsider trying to make sense of post-war Britain,' wrote Paul Dunn in *The Times*.[506] 'Ballard suggests that rave reviews in a newspaper amount to no more than the traditional, empty gush "Darling, you were wonderful!" on first nights,' said Kevin Jackson in the *Sunday Times*. 'I hope he does not really believe this, for in some cases rave reviews can be wholly sincere. Mr Ballard, you are wonderful.'[507]

What few people seemed to remark upon was that Ballard revealed nothing about himself in *Miracles of Life* that was not already known. Beautifully wrought, direct, engaging, unsentimental though surprisingly tender, the first two hundred of the book's two hundred and seventy-eight pages cover the years already covered extensively in *Empire of the Sun* and *The Kindness of Women*, as well as in the dozens of interviews that Ballard had given in the years since the release of his most famous novel.

Although Ballard reflects with great affection on his years of married life and the birth of his children, there is no mention made of the close brush with death suffered by Jim junior and Fay as the result of a leaking gas pipe in their bedroom at 23 The Hermitage, Richmond, the apartment the Ballards occupied immediately before their move to Shepperton and where Bea had been born. The incident only became publicly known when two saved newspaper cuttings were discovered among Ballard's papers at the British Library: 'Three-year-old Jimmy

Ballard and his sister, Fay, two, were taken to hospital unconscious after a disused gas pipe fractured in the nursery of their home in Richmond, today ... Mr and Mrs Ballard gave the children artificial respiration until the ambulance arrived.'[508]

Fay Ballard later referenced the accident in a piece written to accompany her exhibition 'House Clearance', noting that the incident occurred on 8 October 1959 and that it had been her brother who 'accidentally broke a gas pipe in the nursery'.[509] The whole episode must have been terrifying. Certainly it was significant enough for Ballard to save the newspaper clippings. And yet in spite of the many times he spoke about his children in interview he never once mentioned it, or the feelings of fear and acute vulnerability it must have provoked in him.

Mary's death is dealt with in less than a page, and of the years of tumult and successive lovers Ballard writes only that 'after celibacy came a kind of desperate promiscuity, a form of shock treatment in which I was trying to will myself to come alive ... I'm grateful to those friends of Mary's who rallied round and knew that it was time to bring me back into the light.'[510]

He writes lovingly of Claire, his 'partner, inspiration and life-companion for forty years', [511] but there is no hint of their ten-year separation and the dysfunctional behaviour that led to it. 'My son Jim, who was the oldest, grieved deeply for his mother, but we helped each other through, and eventually he regained his confidence and became a cheerful teenager with a charming and witty sense of humour.'[512] No mention of the fact that Jim junior was never able to speak of Mary again, or of the difficulties and altercations that opened a divide between father and son that was never fully healed.

'My friendships with Eduardo Paolozzi, Dr Martin Bax, Chris Evans and Michael Moorcock were important to me but lay on the perimeter of my life. ... My children were at the centre of my life, circled at a distance by my writing,'[513] Ballard insists, but while few would doubt his care for the wellbeing of his family, it is disingenuous of him to claim that his writing, which was so important to him it was essentially indivisible from who he was, was a kind of adjunct. He would never have considered *not* writing.[514] He clearly delighted in parenting his children – but was always secure in the knowledge that half an hour spent watching

Blue Peter when the kids came home from school could easily be made up the following morning.

Ballard made no attempt to maintain a home or a kitchen to a conventional standard — and good for him. But it was in those same hours of not cooking and cleaning that he was able to find the necessary mental and temporal space to be able to work. He joked about being 'a slatternly mother ... the kind of mother of whom the social services deeply disapprove',[515] though he did not seem aware of how differently people might have viewed his behaviour if he had, in fact, been a woman, or of how many women writers caring for young children are expected as a matter of course to put the brakes on their careers.

The fact that Ballard did manage to maintain a loving and nurturing family life alongside his exceptional talent points to enormous resilience and tenacity, but his success as a writer was not a subsidiary clause and he was much more complicated than the selflessly contented father he paints us a picture of in *Miracles of Life*.

The memories Ballard gifts us with are cultivars, curated, smoothed and planed by the polishing motion of a thousand repetitions. *Miracles of Life* is without question the warmest in tone and most enjoyable to read of any book Ballard produced. For anyone unfamiliar with Ballard and wanting to know more I would even say 'start here', so long as they remember that *Miracles* is the official narrative, the version of the truth that Ballard wanted to put on the record. Anyone curious about who Ballard really was would need to dig deeper.

'I only wrote the autobiography because I knew I had advanced cancer,' Ballard says, tellingly.[516] 'In fact my consultant, who looks after me, urged me to write.' On the penultimate page of *Miracles of Life*, Ballard credits Waxman with being the person 'who rescued me at a time when I was exhausted by the intermittent pain and the fears of death that blotted everything else from my mind'.[517]

In the foreword to *The Elephant in the Room*, his 2011 book of stories about the relationship between cancer patients and their doctors, Waxman describes how he had first met Ballard in the nineties when he was treating Claire, and how Ballard had then encouraged him in his own writing.

When he met Ballard again, this time as a patient, he 'was pleased to be able to help him as he had helped me. He was transformed by treatment, and from being dreadfully sick, and in considerable pain, he became remarkably well.'[518] It was during this period of remission that Ballard was able to harness the strength to write *Miracles of Life*. For Waxman, it was the conversations he had with Ballard – the conversations that were intended as the framework for Ballard's unwritten memoir about his illness – that ultimately formed the inspiration behind his own book.

As 2008 wore on, Ballard's remission began to falter. Sometime towards the end of May, he made the decision to leave the house he had occupied for almost fifty years. 'At that point he was very poorly,' Fay Ballard remembers. 'He had been having a lot of chemo and was very sick and weak. He could no longer look after himself in Shepperton.' Claire was anxious to have him come to live with her at Goldhawk Road, where she could care for him properly, though space there was limited. The bedroom that had once been Jenny's would now become Ballard's.

'The room was stuffed with junk,' Fay told me, 'so Jenny took over. She and her girlfriend Annette cleared that space and put all Claire's things in storage, so that I could order the bed, the carpet and the curtains, everything to make the room ready for Daddy to move in.'

After Ballard died it was Jenny who collected the death certificates and helped make the funeral arrangements. By another of those odd quirks of fate, Jenny Walsh was also for a time in close professional contact with Ballard's brother-in-law Tony, who in the late nineties was commissioned by housing campaigner Debby Ounsted to design a project in Willesden for the Octavia Hill Housing Association. Jenny, who had gained a degree in archaeology from Birkbeck College, turned out to be the Association's buildings manager. The two spoke on the phone every week until the project was completed.

Because Claire did not drive, it was Fay who collected her father from Shepperton. 'For the last fifteen years, I had not visited the house. We would always meet Daddy in town. You can't come to Shepperton, he'd say, it's too messy. I still had the key that I had as a teenager. So on the day that he said come and get me, I drove to Shepperton and let myself in. And it was an extraordinary moment because nothing had changed ... I went into the garden and took a photograph of my Dad, which for me was a big moment because this was my revisit to the house, and this was his farewell to the house.'[519]

For several months afterwards and on into the autumn, Fay would continue to drive Ballard back to Shepperton every couple of weeks to check on the house and collect his post. 'My home is a strange sort of museum now where I keep all of my books ... It's very odd. It's like a sort of *time station* – the whole of Shepperton seems very unreal.'[520]

He was increasingly exhausted. Towards the end of July, Claire travelled to Barcelona to attend the opening of 'Autopsy of the New Millennium', a four-month exhibition devoted to Ballard's life and work at the Centre de Cultura Contemporània de Barcelona. The exhibition was the largest of its kind to date, including rare interview and film footage as well as Ballard's early cut-ups and advertiser's announcements. While there, she ran into the writer Hari Kunzru, who she had met the previous October when he came to interview Ballard at her flat.

'Together we walked around Gaudi's La Pedrera; the apartment block's bizarre melting architecture and bourgeois interiors formed another perfectly Ballardian paradox,' Kunzru recalled. 'For Claire it was a difficult afternoon. Barcelona was a place she'd last visited many years previously, on a happy driving holiday with Jim. I tried to comfort her as she cried.'[521]

In September, Ballard sent his agent Maggie Hanbury his outline for *Conversations with my Physician*. Hanbury shopped the proposal at the Frankfurt Book Fair in October, agreeing terms with Clare Reihill at Fourth Estate. Although there was a lot of excitement around the announcement, the hope that *Miracles of Life* would not be Ballard's final work after all, the fact was that Ballard was already too ill to work on the book and it progressed no further; the title was removed from the schedules the following year.

At the end of October, as the Ballard exhibition in Barcelona came to a close, a short video message recorded by V. Vale when he conducted his final interview with Ballard at Claire's flat the week beforehand was relayed to attendees at the Kosmopolis International Festival of Literature. Ballard, wearing a dressing gown, spoke a few words to camera: 'Hello Barcelona. I hope everyone there is enjoying the show, if I'm allowed to call it that. Vale is taking charge of everything, and I leave him to represent me.'

Ballard's condition had deteriorated badly enough for him to have to spend the Christmas of 2008 in Hammersmith hospital. When Fay telephoned Maggie Hanbury to tell her that Ballard might not have long to live, Hanbury went out into the street, hailed a taxi and drove straight to the hospital.

'I was with him for about fifteen minutes. He thanked me for coming and for all I had done for him. That was the last time I saw him. I felt very emotional when I left.'

Ballard was kept in for six weeks in total, a period of time that according to Claire brought back unwelcome memories of Lunghua camp. 'He had that strange sense in the hospital of it being a living organism, draining and feeding patients, the day staff going and the night staff arriving and all these machines winking and blinking. He was feverish and still trying to make sense of it as he had always done.'[522]

Reading over Claire's memories, there are moments when I forget that they are not my own. I remember how after the first day Chris hated being in the Victoria. In the hours that I was not there he felt frightened and alone. Like Ballard, he was no longer strong enough to properly differentiate between dream and reality. On the last evening before he came home he asked if I could stay with him in the hospital overnight. I had understood from our Macmillan nurse Evelyn that there was a pull-down bed I could use. In the event all that seemed to be on offer was a so-called recliner chair, a monstrous, rock-hard contraption covered in a shiny, slippery faux-leather that would only lie flat if you somehow contrived to arrange your bodyweight across the entire length of the seat. God, how I loathed that thing, as ugly and as useless as it was uncomfortable.

The hospital staff were preparing to move Ballard off the main ward and into a private room, for Claire a sure sign that they thought he would not last much longer. I have been told that she became very upset at this time. Quite apart from her grief, the full implications of Ballard's approaching death – how colossally it would affect her life and even her financial security – were pressing in on her. In the will Ballard made soon after his cancer diagnosis, Claire was bequeathed £300,000. A sizeable amount by normal standards, though when considered in the light of Ballard's worth as a whole, not so much. Claire did not own the flat on Goldhawk Road, and whilst there is every chance that Ballard – famously blasé when it came to money matters – did not fully realize that he was leaving Claire only partially provided for, she must have felt extremely vulnerable, all the same.

She was, however, determined to get Jimmy out of hospital and home to Goldhawk Road. I had wondered about how difficult it might have been for her to get the hospital to agree to sign him out. I only had to wield the word 'wife' a couple of times, but they were enough to show me that the word is a powerful weapon. Claire had no official status as Ballard's next-of-kin, and hospital bureaucracy can be appallingly cruel. A later conversation with Fay confirmed my suspicions.

'Daddy hated being in hospital. It was Jon, my husband, who spoke to the clinical staff and persuaded them that Daddy should be released. He was gone for half an hour or so, and whatever he said, he must have said the right things, because after that, we were able to pack up Daddy's stuff, put him in the car and take him to Goldhawk Road, where Claire made him comfortable again.'

This was in early February. Once Ballard was back in the flat, he seemed more peaceful. Both of his daughters visited frequently. Bea remembers bringing her father some of his favourite foods, which she picked up from the local delicatessen. 'We would talk for hours, as he was still eager to hear stories about my children, or what was going on at work. But I could see his health was failing.' Bea last saw her father on the evening before he died. 'Claire had called to say he was not well at all. I raced to get there. It was awful to see him so ill, no longer himself.'

Claire told their friend Will Self how in those final months she would work at her computer during the day, a baby monitor beside her on the desk so she would be able to hear immediately if Ballard needed her. When it was time for her to go to bed she would take the alarm with her. 'When I take it upstairs it's as if I'm carrying his breathing self in the little plastic machine. I hold it very carefully in my hand, like a precious living thing.'[523]

Claire remembered how in the months before Jim's admission to hospital, he was still able to enjoy a visit to Chez Kristof or the

Brackenbury, their favourite restaurant, on Hammersmith Grove, how when driving home they would make plans for a future they both knew could never be realized. 'Why don't we just keep driving, keep going west to Oxford and beyond.'[524]

But their time together, like the River Mallory, had almost run its course. 'It was the greatest joy to me to be able to care for him by myself,' Claire said. 'It was only in the last few days that his illness accelerated rapidly and that was deeply distressing but I am glad to say he was comfortable for most of the time.'[525]

A year and a day from the day Chris died, David Pringle sends me a copy of an email sent by Claire to the poet and novelist Jeremy Reed. Writing just weeks after Ballard's death, Claire describes how she is 'still half-mad with grief', how in the final weeks of his life, they had experienced some intensely happy times as well as difficult ones. She talks of their gratitude for the help they received from Macmillan nurses, most especially one called Angela, who Ballard liked and trusted a great deal. 'I miss Jimmy beyond words,' she writes. 'We had a small family funeral, which was beautifully conducted, warm and inclusive – yet life seems bleaker now. The shock has gone, the real mourning has set in.'[526] Once again, the sense of experience shared is overwhelming to the point of being intolerable. How I wish we could have met.

Ballard died in his sleep during the early hours of Sunday 19 April. He was seventy-eight years old. 'I found it very hard to let him go yesterday,' Claire told a reporter from the *Evening Standard* the following day. 'I lay next to him and stroked his head and just enjoyed the feeling of his face under my hand.'[527]

THIRTY-FOUR

'THE ILLUMINATED MAN'

'I believe in the power of the imagination to remake the world, to release the truth within us, to hold back the night, to transcend death, to charm motorways, to ingratiate ourselves with birds, to enlist the confidences of madmen.'[528]

J. G. Ballard, 'What I Believe'

'Every one of us is a cast of characters. I told myself I was a director putting on a new play. All these people turn up at the audition, and they're all me. Some are more interesting than others, some are more real, some can reach your heart. This happens every morning when I wake up. I have to choose, and I have to be ruthless. You understand that?'[529]

J. G. Ballard, *Kingdom Come*

'I've long thought that biography is deeply untrustworthy on the whole, and that the recollections of friends and acquaintances should be discounted, in the way that senior police officers discount eye-witnesses who claim that "I was sitting next to the gunman when he stood up and shot the pilot."'[530]

J. G. Ballard, letter to David Pringle, 1998

Sometime in the early December of 2023, I happened to hear a recorded interview with the writer Carole Angier about her recently completed biography of W. G. Sebald, *Speak, Silence*.[531] I devoured *Speak, Silence* when it came out in the summer of 2021, immersing myself in it for hours, yellow light pouring in through the wide-angle windows of the sun-room at the rear of our house where I always went to read.

Sebald, who inimitably and perfectly fuses the European passion for the abstract with a British sense of place, is a writer I return to obsessively, simply to sit beside his work, to be in a space with it, to let it set my mind on fire as it always does. Those archaic, labyrinthine sentences, those phantom photographs, the sense of the numinous burning through the fact-filled, the apparently prosaic. Chris read and admired *On the Natural History of Destruction* because the subject matter – the war in the air – was always one of his obsessions. He was interested in Sebald as a writer, his glancing approach to the truth, his incisive intellect, but he could not bring himself to love *Austerlitz*, or at least not as I do. He found it digressive and clotted with detail, a narrative as uneven and broken as a street full of potholes, too hard on the tyres – a mapped route made up of dashes, a precarious track through precipitous mountains, *dangerous for motors*.

I first read *Austerlitz* when I was on a train, travelling to meet him – in Harpenden, I remember that, though I've forgotten why. I remember passing through the deep, damp trench of Farringdon, through Moorgate with its indelible associations (my mother reminded me about the tube crash when I was eighteen. We were on our way to an appointment at Moorfields eye hospital. Even now when I check the date online – 1975 – I don't like to read about the accident. I was nine when it happened. I have trace memories of the headlines) and thinking this is what Sebald is talking about, the layers of history laid one on top of another like soil on a grave. It was like having the world opened. Chris and I discussed the book a hundred times without ever agreeing.

December, like a black hole, and the interview with Carole Angier is like salvage, something precious dug out of the ground and brought into the light. She is talking about the art of biography, about how 'you don't know what you're writing – really, entirely – until you write it.' She tells of how uncomfortable she felt when she was researching her biography of Primo Levi and became aware there was another writer working on his own book about Levi at the same time as her, following up the same sources, almost as if he was shadowing her every move. When the two books were published – less than a year apart – they were like oil and water, completely different both in their composition and viewpoint, and this, for Carole Angier, points to the real truth about biography, which is that it is impossible to tell an objective story.

'It's hugely personal, and in writing about Sebald, that personal angle of approach needed to be part of what the reader experienced – they needed to know. It wouldn't be right to present some apparently objective, third-person narrative account. Because of the gaps in the story it was clear to me from the start that this was a quest biography. That's why I call it *"In search of WG Sebald"*, because I don't claim to have found him, I'm only looking for him.'

I don't claim to have found him, I'm only looking for him. I listened to the podcast a second time, then a third, because it comforted me somehow, and because I kept coming back to those words of hers, and how they explained, so simply and yet with such clarity, what it was I wanted this book to become.

Angier speaks of the importance of talking to witnesses 'before we all die', and I find myself thinking again of the people in *this* story who I have been unable to reach or who have declined to speak to me, how time is running out, how by the time someone else comes to write an account of Ballard's life – which they will, because he is worthy of the attention, and there are multiple layers of his reality still left to be examined – some or all of these silent witnesses will no longer be around.

I keep coming back to something Chris said in the final month of his life, about how when he died, his whole world would vanish with him, all the corridors and halls of memory, the particular view of the world belonging only to him. 'It will all go,' he said, and though he was philosophical about this and so incredibly brave (he kept telling me not to say brave, but there is no other word to use, because that is what he was) his voice was choked nonetheless with the profoundest sorrow. He said that death is like the destruction of a great city and all its libraries, or I said it, I have repeated the words to myself so many times I can no longer remember.

What else is biography but a kind of archaeology, a sifting of debris? We're digging up shards, that's all, pieces of broken pottery and sections of mosaic. Go on to YouTube and search for footage of J. G. Ballard – there is plenty and all of it is interesting but the interview with Tom Sutcliffe in particular is excellent – and you will quickly realize that simply watching him, listening to him talk – the tone of his voice, the clarity of his thinking, the whole vast hinterland of memory and intellect that lies behind the words he speaks – has an immediacy and power that exceeds any number of pages filled with third-party speculation and literary analysis.

Writing a biography is like attempting to remake London from a stretch of cobblestones, a cracked phone case and a dirty beer mat, a discarded crisp packet. Layers of old fliers on an advertising hoarding. A boarded-up curry house. Ridiculous to try, you would think, but then when I think more deeply about these objects, apparently simple but actually not, I begin to wonder if maybe it would be possible, after all. You could make something, anyway, you could make a *version*.

On the day Chris died, I was in the middle of rereading Nabokov's ninth novel *The Real Life of Sebastian Knight*, published in 1941 and the first novel Nabokov wrote in English. This deliberate choice of a second language is one of the novel's major themes. The narrator, Sebastian's brother, says he has a poor command of spoken English. His language is Russian, and the scrap of a burned letter he briefly glimpses is significant to him not for the sense of it, 'but the mere fact of its being in my language'.[532] Sebastian, a famous writer, adopts English as the language he writes in, speaks Russian 'gingerly' and is clearly at pains to leave that part of himself behind. In the narrator and in Sebastian equally, Nabokov evokes his own divided self.

My copy of the novel is one I have owned since I was at Oxford in the early 1990s. The cover image is a self-portrait by Richard Eurich, a second-generation German-Jewish immigrant and a figure so Sebaldian he might be invented, though his father was brought to Britain as a child before Adolf Hitler was even born. Eurich's self-portrait shows him glancing sideways towards the viewer, sensitive mouth and knowing eyes, the image so synonymous with the novel I have come to think of it, I now realize, as a painting of Sebastian Knight himself.

Nabokov, whose subject was the role of art in preserving memory, was as obsessed with biography as Sebald – one of the reasons his presence stalks Sebald's book *The Emigrants* as a kind of ghost. *The Real Life of Sebastian Knight* is filled with false leads, with imaginary enemies and doubles and impostors, a novel few people other than Nabokov completists seem to have read, though it has always been one of my favourites. As a student and so foolishly in love it was the romance of it I adored, those brittle, doomed relationships, those women who managed to be both hyper-intelligent and stupidly faithful, faithful in the Dostoevskian sense – that is, unto madness. Nabokov is a man, after all, a fact I have to move on from or get stuck on forever and where's the point in that?

Now it is the form the novel takes that I am in love with, the biography as investigation into a self, an accumulation of significant, Sebaldian details fifty years before their time. Not wanting Sebastian's story to be hijacked by another, the narrator decides he should be the one to write his brother's biography. Going through Sebastian's belongings after his death, the narrator discovers an envelope filled with photographs of an unknown man received by Sebastian in response to an advertisement he had placed in a newspaper: 'Author writing fictitious biography requires photos of gentleman ... Will pay for photos childhood, youth, manhood to appear in said work.'[533]

What reader of Sebald could read those words without breaking out in goosebumps? Yet there is little doubt Sebastian – like Ballard – would have rejected any advances from prospective biographers. According to his brother, Sebastian was 'that rare type of writer who knows that nothing ought to remain except the perfect achievement; the printed book; that its actual existence is inconsistent with that of its spectre, the uncouth manuscript flaunting its imperfections like a revengeful ghost carrying its own head under its arm'.[534]

Sebastian has instructed his brother to burn unread any biographical materials – in particular a cache of letters. His brother complies, leaving us as readers to throw up our hands in horror, for we care nothing, at that moment, for his moral dilemma (the same as that famously faced by Max Brod, Kafka's executor, as well as Dmitri Nabokov himself on the death of his father) – *we simply want to know what was in the letters.*

What we want to know, and why we want to know it are two of the central questions of the biographer's art. Are we reading to confirm that our hero really was a hero, or to discover that they were secretly a monster? We must already know that except in exceptional cases (and perhaps not even then) they were neither. What we think about less often is the extent to which our opinion might be guided by the person who has taken it upon themselves to tell their story.

Within every biography is an autobiography – that of the biographer themselves, whose reasons for writing the book will inevitably shape it. Will be all over it, in fact, like the fingerprints of the criminal at the scene of the crime.

Chris had a vexed relationship with the idea of biography, with writing non-fiction in general. I was always urging him to produce more of it – more essays, more arguments. His analysis and understanding of literary works was idiosyncratic, unsparing, brilliant. But he grew to dislike writing reviews. He resented the time they took, the attention that would necessarily be deflected from the novel he happened to be working on.

He had previously considered writing a biography of John Wyndham, a writer who had been important to him for as long as Ballard had, though for different reasons. I urged him to commit to the project, arguing that writing about Wyndham would offer him the opportunity to write more generally about science fiction, but he kept backing away from the idea, insisting that no one cared what he thought about science fiction, and he was tired of talking about it.

Chris distrusted all forms of autobiographical writing. For the writer of fiction – for the writer of speculative fiction in particular – he believed the creative source was sacrosanct, a resource that should remain private and closely guarded. He always maintained that Ballard made a mistake when he wrote *Empire of the Sun*, that the work that came after was less intense, less radical, that in revealing the source of his inspiration he had drained himself dry.

When Chris was first diagnosed with cancer, his agent and I tried to persuade him that this book should take on a more personal aspect, that it should touch on his own life as well as Ballard's, that the story of the book should become part of the book. At first, Chris seemed enthused by the idea; the more time passed, the less he seemed able to contemplate writing about himself. When early in November 2023 I suggested that I should take over those parts of the story, he agreed immediately. 'I can't write about that stuff, but you can,' he said. He seemed incredibly relieved.

This was a tough book for Chris to write. At the time he began it, he had been at work on a new novel based around the Shakespeare authorship question. Chris adored Shakespeare and he was fascinated by conspiracy theories and alternative mindsets – the reason he enjoyed Chris Evans's book *Cults of Unreason* so much. One of the truly happy moments of that awful final week of 2023 was being able to tell him I had finally started reading Elizabeth Winkler's *Shakespeare Was a Woman and Other Heresies*, a book that enthralled me almost as much as it had excited him.

'Thank God you got round to reading it before I die,' he said, and we both cracked up. We had less than six weeks left of our time together, yet our ability to laugh as we had always done enabled us to keep hold of who we were.

There were times in the final months of Chris's life when I wondered if it would have been better for him never to have begun writing this book, if he would have been happier working on the novel about Eddy de Vere, island-hopping through the Dream Archipelago in search of artists and deserters to perform in a play he had written, a piece of experimental theatre about a mad king.

We came to think of this book as ours, a way of us continuing to be together after he was gone.

One of the last books I bought for Chris was *Lifescapes*, an extended essay on the art of biography by the obituarist and biographer Ann Wroe. I had hoped he might find it inspiring, but although the gift of the book delighted him – the fact that I had chosen it, the beautiful understatement of its matte grey covers – he was not impressed by it at all as a piece of writing. 'She's just rehashing her old obituaries,' he said, dismissively. 'There's nothing here for me.'

Chris would have preferred Wroe to talk about process, to dig deep into craft. Wroe's insistence on significant detail, on the minutiae – no, the poetry of biography came across to him as self-indulgence. He laid her work aside after just twenty pages, and reading this small, quiet miracle of a book not long after Chris's death (the story of Benson the female carp! The tantalizing conundrum of Perkin Warbeck!) I find myself contemplating once again the perplexing mystery of the distance between us, that no-man's-land we fought over time and again: he liked his non-fiction forensic, factual, declaratory. I want to know about the journey and the writer undertaking it. I love books that seek answers without always getting them, or not at all costs. Chris found such shilly-shallying to be an indulgence and utterly beside the point. How we tussled over Iain Sinclair, Gordon Burn.

At the time of our first coming together I found these differences between us chasm-like, almost frightening; by the end I no longer minded. I understood that they were essential to who we were. What joy, that we could still work ourselves into a lather over the use of the first person. That such things were and are still life and death to us. That he trusted me, by this point in the journey, to complete this adventure for him, to make it right.

'I think to be able to exercise an imagination over a long period of time one has got to be very well stocked in one's childhood with experiences of a pretty radical kind,' Ballard said in a TV interview with Jeremy Isaacs. 'I think I was fortunate in my own case that I did have an extraordinary childhood. I think if my parents had decided not to go out to China in 1929 and I'd been born in a suburb of Manchester I might never have become a writer at all, it's very hard to say. But I think in my own case the very strange and exhilarating and in some ways very cruel world that Shanghai was, fed my imagination.'[535]

Are writers born or are they made? Chris, who *was* born in a suburb of Manchester and whose experience of the second world war was secondhand, examines this very question in an essay he wrote in 2008 called 'Ersatz Wines'. As a child of the 1950s – the Wyndham decade – he initially felt his intellectually straitened, lower-middle-class background very much as an obstacle to becoming a writer. Not that it stopped him. In a career spanning almost six decades, he used the material he felt he had been saddled with as the raw clay for the construction of realities as rich and strange as any of Ballard's. Most notably in his 1981 novel *The Affirmation*, the two worlds – the prosaic everyday and the heightened, photorealistic simulacrum of the imagination – are overlaid, the protagonist drifting between one and the other as all writers do.

If Ballard's *idée fixe* is the dream of violence precipitated by his early exposure to war and captivity, Chris's was always the *re-making*, the reassembly of quotidian reality in a different guise. His novels and stories return again and again to this theme, a metaphorical reworking of his own decision to become a writer. There is no doubt that Ballard's experiences in Shanghai did much to form his literary identity, but this is chance, not destiny, the material he happened to be given. Of the hundreds of others who were in the camp with him, none became writers, or none at least became writers of his calibre. It is not background that makes a writer, but the ambition – wherever it comes from – to make something of it.

'I am in the position of someone performing an autopsy,' Ballard said when asked to describe how he composed his fiction. 'Like all of us when we rent a strange apartment and find traces of the previous occupants – a medical journal, a douche bag, a videotape of an opera – and we begin to assemble from these apparently unrelated materials a hypothesis about who the previous occupants were. We carry out an investigation of our own.'[536]

A resonant description of the biographer's art, yet when the subject of the investigation was himself, Ballard was often resistant, even defensive. In a letter to David Pringle in 1999, he confesses to having turned down three recent approaches from potential biographers, 'largely because I can't face having to be interviewed in detail about my parents, childhood, schooldays, marriage, etc., a huge confrontation with the past I don't think I could cope with.'[537]

Ballard came increasingly to let his own mythology speak for him. The more of Ballard's later interviews you read, the more you find him repeating the same stories of himself to the extent that many of them have been told so often they have acquired the weight of reality, regardless of what actually happened. The way Ballard came to attribute his 1972 car crash to a tyre blow-out is one example of how a convenient theory repeated often enough may be turned into fact. The reports of wild behaviour and outraged sensibilities that have gradually accrued around the 'Crashed Cars' exhibition at the New Arts Lab in 1970 have acquired the patina of urban legend, but they too are almost certainly a fiction.

Writing about the event in *Miracles of Life*, Ballard describes how 'wine was splashed over the cars, windows were broken, and the topless girl was almost raped in the back seat of the Pontiac.'[538] There was a tension in the air, Ballard claims, a kind of sub-audible alarm bell. The destabilizing effect of the cars on the audience was a significant factor in his decision to go ahead and write *Crash* – yet according to the 'topless girl' who does not even get a name in Ballard's account, there was no destabilizing effect, 'it was just three wrecked cars in a very cold warehouse.'

Jo Stanley is a naval historian, with a special interest in the stories of pioneering female and non-binary seafarers. At the time of the 'Crashed Cars' exhibition she was twenty-one, a young person finding her feet on the London arts scene. She was paid £5 to appear naked at the opening, and assumed she would be taking part in an exhibition launch, a kind of happening. She did not know in advance that she would be the only person who would be naked, which is why she insisted that she would only appear topless – not, as Ballard claimed later,[539] because she was unduly disturbed by the sight of the cars. She felt confused about what she was supposed to be doing and it was the head of the video team, Hoppy Hopkins, who suggested that she circulate with a microphone, asking spectators to comment on what they saw.

'I would say that it was a really dismal non-event,' she said in a recent interview. 'It was absolutely not an orgy. It was boring. It felt really flat. Lots of the people there were journalists, getting a bit of free wine and wondering how to write it up the following day.'[540]

She did briefly sit in the back of the Pontiac – one of the journalists covering the event described how Stanley 'giggled and snogged and clowned with some other young people sitting merrily in the centre crashed car, all its windows gone and wine glasses littering the bonnet and roof'[541] – but no one tried to assault her, and she found it reprehensible of Ballard to suggest that they did. As for the Hare Krishnas who were supposed to have daubed the cars with white paint, they were never there, or at least not at the opening.

Then there is the endlessly repeated story of Catherine Storr's inflammatory reader's report on *Crash* the novel. In his recent monograph, *J. G. Ballard's* Crash: *a critical companion*,[542] the academic and science fiction specialist Paul March-Russell traces the progress of Storr's report from hearsay to 'fact'. Ballard first makes reference to the report in 1974 in his interview with Alan Burns, claiming that Storr 'wrote the most damning and vituperative reader's report they'd ever received'.[543] By the time of his interview with Graeme Revell for *ReSearch* in 1983,[544] the report has been embellished with the injunction 'Do Not Publish'.

March-Russell's own deep dive into the archives of Jonathan Cape at Reading University revealed something still more unexpected: Storr's infamous reader's report appears not to exist. Tom Maschler, who professed himself 'knocked over' by the book's impact,[545] shared the manuscript with several other readers as well as Storr. Some loved it, others hated it, but all considered that it was too long.[546] The book's copy-editor Mike Petty suggested that Storr had disapproved of *Crash* – she might even have made negative remarks about the state of the author's mental health – but that she had similarly objected to Martin Amis's *The Rachel Papers*, that senior readers, of whom Storr was one, 'would say this sort of thing all the time' and that Ballard had attached undue significance to the whole episode.

'I have a scientific imagination,' Ballard said to Will Self in 1995. 'My fiction is not generated by my emotions but by a natural inquisitiveness.'[547] He liked to play on this idea of himself as the dispassionate observer, untouched by ego – the invariably genial, immaculately courteous Jim Ballard of the TV interviews, of the many polite and humorous postcards sent in reply to sometimes importunate questions from readers and fans. But Ballard could be ruthless in protecting his reputation.

Both Michael Moorcock and J. G. Ballard claim to have invented the other, to have been the 'true' instigator of radicalism at *New Worlds*; there is no way of knowing now whose version is more accurate, and in a sense it is pointless to keep arguing over it. What is true beyond doubt is that the two were for a time hugely important in each other's lives, that the combination of Moorcock's energy and Ballard's brilliance created an atmosphere of possibility that might never have existed had the two of them not become friends and, for a time at least, frenemies.

But for Ballard, work would always trump friendship: the withering contempt he showed for the work of Keith Roberts during the row over the editorship of *Impulse*, his sudden freezing out of the Baxes in the early nineties, the two letters he wrote to Iain Sinclair venting his anger and frustration at what he perceived to be Moorcock's intrusion into his personal legend – all are revealing of more than momentary vexation.

Early in 2005, Ballard received a letter from the Venezuelan photographer Victor Sira, sending him a copy of a work by the American conceptual artist and photographer Richard Prince, who was to have an exhibition at the Whitechapel Gallery later that year. The work was a fake interview originally published in the avant-garde art magazine *ZG* in 1985 but purporting to be from 1969, in which 'J. G. Ballard' questions the then-eighteen-year-old Prince on – among other things – how he became 'a citizen of British Airways'.

The piece is deadpan and frequently funny and moreover, the 'Ballard' character is transparently not Ballard. Nonetheless, Ballard was not amused. He had not heard of Richard Prince, and seemed concerned that the interview might be taken at face value. He condemned it as 'a pedestrian and utterly worthless piece of work', and went on to say that he strongly resented 'being co-opted in this third-rater's self-flattering exercise'.[548] He then lambasted Sira himself for condoning what Prince had done.

That Ballard did not appreciate the joke was a double irony, given that Prince's first series of artworks had been entitled simply 'jokes'. Prince, a friend of Jeff Koons and Damien Hirst, shares common ground with both the American Pop artists and the YBAs. Given his strong interest in fakery and the recontextualizing of previously existing images, it is not surprising that his work has aroused controversy on multiple occasions, though one would have thought his obsession with advertising imagery would have generated at least a spark of fellow-feeling in Ballard.

The vehemence of Ballard's reaction is in stark contrast to the 'gentleman Jim' persona more usually on display in his correspondence, and as we have already seen, it was not a one-off. Ballard's frequently expressed nonchalance with regard to his fame was a grounding tenet of his personal mythos; as with everything in Ballard's life, the truth is more complicated. Though he did not care about the material trappings that fame often brings with it, he believed his work mattered, not just to himself but to the world of letters. He joked about burning his manuscripts, yet preserved them all, and a wealth of other literary artefacts besides. He left nothing to chance.

That he never stopped caring about how his work was perceived can be seen from a letter he wrote to the translator Bernard Sigaud the year before he died. Sigaud, who remains passionate about Ballard's writing and who had previously translated a number of Ballard's works into French, had written to ask if his rendition of one of Ballard's short stories might be included in the French science fiction magazine *Lunatique*. Ballard refused, adding that *Lunatique* represented 'the kind of fantasy SF I've tried so hard to get away from'.⁵⁴⁹

This episode has an interesting aftermath. Visiting Ballard's archive at the British Library after Ballard's death, Sigaud was excited to discover that it contained the manuscript pages of an unpublished *Vermilion Sands* story – the 'unsuccessful tyro effort' referred to by Chris several hundred pages ago. The typescript is undated but as the story references Disneyland, which opened in 1955, it was most likely written somewhere around that time.

Chris Beckett described how he had discovered the manuscript while cataloguing the archive: 'Its survival seems to have been accidental, insofar as its untitled parts were discovered ungathered and seemingly unloved: I came upon fifteen of seventeen annotated typescript sheets in the bottom of a box with an assortment of other loose fragments; but the final two sheets were found in another box, reused as if discarded, folded around other papers.'⁵⁵⁰

Sigaud made a copy of the manuscript and later showed it to David Pringle, who re-edited it to include some of the material that Ballard had crossed out – by now they had given it the title 'The Hardoon Labyrinth'. Sigaud translated the story into French and sought permission to publish it as part of an upcoming French edition of *Vermilion Sands*. Sigaud believed he had complied with the necessary protocols, though in fact that turned out not to be the case. The collection, published in 2013 by Editions Tristram, was effectively illegal, and had to be pulped. A few dozen copies – mainly those sent out in advance to sales reps and reviewers – escaped their death sentence and remain at large, wafting their way – like the sand rays portrayed on their covers – through the mysterious byways of the underground book trade.

That Bernard Sigaud also happens to be my French translator, and Editions Tristram my French publisher is one of those points of interconnectedness that have come to characterize this book's journey.

The draft manuscript of 'The Hardoon Labyrinth' is around 9,000 words in length, and tells the story of a young man, Max Caldwell, who takes a temporary job in Vermilion Sands as secretary to an eccentric millionaire. Hardoon – no doubt a prototype for the villain in *The Wind from Nowhere* – is obsessed with the nature of time as a sixth sense, and also with the ever-expanding shanty town of architectural follies to the rear of his mansion.

'The Hardoon Labyrinth' has all the hallmarks of the canonical *Vermilion Sands* stories and, had Ballard found the time or inclination to finish it, would have formed a natural part of the collection. The manuscript as it stands is littered with the errors and inconsistencies that are inevitably present in any first draft.

Speaking in 2002 about the posthumous release of an uncompleted work by Douglas Adams – a notorious perfectionist – Ballard leaves no doubt as to his views on the matter: 'There's a lot of magic involved in writing a novel,' he insists. 'Like Houdini, we try to pull off a surprise ending, and I think that, in the same way, nothing should be performed unless it's perfect. Cobbling together a first draft that would have been subject to a huge number of further drafts and revisions is a bit like turning the novelist into a second-rate conjuror.'[551]

It is inconceivable that Ballard, whose drafting process shows how rigorous he was in perfecting his work prior to publication, would have wanted or allowed 'The Hardoon Labyrinth' to be read in its unfinished form. So far as Chris was concerned, Sigaud's abortive attempt to get the story published was itself a kind of folly. A fictional retelling of the incident appeared in *Reports From the Deep End*, an anthology of short fiction inspired by J. G. Ballard and published by Titan Books in 2023. Editors Rick McGrath and Maxim Jakubowski were eager to publish 'The Hardoon Labyrinth' itself in the same anthology. Their request was denied.

The story has seemed to cast a negative spell over all those who have tangled with it, as such lost texts often do. Judging by his response to similar infringements, Ballard would not have been amused, though late in 2025, and at the last possible moment for reporting it here, I have a conversation that makes me consider the uncharted passageways of 'The Hardoon Labyrinth' in a different light. I am in Paris to be announced the winner of a literary prize, and in a bistro just off the Boulevard Saint-Germain, my publishers, Jean-Hubert Gailliot and Sylvie Martigny of Editions Tristram ask me eagerly how this manuscript is faring on its journey towards publication. There are things I can speak of and things I choose not to, though even in the silences I can sense their compassion, their unwavering belief in my ability to put words on the page. Then they relate to me an anecdote I have not heard before, of how they first made contact with Ballard in the early 2000s by looking him up in the telephone directory. His name and address were listed, like anyone else's – BALLARD, James Graham, 36 Old Charlton Road, Shepperton – together with his telephone number. Jean-Hubert performs an amusingly lifelike impression of how Ballard sounded when he picked up the phone: those well-rounded vowels, tempered by a habitual underlying distrust of anyone who might dare to drag him away from his work-in-progress. He and Sylvie were calling, Jean-Hubert explained, to ask for permission to publish a new translation of *The Atrocity Exhibition*. 'Of course,' Ballard said. His realization that these were book people made him immediately more expansive, more relaxed. 'Only you will have to make sure you are working from the new edition. It's just come out.'[552]

They were to meet Ballard in person only once, at the London Book Fair, the year before he died. 'You could see that he was ill,' Sylvie says, 'but he was still magnificent.' Claire was with him, and the four of them spent an hour together, talking about the soon-to-be-published *Miracles of Life*, and the second instalment of the Tristrams' three-volume compendium of Ballard's short stories, not destined to appear until after his death.[553] 'We liked Claire very much,' Sylvie adds, and here, so late in the day, the circle closes and I find myself face to face with them, Jim and Claire, chatting with my friends, who I love dearly, and who in the sharing of their memories have become a part of this narrative as they always have been, as they were before I was. There is a silence at the heart of the labyrinth that deserves to be broken, a monster made of words that will one day escape. Words are wayward by nature and so are writers. There are those who cannot grasp this, who care more for how the dead might appear to the living than for the life of the text. Vermilion Sands remains closed to them, a lost estate.

Chris always wanted to write about Paris but aside from abandoned scraps he never did. In the Jardin du Luxembourg it is early November and 17 degrees. Next week the temperature will fall and winter will arrive, but not quite yet. Children run and play in the golden light that seeps between the trees, and I wonder if I will ever be able to remake my relationship with this city – beloved city, enchanted city – in a way that does not feel characterized by its emptiness, its insurmountable lack. Here in Paris especially I feel the gulf of Chris's absence, the fact that others have already begun to see him as part of the past.

Chris's practical working methods were remarkably similar to Ballard's: his strict insistence on writing proper second drafts, also his tendency to augment successive drafts, increasing the word count rather than cutting — what Chris Beckett describes as 'a compositional principle of enlargement'[554] and what my Chris called 'thickening'. But their likeness to one another goes deeper even than that. It is not surprising that *Miracles of Life* became one of Chris's favourites of Ballard's texts. With its clarity of purpose, its uncluttered line, its carefully curated account of a messier reality it in many ways represents the version of this book that Chris wanted to write.

The book we have created together is more difficult to categorize. Chris interpreted Ballard's later life as he interpreted his own, insisting there was nothing to see here, just a man in a room, writing. Watching back our Zoom calls with Fay and with Beatrice, I cannot help noticing how frequently our conversations begin to take on the aspect of running battles: Chris, at pains to reassure both sisters he has no intention of trying to lift the lid on matters they might consider too personal; me — sometimes visibly frowning — attempting gently but persistently to do exactly that.

The world in which Ballard's journey as a writer began belongs far more to Chris than it does to me. It is a story I have acquired — through reading and through listening, through the gradual accretion of facts or if not facts, theories; through the repeated recitations of particular anecdotes, through osmosis. This imported past is a difficult burden, one I carry in the knowledge that I have had for a long time and always held as a comfort: that we are all of us reinvented each second, that yesterday's truth has already shifted a little, that we can never quite grasp it.

So much more than the life, in any case, taking on this strange endeavour has sent me back to the work.

'A text's unity lies not in its origin, but in its destination,' argues Roland Barthes in *The Death of the Author*, and while I would not go the whole hog and maintain as Barthes does that the personality and biography of the writer is of no account, I would argue absolutely and without apology that the writer's life is only of interest insofar as the work they have produced can withstand the Barthes test.

Ballard's work can survive the Barthes test and wipe the floor with it. Few writers of the past fifty years have showed such singularity of vision and strength of purpose in exposing the workings and mysteries of the human mind. Still fewer have created such a unique and powerful language with which to do so, an iconography as beautiful as it is savage. Ballard has given us a key to the century, a means of coming closer to an understanding of the state we're in.

Like Nabokov, Ballard did not believe in God, but he believed in art. Open any of Ballard's novels, and it is the wildness of his conceits, that vertiginous sense of unsafety that drives you forward, the feeling Chris described – that has been described by many – as uniquely 'Ballardian'. What you may know or think you know about the author slips away: the contentions, assumptions and gossip, the he-said and she-said that can never now be challenged or proven because the man himself is dead and cannot respond. Judging by his dismissive comments about secondary sources, Ballard would have given short shrift to much of the rumour and speculation that has begun to come out of the woodwork in the years since his death.

'I'm glad I didn't write this book when he was alive,' writes John Baxter in his epilogue to *The Inner Man*. 'It would have taken a stronger will than his to confront the realities of his troubled life.'[555] I would counter that few wills have proven stronger, and my guess is that Baxter, knowing that full well, simply wouldn't have dared.

We gather facts because once a person is gone from the world the facts – precious splinters of glass – are all we have to cling to, and I am as guilty as any in my eagerness to discover facts I have no business knowing.

What does that say about biography, except that those who were not there are almost bound to get it wrong. Even my own version of my own life, written at a distance, already, of months, will be more rounded than it should be, more considered and thus, in a sense, distorted. Such errors cannot be helped, but I can tell you now that the truth of certain moments is contained more in the scatter of words I wrote in the small hours, in the sparsely notated measures of Tavener and Britten heard at 3 am when the love of my life lay dying and I — confused, shaken, exhausted — was at my lowest ebb, than in any 'facts' or perfected details I might reveal afterwards.

Text, though, is rarely a dry thing; it has a habit of telling tales.

'What I am interested in — what I think readers will be interested in — is his inner life, the life of his mind,' says Carole Angier of W. G. Sebald. 'I don't think that the gap of his marriage, which I had to leave as a gap, is all that crucial in understanding what I am trying to understand, which is his creative, artist's mind.' With the voices of Sebald's wife and daughter notably missing from Angier's biography, any return to Sebald's text will reveal an uncanny mirroring of this omission. In all of Sebald's works, there is not a single woman that appears as a primary participant. What women there are, are supporting cast, and barely that. The most intense relationships in *The Emigrants* are those heightened, ineffable bromances between mismatched men; in Austerlitz, it is the *Liebestod* between Jacques Austerlitz and the ghosts of his past.

Sebald has written his truth himself, and it is all in plain sight. The same can be said of J. G. Ballard, whose insurmountable aloneness and emotional distance is hard-wired into every one of his solitary doctors. Whose angers and griefs, though deeply buried, resurface in every book. Whose innate conservatism and desire for change mount running battles with one another through the pages of each of his narratives and whose hunger for the love of women is forever at odds with his need for privacy. Even his estrangement from his son can be revealed through text, in this case his will, which leaves Jim junior a fraction of the sum bequeathed to each of Ballard's daughters.

'I would say that I quite consciously rely on my obsessions in all my work,' Ballard admitted to Thomas Frick in his interview for *The Paris Review* in 1983. 'That I deliberately set up an obsessional frame of mind ... All obsessions are extreme metaphors waiting to be born. That whole private mythology, in which I believe totally, is a collaboration between one's conscious mind and those obsessions that, one by one, present themselves as stepping stones.'[556] Later in the same interview and speaking about the occasional integration of found texts into his work, Ballard describes how he transcribed a secret tape recording he made of Claire in a rage and used it in the closing pages of *Concrete Island*. 'Well, secret is the wrong word,' Ballard adds. 'She was simply too angry to notice that I had switched the machine on.'

Men have all too frequently weaponized women's anger as 'proof' that they are crazy, and when I first read about Ballard taping Claire without her permission I feel outraged, that he would treat her with such belittling indifference. I jot down some notes about Ballard's sexism, about it being obvious that it was this kind of emotional detachment that led to the breach in their relationship in the 1970s. When I seek out the relevant passage in *Concrete Island* some weeks later, I assume I already know what I will discover.

What I find, in fact, is tenderness, abjection, the ineradicable closeness of two people involved in a struggle that neither can win.

> You'll get yourself run over, baby. Thank God you'll soon be out of my life. You ought to live in an Oriental bazaar. I loved you dearly and you buggered it up. Just twelve hours and you'll be gone. Who wants relationships? You bore me right now. You never had any love and affection as a child. Don't commit any acts of violence tonight. There are lots of nice children here. Why are you such a shit? That fucking American girl ... So conceptual. She's so brilliant, I know.
>
> Maitland stood up and stepped over to her. Holding off her strong arms, he pulled her shoulders against his chest. He soothed and comforted her, brushing the wet hair from her face ... They sat on the bed together in the warm room.[557]

I had thought it would be Emma Tennant the two would be fighting over, though clearly — devastatingly — it is Pam Zoline. All their pain is laid bare in this passage, and I am shattered, burst wide open by the pathos of it. That Ballard can see himself so clearly, the selfish need for validation that is part of his aloneness, a thing he cannot relinquish even as he sees it destroying the person he cares for most.

The text does not apportion blame to either of them; it describes what is.

Reading Claire's recorded words at this distance of decades I find myself in tears. It is the last day of July and I have been sad this week anyway. I am in the final stages of clearing the house, taking apart the infrastructure of our life together and in this moment I am overcome by one thought above all: how they are gone beyond reach. They're all dead, I cry aloud. Jim, Claire, Chris – they're all dead.

The summer is at its zenith and here, alone in what remains of our home I am inconsolable. I find myself wishing I could talk to Claire, yet it is Claire, most of all, who I have had trouble in bringing to life in my mind as well as on the page. There are conflicting accounts of her, contradictions I cannot rely on or repeat because they are hearsay. There are people I have wanted to talk to who knew Claire well, who I have tried to contact, but for reasons that remain elusive they have – like Ute and Anna Sebald – kept their silence. Having the right to remain silent is such an absolute it is written into our law, and in spite of my sadness – for sadness is what I feel, most of all, the ache of absence, regret for voices that might now be lost, conversations that have never taken place – I find myself in sympathy with their decision. What gives me the right to be asking these questions, after all?

It is only later, in the autumn, when I have more or less given up hope of making further headway, that I stumble across a link to a video recording of Claire made at a symposium called 'Ballardian Architecture: Inner and Outer Space', a day conference organized by the RA Architecture Programme that took place in the Reynolds Room at the Royal Academy of Arts, London, on Saturday 15 May 2010. And for a mercy the link still works, the video still plays, and as I watch it I find myself seized by the impulse to go back, to start Jimmy's story again from a different angle.

But it is in the nature of quests that they keep you moving forward, that they force you to change.

Claire is the last speaker on the programme and she talks for ten minutes. Seeing her on stage – above all, hearing her speak – feels nothing short of magical. It is as if she has stepped forward to talk to me personally, as if against all odds she has crossed time to be here, to add her voice to this conversation as I have wished for her to do.

Her voice is calm, warm, resonant, a rich contralto. Her presence is focused and engaged. She speaks about Ballard and his work in a way that is both intimate and full of insight. There is an energy that emanates from her, an attractiveness that none of the photos I have seen are able to convey. Speaking about the day's conference and how much she has enjoyed it, she adds that 'my instinct is to go rushing home to tell him all about it. It feels terrible, really, that I can't.'

Words I have spoken so many times myself I am afraid the people who know me will soon be bored by them. Words that reveal to me more than any other something of how their life together must have been.

'Of course he was a terrific tease. He really, really liked to keep everyone guessing, and you had to use your own judgement about when he was teasing and when he was serious. Because the two overlapped and sometimes, did he even know himself? I'm not too sure. He kept us on our toes.'

She talks of how Jim envied her, that she grew up in London, that she could literally touch her childhood. Of a pilgrimage they made together to visit the grave of Le Corbusier. Of his love of empty hotel dining rooms, that sense of vacancy. 'Heathrow was the only airport he would ever use, because it was quite close to home. The sense of freedom, the sense of flying, the sense of impermanence, of movement, of mobility that excited him so much.'

She describes how Ballard truly couldn't see any reason why there shouldn't be an elevated highway branching off from the Westway, carving a swathe through St John's Wood, Hampstead, Highgate, all those buildings of red-brick London he so disliked. And as for where it would stop? Well, wherever he wanted to get off. How he never stopped feeling that he didn't belong, even in those landscapes that he had made his own.

'But the one thing I would say,' Claire adds by way of conclusion, 'is that when you next go on the Westway and drive west, particularly if it's at sunset, with those amazing skies, or dusk when you've got clouds, or just when that very disappointing development at Paddington is lit up, and looks lovely for once, think of him driving with you, because he'll be there.'

ACKNOWLEDGEMENTS

My thanks to Fay Ballard and Beatrice Ballard, who have both given generously of their time and of their memories. Among J. G. B.'s family and friends my thanks and appreciation go out also to Tony Richardson, Margaret Ballard-Richardson, Maggie Hanbury, Barney Cokeliss, Harley Cokeliss, John Gray, Iain Sinclair, Michael Moorcock, Lindsay Fulcher and Pamela Zoline. The sharing of memories is a powerful and sometimes painful act and my gratitude for the contributions of those who knew Ballard personally, some for a brief while, others for many years is enormous and unstinting. To David Pringle, who was there from the beginning and even before that, and who gave significant attention to each and every random Ballard query I threw at him during the course of my work, I can only say that this book could not have existed without you. To Chris's agent Max Edwards, to my agent Anna Webber, to our editors Tomasz Hoskins and Declan Ryan and to everyone at Bloomsbury who kept believing in this book even though it is not the book you originally signed up for, thank you for being there, thank you for staying there – you helped me more than you know.

To Greg Buzwell, Eleanor Dickens and Callum McKean at the British Library and to Adam Roberts for making the introduction – there are no words for what your involvement in our lives and work has meant to me and would, one hundred per cent, have meant to Chris. To Chris Beckett at the British Library, so many thanks for your wonderful work in cataloguing and writing about the J. G. Ballard archive. To Rick McGrath, Simon Sellars and Mike Holliday for the veritable treasure house of Ballardian information, memorabilia and original research you have undertaken and made available online – though you may not have been aware of it, you have been with me throughout! To Bernard Sigaud for revealing to us the secrets of 'The Hardoon Labyrinth', to Sylvie Martigny and Jean-Hubert Gailliot for your love and support and for being such staunch promotors of Ballard's work in France. To Jon Riley for your caring and patience. To Cyril Leuthy and Denis Gaubert for your intelligence and commitment, and for a magical two days of business more or less as usual.

To the friends, family and colleagues – many of whom are named in this book – who offered their love and support and commitment to Chris and me through the months of 2023 and 2024. Words are insufficient, except to say thank you for being in our lives and from me especially thank you for being there for Chris, who loved you all: Leigh Kennedy, Simon Priest, Elizabeth Priest, Monica Allan, Barbara Mosey, Emma Swift, James Long, Matt Hill, Suze Hill, Anne Charnock, Garry Charnock, Mark Blacklock, Martin MacInnes, Adna Dumitrescu, Aliya Whiteley, Nick Whiteley (Sussex), Chris Johnstone, Anne Johnstone, John Clute, Judith Clute, Liz Hand, Mike Harrison, Cath Phillips, Lisa Tuttle, Colin Murray, Emily Murray, Meg MacDonald, Wendy Aldiss, David Langford, Sam Thompson, Paul Kincaid, Helen Marshall, Vince Haig, Paul Vincent, Janet Bentley, Carole Johnstone, Iain Black, Bob Millington, Rojelio Fojo and to every single person who wrote to me in the wake of Chris's death, expressing condolences and sharing memories, and also to those who were present at Chris's memorial event at the Glasgow Worldcon in the summer of 2024, I want you all to know that you made a real difference.

To my dad, Stuart Allan, who also died during the writing of this book, thank you for our last conversation and for being my father.

To the staff of the Royal Alexandra Hospital, Paisley, the Beatson Cancer Centre, Hyndland, Glasgow, the Victoria Hospital, Rothesay and Inverclyde hospital, Branchton, to the district nurses and care workers on the Isle of Bute who helped me to keep Chris at home where he wanted to be – to every single person involved in Chris's care through the NHS, my boundless love and thanks. Ben Fulton, Vivienne MacLaren, Kate Canavan, Derek Doherty, James Paxton, Nick Whiteley (Glasgow), Pam Dalrymple, Kitty Reid, Barbara, Agnes, Julie, Katie, Julie 2, Janey, Lindsey, Lindsey 2, Paula, Iona, Ross, Leanne, Anna. To Asha, Marta and Angela at the Finesse Dental Practice, Paisley – you were marvellous to Chris and he would have wanted you mentioned here. To Sandra Cobain, who officiated at our wedding and who was such a help to me later with filing official paperwork, and to Amy, who was there, too. To Craig McKellar and McKellar Funeral Services – you could not have been more compassionate or efficient. I know there will be some names I have inadvertently missed, but believe me, none of you are forgotten. To Gianna Zavaroni, Kim Kernaghan and Alison Dallas at the Bute Law Practice, thank you for your work on my behalf and for making a difficult process so much easier. Above all, to Evelyn Glass, our good angel – not just for your care of us but for the work you do, the compassion you show, the knowledge you pass on – I seriously do not know how I would have coped without you, so this book, at least in part, is for you.

And most of all, to my beloved Chris. We did it, my lovely – I told you we would. The work is complete and the book is here. Ever thine, ever mine, ever ours.

BIBLIOGRAPHY

What follows is by no means a complete bibliography of either the works of J. G. Ballard or works pertaining to J. G. Ballard, but rather a list of the works, and the specific editions of those works, that have been referred to or consulted in writing of *The Illuminated Man*.

WORKS BY J. G. BALLARD
Novels
The Wind From Nowhere, Berkeley 1962
The Drowned World, SF Book Club edition 1964
The Drought, Flamingo (paperback reissue) 1993
The Crystal World, Cape 1966
The Atrocity Exhibition, Flamingo (annotated paperback edition) 1993
Crash, Cape 1973
Concrete Island, Cape 1974
High-Rise, Cape 1975
The Unlimited Dream Company, Cape 1979
Hello America, Cape 1981
Empire of the Sun, Gollancz 1984
The Day of Creation, Gollancz 1987
Running Wild, Hutchinson 1988
The Kindness of Women, HarperCollins 1991
Rushing to Paradise, Flamingo 1994
Cocaine Nights, Flamingo 1996
Super-Cannes, Flamingo 2000
Millennium People, Flamingo 2003
Kingdom Come, Fourth Estate 2006

Autobiography
Miracles of Life: Shanghai to Shepperton, Fourth Estate 2008

Short Story Collections
The Four-Dimensional Nightmare, SF Book Club edition 1964
The Terminal Beach, Gollancz reissue 1985
Vermilion Sands, Cape 1973
Low-Flying Aircraft, Cape 1976
Myths of the Near Future, Cape 1982
Memories of the Space Age, Arkham House 1988
War Fever, Collins 1990

Non-Fiction
A User's Guide to the Millennium: Essays and Reviews, Picador 1996

WORKS ABOUT J. G. BALLARD
House Clearance, Fay Ballard, Aldgate Press 2014
The Inner Man: The Life of J. G. Ballard, John Baxter, Weidenfeld & Nicolson 2011
J. G. Ballard: Selected Non-Fiction 1962–2007, ed. Mark Blacklock, MIT Press 2023
The Imagination on Trial: British and American writers discuss their working methods, eds Alan Burns and Charles Sugnet, Allison & Busby 1981
'The Angle Between Two Walls': The Fiction of J. G. Ballard, Roger Luckhurst, Liverpool University Press 1997
J. G. Ballard's Crash, Paul March-Russell, Palgrave Macmillan 2024
Extreme Metaphors: interviews with J. G. Ballard 1967–2008, eds Simon Sellars and Dan O'Hara, Fourth Estate 2012
Crash: David Cronenberg's post-mortem on J. G. Ballard's 'trajectory of fate', Iain Sinclair, BFI Publishing 1999
'J. G. Ballard', V. Vale/Andrea Juno, ReSearch Publications 1984

MISCELLANEOUS
'Enemy Subject' No 20/61: Life in a Japanese Internment Camp 1943–45, Peggy Abkhazi, Sutton Publishing Ltd 1995
The Shape of Further Things, Brian Aldiss, Faber & Faber 1970
Empire Made Me: An Englishman Adrift in Shanghai, Robert Bickers, Penguin 2004
Eduardo Paolozzi at New Worlds, David Brittain, Savoy Books 2013
Champions Day: the End of Old Shanghai, James Carter, WW Norton 2020
My Dear Hugh: Letters from Richard Cobb to Hugh Trevor-Roper and others, ed Tim Heald, Frances Lincoln 2011
Captive in Shanghai, Hugh Collar, OUP 1991

Gollancz: The Story of a Publishing House 1928–78, Sheila Hodges, Gollancz 1979
Steven Spielberg: a biography, Joseph McBride, Simon & Schuster 1997
New Worlds: An Anthology, ed. Michael Moorcock, Flamingo 1983
Little Foreign Devil, Desmond Power, Pangli 1996
Sin City, Ralph Shaw, Sphere 1992
Burnt Diaries, Emma Tennant, Canongate 1999
The Elephant in the Room: Stories About Cancer Patients and their Doctors, Jonathan Waxman, Springer 2011

CHAPTER TITLES

Chris selected his chapter titles from among Ballard's own and I continued to follow his lead as the book progressed. Here is the list of chapters, and the books their titles came from.

'The White Hotel' – *The Crystal World*
'The Paradises of the Sun' – *The Drowned World*
'Journey Towards the Rain Planet' – *The Day of Creation*
'The Eve of Pearl Harbor' – *Empire of the Sun*
'A Landscape of Airfields' – *Empire of the Sun*
'A New Arrival' – *Rushing to Paradise*
'The Man with the White Smile' – *The Drowned World*
'The Abandoned Aerodrome' – *Empire of the Sun*
'The Unlimited Dream Company' – *The Unlimited Dream Company*
'Exit Strategies' – *Kingdom Come*
'Out of the Night and into the Dream' – *The Day of Creation*
'Danger in the Streets of the Sky' – *High-Rise*
'The Children's Sanctuary' – *Millennium People*
'The Naming of New Things' – *The Day of Creation*
'Appointment with a Revolution' – *Millennium People*
'The Sign of the Crab' – *The Drought*
'The Depot of Dreams' – *Millennium People*
'Preparations for Departure' – *High-Rise*
'A Season for Assassins' – *Millennium People*
'The House of Women' – *The Day of Creation*
'The Burning Car' – *Concrete Island*
'The Causeways of the Sun' – *The Drowned World*
'A Decline in Property Values' – *Millennium People*
'The Evening's Entertainment' – *High-Rise*
'Giving Himself to the Sun' – *Millennium People*
'The Great American Desert' – *Hello America*
'The Third Nile' – *The Day of Creation*
'Through the Crash Barrier' – *Concrete Island*

'I Give Myself Away' — *The Unlimited Dream Company*
'The Road to Shanghai' — *Empire of the Sun*
'The Predatory Birds' — *High-Rise*
'Too Soon, Too Late' — *The Drowned World*
'The Upholstered Apocalypse' — *Millennium People*
'Absolute Zero' — *Millennium People*
'A Task Completed' — *Millennium People*
'The Illuminated Man' — *The Crystal World*

UNATTRIBUTED QUOTES
In the chapter 'Absolute Zero', readers may recognize small fragments of quotations from other works. My thanks to Ervin Drake, Ludwig van Beethoven, William Wordsworth, Boris Pasternak, Felicia Hemans, Max Colpet, Joan Lindsay and Alan Garner.

NOTES

PROLOGUE 'THE WHITE HOTEL'

1 'Shameless Autobiography, or, How I Started Reading the Works of J. G. Ballard', *JGB News* 11, April 1984.
2 *Earth is the Alien Planet*, David Pringle, Borgo Press 1979.
3 *J. G. Ballard: A Primary and Secondary Bibliography,* David Pringle, GK Hall 1984.

INTRODUCTION 'THE PARADISES OF THE SUN'

4 *Anticipations*, edited by Christopher Priest, Faber & Faber 1978, which includes Ballard's story 'One Afternoon at Utah Beach.'

CHAPTER 1 'JOURNEY TOWARDS THE RAIN PLANET'

5 Probably named after William Pitt Amherst, 1st Earl Amherst. Lord Amherst was Governor-General of India between 1823 and 1828. In 1816, as Ambassador Extraordinary to the court of the Jiaqing Emperor, he refused to kowtow to the emperor and was refused all diplomatic access thereafter.
6 J. G. Ballard, *Miracles of Life*, 2008.
7 Ballard, interviewed by Catherine Bresson, 1982; Ballard, interviewed by Thomas Frick, 1983.
8 Interview with David Pringle, 1981; Ballard, 'Licence to Kill', *Sunday Times*, 21 February 1999; Ballard, 'The End of My War', *Sunday Times*, 20 August 1995.
9 Irene Duguid Kilpatrick, in conversation with Rick McGrath and David Pringle in 2008.
10 Ballard, *Miracles of Life*, 2008.
11 Ballard, interviewed by Catherine Bresson, 1982.
12 Ballard, *Miracles of Life*, 2008; Ballard, interviewed by James Goddard and David Pringle, 4 January 1975.
13 Ballard, interviewed by Danny Danziger, *Independent*, 16 December 1991.

14 Ballard, interviewed by David Pringle, 24 July 1981.
15 'Strange Fiction' by James Campbell, *Guardian,* 14 June, 2008.
16 Ballard, interviewed by Hari Kunzru, 31 October 2007 (Waterstones internal magazine).
17 Ballard, *Miracles of Life*, 2008.

CHAPTER 2 'THE EVE OF PEARL HARBOR'

18 Ballard, *Miracles of Life*, 2008.
19 *Captive in Shanghai*, Hugh Collar, 1990
20 Ballard, 'Unlocking the Past', *Telegraph*, 21 September 1991.
21 Ballard, *Miracles of Life*, 2008.
22 Ballard, *Miracles of Life*, 2008.
23 Ballard, 'The End of My War', *Sunday Times*, 20 August 1995.
24 Desmond Power, *Little Foreign Devil*, 1996.
25 Ballard, *Miracles of Life*, 2008.
26 Ballard, *The Pleasure of Reading*, edited by Antonia Fraser, 1992.
27 Ballard, *Miracles of Life*, 2008
28 Ballard, *The Pleasure of Reading*, edited by Antonia Fraser, 1992.
29 Ballard, on Radio 2, 2006; Ballard, *Miracles of Life*, 2008; Peter Linnett, *The Writer*, June 1973.
30 Ballard, *Miracles of Life*, 2008.
31 James Carter, *Champions Day*, 2020
32 Ballard, interviewed by James Goddard and David Pringle, 4 January 1975; Ballard, *Miracles of Life*, 2008.
33 Ballard, *Miracles of Life*, 2008.
34 Ballard, *Miracles of Life*, 2008.
35 Ballard, *Miracles of Life*, 2008.
36 Ballard, interviewed by James Goddard and David Pringle, 4 January 1975; Ballard, *Miracles of Life*, 2008.
37 Peggy Abkhazi, 'Enemy Subject', 1995.
38 Hugh Collar, *Captive in Shanghai*, 1990.
39 Peggy Abkhazi, 'Enemy Subject', 1995.
40 Robert Bickers, *Empire Made Me*, 2003.
41 Hugh Collar, *Captive in Shanghai*, 1990.

CHAPTER 3 'A LANDSCAPE OF AIRFIELDS'

42 Robert Bickers, *Empire Made Me*, 2003.
43 Ballard, 'Look Back at Empire', *Guardian*, 2006.
44 Ballard profile by Claire Tomalin, *Sunday Times*, 9 September 1984.
45 Desmond Power, *Little Foreign Devil*, 1996.

46 Peggy Abkhazi, *'Enemy Subject'*, 1995.
47 Ballard, *Miracles of Life*, 2008.
48 Ballard, interviewed by Lynn Barber, 1991.
49 Ballard, *Miracles of Life*, 2008.
50 Emma Tennant, *Burnt Diaries*, 1999.
51 Ballard, interviewed by David Pringle, 1981.
52 Peggy Abkhazi, *'Enemy Subject'*, 1995 – Foreword by Ballard.
53 Sophie Kummer, *Hendon Times*, 2004. The reference to 'Braidwood' was to Mr W. G. Braidwood, a senior executive in the Shell Oil Company, and another prominent member of the camp.
54 Ballard, quoted in Ian Bradley, *Oh Joy, Oh Rapture!: The Enduring Phenomenon of Gilbert and Sullivan*, OUP 2005.
55 Robert Goralski, *World War II Almanac, 1931–1945*, 1981.
56 Ballard, interviewed by Lynn Barber, 1981.
57 Ballard, interviewed by David Pringle, 1981.
58 Ballard, *Miracles of Life*, 2008.
59 Ballard, *Miracles of Life*, 2008.
60 Irene Duguid Kilpatrick, letter to *The Times*, 1 September 1984.
61 Ballard, *Miracles of Life*, 2008.
62 Mrs Irene Duguid Kilpatrick, letter to Rick McGrath, 29 April 2007.
63 Irene Duguid Kilpatrick, letter to *The Times*, 1 September 1984.
64 Ballard, 'Media Games', *Daily Telegraph*, 1992.
65 Ballard, *Miracles of Life*, Chapter 8, 2008.
66 Ballard, interviewed by Matthew Leonard, *ABC Radio 24 Hours*, January 1992.
67 Ballard, *Miracles of Life*, Chapter 9, 2008.
68 Ballard, 'The Last Real Innocents', *New York Times*, 1991.

CHAPTER 4 'A NEW ARRIVAL'

69 Raymond Tait, 'J. G. Ballard at The Leys School', *Deep Ends* 2014.
70 Interview with Martin Amis, *Observer Magazine*, 2 September 1984.
71 Barrie Page, *Old Leysian Newsletter*, circa 2010.
72 Tony Thornton to Raymond Tait, 13/09/04.
73 Notes by Raymond Tait, 2007, based on his research at The Leys School in the 1990s.
74 Ballard, *Miracles of Life*, p121.
75 Emails (November 2011) to David Pringle from Desmond Power, a friend of Bill Weight's in Canada, where he later relocated. Weight told Power that Ballard had been expelled from his grandparents' home for 'gross misconduct' and 'unspeakable behaviour', the nature of which he did not divulge. Bill Weight died in Vancouver in 2002.

76 Ballard, interviewed by David Pringle, 23 September 1984.
77 Thomas Frick interview, *Paris Review* 1983.
78 Ballard, interviewed by David Pringle, 24 July 1981.
79 Raymond Tait, 'J. G. Ballard at The Leys School', *Deep Ends* 2014.
80 Raymond Tait, 'J. G. Ballard at The Leys School', *Deep Ends* 2014.
81 Ballard, interviewed by Lynn Barber, 27 December 1981; Ballard, interviewed by David Pringle, 24 July 1981.
82 Ballard, *The Kindness of Women*, 1991; Ballard, *Miracles of Life*, 2008.
83 Mark Thomas, 'The Rules of Autogeddon: death, sex and law in J. G. Ballard's *Crash*', Griffith Law Review 2011, Jonathan McCalmont, 'A Benign Psychopathology: the films of J. G. Ballard', ruthlessculture.com 2010, David Kopacz interview 1997 beingfullyhuman.com 2016 among many others.
84 Ballard, 'Raising the Dead', *Sunday Times Magazine*, 7 March 1999 – apparently an oral piece, but no interviewer was named.
85 Ballard, *Miracles of Life*, 2008.
86 William Spencer, interviewed by David Pringle, *Interzone 79*, January 1994.
87 Spencer, notes written in 2010.
88 Ballard, *Miracles of Life*, 2008.
89 Alison Carter, 'Talking to J. G. Ballard about King's', *King's Parade*, Autumn 2000.
90 Ballard, interviewed by David Pringle, 24 July 1981.
91 Ballard, interviewed by David Pringle, 24 July 1981.
92 Ballard, *Miracles of Life*, 2008.
93 Ballard, interviewed by David Pringle, 24 July 1981; William Spencer, notes to Pringle, 2010.

CHAPTER 5 'THE MAN WITH THE WHITE SMILE'

94 William Spencer, interviewed by David Pringle, *Interzone 79*, January 1994.
95 Ballard, interviewed by David Pringle, 24 July 1981.
96 Ballard, interviewed by David Pringle, 24 July 1981; Ballard, *Miracles of Life*, 2008,
97 Ballard, interviewed by David Pringle, 24 July 1981; Ballard, interviewed by Ken Bruce, BBC Radio 2, 10 September 1984.
98 Ballard, interviewed by Marianne Brace, *Independent*, 15 September 2006.

CHAPTER 6 'THE ABANDONED AERODROME'

99 Ballard, interviewed by David Pringle, 24 July 1981.
100 Ballard, interviewed by Ralph Rugoff, *Frieze 34*, May 1997.

101 Ballard, *The Kindness of Women*, 1991.
102 Ballard, interviewed by Mark Pauline, June 1986
103 Ballard, *Miracles of Life*, 2008.
104 Ballard, interviewed by Chris Hall, *spikemagazine.com*.
105 Ballard, *Mysteries of Life*, 2008.
106 Ballard, postcard to the book collector Angharad Ryder, undated but circa September 1987.

CHAPTER 7 'THE UNLIMITED DREAM COMPANY'

107 Ballard, interviewed by J. Goddard and D. Pringle, 4 January 1975.
108 Ballard, interviewed by Martin Fenner, *Night Out 5*, November 1982.
109 Ballard, interviewed by J. Goddard and D. Pringle, 4 January 1975.
110 Ballard, *Miracles of Life*, 2008.
111 Ballard interview, Julian Dibbell, *Spin*, Feb 1989.

CHAPTER 8 'EXIT STRATEGIES'

112 Ballard, interviewed by David Pringle, 24 July 1981.
113 Ballard, interviewed by David Pringle, 24 July 1981.
114 Ballard, *Miracles of Life*, 2008.
115 From a profile of Ballard in *New Worlds,* December 1956.
116 Ballard, *Miracles of Life*, 2008.
117 Ballard, letter to Mike Bonsall, September 2007.
118 *Chiswick Timeline of Writers & Books*, chiswickbookfestival, April 2019.
119 Ballard, interviewed by David Pringle, 24 July 1981,
120 Ballard, 'Public Lending Right: A Symposium', *New Review*, December 1975.
121 Ballard, Anthony Denselow interview, *Sunday Times*, 1988.
122 Ballard, Pringle interview, 1981.
123 Ballard, Pringle interview, 1981.
124 E. J. Carnell, *Preface* in James Goddard, *J. G. Ballard: A Bibliography*, 1970.
125 Ballard, Pringle interview, 1981.
126 Ballard, 'Sculptors Who Carve the Clouds,' *Independent*, 24 October 1992.
127 Robin Chand: full name Dhun Robin Chand, a friend of Ballard's from The Leys school, Cambridge.
128 *New Worlds SF,* December 1956.
129 Ballard, 'The Widest Windows onto the New', *Aloud* [Toronto], 1992.
130 Ballard, *Miracles of Life*, 2008.
131 Ballard, Pringle interview, 1981.
132 Ballard, Anthony Denselow interview, *Sunday Times*, 1988.

133 Brian Aldiss, *The Shape of Further Things*, 1970.
134 Ballard, Pringle interview, 1979.
135 Ballard, 'A Personal View', *Cypher*, May 1974.
136 Ballard, Pringle interview, 1981.
137 *New Worlds SF*, November 1959.

CHAPTER 9 'OUT OF THE NIGHT AND INTO THE DREAM'

138 Ballard, Goddard/Pringle interview.
139 *New Worlds SF 111*, October 1961.
140 Ralph Shaw, *Sin City*, 1973.
141 Ballard, *Miracles of Life*, 2008.
142 Ballard, Goddard/Pringle interview, 1975.
143 Files of Victor Gollancz Ltd.
144 Sheila Hodges, *Gollancz: The Story of a Publishing House*, 1978.
145 Ballard, *Books and Bookmen*, July 1970.
146 'J. G. Ballard and the Drowned World of Shanghai', Graham Matthews, *J. G. Ballard: Landscapes of Tomorrow*, eds Richard Brown, Christopher Duffy, Elizabeth Stainforth, Brill Rodopi 2016
147 Ballard, interview Goddard/Pringle, 1975.

CHAPTER 10 'DANGER IN THE STREETS OF THE SKY'

148 Ballard, *Miracles of Life*, 2008.
149 Ballard, draft of *Miracles of Life*, British Library, p174.
150 Ballard, 'Deep End', in *The Terminal Beach*, 1964.
151 Ballard, *Miracles of Life*, 2008.
152 Fay Ballard, 16 May 2015, corridor8.co.uk.
153 Ballard, *Miracles of Life*, 2008.
154 Fay Ballard, 16 May 2015, corridor8.co.uk.
155 Ballard, Jonathan Weiss interview, 2005.
156 Ballard, Tom Shone interview, *New Yorker*, 1997,
157 Ballard, *Miracles of Life*, 2008.

ELEVEN 'THE CHILDREN'S SANCTUARY'

158 Ballard, *The Kindness of Women*, pp. 138, 145.
159 'J. G. Ballard's daughter on the mother who could never be mentioned', Chris Hall, *Guardian*, 20 June 2014.
160 Manser was offered a CBE in 1988, an offer he declined on account of the then Prince Charles's infamous attack on contemporary architecture. He did however accept the honour when it was offered again in 1993.

CHAPTER 12 'THE NAMING OF NEW THINGS'

161 Michael Moorcock, *ballardian.com*, 2007.
162 Ron Bennett, *Skyrack 64*, 16 March 1964.
163 Michael Moorcock, *New Worlds*, March 1965.
164 Algis Budrys, 'Galaxy Bookshelf', *Galaxy*, December 1966.
165 Brian Aldiss, *The Twinkling of an Eye*, 1998.
166 Ballard, Vale & Revell interview, 1985.
167 Brian Aldiss, *The Twinkling of an Eye*.
168 Brian Aldiss, 'Science Fiction Report from Rio', *Observer*, 6 April 1969.
169 Ballard, interviewed by David Pringle, 1979.
170 Ballard, 'A Personal View', *Cypher*, May 1974.
171 Ballard, interviewed by Alexandre Matias of *Folha de São Paulo*, Brazil, 26 May 2005.

THIRTEEN 'APPOINTMENT WITH A REVOLUTION'

172 Ballard, *Miracles of Life*, p. 188.
173 Ballard, *Miracles of Life*, p. 157.
174 Ballard, *Miracles of Life*, p. 157.
175 Ballard, 'Myth-Maker of the 20th Century', *New Worlds 142*, May/June 1964.
176 Moorcock, 'A New Literature for the Space Age', *New Worlds 142*, May/June 1964.
177 'They Flooded the Place Afterwards', Christopher Priest blog 27/09/2012.

CHAPTER 17 'A SEASON FOR ASSASSINS'

178 Ballard, interviewed by David Pringle, 24 July 1981.
179 Ballard, letter to David Kopacz MD, 2 October 1997, not published until 7 October 2016.
180 James Naughtie, interview with Ballard, BBC Radio 4, 2008.
181 Moorcock, email to Christopher Priest, 24 August 2023.
182 David Pringle, *You and Me and the Continuum: In Search of a Lost J. G. Ballard Novel*, 1993.
183 Ballard, Introduction to 'You and Me and the Continuum', *Impulse 1*.
184 Marc Haefele, former assistant to Larry Ashmead at Doubleday, in an e-mail forwarded to David Pringle by Michael Moorcock, 24 April 2009.
185 Ballard, annotations to *The Atrocity Exhibition*, RE/Search 1990.
186 Ballard, annotations to *The Atrocity Exhibition*, RE/Search 1990.

187 Ballard, letter to Jonathan Weiss, 12 December 1997, photocopied and distributed with information about the film at special theatrical showings, film festivals.
188 Ballard, *Miracles of Life*, p. 193.
189 Ballard, interview with Alan Burns, *The Imagination on Trial*, Allison & Busby 1981, p 25.
190 Ballard, 'Terminal Documents', *Ambit 27*, Spring 1966.
191 Ballard, William Burroughs obituary, *Mail & Guardian* (South Africa), 8 August 1997.
192 Priest, 'A View of Suburbia', *Speculation 27*, September–October 1970.
193 'James the Great', *Guardian*, 11 October 1990.
194 Ballard, *Miracles of Life*, p. 193.

EIGHTEEN 'THE HOUSE OF WOMEN'

195 Ballard, *Miracles of Life*, p. 204.
196 Ballard, *Miracles of Life*, p. 205.
197 'The Widest Windows onto the Now', *Aloud*, 1992.
198 Claire Walsh Obituary, Will Self, *Guardian*, 14 October 2014.
199 Claire Walsh interview, Tim Adams, *Observer*, 26 April 2009.
200 'Venus Smiled: a tribute to Claire Churchill', Ballardian.com 21 October 2014.
201 John Baxter, *The Inner Man*, p. 187, 229.
202 Interview with David Pringle 1979, published in *J. G. Ballard: A Primary and Secondary Bibliography*, ed. David Pringle, G. K. Hall 1984.
203 Emma Tennant, *Burnt Diaries*, p. 29.
204 Emma Tennant interview, *Sunday Times*, 21 August 2011.
205 Vale interview, ReSearch Publications 1984.
206 Emma Tennant, *Burnt Diaries*, p. 30. The identity of the poet remains unknown, though David Pringle has suggested that the initials – L.T. – might be those of Lorna Tracy, the US-born wife of the poet Jon Silkin and a contributor to *Bananas 12*, autumn 1978.
207 Pamela Zoline, 'Crashing Cars', *New Worlds 224*, July 2024.
208 Letter from Hilary Bailey to Fay Ballard c2011/12.
209 John Baxter, *The Inner Man*, p. 306.
210 'Bea Ballard: These terrible lies about my father have sullied our lives', Peter Stanford, *The Telegraph*, 18 December 2011.
211 'Whatever Became of Jim?' Jeannette Kupfermann, 10 April 1988.
212 Ballard, *Miracles of Life*, p 228.
213 Deborah Levy, introduction to *Kingdom Come*, reprint edition, Fourth Estate 2014.
214 John Baxter, *The Inner Man*, p. 150.

215 'I remember my wife being outraged when she read ["The Overloaded Man"] and rightly so. The marriage described here, and those that follow it, has no basis in my own life. Yet from what forgotten experience stems this obsessive and often repeated image of the predatory woman and the husband retreating into his own mind.' Ballard, in the introduction to *The Best of J. G. Ballard*, Orbit 1977.

216 'My wife, when she was alive would say "why all these strange women in your stories?" I had a very happy marriage with her, and we were extremely close, yet I produced all these odd women.' Ballard, interviewed by Lynne Fox 1991, *J. G. Ballard: Conversations*, ed. V. Vale ReSearch Publications 2005.

CHAPTER 19 'THE BURNING CAR'

217 Ballard, letter to Luca Del Baldo, 18 May 1993.
218 Harley Cokeliss was then known as Harley Cokliss, the name as it appears in the credits for the film.
219 Clare Boylan interview, *Guardian*, 5 September 1991.
220 Rick Poynor, 'Collapsing Bulkheads: The Covers of *Crash*', *Eye*, Summer 2004.
221 Ballard, annotations to *The Atrocity Exhibition*, RE/Search 1990.
222 Jonathan Rosenbaum, https://jonathanrosenbaum.net/2023/11/sex-drive/ quoting from the introduction to *Crash* by Ballard, 1997.
223 Ballard, *Street Life* interview, 1976.
224 Ballard, *Crash*, Chapter 4.
225 Ballard, *Crash*, Chapter 19.
226 Bruce Sterling, 'David Cronenberg mulling over J. G. Ballard's *Crash*', *Wired* 2015.
227 Iain Sinclair, *Crash*, BFI Publishing 1999.
228 Church Car Park, Exchange Road, Watford.
229 Ballard, *The Atrocity Exhibition*, p. 158, Flamingo edition 2001.
230 Ballard, *The Atrocity Exhibition*, p. 157, Flamingo edition 2001.
231 *Nick Drake: The Life*, Richard Morton Jack's 2023 biography of Nick Drake, provides a fascinating insight into the life and times of this unique singer, including a wealth of testimony from his sister Gabrielle.
232 Ballard, Hans Ulrich Obrist interview, *Extreme Metaphors*, p. 387.
233 Introduction to the French edition of *Crash* (1974) *J. G. Ballard: Selected Nonfiction 1962–2007*, edited by Mark Blacklock, MIT Press 2023.
234 Ballard, interview with Will Self 1995, *Extreme Metaphors*, p. 310.
235 Ballard, *Repsychling 1*, 1975.
236 Ballard, *Repsychling 1*, 1975.

237 Ballard, Mike Bygrave interview, *Radio Times*, 13 December 1973.
238 Michael Moorcock, interview with Iain Sinclair, *Crash*, BFI Modern Masters 1999, p. 96.

CHAPTER 20 'THE CAUSEWAYS OF THE SUN'

239 Bea Ballard, conversation with Christopher Priest, 13 October 2023.
240 Ballard, Christopher Evans interview, *Penthouse*, April 1979.
241 Ballard, 'Are We Over the Moon?' *Telegraph*, 16 July 1994.
242 Charles Platt, e-mail to David Pringle, January 2008.
243 Stuart Wavell, 'Space: The Final Phut', *The Times*, 31 August 2003.
244 Ballard, 'The Diary of a Mad Space Wife', *Vogue*, December 1979.
245 'Thirteen to Centaurus', *Amazing Stories*, April 1962.
246 'Passport to Eternity', *Amazing Stories*, June 1962.
247 'The Time-Tombs', *Worlds of If*, March 1963.
248 'Report on an Unidentified Space Station', *City Limits*, December 1982.
249 'The Cage of Sand', *New Worlds*, June 1962.
250 'The Dead Astronaut', *Playboy*, May 1968.
251 'Memories of the Space Age', *Interzone*, Summer 1982.
252 'A Question of Re-Entry', *Fantastic Stories*, March 1963.
253 Ballard, Introduction, *Myths of the Near Future*, Viking 1984.

CHAPTER 21 'A DECLINE IN PROPERTY VALUES'

254 Ballard, *The Drowned World*, 1962.
255 Charles Platt, private email to David Pringle 2008.
256 Ballard, *Miracles of Life*, pp. 211-12.
257 Ballard, *Miracles of Life*, p. 213.
258 June Rose, *Sunday Mirror*, 19 May 1968.
259 *SF Digest*, June 1976.
260 4 February 1978.
261 Ballard, *Miracles of Life*, pp. 212–13.
262 Ballard, *The Kindness of Women*, p. 72.
263 Ballard, *The Kindness of Women*, p. 254.
264 Ballard, *The Kindness of Women*, p. 254.
265 Ballard, *Miracles of Life*, pp. 217–18.
266 Ballard, *Miracles of Life*, pp. 216–17.
267 Vol. 182, 1971.
268 *Desert Island Discs*, Sunday 2 December 1990.
269 *Desert Island Discs*.
270 *Desert Island Discs*.

271 *Desert Island Discs.*
272 Review, Friday 1 October 1971.
273 Ballard, *Miracles of Life*, pp. 219–20.
274 *Archive on 4: Self on Ballard*, Saturday 26 September 2009.
275 *Archive on 4: Self on Ballard*, Saturday 26 September 2009.
276 'My Hero J. G. Ballard', Will Self, *Guardian*, 14 November 2009.
277 John Gray, 'The Night that Changed My Life', *New Statesman*, 6 December 2018.

CHAPTER 22 'THE EVENING'S ENTERTAINMENT'

278 'From Here to Dystopia', Ballard interviewed by Mick Brown, *Telegraph Magazine*, 2 September 2006.
279 'Free Association', a short interview with Ballard and his daughter Fay, by Anthony Denselow, *Sunday Times Magazine*, March 1988.
280 Ballard, interviewed by James Fallon, 1 April 1988.
281 Ballard, interview with Peter Linnett, *The Writer* magazine.
282 'How I Write', Ballard interviewed by Jerome Boyd Maunsell, *The Times*, 16 September 2000.
283 'How I Write', Ballard interviewed by Jerome Boyd Maunsell, *The Times*, 16 September 2000.
284 V. Vale, interview with Ballard, excerpted from the original, ReSearch 8/9, 1982.
285 Ballard, Peter Linnett interview, *The Writer*, February 1973.
286 Ballard, quoted in the *Daily Mail*, 23 November 1992.
287 Ballard, interviewed by Toby Litt, 10 July 2006.
288 Bea Ballard, conversation with Christopher Priest, 13 October 2023.
289 Bea Ballard, *Deep Ends*, 2016.
290 Ballard, David Pringle interview, 1995.
291 Ballard, interviewed by Vale, ReSearch.
292 Ballard, interviewed by Jim McClellan and Steve Beard, *J. G. Ballard: Traveller in Hyper-Reality*, i-D, November 1987.
293 Ballard, interview with David Pringle, 21 August 1987.
294 Ballard, interviewed by Solveig Nordlund, *Future Now* 1986.
295 Ballard, interviewed by Andrew Dorey and Joseph Nicholas, 'Unlimited Dreams', *Vector 96*, December 1979.
296 'Unlimited Dreams', *Vector 96*.
297 Ballard, *The Unlimited Dream Company*, p. 13.
298 Ballard, *The Unlimited Dream Company*, p. 9.
299 Ballard, 'The Art of Fiction', Thomas Frick, *Paris Review*, 1984.
300 Pringle, *News from the Sun* 7, October 1982.

301 In his interview with V. Vale in 1982, Ballard had spoken about wanting to have a cruise missile stationed at the bottom of his garden: 'This beautiful bird sitting there waiting to fly towards the air will give me a real sense of involvement with the world.'
302 Pringle, *News from the Sun 8*, June 1983.
303 Ballard, interview with David Pringle, *Interzone 51*, September 1991.

CHAPTER 23 'GIVING HIMSELF TO THE SUN'

304 'The Artist as a Young Prisoner', an interview with Ballard by Claire Tomalin, *Sunday Times*, 9 September 1984.
305 Ballard, interviewed by Elizabeth Dunn, *Telegraph*, 9 November 1991.
306 Hugh Collar, *Captive in Shanghai*, 1990.
307 Pamela Battle, 'Survivors of a Japanese Camp', the *Observer*, 30 September 1984.
308 In *Miracles of Life*, Ballard names his friend as Bobby Henderson, though subsequent research by David Pringle after Ballard's death revealed that the boy was actually named Bobby, or Robert Patterson. His son, a retired airline pilot also named Robert, confirmed to Pringle that his father had been in Lunghua camp, and that he had indeed known Ballard.
309 Ballard interviewed before an audience at the ICA by Matthew Hoffman: *Writers in Conversation: J. G. Ballard*, 27 September 1984.
310 John Sutherland, 'The Great Exhibition', London Review of Books September 1984.
311 Allan Prior, *Daily Mail*.
312 Nicholas Shrimpton, *Sunday Times*.
313 Robert Nye, *Guardian*.
314 Philip Howard, *The Times*.
315 Richard Cobb, *My Dear Hugh*, 2011.
316 Malcolm Edwards, *Fictionmags* online discussion forum, 15 March 2016.
317 Ballard, letter to Peter Brigg, 4 October 1985.
318 Joseph McBride, *Steven Spielberg: A Biography* (1987).
319 Les Mayfield, *The China Odyssey* (a film about the making of *Empire of the Sun*), 1987.
320 Ballard, interviewed by David Pringle, 14 November 1988.
321 Ballard, 'Look Back at Empire', *Guardian*, March 2006.
322 Ballard, 'In Your Dreams', *Observer*, 1998.
323 Ballard, interviewed by Peter Halley and Bob Nickas, *Index*, November 1996.
324 Ebert, *Chicago Sun-Times*, 11 December 1987.
325 Sollars, Bays, *Montreal Gazette*, 29 December 1987.

326 Steve Absalom, 'Royal Film of Hell Camp is "Nonsense" Say Women', *Daily Mail*, 30 March 1988.
327 'Memories Scarred by Brutal Treatment', Paul Stimpson/Grace Kendal-Ward, *Gloucestershire Echo*, 11 August 1995.
328 Roger Clarke, *Independent*, 11 March, 1999.

CHAPTER 24 'THE GREAT AMERICAN DESERT'

329 Ballard, interviewed by John Sutherland, *Good Book Guide*, 2000.
330 Ballard, 'Last Gasp for the American Dream', *Guardian*, 2003.
331 Tom Stoppard, *New-Found-Land*, Ambience/Almost Free Playscripts, 1976.
332 Ballard, interviewed by David Pringle, 1995.
333 Martin Amis, the *Observer*, 7 June 1981.
334 Letter from Charles Platt to David Pringle, published in *News from the Sun*, New Year 1981/82.
335 Gregory Benford, review of the Carroll & Graf edition of *Hello America*, in the *New York Times*, 16 October 1988.
336 Ballard, V. Vale interview, ReSearch 1984.
337 Claire Walsh, interviewed by Robert Mendick, *Evening Standard*, 20 April 2009.
338 Ballard, *Miracles of Life*, pp. 230, 231.
339 Walsh, Adams interview, *Observer* 26 April 2009.
340 Mendick, *Evening Standard*.
341 Adams, *Observer*.

TWENTY-FIVE 'THE THIRD NILE'

342 Ballard, interview with Mark Pauline (1987), *Conversations with J. G. Ballard*, ReSearch 2005.
343 Ballard, 'An Appreciation', Brigid Marlin: Paintings in the Mische Technique exhibition catalogue 1991.
344 Ballard, *Independent*, 29 January 1994.
345 Brigid Marlin, 'A Temporarily Tame Tiger', interview by Andrew Bishop Ballardian.com January 2012.
346 'A Temporarily Tame Tiger'.
347 'A Temporarily Tame Tiger'.
348 'A Temporarily Tame Tiger'.
349 Ballard, letter to Brigid Marlin 20 October 1986.
350 'Return to the Source', review by Christopher Priest, *New Statesman*, 11 September 1987.
351 Ballard, interview with Paul Gray, *Time* magazine, 25 April 1988.

352 Ballard, *The Day of Creation*, p. 230.
353 Samuel R. Delany, *New York Times*, 19 May 1988
354 Ballard, *The Day of Creation*, p. 101.
355 Ballard, *The Day of Creation*, p. 156.
356 Ballard, interviewed by Phil Halper and Lars Iyer, 'The Visitor', *Hardcore 8*, 1992, *Extreme Metaphors*, p. 268.
357 Ballard, interviewed by Philip Dodd, *Night Waves*, BBC Radio 3, 16 September 2003.
358 Ballard, *The Day of Creation*, p. 151.
359 Ballard, *The Day of Creation*, p. 101.
360 Ballard, *The Day of Creation*, p. 254.
361 Ballard, *War Fever*, pp. 52–3.
362 Ballard, *War Fever*, p. 58.
363 Ballard, interviewed by Jon Savage, *Search and Destroy 10*, 1978, *Extreme Metaphors*, p. 117.
364 Ballard, Vale interview, ReSearch 1984.
365 Ballard, *Running Wild*, p. 2.
366 *Running Wild*, p. 56.

CHAPTER 26 'THROUGH THE CRASH BARRIER'

367 Ballard, 'This Boy Does Talk. Who is he?' *Guardian*, 1 June 2002.
368 Ballard, 'The Prophet', 23 July 2005.
369 Ballard, interviewed in *Close-Up*, BBC, 3 April 1995.
370 Ballard, interviewed by Matthew Leonard, *ABC Radio 24 Hours*, January 1992.
371 Ballard, Iain Sinclair interview, 1998.
372 Ballard interviewed by German critics Jörg Krichbaum and Rein A. Zondergeld, for the fan magazine *Quarber Merkur*. Back-translation from the German by Dan O'Hara.
373 Ballard, interviewed by James Verniere, *Twilight Zone*, June 1988.
374 Ballard, Adam Pirani interview, *Starlog*, 1988.
375 David Pirie, *A Heritage of Horror: English Gothic Cinema 1946–72*, 1973.
376 Ballard, 'Sweet Smell of Excess', *Independent on Sunday*, 1990.
377 Ballard, Jon Savage interview, *Search & Destroy 10*, 1978.
378 Ballard, 'Losing It at the Movies', *Sunday Times*, 1996.

CHAPTER 27 'I GIVE MYSELF AWAY'

379 *The Kindness of Women*, review by Charles Platt, *New York Review of Science Fiction*, 1992.
380 Ballard, letter to David Pringle, 13 October 1993.

381 Ballard, *The Kindness of Women*, p. 135.
382 Saturday 28 September 1991.
383 Friday 20 September 1991.
384 Sunday 22 September 1991.
385 Sunday 29 September 1991.
386 Ballard, *The Kindness of Women*, p. 277.

TWENTY-EIGHT 'THE ROAD TO SHANGHAI'

387 Ballard, *The Kindness of Women*, p. 60.
388 Ballard, interview with Richard Kadrey published *Interzone 51*, 1991.
389 *J. G. Ballard: A Reader's Guide*, Peter Brigg, Starmont House 1985.
390 Ballard, letter to Peter Brigg, 5 February 1986.
391 Ballard, letter to Peter Brigg, 29 December 1984.
392 'Unlocking the Past', *Daily Telegraph*, 21 September 1991.
393 *Desert Island Discs*, BBC Radio 4, 30 August 1992.
394 *Desert Island Discs*.
395 21 July 1991.
396 25 July 1991.
397 Ballard, interview with Eleanor Wachtel, *Writers and Company*, CBC Radio, 1993.
398 Ballard, *Miracles of Life*, p. 269.
399 Ballard, email to Rick McGrath, 22 October 2007.

CHAPTER 29 'THE PREDATORY BIRDS'

400 Ballard, interviewed by Will Self, 'A Horror Story from Paradise', *London Evening Standard*, September 1994.
401 Review by Scott Bradfield, 16 *Independent,* September 1994.
402 *Kirkus Reviews*, 19 March 1995.
403 Ballard interview *Newsday,* 21 May 1995.
404 Ballard interviewed by Andrew Billen, *Observer*, 7 August 1994.
405 Ballard, *Rushing to Paradise*, p. 130.
406 Ballard, interviewed by Alex Burns, *Revelation*, summer 1994.
407 Ballard, *Rushing to Paradise*, p. 86.
408 Ballard, interviewed by Jeannette Kupfermann, *Mail on Sunday*, 10 April 1988.
409 Chris Petit, *Elle* (US edition), October 1989.
410 Malcolm Edwards, bookbrunch.co.uk 20 April 2009.
411 Jeannette Kupfermann, *Mail on Sunday*, 10 April 1988.
412 Ballard joked to David Pringle in 1979: 'When I took up reviewing for the *New Statesman* I was very reluctant to do it, so I said that . . .

I would only criticize or find fault with a book if I'd read it. If I hadn't read it, I'd always give it a good review. It was only fair.' David Pringle, 'Interview', in *J. G. Ballard: A Primary and Secondary Bibliography* (Boston: G. K. Hall 1984), 14.

413 'The thing is, Jim read virtually no fiction. In the roughly fifteen years I worked with him, I believe the only novel he read was *The Wasp Factory*, which he enjoyed. Latterly, he may have read some of Will Self's work – he certainly says in his autobiography that he had – but I wouldn't bet on it. One of his most polished anecdotes, which I heard him recount a few times, described the satisfying noise a copy of *Midnight's Children* (sent to him by the publisher) made as it hit the bottom of his dustbin.' Malcolm Edwards, in a webchat for the *Guardian*, 25 March 2016.

414 John Baxter, *The Inner Man*, p 164.
415 Christopher Priest, blog, 4 August 2011.
416 Live interview London, 14 September 2006.

THIRTY-ONE 'THE UPHOLSTERED APOCALYPSE'

417 Ballard, 'The End of My War', *Sunday Times*, 20 August 1995.
418 Published in *Interzone 106*, March 1996 – a J. G. Ballard special issue.
419 Ballard, Vale interview, ReSearch 1984.
420 Ballard, *Observer*, 31 December 1995.
421 Ballard, *Sci-Fi Universe*, 6 April 1995.
422 Ballard, *Cocaine Nights*, p. 146.
423 Ballard, *Cocaine Nights*, pp. 34–5.
424 Ballard, review of *King of Cannes* by Stephen Walker, *Guardian*, 1 June 2002.
425 *Daily Mail*, 9 November 1996.
426 Gordon van Gelder, fictionmags (online discussion forum), 21 May 2012.
427 Salman Rushdie, 'Reflection: *Crash*', *The New Yorker*, 15 September 1997.
428 Ballard, interview with Mary Wakefield, *The Spectator*, 18 August 2001.
429 Ballard, *Independent*, 30 December 2003.
430 Ballard, interviewed by Hans Ulrich Obrist, 'Beck's Futures' ICA April 2003, *Extreme Metaphors*, p. 388.
431 Ballard, interview with John Hughes 1996, unpublished.
432 Ballard, 'Time and Tacita Dean', introduction to exhibition catalogue, Tate Publishing 2001.
433 Dennis Lim, *Village Voice*, March 1998.
434 Ballard, 'In the Voyeur's Gaze', *Guardian*, 25 August 1989.
435 Ballard, *Super-Cannes*, p. 202.
436 Ballard, *Super-Cannes*, p. 74.
437 Ballard, *Super-Cannes*, p. 376.

438 Ballard, *Super-Cannes*, p. 178.
439 Solveig Nordlund, interview with Rick McGrath, 2008.
440 *Daily Telegraph*, 16 November 2000.
441 Ballard, letter to Rick McGrath, 18 April 2001.
442 Ballard, 'Bursting the Bubble', *Daily Telegraph*, 6 January 2000.
443 Ballard, interviewed by Tom Sutcliffe, 'The Shopping Mall Psychopath', 14 September 2000.
444 *Musica Repubblica*, 21 January 2000.
445 Ballard, interviewed by Giles Whittell, 8 November 2001.
446 'One Year On: A Special Report', *Independent*, 11 September 2002.
447 'The Martians and Us', BBC4, September 2006.
448 'One Month On', *Guardian*, 11 October 2001.
449 'One Month On'.
450 Ballard, interviewed by Edward Docx, *Daily Express*, 23 September 2000.
451 Ballard, *Guardian*, 14 March 2002.
452 Ballard, *Millennium People*, p. 11.
453 Ballard, *Millennium People*, p. 140.
454 Ballard, *Millennium People*, p. 80.
455 Ballard, *Millennium People*, pp. 150–1.
456 Ballard, letter to David Pringle, 9 June 2004.
457 Ballard, *Millennium People*, pp. 139–40.
458 André Gide, *Les Caves du Vatican*, 1914, translated as *Lafcadio's Adventures*.
459 Ballard, *Millennium People*, p. 176.
460 Ballard, *Millennium People*, p. 138.
461 Ballard, *Millennium People*, p. 173.
462 Ballard, *Millennium People*, p. 182.
463 Ballard, *Millennium People*, p. 127.
464 Sam Leith, *Daily Telegraph*, 11 November 2000.
465 Ballard, interviewed by Tania Branigan, *Guardian*, 22 December 2003.

THIRTY-THREE 'A TASK COMPLETED'

466 Ballard, interviewed by Eleanor Wachtel, CBC April 1993.
467 Chris Hall, 'Relics of a Red-hot Mind', *Guardian*, 4 August 2011.
468 Ballard, letter to Mike Hodges, 20 February 2002.
469 Ballard, *Sunday Telegraph*, 25 January 2004.
470 Nick Rossiter obituary, *Independent*, 2 August 2004.
471 Ballard, interviewed by Agnes Ortega, *Pagina12*, Buenos Aires, 24 July 2005.
472 Ballard, interviewed by Simon Sellars, Ballardian.com 29 September 2006, *Extreme Metaphors*, pp. 439-40.
473 Iain Sinclair, personal email.

474 Andrew Rossabi was also an editor of *Crash*. Fay Ballard wrote to Iain Sinclair on the subject of his inscribed copy of *Love & Napalm: Export USA*: 'Daddy knew the Rossabis very well in the late 1960s / early 70s around the time he saw a lot of Mike Moorcock. They used to visit Shepperton or we'd have Sunday lunch at their flat in West London. I think he was a writer and I gather that he interviewed William Burroughs for *Mayfair* magazine. Daddy lost touch with them after they separated. Monique married her cancer surgeon and I don't know what happened to Andrew.

'However, Andrew Rossabi became president of the Richard Jefferies Society (2010 – 2015) and I recognized him immediately from his recent photograph. I haven't read *After London* but I'm sure you know it well. It feels a bit mysterious and magical that this particular copy has found its way to you!'

475 *The Late Show*, 12 March 1991. The segment was filmed by Mary Harron, who went on to direct the cult movies *American Psycho* and *I Shot Andy Warhol*.

476 Sinclair, *Crash*, pp. 76, 77 BFI 1999.

477 25 October 2002.

478 Reported in the *Guardian*, Thursday 10 February 2005.

479 Ballard, interviewed by Sarah O'Reilly in 2007, published as an appendix to the 2015 pb edition of *Kingdom Come*.

480 Ballard, *Kingdom Come*, p. 4.

481 Ballard, *Kingdom Come*, p. 6.

482 Ballard, *Kingdom Come*, p. 70.

483 Ballard, *Kingdom Come*, p. 99.

484 Ballard, *Kingdom Come*, p. 16.

485 Ballard, *Kingdom Come*, p. 33.

486 Lionel Shriver, *Daily Telegraph*, 9 September 2006.

487 Ursula Le Guin, *Guardian*, 9 September 2006.

488 Phil Baker, *Observer*, 3 September 2006.

489 Ballard, *Kingdom Come*, p. 248.

490 Ballard, *Kingdom Come*, p. 224.

491 Ballard, *Kingdom Come*, p. 223.

492 Ballard, *Kingdom Come*, p. 247.

493 Ballard, *Kingdom Come*, p. 275.

494 Ballard, *Kingdom Come*, p. 163.

495 The Three Bears of the Metro-Centre are directly inspired by the three animatronic 'singing bears' that at one time graced the atrium of the Bentall Centre in Kingston-Upon-Thames, just down the road from Ballard in Shepperton.

496 Ballard, *Kingdom Come*, p. 265.
497 *Desert Island Discs*, BBC Radio 4, 2 February 1992. When asked by Sue Lawley how he felt about being sentenced to life on a desert island, Ballard replied that he had 'lived like a castaway all these years. I think I would enjoy it very much.' He described how as a boy in Shanghai, he had been given a wind-up gramophone, but with only one record, 'The Teddy Bears' Picnic', recorded by Henry Hall and his Orchestra in 1932, which he played so many times that for the whole of his twenties and thirties he could not bear to listen to it. 'Curiously, about ten years ago, I began to like it again, and now I could hear it forever.'
498 Daniel O'Donohue, BBC Northwest, 1 October 2024.
499 Ballard, *Kingdom Come*, p. 100.
500 BBC Radio 4, *Today*, 10 October 2024.
501 'I hate shopping! It drives me mad. I do as little of it as possible. A big retail park is my idea of hell. Every so often I need to buy a new washing machine and it leads me into a nervous breakdown.' Ballard, 'Papering Over the Cracks' interview with Sarah O'Reilly 2007, published as appendix to pb edition of *Kingdom Come*, 2014.
502 Ballard, *Miracles of Life*, p. 277.
503 Martin Amis, *Guardian*, 25 April 2009.
504 Ballard, interviewed by Donald Morrison, 9 October 2006, *Time Magazine*, Vol. 168, No 16.
505 Sarah Finley, *The Bookseller*, 31 August 2007.
506 Paul Dunn, *The Times*, 9 February 2008.
507 *Guardian*, 'Critical Eye', 9 February 2008.
508 *Evening Standard*, 8 October 1959.
509 Fay Ballard, 'House Clearance', *Memory Network*, 1 June 2015.
510 Ballard, *Miracles of Life*, p. 205.
511 Ballard, *Miracles of Life*, p. 230.
512 Ballard, *Miracles of Life*, p. 203.
513 Ballard, *Miracles of Life*, p. 226.
514 'I know that if I don't write, say on holiday, I begin to feel unsettled and uneasy, as I gather people do who are not allowed to dream.' Ballard, Thomas Frick interview *Paris Review* 1984, *Extreme Metaphors* p. 183.
515 Beatrice Ballard, *Daily Mail*, 18 June 2011.
516 Ballard, interviewed by Philip Dodd, *Night Waves*, BBC Radio 3, 30 January 2008.
517 Ballard, *Miracles of Life*, p. 277.
518 Jonathan Waxman, *The Elephant in the Room*, p. x.
519 Fay Ballard, corridor8.co.uk, 16 May 2015.

520 Ballard, interviewed by V. Vale, October 2008, 'In Celebration of J. G. Ballard', ReSearch Publications 2016.
521 Hari Kunzru, 'Ballard in Memoriam', *Granta*, 22 April 2009.
522 Claire Walsh, interviewed by Tim Adams, *Observer*, 26 April 2009.
523 Will Self, 'The Mind Child', *Granta 107*, 2009.
524 Claire Walsh, Tim Adams interview, 26 April 2009.
525 Robert Mendick interview, *Evening Standard*.
526 Email from Claire Walsh to Jeremy Reed, 15 May 2009.
527 Robert Mendick interview, *Evening Standard*.

THIRTY-FOUR 'THE ILLUMINATED MAN'

528 Ballard, 'What I Believe', *Interzone #8*, Summer 1984.
529 Ballard, *Kingdom Come*, p. 140.
530 Ballard, letter to David Pringle, 18 June 1998.
531 Alice Kent speaks to Carole Angier, The Writing Life podcast, September 2021.
532 Vladimir Nabokov, *The Real Life of Sebastian Knight*, p. 32.
533 Nabokov, *The Real Life of Sebastian Knight*, p. 34.
534 Nabokov, *The Real Life of Sebastian Knight*, p. 30.
535 Ballard, *Face to Face with Jeremy Isaacs*, BBC2, 7 November 1989.
536 Ballard, interviewed by Will Self, *Junk Mail*, Bloomsbury 1995, *Extreme Metaphors*, p. 316.
537 Ballard, letter to David Pringle, 7 July 1999.
538 Ballard, *Miracles of Life*, p. 240.
539 Ballard, *Miracles of Life*, p. 239.
540 Jo Stanley, 'J, G. Ballard's *Crash*', *Free Thinking*, BBC Radio 3, 7 December 2023.
541 'Artful Accidents', *New Society* 9 April 1970 p. 588.
542 Paul March-Russell, *J. G. Ballard's Crash*, Palgrave Macmillan 2024.
543 Ballard, interview with Alan Burns, *The Imagination on Trial*, ed. Alan Burns and Charles Sugnet, Allison & Busby 1981.
544 *ReSearch*, p. 144.
545 Cape correspondence, 5 April 1972.
546 Cape correspondence, 3 May 1972.
547 Will Self interview, *Extreme Metaphors*, p. 316.
548 Ballard, letter to Victor Sira, 14 March 2005.
549 Ballard, letter to Bernard Sigaud, 13 March 2008.
550 Chris Beckett, 'The Progress of the Text: the papers of J. G. Ballard at the British Library', *British Library Journal* 2011.
551 Ballard, *Independent on Sunday*, 17 February 2002.

552 The Tristram edition was to appear in 2003 as *La Foire aux Atrocités*, translated by Bernard Sigaud and including the introduction to the 1990 annotated edition by Andrea Juno and V. Vale together with the introduction by William Burroughs and an afterword by Francois Rivière.
553 Ballard, *Nouvelles complètes Vol 2 1963 – 1970*, Editions Tristram 2009.
554 Beckett, 'The Progress of the Text'.
555 Baxter, *The Inner Man*, p. 345.
556 Ballard, interviewed by Thomas Frick, 'The Art of Fiction', *Paris Review* 94, winter 1984.
557 Ballard, *Concrete Island*, pp. 165–6.

PHOTO PERMISSIONS

Every effort has been made to track down the photographers of the photos used in the book.

Frontispiece: Ballard as photographed by Barney Cokeliss at Old Charlton Road, 1990.

1. Ballard and his 1958 collage. (Photo courtesy David Pringle, photographer unknown).
2. 'Mother Reinstated' © Fay Ballard 2012.
3. Ballard with Fay, Beatrice and Jim junior at Old Charlton Road, Shepperton, 1965. (Photo courtesy Fay Ballard.)
4. Michael Moorcock, 2009. (Photo by Rick McGrath.)
5. Christopher Priest (left), Brian Aldiss (right) with their editor Charles Monteith of Faber & Faber, London, 1970. (Photographer unknown).
6. Christopher Priest (centre) at the 'Phun City' music festival, Patching, West Sussex, 1970. (Photo by Richard Howett).
7. Martin Bax looks on as Ballard presents Ann Quin with first Prize in Ambit's 1968 competition for 'stories written under the influence'. Quin's drug of choice was the contraceptive pill Orthonovin 2. (Photographer unknown.)
8. 'Homage to Claire Churchill', the first of Ballard's Advertiser's Announcements, published in *Ambit* 32, summer, 1967 © John Blomfield. Photo courtesy of the Ballard Estate.
9. Lindsay Fulcher in 1984. (Photo courtesy Lindsay Fulcher).
10. J.G. Ballard, 1987. (Photo by Bettmann/Getty Images.)
11. Ballard looks out on the garden at Old Charlton Road for the final time. (Photo by Fay Ballard.)

12 Beatrice Ballard at her father's memorial event in 2009. (Photo by Rick McGrath.)
13 Film director Solveig Nordlund 2009. (Photo by Rick McGrath.)
14 Christopher Priest and Fay Ballard, Eleven Spitalfields, London, 2014. (Photo by Nina Allan.)
15 David Pringle at the Kelpies, Falkirk, 2016. (Photo by David Herd.)
16 'Flipper 3' © Fay Ballard 2012.
17 Ballard in 1988, pictured with Brigid Marlin's reconstruction of 'The Violation' by Paul Delvaux (1936). (Photo by David Levenson/Getty Images.)
18 Christopher Priest and Nina Allan, Straad, Isle of Bute, 2018. (Photo by Mary Turner.)

INDEX

10th Victim, The (film) 134

Abkhazi, Peggy (née Pemberton-Carter) 37, 43
Abraham, Isaac 43–4
Adamski, George 111–12
Adjacent, The (Priest) 341
Affirmation, The (Priest) 155, 432
Afire (film) 347
After London (Jeffries) 243
'Air Disaster, The' (Ballard) 190–1
Airside (Priest) 394, 401
Aldiss, Brian W. 84, 143, 233, 248, 280, 351, 393
  Ballard family and 109–10, 119
  and conventions 89, 90, 127, 133–5
  in *New Worlds* 129
  Penguin Science Fiction anthology 3
Aldiss, Margaret 109–10
Alicante, Spain 110, 112–14
Alien (film) 306–7
Allan, Monica 341
Alphaville (film) 305
Ambit (magazine) 131, 174, 245, 284–5
American New Wave 131–2
American Story, An (Priest) 401
Amis, Kingsley 22, 23, 101, 109–10, 122
Amis, Martin 281, 411
Anderson, Poul 133–4
Angier, Carole 425, 426–7, 442
Anthony Richardson & Partners 121
Antonioni, Michelangelo 198, 305
Aparelho Voador a Baixa Altitude (film) 360, 361–2
Arkham House (American publisher) 221
Arquette, Rosanna 208
Asimov, Isaac 76, 77, 131, 134, 249
Astounding Science Fiction (magazine) 76
Atrocity Exhibition, The (Ballard) 60, 130, 139, 172–80, 228, 324, 403
  annotations 176, 205, 212–13
  Author's Note 176
  chapter headings, lack of 256–7
  and *Crash* 145
  'Crash!' 203, 205, 212–13
  extreme imagery 182
  Financial Times review 176

'The Generations of America' 177
  list of references 177–8
  Love and Napalm: Export USA (American edition) 176
  Priest and 165–6
  reception 181
  translation of 439
  'You and Me and the Continuum' 173–4, 175–6, 213
Atrocity Exhibition, The (film) 179–80, 357
Austerlitz (Sebald) 426, 442
Autopsy of the New Millennium exhibition, Barcelona 420

Bacon, Francis 138
Bailey, Hilary 109, 129–30, 198, 199
Baker, Phil 408
Bale, Christian 273, 277
Balgarnie, William H. 57–8
Ballard, Beatrice (Bea) 91, 119, 120, 122, 185, 199, 298–9
  and BBC film *Crash!* 214
  breast cancer 399
  and Claire 188
  description of typical day 255
  on father's interest in film 305–6, 307
  on father's lack of interest in material possessions 329
  husband, death of 398–9
  marriage 328
  and mother's death 114, 117, 118
  on *Running Wild* 301
  visits father at Goldhawk Road 422
  Zoom calls with 440
Ballard, Edna (née Johnstone) 14, 16, 25, 55, 57, 120, 123, 332
Ballard, Emma 16
Ballard, Ernest 16, 25
Ballard, Fay 88, 124, 189–90, 232, 240–1, 243, 245, 250, 299, 320
  and BBC film *Crash!* 214
  close brush with death 416–17
  on *Conversations with my Physician* 396
  family life 120, 122, 242, 400

on father's car accident 216
on father's girlfriends 185, 186, 287
'House Clearance' series 118–19, 196, 211, 417
marriage 328
and mother's death 113, 114, 117–19
moves father out of Shepperton 419–20
Zoom calls with 440
Ballard, J. G. (James Graham)
and alcohol 188–90
and American cars 279
autobiography 28–9, 32, 41, 47, 49–52
and biography 433
in Cambridge 55–8
cancer 396–7
car crash 215–16
condensed novels 173–4
daily life 329–30
and digital technology 401–2
early jobs 65–8
childhood and adolescence 10–11, 13–22, 23–4, 26–32, 171–2
early years as writer 23
education 32–3, 35–6, 42–3, 55–7, 59–64
family life 254, 399–400, 417–18
and film 303–7
grandchildren 328–9
health issues 362, 396–8, 411–12, 413–14, 415–16, 421
house 250–1
influences on 32, 80, 86–7
interests 57, 59, 69
interned by Japanese 10, 14, 19, 21
and Joseph Conrad 295–6
journalism 87–8
on jury of film festival 303–4
last days at Goldhawk Road 422
lifestyle 249–51
medicine at King's College, Cambridge University 58, 59–63
on middle class 364–5
and Moorcock 119, 127–8, 173–4, 181, 185–6, 188–9, 200, 201, 202, 216, 242, 330–1, 413–15, 417, 435
moves out of Shepperton 419–20
and *New Worlds* 84–6, 90, 91–2, 94, 98, 106, 129, 141, 144, 174, 186, 401, 435
notebooks 394–6
portrait box 195–6
portrait by Marlin 290–2
public library work 83
relationship with father 15, 35–6, 254, 299
and Richard Prince 435–6
and ruined casino 36
and television 255–6
trauma, possible effects of 172–3
turns down CBE 368–9

and US space program 255
USA tour 274, 279, 317
voyage to England 14–16, 19–21
will 421–2
working method 251–3
on writing fiction 432–3
Ballard, James senior 25, 42, 43–4, 45–8, 57, 123–4
relationship with JGB 15, 35–6, 254, 299
in Shanghai 15, 34, 35–6
Ballard, Jim junior 83, 120, 122, 185, 298–9, 416–17
Ballard, Margaret, *see* Richardson (née Ballard), Margaret
Ballard, Mary (née Matthews) 80–3, 98, 109–10, 113–15, 117–19, 173
Bananas (magazine) 190–1, 264, 360
Barcelona: Centre de Cultura Contemporània de Barcelona 420
Barstow, Stan 22, 23
Barthes, Roland 440–1
Bax, Judy (née Osborn) 241, 242
Bax, Martin 131, 241–2, 245
Baxter, Jeanette 415
Baxter, John 129, 199, 201, 441
Bayley, Barrington (Barry) 127, 129
Bays, Daniel 275
Baz, Helen 185, 186
BBC 364
BBC Radio Scotland 326
BBC2 *The Late Show* 403
BBC4 J. G. Ballard season 368
The Book Programme 234
Bookmark documentary (*Shanghai Jim*) 315–16, 318–19, 368
Desert Island Discs 318
Radio 3 *NightWaves* 296
Saturday Night Clive 399
Beatson Cancer Centre, Glasgow 154–64, 165
Becker, Harold 272
Beckett, Chris 392, 437, 440
Beckett, Samuel 141
Benford, Gregory 282
Bentham, Jeremy 195
Bentley, Janet 341
Berkley Books, New York 98, 100, 111
Bester, Alfred 133–4
Billenium (Ballard) 100
'Billennium' (Ballard) 111
biographies 2, 426–30, 433, 441–2
Birley, D.S. 62
Bishop, Andrew 290
Bitter Fame (Stevenson) 2
Blackburn, John 284
Blade Runner (film) 307
Blair, Tony 356, 363

Blake, William 259
Blethen, Elizabeth 186
Bloch, Robert 133
Bloomsbury Group 61–2
Blow-Up (film) 198
Blunt, Anthony 121
Bonfiglioli, Kyril 128, 173–4
book fairs
   Frankfurt Book Fair 420
   London Book Fair 439
Book Now literary festival, Richmond 362
Book of Knowledge, An Encyclopaedia for Readers of All Ages, The 67
Bookseller, The 415
Botten, Bill 204, 258
Bottomley, Virginia 355
Boulle, Pierre 264
Bounds, Sydney J. 129
Boyd, William 314
BRA (British Residents Association) 37–8, 268
Bradbury, Ray 76, 131, 134
Braddon, Russell 264
Bradfield, Scott 326
Bragg, Melvyn 271
Braine, John 22
Bridge on the River Kwai, The (Boulle) 264
Brigg, Peter 272, 317–18
Brighton Worldcon (Seacon, World Science Fiction Convention), Brighton 234
British Baker, The (trade magazine) 87
British Library, London 391, 392–3, 437
British New Wave (New Wave in Science Fiction) 5, 125–7, 131, 132, 145, 186, 192, 194, 198, 260
British Pop Art 137–8
British Residents Association (BRA) 37–8, 268
Brodsky, Joseph 190
Brooke-Rose, Christine 141, 142, 180
Brookner, Anita 271
Brothers of the Head (Aldiss) 280
Brunner, John 84, 90, 127, 129, 133–4, 183–4, 351, 352
Budrys, Algis 100–1, 132
Bug Jack Barron (Spinrad) 180
Burgess, Anthony 204, 208
Burns, Alan 141, 142–3, 180, 181, 434
Burns, Jim 280
Burnt Diaries (Tennant) 191
Burnt-Out Case, A (Greene) 107
Burroughs, William S. 128, 129, 141, 144, 145, 146, 181–3, 184
Buster (Burns) 142
Bute Highland Games 168–9
Bute, Isle of 124
Butler, Bill 183–4

Cabinet of Dr Caligari, The (film) 58
'Cage of Sand, The' (Ballard) 221–2, 245

Calder circle 143, 180
Calder, John 141, 142, 143, 146
Calico Printers' Association 25
Cambridge Film Society 58
Campaign for Nuclear Disarmament (CND) 326
Capa, Robert 53
Carnell, Edward (Ted) John 84–6, 87, 89, 90, 98, 128, 173
Carpentier, Alejo 101
Carter, Alison 62
Carter, Angela 190
'Casey Agonistes' (McKenna) 162, 165
Cervantes, Miguel de 3
Champagne, Terry 146
Chand, Dhun Robin 56, 87
Charnock, Anne and Garry 334, 339, 388
Charnock, Graham 183
Chase, Chevy 273
Chemistry & Industry (trade magazine) 87–8
Cherwell (student newspaper) 319–20
China Film Co-Production Corporation 272
China Printing and Finishing Company 15, 25
Chirico, Giorgio de 87
Christopher, John 85
'Chronopolis' (Ballard) 93
Churchill, John 187
Churchill, Winston 237–8
Clare, Anthony 49
Clarke, Arthur C. 76, 92, 133–4
Clement, Hal 100–1
'Cloud-Sculptors of Coral D, The' (Ballard) 174, 218
Cloutier, Suzanne 304
Clute, John 193, 194, 340, 341
Clute, Judith 193, 340
CND (Campaign for Nuclear Disarmament) 326
Cobain, Sandra 341
Cobb, Richard 271
Cocaine Nights (Ballard) 352–4, 359, 410
Cohen, Gerald 194
Cokeliss, Barney 211, 212, 320–1
Cokeliss, Harley 203, 210–12, 213, 240, 368
Cold Heaven (film) 304
Coldstream, William 193–4
Collar, Hugh 37
Collyn, George 129–30
Complete Short Stories of J. G. Ballard, The 262
'Concentration City, The' (Ballard) 87
Concrete Island (Ballard) 216, 225–8, 257, 305, 442–3
Conrad, Joseph 32, 101, 107, 295–6
Conversations with my Physician (Ballard) 392–3, 396–7, 420
Corgi Books 128
Cowley, Jason 243
Crash (1996 film) 208, 209–10, 354–5, 403–4

Crash (Ballard) 10, 77, 145, 203–8, 209, 212, 213, 214–15, 231, 286, 324, 392
   chapter headings 256–7
   reader's report on 434–5
'*Crash!*' (1971 BBC film) 203, 210–12, 213–14
'Crash!' (Ballard) 203, 205, 212–13
Crash - David Cronenberg's Post-Mortem on J. G. Ballard's 'Trajectory of Fate' (Sinclair) 210
'Crashed Cars' exhibition 211, 214, 433–4
Croft-Murray, Edward 121
Cronenberg, David 208, 209, 210, 354–5
'Cry Hope, Cry Fury!' (Ballard) 174, 218
Crystal World, The (Ballard) 106–7, 110, 244, 257, 408
Cults of Unreason (Evans) 233
Curious Cage, A / Enemy Subject (Abkhazi) 43
Curson Smith, Richard 368

Daily Mail 355
Dardis, Tom 98
Dassin, Jules 304
Davidson (née Matthews), Peggy 81, 119
Davies, Gavyn 364
Day of Creation, The (Ballard) 292–6
de Porta, Filippo 363
'Dead Astronaut, The' (Ballard) 222
'Dead Time, The' (Ballard) 264–5
Dean, Tacita 357
Death of the Author, The (Barthes) 440–1
'Deep End' (Ballard) 111
Defoe, Daniel 227
Delaney, Shelagh 22
Delany, Samuel R. 294–5
Delvaux, Paul 289–90, 398
Dempsey, Mike 183–4
Desert Island Discs 318
Diana, Princess of Wales 355–6
Dick, Philip K. 277
Dick, William (Bill) E. 87, 88
Dickens, Charles 12
Digby Wills Ltd 66
Disch, Thomas M. 190–1, 193, 194, 198
Ditchburn, R. 232–3
Docx, Edward 364
Dodd, Philip 296
Dolce Vita, La (film) 305
Don Quixote (Cervantes) 3
Doubleday & Company 176
Dr Strangelove (film) 305
Drake, Gabrielle 203, 214
'Dream's End' (Kuttner) 92
Drought, The / The Burning World (Ballard) 104–5, 257, 259, 305
'Drowned Giant, The' (Ballard) 60
Drowned World, The (Ballard) 100–4, 122, 227, 243, 257, 259, 408
Dunn, Paul 416

Duras, Marguerite 142
Dworkin, Andrea 327
Dylan, Bob 9

'Earthworks, The' (Blackburn) 284
Ebert, Roger 274–5
Editions Tristram (French publisher) 437, 438–9
Edwards, Malcolm 261, 271, 330
Elephant in the Room, The (Waxman) 418
Eleven Spitalfields gallery, Whitechapel 196
Elliott, Freda Madge 239
Ellison, Harlan 352
Emigrants, The (Sebald) 428, 442
Emin, Tracey 356–7
Empire of the Sun (Ballard) 10, 48, 49, 77, 260–2, 263, 264–72, 275–6, 292, 324
   and Booker Prize 208–9, 270–1
   complaints about accuracy 48, 268–9
   Guardian Fiction Prize 271
   James Tait Black Memorial Prize for Fiction 271
   reviews 267, 270
Empire of the Sun (film) 48, 179, 208, 268, 272–7, 368
   complaints about accuracy 275–6
   premiere 273–4
   reviews 274–5
Emshwiller, Ed 74
Encounter (magazine) 174
'End-Game' (Ballard) 254
End of a Hate (Braddon) 264
England Swings SF (Merril) 186
'Enormous Space, The' (Curson Smith) 368
Entropy Exhibition, The (Greenland) 260
Equinox (Figes) 142
'Equinox' (Ballard) 106, 110, 129
'Ersatz Wines' (Priest) 432
'Escapement' (Ballard) 84–6
Esquire magazine 182
Eurich, Richard 428
Europe After the Rain (Burns) 142–3
Evans, Christopher Riche 231–4, 235–6
Evans, Luke 231
exhibitions
   Autopsy of the New Millennium exhibition, Barcelona 420
   'Crashed Cars' exhibition 211, 214, 433–4
   'House Clearance' exhibition 118–19, 196, 211, 417
   'This is Tomorrow' exhibition, Whitechapel Gallery 137–8
   YBA 'Sensation' exhibition 356–7
Extremes, The (Ballard) 301

Faber & Faber 140, 145
Fantastic Universe (magazine) 75
Farmer, Philip José 133–4
Fellini, Federico 305

Field, Andrew 321
Field, Ophelia 321
Figes (née Unger), Eva 141–2
film festivals
   Gothenburg Film Festival, 2 February 2002: 360
   MystFest film festival 303
   Rotterdam Film Festival 357
   Third Annual International Film Festival, Rio de Janeiro 133
Fonseca, Isabel 411
Forge, Andrew 194
Forster, E. M. 61–2
Four-Dimensional Nightmare, The (Ballard) 3–4, 140
Fourth Estate 415, 420
Frank, Reinhard 56
Frankfurt Book Fair 420
Frazer, Rupert 273
Frick, Thomas 442–3
Frost, David 305
Fulcher, Lindsay 283–6
Fullmer, Nancy 232
Fulton, Ben 167–8

Gailliot, Jean-Hubert 438–9
Galaxy Science Fiction 74, 75, 77, 84
'Garden of Time, The' (Ballard) 407
Gartnavel Hospital, Hyndland 337
Gaubert, Denis 412–13
'Generations of America, The' (Ballard) 177
Glamour, The (Priest) 391
Glass, Evelyn 333–4, 373, 374, 375, 421
Gnome Press 87
Godard, Jean-Luc 305
Goldbert, Cyril (later Peter Wyngarde) 43
Golding, William 230
Goldsmith, Cele 80, 97
Goldstein, Dan 284
Gollancz (publisher), *see* Victor Gollancz Ltd
Gollancz, Victor 100–1
Goodbye, Mr Chips (Hilton) 57–8
Górecki, Henryk: Symphony No 3: 357
Gothenburg Film Festival, 2 February 2002: 360
Grant, Duncan 61–2
Gray, John 243–5, 316–17
Green, Joseph 129
Greene, Graham 32, 107, 270, 295
Greenland, Colin 260
Greenpeace 326
Grimwood, Brian 155
Groundhog Day (film) 388
Grove Press 176
Guardian 204
Guest, Val 306
Guilherme, Miguel 360
Guilty (Kavan) 143

Haden-Guest, Anthony 183–4
Hamilton, Richard 137–8
Hammer Films 306
Hammersmith Hospital 421
Hanbury, Maggie 261–2, 420, 421
Harding, Lee 129
'Hardoon Labyrinth, The' (Ballard) 437–8
Hardoon, Silas Aaron 99
Hare, David 369
HarperCollins 262
Harris, Henry 59
Harrison, Harry 129, 133–4, 135, 280
Harrison, M. John (Mike) 132, 147, 150, 170, 183
Harrogate Festival of Arts and Sciences 145–6
Harvey, Marcus 357
Havers, Nigel 273
Hawes, Keeley 231
Heald, Tim 271
Heart of Darkness (Conrad) 295
'Heat Death of the Universe, The' (Zoline) 192, 198–9
Heinlein, Robert A. 76, 131, 133–4, 249
Helliwell, Brian Victor Ellington 56
Hello America (Ballard) 256, 279–83, 324
Henderson, John 82
Henderson, Judith 239
Henderson, Nigel 239
Henn, Tom 61
Herzog, Werner 293
Hidden Treasure, The (Tavener) 387
Hiddleston, Tom 231
High-Rise (Ballard) 77, 122, 225, 228–31, 257
High-Rise (film) 230–1
Hill, Matt 196, 341, 388
Hilton, James 57–8
Hirohito, Emperor of Japan 51
Hirst, Damien 356–7
Hodges, Mike 398
Hoffman, Matthew 269
Home (TV play) 368
Honderich, Ted 194
Horn, Rebecca 357
Hornby, Nick 314
Hospital Ship, The (Bax) 242
hospitals
   Beatson Cancer Centre, Glasgow 154–64, 165
   Gartnavel Hospital, Hyndland 337
   Hammersmith Hospital 421
   Inverclyde Royal Hospital, Branchton 336
   Royal Alexandra Hospital, Paisley 152–5, 166–7
   Victoria Hospital 372–3, 421
Hotel du Lac (Brookner) 271
'House Clearance' exhibition 118–19, 196, 211, 417
Houston, Donald 368
Howard, Elizabeth Jane 109–10
Howard, Philip 270

Hughes, Ted 190, 283
Humphrey, W. G. 55
Hungerford shooting tragedy 300–1
Hunter, Holly 208
Hutchinson (publishers) 299–300
Hyashi, Mr (camp commandant) 47

ICA (Institute of Contemporary Arts), London 203
Ice (Kavan) 143
IKEA store, Tottenham: riot 405–6
'Illuminated Man, The' (Ballard) 106, 129, 254
Impulse (magazine) 173–4, 330–1
Incredible Shrinking Man, The (Matheson) 92
Independent Group 137
Indoctrinaire (Priest) 145
Inner Man, The (Baxter) 199, 441
Institute for Research into Art and Technology (New Arts Laboratory), Camden 193, 194–5, 203, 211, 433
Institute of Contemporary Arts (ICA), London 203
International Times (magazine) 174
Interzone (magazine) 4, 12, 296–7
Inverclyde Royal Hospital, Branchton 336
Irons, Jeremy 231
Isaacs, Jeremy 432
ITV: *Jonathan Ross Show* 399

Jackson, Kevin 416
Jakubowski, Max 183–4, 438
James, M. R. 233
Japan 51
  invasion of Manchuria 17, 26–7
  occupation of Shanghai 14, 17–18, 29, 31, 33–6, 37–8
  Pearl Harbor 33
Jefferies, Richard 243
John Menzies (retailer) 180
Johnson, B. S. 141, 180, 181, 184
Johnstone, Archibald and Sarah Annie 21–2
Johnstone, Christopher 153–4, 388
Jonathan Cape (publisher) 175, 203–4, 261, 280, 360
Jones, Langdon 129–30
Jordan, Hashemite Kingdom of 20
Journey to Orion (film) 361
Jump, Amy 230–1
'Just what is it that makes today's home so different, so appealing?' (Hamilton) 137–8

Kadrey, Richard 317
Kane, Pat 326
Kavan, Anna 143, 151
Kemp, Peter 314
Kempeitai (Japanese military police) 34
Kendal-Ward, Arthur 30

Kendal-Ward, Clifford 30
Kendal-Ward, Grace 30, 276
Kendal-Ward, Hugh 30
Kendal-Ward, Malcolm 30, 317
Kendal-Ward, Vernon 30
Kennedy, Leigh 155–6, 387
Keswick, W. J. 38
Keynes, Maynard 61–2
Kilpatrick, Irene (née Duguid) 19, 48
Kindness of Women, The (Ballard) 59, 91, 117, 135, 234–5, 309–14, 315, 324
King, Stephen 150–1
Kingdom Come (Ballard) 402, 405–11, 425
King's Parade (newsletter) 62
Kingsley, Charles 32
Kipps (Wells) 12
Kirby, Michael 179
Kirkus Reviews 227–8, 326
Kitaj, R. B. 194
Klaas, Brian 410
Knight, Damon 98, 133–4
Kopacz, David R. 172–3
Kosmopolis International Festival of Literature 420–1
Koteas, Elias 208
Kubrick, Stanley 92, 291, 305, 307
Kunzru, Hari 420
Kupfermann, Jeannette 199–200, 330
Kurosawa, Akira 305
Kustow, Michael 189–90
Kuttner, Henry 92

Landscapes of the Night (Evans) 233
Last Dangerous Visions anthology (Ellison) 352
Le Guin, Ursula 407–8
Lean, David 272
Leavis, F. R. 61
Lee, Hermione 271
Leith, Sam 368
Lessing, Doris 143
Leuthy, Cyril 412–13
Lever, James 354
Levy, Deborah 143, 200
Lewis, Wyndham 87
Leys School, Cambridge 55–8
Life (US magazine) 177
Lifescapes (Wroe) 431
Lifton, John 193
Lim, Dennis 357
Limbo '90 (Wolfe) 87, 92
Linnett, Peter 253
literary festivals
  Book Now literary festival, Richmond 362
  Kosmopolis International Festival of Literature 420–1
Lobanov-Rostovsky, Orlando Mark 284
London Book Fair 439

London Orbital (autofictional documentary) 402, 404–5
London Review Bookshop 143
Look (US magazine) 177
Lord of the Flies (Golding) 230
Love and Napalm: Export USA (Ballard) 176
'Love in a Colder Climate' (Ballard) 321
Low-Flying Aircraft (film) 360, 368
'Low-Flying Aircraft' (Ballard) 191, 360–1, 362
Lowry, Malcolm 58
Lucas, Sarah 356–7
Lunatique (French science fiction magazine) 436–7

McGrath, Rick 319, 362, 402, 438
MacInnes, Martin 148, 413
Mackelworth, R. W. 129
McKenna, Richard M. 162, 165
Maclaren Group 87, 128
MacLaren, Vivienne 336, 337–8
Mad Max 2 (film) 281, 307
Madersbacher, Fred 133
Magazine of Fantasy & Science Fiction, The 77, 97
Mahler, Marian 150
Maitland, Sara 190
Malcolm, Donald 129
Malkovich, John 273
Mandelstam, Osip 190
Manser, Michael 121
March-Russell, Paul 434–5
Marinetti, Filippo Tommaso 205
Marinho, Margarida 360, 362
Marlin, Brigid 250, 285, 289–92
Martigny, Sylvie 438–9
Maschler, Tom 203–4, 261, 435
Masson, David I. 129–30
Mastroianni, Marcello 134
Matheson, Richard 76, 84, 92
Matias, Alexandre 135
Matthews, Arthur 81
Matthews, Betty 81, 119
Matthews, Dorothy (née Vernon, Granny Matthews) 81, 82, 115, 119, 185
Matthews, Graham 103
Matthews, Helen Mary Nance, *see* Ballard, Mary
Matthews, Mary 80–3
Matthews, Peggy, *see* Davidson (née Matthews), Peggy
Matthews, Reverend P. C. 32–3
Memories of the Space Age (Ballard) 221–4, 245
  'The Cage of Sand' 221–2, 245
  'The Dead Astronaut' 222
  'Memories of the Space Age' 222–3, 245
  'Myths of the Near Future' 223–4
  'News from the Sun' 223–4
  'A Question of Re-entry' 223
'Memories of the Space Age' (Ballard) 222–3, 245

Merril, Judith 87, 98, 133–4, 135, 186
Miéville, China 321
Mighty Micro, The (Evans) 234, 235
Millennium People (Ballard) 365–8, 392, 410
Miller, George 281
Miller, Henry 60
Miller, Sienna 231
Milton (Blake) 259
Mind at Bay (anthology) 233
Mind in Chains (anthology) 233
Minority Report (film) 277
Miracles of Life (Ballard) 48, 50, 262, 267, 287, 411, 415–18, 420, 433–4
Mirror, The (Delvaux) 290
Misek, Richard 320
Monteith, Charles 145
Moorcock circle 189, 190, 192, 198
Moorcock, Linda 413–14
Moorcock, Michael (pseudonym James Colvin) 126–9, 187, 194, 199, 236, 241, 356, 413–15
  and Ballard 119, 127–8, 173–4, 181, 185–6, 188–9, 200, 201, 202, 216, 242, 330–1, 413–15, 417, 435
  and Ballard family 109, 198
  and British New Wave 126–7, 132, 260
  and Evans 231, 234
  and literary conferences 146
  'A New Literature for the Space Age' 144
  and *New Worlds* 128–30, 144, 173–4, 180–1, 260, 331, 435
  and Priest 140
  The Shores of Death 129
Morgan, Dan 129
Morrison, Rui 360
Murray, Bill 388
Murray, Colin 388
Murray, Isobel 176
My Dear Hugh: Letters from Richard Cobb to Hugh Trevor-Roper and others (Cobb) 271
Myra (Harvey) 357
MystFest film festival 303
'Myth Maker of the 20th Century' (Ballard) 129, 144
Myths of the Near Future (Ballard) 264
'Myths of the Near Future' (Ballard) 223–4

Nabokov, Vladimir 321, 428–9
Naked Island, The (Braddon) 264
Nanking, Treaty of 26
NASA 219–20
NATO (North Atlantic Treaty Organization) 69
Neurath, Eva 261
New Arts Laboratory (Institute for Research into Art and Technology), Camden 193, 194–5, 203, 211, 214, 433
New-Found-Land (Stoppard) 279–80

'New Literature for the Space Age, A' (Moorcock) 128, 144
New Maps of Hell (Amis) 101
New Statesman 292–4
New Wave in Science Fiction (British New Wave) 5, 125–7, 131, 132, 145, 186, 192, 194, 198, 260
New Worlds (magazine) 98, 128–31, 140, 146, 180, 190, 219, 351, 403
   Ballard and 84–6, 90, 91–2, 94, 98, 106, 129, 141, 144, 174, 186, 401, 435
   Carnell and 84–6, 98, 173
   'Crashing Cars' (60th anniversary edition) 195
   Moorcock and 128–30, 144, 173–4, 180–1, 260, 331, 435
   Paolozzi and 236
   Zoline and 192, 193, 194, 195, 198–9
New Writings in SF 128
New York Times 204
'News from the Sun' (Ballard) 223–4
Newton, Helmut 398
Nordlund, Solveig 258, 360, 361–2, 368
North Atlantic Treaty Organization (NATO) 69
'Notes Towards a Mental Breakdown' (Ballard) 190–1
Nova Publications Ltd 84
'Now: Zero' (Ballard) 93
'Nuclear Man' (Paolozzi) 137–8
Nye, Robert 270

'Object of the Attack, The' (Ballard) 296–8, 299
Obrist, Hans Ulrich 214
Octavia Hill Housing Association 419
On the Natural History of Destruction (Sebald) 426
Opium Wars 26
Orr, Deborah 411
Orwell, George 248
Osborn, George 42, 55, 242
Osborne, John 22, 23
Ounsted, Debby 419
Out (Brooke-Rose) 142
'Out of the Unknown': 'Thirteen to Centaurus' TV adaptation 368
Oxford Mail 204

Page, Barrie 56
Paglia, Camille 327
Pangborn, Edgar 74
Pantoliano, Joe 273
Paolozzi, Eduardo 137–8, 194, 233, 236–41, 400
Paolozzi, Rodolfo 237, 238
Paris 438–40
Passages (Quin) 143
Passport to Eternity (Ballard) 100
'Passport to Eternity' (Ballard) 79–80, 221
Pauline, Mark 289

Paxton, James 154
Peake, Mervyn 244
Pearl Harbor 33
Pemberton-Carter, Peggy 37, 43
Penguin Science Fiction 3
Peter Owen (publisher) 143
Petit, Chris 329, 402
Petrie-Hay, Victoria 260–1
Petty, Mike 435
Petzold, Christian 347
Phillips, Cath 170
Phillips, Leslie 273
Phun City outdoor rock festival 183–4
Pirie, David 306
Planet Story (Harrison) 280
Plath, Sylvia 2
Platonov, Andrei 190
Platt, Charles 129–30, 219, 231, 281–2, 310
Poe, Edgar Allan 87
Pohl, Frederik 76, 84, 100–1, 134
Polkinghorn, Stephen 34
Priest, Christopher 7–8, 143, 413
   and Ballard book 430–1
   cancer diagnosis 154–6, 166–8
   chemotherapy treatment 336, 337–8
   contributions to *New Worlds* 130
   and digital technology 400
   early life 11–12, 139–40
   at home after treatment 333–6
   last days 343–4, 345–50, 371–89
   last weeks/months 151–2, 412–13, 431
   marriage 338–9, 340–1
   medical issues 7, 147–50, 152–6, 157, 166–8
   notebook 150–1, 158
   at Phun City outdoor rock festival 183–4
   and popular culture 400–1
   radiotherapy treatment 338, 342–3
   reviews by 292–4
   and SF 247–9
   steroid-induced nightmares/hallucinations 157–64
   in Victoria Hospital 421
   working method 253, 393–4, 440
   WORKS
      The Adjacent 341
      The Affirmation 155, 432
      Airside 394, 401
      An American Story 401
      'Ersatz Wines' 432
      The Glamour 391
      Indoctrinaire 145
Priest, Elizabeth (Lizzy) 147, 156, 340, 387
Priest, Simon 147, 156–7, 340, 387
'Prima Belladonna' (Ballard) 85, 86, 87, 217–18
Prince, Richard 435–6

Pringle, David 3–4, 5–7, 315, 402, 414, 423
   and Ballard 260, 309, 311, 331–2, 351, 433
   Ballard chronology 2, 5, 12, 395, 412
   Ballard newsletter 259, 317
   bibliography of Ballard's work 4
   brain tumour 5–6
   Priest and 1–2, 6, 12
   and unpublished Vermilion Sands story 'The Hardoon Labyrinth' 437
Prior, Allan 270
Proudman, Anthony 57

'Question of Re-entry, A' (Ballard) 223
Quin, Ann 141, 143, 180
Quinn, Marc 356–7

RAF (Royal Air Force) 69–72, 79–80
Ramis, Harold 388
Rashomon (film) 305
Raven, Simon 61
RCAF (Royal Canadian Air Force) 70–1
Real Life of Sebastian Knight, The (Nabokov) 428–9
Redgrove, Peter 190
Reed, Clifford C. 129
Reed, Jeremy 423
Reihill, Clare 415, 420
'Report on an Unidentified Space Station' (Ballard) 221
Reports From the Deep End (anthology of short fiction) 438
Revell, Graeme 434
Rhine, J. B. 232
Richard, Emily 273
Richardson, Candida 121
Richardson (née Ballard), Margaret 15, 18, 57, 120–1, 122, 123, 369
Richardson, Miranda 273
Richardson, Tony (Anthony) 120–2, 123–4, 419
Richardson, Victoria 121
Robbe-Grillet, Alain 142
Roberts, Keith 129–30, 330–1
Roberts & Vinter 128
Robinson Crusoe (Defoe) 227
Robinson, Robert 234
Roeg, Nicolas 304
Rome, David 129
Rose, Laurie 231
Rose Madder (King) 150–1
Rossabi, Monique and Andrew 403
Rossiter, Alice 329
Rossiter, Nick 328, 398–9
Rossiter, Pandora 328
Rotterdam Film Festival 357
Rowlands, Ted 271
Royal Air Force (RAF) 69–72, 79–80
Royal Alexandra Hospital, Paisley 152–5, 166–7
Royal Canadian Air Force (RCAF) 70–1

Rubinstein, Hilary 101
Runcie, James 315, 318
Running Wild (Ballard) 256–7, 299–300
Rushdie, Salman 356
Rushing to Paradise (Ballard) 324–8
Ryan, Michael 300

Saatchi, Charles 356–7
Sand Pebbles, The (McKenna) 165
Sanz, José 133
Sargent, John Turner 176
Sarraute, Nathalie 142
Savage, Jon 298
Science Fantasy (magazine) 84, 86, 128
Science Fiction Adventures (magazine) 84
science fiction conventions
   Seacon, World Science Fiction Convention, Brighton 234
   world convention of SF fans in London 88–9
   World Science Fiction Convention, Glasgow (1995) 351–2
science fiction magazines
   Ambit 131, 174, 245, 284–5
   American magazines 71
   Astounding Science Fiction 76
   Fantastic Universe 75
   Interzone 4, 12, 296–7
   Lunatique 436–7
   The Magazine of Fantasy & Science Fiction 77, 97
   Science Fantasy 84, 86, 128
   Science Fiction Adventures 84
   Vector 258
   see also *New Worlds*
Scott, Ridley 306
Seacon, World Science Fiction Convention, Brighton 234
Search & Destroy (San Francisco-published punk paper) 298
Seaways (nautical journal) 187
Sebald, W. G. 425–6, 428, 442
Seed and the Sower, The (van der Post) 264
Self, Will 242–3, 411
Sellars, Simon 402
Sellings, Arthur 129
Seymour-Smith, Martin 204
SF: '57, The Year's Greatest Science Fiction and Fantasy (anthology) 87
Shakespeare Was a Woman and Other Heresies (Winkler) 431
Shanghai 14–15
   Ash Camp 39
   British Residents' Association (BRA) 37–8, 268
   French Concession 17–18, 26, 27–8, 34, 35
   Greater Shanghai Municipality 34
   Hongqiao International Airport 31
   International Settlement 14, 17, 18, 26, 27–30, 32, 34, 38

Japanese occupation 14, 17–18, 29, 31, 33–6, 37–8, 39
  Lunghua internment camp 19, 39–47, 48, 123, 316
  Lunghua Pagoda 40, 47
  Lunghua Sophomores 44
  Pootung camp 39
  repatriation negotiations 37
Shanghai, Battle of 17, 27, 34
Shanghai Film Studios 272
Shanghai Jim (TV documentary) 315–16, 318–19, 368
Shanghai Municipal Council (SMC) 27, 29, 37, 38
Shapiro, Robert 272
Sheckley, Robert 74, 76, 84, 133–4, 135
Sher, Anthony 368
ships
  HMS *Peterel* 34
  HMS *Prince of Wales* 35
  HMS *Repulse* 35
  RMS *Empress of Scotland* 70
  SS *Arandora Star* 238
  SS *Arawa* 14, 15–16, 19–20, 315
  USS *Wake* 33–4
Shores of Death, The (Moorcock) 129
Shrimpton, Nicholas 270
Shriver, Lionel 407
Sigaud, Bernard 436–7
Sillitoe, Alan 22
Simak, Clifford D. 74
Sinclair, Iain 210, 242, 287, 331, 402–5
Sinclair, May 233
Sir John Soane's Museum 123
Sira, Victor 435–6
Sladek, John 190–1, 193, 233
SMC (Shanghai Municipal Council) 27, 29, 37, 38
'Smile, The' (Ballard) 60, 190–1
Smithson, Alison 137–8
Smithson, Peter 137–8
Só, Rita 360
Sollars, Stella 275
Sort of Life, A (Greene) 270
'Sound-Sweep, The' (Ballard) 91, 93–4
space age 218–20
space travel 220–1
Spader, James 208
Speak, Silence (Angier) 425, 442
Spencer, William (Bill) 60, 61, 65
Spielberg, Steven 48, 50, 208, 209, 262, 272, 274, 277, 368
Spinrad, Norman 146, 180
Sports Illustrated 204
Stanley, Jo 433–4
Star Trek 77
Star Wars 77
Stevenson, Anne 2
Stevenson, Robert Louis 32

Stokes, Isabella 328
Stokes, Jonathan 328, 422
Stokes, Matthew 329
Stoppard, Tom 48, 272, 279–80
Storey, David 22
Storm-Wind (Ballard) 98, 99
Storr, Catherine (née Peters) 204, 434–5
Stowell, Gordon 67
Straw Dogs (Gray) 243
'Studio 5, The Stars' (Ballard) 218
Studio International 237
Stunt Pilot, The (Ballard), *see Unlimited Dream Company, The* (Ballard)
Such (Brooke-Rose) 142
Sun Yat-sen 26
Sunday Times 227–8
Sunset Boulevard (film) 93, 305
Super-Cannes (Ballard) 357–60, 410
Sutcliffe, Tom 363, 364, 368
Sutherland, John 270
Swaim, Bob 304
Swift, E. J. 372

T-Men (film) 61
Tarzan Adventures (magazine) 127
Tavener, John 387
Tennant, Emma 190–2, 199, 250, 283, 310
Terminal Beach, The (Ballard) 106, 110–11, 402–3
'Terminal Beach, The' (Ballard) 110, 112
'Terminal Documents' (Ballard) 181
terrorist violence
  Madrid 398
  9/11 (World Trade Center) 363, 364
  7/7 London bombings 400
Thatcher, Margaret 260, 289, 301, 327, 404
Third Annual International Film Festival, Rio de Janeiro 133
'Thirteen to Centaurus' (Ballard) 220, 361, 368
'This is Tomorrow' exhibition, Whitechapel Gallery 137–8
Thomas, Jeremy 209
Thornton, Tony 56, 57
'Thousand Dreams of Stellavista, The' (Ballard) 218
Three Studies for Figures at the Base of a Crucifixion (Bacon) 138
Tildesley, Mark 231
Time (US magazine) 177
'Time-Tombs, The' (Ballard) 221
Titan Books 438
Tookey, Christopher 210
Towards Crash (film) 368
'Track 12' (Ballard) 3
Transatlantic Review (magazine) 174
Transjordan, Protectorate of 20
Trocchi, Alexander 183
Tsvetayeva, Marina 190

Tubb, E. C. 127, 129, 130
Tuttle, Lisa 148, 388
2001: A Space Odyssey (Clarke) 92, 134
2001: A Space Odyssey (film) 92, 134, 307

Under the Volcano (Lowry) 58
Unger, Deborah Kara 208
Unlimited Dream Company, The (Ballard) 251, 258–9, 392
User's Guide to the Millennium, A (Ballard) 351

Vale, V. 191, 298, 420–1
van der Post, Laurens 264
van Gelder, Gordon 356
van Vogt, A. E. 131, 133
Vance, Jack 80
Vanishing Point (film) 307
Varsity (magazine): Crime Story Competition 62–3
Vector (SF quarterly) 258
'Venus Hunters, The' (Ballard) 111–12
'Venus Smiles' (Ballard) 87
Vermilion Sands (Ballard) 174, 217–18, 245, 321, 323–4
   'The Cloud-Sculptors of Coral D' 174, 218
   Cry Hope, Cry Fury!' 174, 218
   French edition of 437
   'Prima Belladonna' 85, 86, 87, 217–18
   'Studio 5, The Stars' 218
   'The Thousand Dreams of Stellavista' 218
Vernon, Dorothy, *see* Matthews, Dorothy (née Vernon)
Victor Gollancz Ltd 100–1, 111, 260–1
Victoria Hospital 372–3, 421
Victorian Society 122
Vietnam War 177
Violation, The (Delvaux) 290
'Violent Noon, The' (Ballard) 62–3
Voices of Time, The (Ballard) 100
'Voices of Time, The' (Ballard) 91, 93, 94–6

W. H. Smith (retailer) 180
Wain, John 22
'Waiting Grounds, The' (Ballard) 91–3, 257
Walker, Alexander 210, 355
Wallace, F. L. 74
Wallis, Barnes 233
Walsh, Claire (née Churchill) 186–8, 189–90, 191–2, 241, 243, 244, 286–8
   'Ballardian Architecture: Inner and Outer Space' symposium video recording 444–5
   and cancer 332
   and digital technology 401–2
   and JGB's last days at Goldhawk Road 422–3
Walsh, Jenny 186, 188, 397, 419
Walsh, Michael 186

Waterhouse, Keith 22
Wavell, Stuart 219
Waverley Book Company 67
Waverley Encyclopedia of General Information, The 67–8
Waxman, Jonathan 392–3, 396, 397, 418–19
Weight, Bill 57
Weiss, Jonathan 179, 357
Wells, H. G. 12, 248
Wesker, Arnold 22
'What I Believe' (Ballard) 425
Wheatley, Ben 230–1
When Dinosaurs Ruled the Earth (film) 306
Whitechapel Gallery: 'This is Tomorrow' exhibition 137–8
Whiteley, Nick 166–7
Whitford, Frank 237
Whittell, Giles 363
Wilder, Billy 93
Wilhelm, Kate 133–4
Williams, Heathcote 190
Wilson, Colin 22, 23
Wind from Nowhere, The / Storm-Wind (Ballard) 98–100, 254, 257, 392
Winkler, Elizabeth 431
Wish I Was Here (Harrison) 147, 150
Wolfe, Bernard 87, 92
Wolfers, John 261
Wollaston, Keith 57
Wollaston, Nicholas 314
Wollheim, Richard 194
World Science Fiction Convention, Glasgow (1995) 351–2
World Trade Center: 9/11 terrorist attacks 363, 364
World Versus America (*VUS1*, Ballard) 392, 394, 395–6
World War II: 13–14, 44, 47
Wright, Randall 315
Wroe, Ann 431
Wycombe Air Park 79
Wyndham, John 85, 89, 90, 248, 430
Wyngarde, Peter (previously Cyril Goldbert) 43

Yamashita, Mr (camp commandant) 47
Yevtushenko, Yevgeny 340–1
'You and Me and the Continuum' (Ballard) 173–4, 175–6, 213
Young, Aida 306
Young British Art (YBA) 356–7

Ziff Davis magazines 97
Zoline, Pamela 190, 192–9
   and *New Worlds* 192, 193, 194, 195, 198–9
'Zone of Terror' (Ballard) 93